管理学：全球化视角

主　编　李　慧

副主编　李敬强　李　辉

南开大学出版社

图书在版编目(CIP)数据

管理学：全球化视角：汉英对照 / 李慧主编. —
天津：南开大学出版社，2017.8
ISBN 978-7-310-05392-6

Ⅰ.①管… Ⅱ.①李… Ⅲ.①管理学－高等学校－教
材－汉、英 Ⅳ.①C93

中国版本图书馆 CIP 数据核字(2017)第 133281 号

版权所有　侵权必究

南开大学出版社出版发行
出版人：刘立松
地址：天津市南开区卫津路 94 号　　邮政编码：300071
营销部电话：(022)23508339　23500755
营销部传真：(022)23508542　　邮购部电话：(022)23502200
*
三河市天润建兴印务有限公司印刷
全国各地新华书店经销
*
2017 年 8 月第 1 版　　2017 年 8 月第 1 次印刷
297×210 毫米　16 开本　22.75 印张　2 插页　630 千字
定价：55.00 元

如遇图书印装质量问题,请与本社营销部联系调换,电话:(022)23507125

作者简介

李慧，女，天津理工大学国际工商学院副教授、硕士生导师；毕业于中国人民大学商学院，获管理学博士学位，研究方向为品牌管理和城市营销。曾到美国南加州大学、美国得州大学圣安东尼奥分校、加拿大汤姆逊大学、加拿大皇家路大学进行学术访问和交流；主持和参与过 10 余项国家级、省部级课题，出版专著 2 部，发表论文 10 余篇；主讲"管理学"课程 12 年，其中双语课程 8 年。

李敬强，男，北京物资学院商学院讲师；毕业于中国人民大学商学院，获管理学博士学位，研究方向为企业社会责任与品牌管理、农村居民消费行为；先后参与国家社会科学基金项目、国家自然科学基金项目等 7 项课题，发表论文近 20 篇，参与编写"21 世纪普通高等教育规划教材"1 部，其他著作 3 部，主讲"管理学"课程 5 年。

李辉，男，中国人民公安大学公安管理学院讲师；毕业于中国人民大学商学院，获管理学博士学位，研究方向为公安管理和企业管理理论；主持和参与过 5 项国家级、省部级课题，发表论文 30 余篇；参与编写"中国人民公安大学十二五规划教材"2 部，其他著作 1 部；主讲"公安管理学""警察组织行为学"等课程。

序 言

　　管理学是一门系统研究人类社会管理活动中的基本规律和一般方法的科学，是管理科学的一门基础课程，它涉及哲学、社会学、心理学、决策科学等多个学科，是一门综合性的交叉学科。随着我国国际化水平的不断提升和大学生国际化素质培养要求的提出，越来越多的高校已开设或正着手开设管理学双语课程。在多年的双语教学实践中，我们发现，虽然目前翻译、编著的管理学相关教材已经有数十种，但是适合双语教学的教材并不多见。许多学校选用全英文影印版教材作为本科生教学用书，但在实际使用中，本科生学习全英文版教材的难度较大，而现有的双语教材多是在英文教科书的基础上辅以简单的中文术语解释，且所学案例多源自北美。在对中国学生的双语教学中，缺少以中文思想为主线、英语解释为辅助的适合我国管理学双语教学的教材。这为教师进行双语授课增加了难度。也正是这个原因，促使我们萌生了编写一本适合我国学生的管理学双语教材的想法。

　　本教材由编著者们将多年的双语授课讲稿和双语教学心得进行整理，设计中文理论配合英文术语解释、融入中国本土案例、增加全球化视角的全新范式。通过英文解释，尽可能汲取外文原版教材的精华；通过中文讲述，帮助读者系统梳理管理学理论精髓；通过中国本土案例的融入，让读者对中国背景下的管理理论有更深刻的理解；通过全球化视角，扩展读者对管理学前沿知识理论的了解，掌握全球化背景下管理实践的特点。这一编著模式更适合我国读者进行管理学的双语学习，既能深入理解管理学理论，又能掌握管理学基本的英文术语和理论思想；既能融入中国本土情境，又能培养读者的国际化视野。本教材定位为双语教学的理论教程，可以为广大的工商管理专业学生、企业家，以及对管理学感兴趣的读者提供完整的管理理论思想。

　　本教材的主要特色体现在以下几个方面。

- 中英双语：管理学理论的介绍由中英双语两部分构成，基本的理论保持英文版本的原汁原味，用中文来对理论进行扩展和解释，便于读者进行中英对照学习。

- 易于学习掌握：本教材每一章节均由学习目标、主要内容、开篇案例、关键概念、讨论问题和综合案例构成。"学习目标"有助于读者带着问题，有目的地去阅读；"主要内容"让读者了解本章主要内容构成；"开篇案例"有助于读者融入管理实践，掌握管理理论在实践中的应用；"关键概念"和"讨论问题"有助于读者进行课后总结和自测；"综合案例"有助于提升读者综合运用管理理论的能力。

- 中国本土案例与国际企业案例结合：本教材每一章节中都有多个全球化视角的案例介绍，其中保留了一些比较经典的国外知名企业案例，也增加了一些新兴的国际化企业案例，同时，更融入了许多中国知名企业的管理案例，通过中国本土案例和国际企业案例的对比和分析，有助于读者在扩展国际化视野的基础上，更加准确地理解中国背景下管理实践的特色。

- 教辅材料丰富：除了每一章后的关键概念、讨论问题和综合案例之外，本教材还提供配套的英文版的习题集及演示文稿（PPT 课件），为教师授课提供便捷的辅助手段，也有利于读者自学时进行自测和综合思考。

　　本教材由天津理工大学李慧博士担任主编，北京物资学院李敬强博士和中国公安大学李辉博士担任副主编。其中，李慧博士负责设计整本教材的框架、范式，并撰写第一章、第二章和第八章；李敬强博士负责撰写第三章、第四章和第五章；李辉博士负责撰写第六章、第七章和第九章；最后由李慧博士负责全书审校和统稿。参加教材编写和修订工作的还有傅文利老师、陈燕老师、张晓丹老师，硕士研究生谷园园同学、本科生杨孟杭同学、隋雨瞳同学、王梦梅同学、王馨悦同学在本教材的校对和排版工作中付出了辛苦的努力。本教材凝聚了所有参编人员的辛勤汗水和智慧结晶。

在本教材编写过程中，获得了天津理工大学教材建设基金的资助（项目号：JC15-03），在此非常感谢学校给予我们的支持。非常感谢南开大学出版社王乃合主任的理解和支持，本教材从开始设想框架到书稿完成，多次校对，几易其稿，王乃合主任不厌其烦、工作细致，才能够使得本教材及时与读者见面。这里，还要特别感谢我们的家人。教材的编写工作异常清苦，我们占用了许多假日时光来商讨教材编写细节，未能陪在家人身旁，没有他们的理解和包容，我们很难编写完成这部教材。感谢所有为本教材的出版付出辛劳的人们！

我们在编写过程中，竭尽全力保证准确，不敢有半点疏忽。但是，鉴于作者水平有限，全书一定有许多不妥之处，敬请读者批评指正。

李慧

2016 年 3 月 24 日于明理湖畔

目　录

图目录

表目录

第一章　管理的基本概念

学习目标

1. 解释管理的概念和管理的目的
2. 界定管理的基本职能
3. 辨析效率、效果和生产率之间的关系
4. 理解管理的属性
5. 描述多元化社会及优选环境的本质

Learning Outcomes

1. Explain the nature and purpose of management.
2. Define the managerial functions.
3. Differentiate among efficiency, effectiveness, and productivity.
4. Understand the attributes of management.
5. Describe the nature of the pluralistic society and selected environments.

主要内容

第一节　管理的定义
第二节　生产率，效率和效果
第三节　管理的属性
第四节　管理与环境

Contents

1.1 Definition of Management
1.2 Productivity, Efficiency and Effectiveness
1.3 Attributes of Management
1.4 Management and Environment

第一节　管理的定义

Dear Dr. Dorothy,

I work 30 hours a week at a nearby auto rental center and have managed to organize classes around my work schedule. Two months ago I was promoted to shift supervisor, which is awesome. In my new job I have to schedule and supervise counter and phone employees, and also the maintenance and security people. Plus I must step in with difficult customers, and I have to reconcile financial figures at the end of the shift. Here's the problem: I have to stay late, usually two to three hours every day. My employees just can't handle customers at night, so I end up spending a lot of time handling this rather than my new management tasks. If I don't do something soon, I'm going to have to either quit my job or drop out of school.

Cloneless in Wichita

Dear Cloneless,

You have the new manager disease: can't-let-go-itis. You no doubt got promoted because you breezed through customer interactions in a way that left customers happy and time to spare. Now, though, dear friend, your job is to manage the work of others, not do it yourself. Making the shift from doer to manager is more complicated than most college students (or other grown-ups, for that matter) appreciate. But you have an incessant desire to do that which you have done well.

Because you've got promoted, Dr. Dorothy can feel confident that you are not deluding yourself about how well you handle the customers. You have to learn to let go and allow your employees to do their jobs themselves rather than have you meddle, which is precisely how they see it—take Dr. Dorothy's word for it. If you see that they are not talking to customers the way you want, coach them, or send them to training. And if they are really bad, fire them! Before you do that, however, make sure the real problem is not your own need to control and to have things done in your way. Dr. Dorothy assures you that if you learn to let go, delegate, and empower, this will make you a better person in other relationships, too.

（案例来源：Richard L. Daft and Dorothy Marcic 著．高增安，马永红改编. *Management*（6th edition）．北京：机械工业出版社，2010，p. 38）

　　案例中 Cloneless 遇到的问题，是许多管理者在职业发展生涯过程中也会遭遇的困惑。Cloneless 得到提升的原因是他勤奋的工作态度、卓越的工作效果和良好的顾客满意度，可以说，提升是作为对他工作努力的一种奖励。但是面对新的工作，Cloneless 却感觉麻烦重重，将新工作中的各项任务独自担起，却缺少与下属的沟通和对下属的委任。Cloneless 作为一名管理者，却过于忙着亲自做具体事情，不懂得如何通过与他人分工协作来把事情完成，这是他亟待解决的问题。管理是一门"借力打力"的艺术，需要管理者通过对他人的指挥和激励，来克服工作过程中的种种阻力，最终实现组织的目标。本节将围绕管理的意义、管理的基本概念以及管理的目标展开讨论。

一、为什么要学习管理？

　　人类掌握管理的本领，可以说是由来已久。从人类以群体的方式去实现个人无法实现的目标开始，管理就已成为确保群体成员高效合作的一个基本工具。无论是古代的群居群猎，还是现代社会中的团队合作，其核心作用都是一样的，即集结个人的力量，以发挥集体更大的作用。

　　管理是伴随着组织的产生而产生的。所谓组织（Organization)，是人们为了实现共同的目标而彼此结成的有机整体。组织的类型既包括营利性组织，如银行、饭店、便利店等，也包括非营利性组织，如学校、慈善基金、公立医院等。简言之，组织就是为着共同奋斗目标，共同完成一系列相关任务的一群人的集合。一个组织应该有明确的目标、志同道合的成员和系统化的组织架构。为了实现组织的目标，组织的成员必须合作，也就产生了管理。管理是协调个人努力所必不可少的要素，是组织活动的一个极为重要的组成部分，它存在于各种类型的组织当中。

　　随着社会经济的发展、国际化的进程加速以及 21 世纪对人才争夺的白热化，管理对企业的重要作用越来越显著。有人已经将管理同土地、劳动和资本并列称为社会的四种经济资源。1998 年，海尔著名的"激活休克鱼"（Activating Stunned Fish）案例被正式纳入哈佛教材案例库，成为写入哈佛教材的第一个中国企业案例。所谓"激活休克鱼"，是指选择那些硬件条件很好但是管理跟不上、由于经营不善导致效益不佳的企业，通过收购的方式，引入一整套行之有效的管理制度，把握住市场，使企业起死回生。海尔在收购"休克鱼"企业之后，常常会派去一批人马，将海尔先进的管理方法和成熟的管理经验带过去，在被兼并企业里面将海尔的管理模式进行复制，通过无形的管理模式盘活有形资产。"激活休克鱼"的管理方法为海尔在短短时间内盘活上亿资产，实现了低成本扩张。由此可见，在国际化的激烈竞争中，管理已成为企业竞争获胜的关键要素之一，良好的管理可以使企业获得迅速发展，取得事半功倍的效果。

✍ **Why Should We Study Management?**

Management is an essential tool to enable individuals to make their best contributions to group goals.

An organization is a systematic arrangement of people brought together to accomplish some specific purpose.

Management applies to any kind of organization.

3

Global Perspective

Haier：Activating Stunned Fish

With the help of Haier's invisible capital of culture in activating "stunned fish" enterprises, its "diversified development" phase started in the early 1990s. This helped Haier save much of the cost of diversified expansion and woke up the so-called "stunned fish," which once again became competitive in the market. A good example is Qingdao Hongxing, a producer of electrical appliances that had once been famous but was on the verge of collapse in 1995 due to poor management. Haier applied its cultural values and new management approaches, such as the OEC management pattern, and utilized Hongxing's tangible capital without any financial input. Hongxing was rejuvenated in three months' time and began to show profit in the fourth month. Because of the infusion of Haier's culture, Hongxing, now Haier's producer of washing machines, not only became vigorous again, but also helped to activate several other "stunned fish" such as Shunde Aide (a washing machine firm), by applying Haier's culture and management pattern (OEC) in a similar manner.

二、管理的定义

　　古今中外对于管理的概念界定至今并没有一种统一的说法。古汉语中，"管"的意思是规范、法则，有时候也用作动词，意为统率、主宰、主管；"理"的意思是整治土地、治疗疾病，用作动词讲时指的是治理、处理事务。所以，管理指的是管人理事、管辖约束、约束与引导。当代的《世界百科全书》认为，管理就是对工商企业、政府机关、人民团体以及其他各种组织的一切活动的指导，它的目的是要使每一行为或决策有助于实现既定的目标。虽然与古代解释的说法不同，但异曲同工，其核心思想都是想说明管理是一种有目的的指导行为。

　　不同的学者也分别就管理给出了不同的概念界定：

　　福莱特认为，管理是通过其他人来完成工作的艺术；

　　法约尔认为，从职能的角度来看，管理是计划、组织、指挥、协调和控制；

　　西蒙提出了管理决策论，将"决策"一词从广义予以理解，认为它和"管理"一词几近同义，管理就是决策；

　　罗宾斯认为，管理指的是和其他人一起并且通过其他人来切实有效地完成活动的过程；

　　孔茨提出了协调论，认为从广义来讲，管理就是协调员工的工作。

✍ **Definition of Management**

Management is a too complex concept for one definition to capture accurately.

Scholars give different ideas about management.

Stephen P. Robbins: Management refers to the process of getting things done, effectively and efficiently, through and with other people.

在当今社会，人才在组织发展中的作用日益显现。在全球化的视角下，优秀的人才可能来自不同的国家和地区。摆在管理者面前的一个难题，就是如何让有着不同文化背景的员工很好地沟通、协调、配合，最终实现组织的目标。因此，协调工作应该是 21 世纪管理者们必须要完成的一项重要工作内容。基于此，本书选择孔茨的概念界定来解释管理的内涵。管理是设计和维持一种环境，让人们以团队的方式工作，最终有效地实现组织既定目标的过程。

该定义包含着以下四层含义。

（一）管理是一个过程

早在 20 世纪早期，著名管理学家亨利·法约尔就提出，管理者必须履行五个管理职能，即计划、组织、指挥、协调和控制，他将这五个职能概括为管理过程。后来的学者基于法约尔的观点，将管理的过程概括为四个（计划、组织、领导、控制）或者五个职能（计划、组织、人员配备、领导、控制）。本书选取孔茨的协调论作为界定管理内涵的标准，因此认同管理是包括五个职能的过程，即计划、组织、人员配备、领导、控制。

计划（Planning）是组织选择使命、目标和实现这些目标的行动方案。

组织（Organizing）是在组织中有目的地建立一个架构，分配成员的角色。

人员配备（Staffing）是为组织结构填充并不断填充合适人员的过程。

领导（Leading）是影响他人使其自愿的为组织目标做贡献。

控制（Controlling）是测量并纠正个人和组织的绩效，以确保计划的实施。

管理由计划、组织、人员配备、领导、控制等一系列相互关联、连续进行的活动构成。

（二）管理是在一定的环境下进行的

管理不能离开环境在真空中进行。不同的组织环境会产生迥异的管理问题，需要采用特定的管理方法进行解决。管理与环境的依存关系在全球化背景下更为明显。在国内贸易中，企业管理者在发展战略方面可以遵循以民族为中心（Ethnocentric Orientation）的原则，但是当企业走上国际化的竞争舞台，需要在海外设立营销公司、分支机构，甚至建厂的时候，以全球为中心（Geocentric Orientation）的原则可能会助企业发展一臂之力。

Management is the process of designing and maintaining an environment in which individuals, working together in groups, efficiently accomplish selected aims.

❖ Management is a process.

Break management down into five managerial functions in this book. They are planning, organizing, staffing, leading, and controlling.

Planning: selecting missions and objectives as well as the actions to achieve them.

Organizing: establishing an intentional structure of roles for people to fill in an organization.

Staffing: filling, and keeping filled, the positions in the organization structure.

Leading: influencing people so that they will contribute to organizational and group goals.

Controlling: measuring and correcting individual and organizational performance to ensure that events conform to plans.

❖ Management operates in a certain environment.

Ethnocentric orientation: the style of the foreign operations is based on that of the parent company.

Geocentric orientation: the entire organization is viewed as an interdependent system operating in many countries.

（三）管理需要通过综合组织中的各种资源来实现组织的目标

　　管理者的一项重要工作就是管理组织中的各种资源。管理者必须确保有效地使用资源，而且还要使用这些资源实现组织目标的最大化。组织的资源包括财务资源、人力资源、硬件环境资源（如厂房和设备）、技术资源等多项内容。管理者需要做的是，首先明确企业所拥有的资源，其次对目标进行分析，根据目标对资源进行有效分解，然后在资源的使用过程中不断的监控和调整，最终实现组织的目标。在诸多资源中，管理者在全球化的背景下应尤其关注对人力资源的整合和利用。正如 Xerox 的前 CEO Mulcahy 所说的那样，管理者的作用是吸引员工，激励员工，留住员工，使 Xerox 成为员工们的最佳选择，这是公司成功的关键要素之一。

◇ It's very important to manage the organization's resources to realize its objectives.

Global Perspective

Xerox：Staffing with the Best Human Capital

Anne Mulcahy, former chairman and CEO, is largely credited with turning around that company's performance. But Mulcahy claims Xerox employees were responsible for the turnaround. She stated that, "attracting them, motivating them, keeping them—making Xerox an employer of choice—are critical to our drive back to greatness." These comments suggest that staffing the organization with the best human capital possible and further developing the knowledge and skills of employees are critical for the success.

（四）管理是为了实现组织的目标

　　管理是一个有意识、有目的的过程，是为了实现组织的目标而服务的。对于组织的目标，应该有广义的理解。营利性组织的目标可能是获取更多的利润，即经济目标，但同时，它也可能希望获得社会的认可、较好的公司形象，即社会目标。管理的作用就在于集合所投入的各种资源，如人、财、物和信息资源，并对其进行有效的配置和运用，最终确保组织在活动过程中能够保质、保量、按期、低成本的实现产出，即：提供产品或服务，实现组织目标。如图 1-1 所示。

◇ Management is to achieve organization's goals.

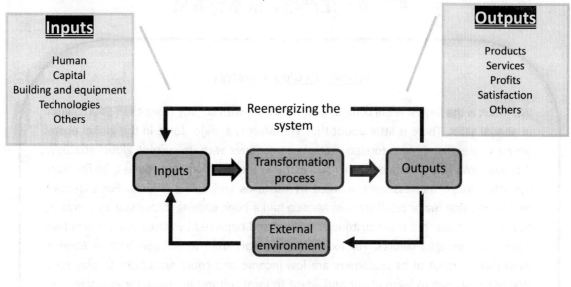

图 1-1　投入-产出模型

Figure 1-1　Input-Output Models

（资料来源：改编自 Heinz Weihrich, Mark V. Cannice and Harold Koontz. *Management: A global and Entrepreneurial Perspective* (13th edition). 北京：经济科学出版社，2011，p. 22）

三、管理的目标

　　管理是组织的一个职能，是实现组织目标的工具，因此管理的目标并不是孤立存在的，必须围绕着组织的目标进行管理。因此，管理的目标必须与组织发展目标相一致。正如前一节所描述的那样，尽管不同类型的组织目标可能有所不同，但终极目标都是使组织以尽量少的资源尽可能多地完成预期的合乎要求的目标。

　　管理的目标同样关注投入产出率。无论哪个层级的管理者，其管理的核心目的是创造盈余。对于盈余，应该有广义的理解。许多人将盈余理解为企业的利润。对于营利性企业来说，盈余可能更多地强调利润层面，但是不仅限于利润。例如，对于上市公司来说，如何保护股东价值也是管理的目标之一；对于百年老字号企业来说，维持良好的品牌声誉也是管理的目标之一；对于服务型企业来说，创造更高的顾客满意度也是管理的目标之一；对于人才紧缺的企业来说，培养优秀的人才也是管理的目标之一。利润、股东利益、品牌声誉、优秀人才等，都是盈余的具体体现。管理的目的是创造一种优良的环境，使人们以最少的资源实现组织的目标，即创造更多的盈余。

✎ **The Goal of Management**

The goal of management should match an organization's mission and strategy.

The aim of all managers should be to create a surplus, by establishing an environment in which people can accomplish group goals with the least amount of time, money, materials, and personal dissatisfaction.

第二节 生产率、效率和效果

Wal-Mart's Global Strategy

Wal-Mart is the largest retail company in the world, with slightly more than $400 billion in annual sales. There is little doubt that Wal-Mart is a major force in the global economy and has many more foreign markets to conquer with its current global strategy. Although Wal-Mart has been highly successful in the U.S. domestic market, its first forays into foreign markets were marked by mistakes and a few failures. For example, Wal-Mart's first major retail store in Mexico had a huge parking lot, similar to stores in the United States, but most customers arrived and departed by buses. And, it also had some early product failures. For example, Wal-Mart tried to sell golf balls in Mexico even though most of its customers are low-income and could not afford to play golf. Wal-Mart has had to learn about and adapt to local culture: in Japan, for example, low prices are equated with low-quality goods and few customers buy large quantities because of very small living quarters. Yet, the company has learned from its early mistakes and has been more successful in its later entries into foreign markets. As an example, Wal-Mart has 260 retail outlets and almost 90,000 employees in China. All of its stores in China are operated by Chinese general managers. According to Ed Chan, Wal-Mart's China former CEO, all of the management team are passionate about Wal-Mart's values. Wal-Mart sources many of its products locally within China as well, helping to keep costs low.

Wal-Mart was successful relative to most retailers during the recent recession. Overall, it experienced sales growth, and its international division was a major contributor because U.S. sales declined. Approximately 25 percent of Wal-Mart's annual sales come from its international business. In fact, if its $100 billion international business were a stand-alone company, it would be among the top five retailers in the world. Wal-Mart has plans to increase this unit by entering more markets with major operations such as India and Russia. In addition, the company plans to greatly reduce its costs by moving to global sourcing directly from the manufacturers, where possible. This move alone is expected to save the company billions of dollars. Through these efforts, Wal-Mart CEO David Duke expects the company to maintain its momentum as the global economy continues to improve.

（案例来源：改编自 Michael A. Hitt，J. Stewart Black，and Lyman W. Porter. *Management* (3rd edition). 北京：中国人民大学出版社，2013，p. 7）

作为全球最大的零售商，沃尔玛的全球化战略是比较成功的。但正如案例所述，在战略实施过程中，是选择全球化采购还是本土化采购？是选择全球统一配送还是本土配送？是在全球所有分公司采用一样的产品种类，还是针对各国因地制宜？是由母公司选派管理人员，还是管理人员当地化？这些是沃尔玛必须要面对和抉择的问题。任何公司在发展中都会遇到问题，它们对问题不断进行分析和解决，旨在最终实现组织的目标，即：以尽量少的资源来尽可能多地完成预期的目标。对管理目标的理解还有另一种视角，即提高生产率。本节将围绕生产率、效率、效果的内涵展开讨论。

一、什么是生产率？

组织的目标是以尽可能少的资源来尽可能多地完成预期目标。在管理过程中，为了实现这一目标，就必须提高效率、增强效果，提高生产率。第二次世界大战后，美国已成为世界上生产率最高的国家，但是从 20 世纪 70 年代起，生产率开始下滑，进入 21 世纪后尤为严重，所以 2011 年美国总统奥巴马（Barack Hussein Obama）提出，充分发挥工人的生产效率，是提高国家竞争力的关键要素。

☞ **What Is Productivity**？

对于生产率（Productivity）的解释有很多种，学者们对其定义仍有争论。总体上来说，生产率是在一定时期内、基于约定产品质量的投入产出比，可以通过总产出除以劳动投入来计算，衡量的是每单位投入的产出量。即：

$$生产率=总产出/总投入$$

Productivity: The output-input ratio within a period with due consideration for quality.

其中，总投入包括组织的人力、资本、设备、技术等投入，总产出包括产品、服务、利润、满意度等多个要素。根据这个定义，我们可以看出，提高生产率有如下几种途径：（1）在相似投入的情况下，增加总产出；（2）在相似产出的情况下，减少总投入；（3）在减少总投入的同时，增加总产出。在过去关于提高生产率的研究中，多聚焦于劳动生产率，事实上，管理中的生产率更多地强调综合效应，人力、资本、技术都属于投入，应该通过管理，整合资源，减少总投入，增加总产出，进而提高生产率。

Inputs include human, capital, equipment, technologies, and others.

Outputs include products, services, profits, satisfaction, and others.

二、效率和效果

"效率"（Efficiency）和"效果"（Effectiveness）是经常成对出现的一组管理学术语，也是生产率在组织绩效中的具体体现。效率，从字面上解释，是指单位时间内完成的工作量。在管理学中，效率是指有效地使用资源以完成既定的目标。由于在组织运营过程中，所投入的资源往往是稀缺的，因此提高管理的效率，往往强调的是使资源成本最小化。但是，仅仅有效率是远远不够的，管理还必须实现预定的目标，即追求活动的效果。效果，从字面上解释，是由某种因素造成的结果。在管理学中，效果特指目标的实现。当管理者实现了组织的目标时，我们就说，他们的工作是有效果的。

☞ **Efficiency and Effectiveness**

Effectiveness is the achievement of objectives.

Efficiency is the achievement of the ends with the least amount of resources (time, money, etc.).

效率和效果是互相联系的。效率强调活动方式，关注对资源的利用，所以只有效率高或效率低，不存在好与坏；而效果涉及活动的结果，可能如期而至，也可能谬之千里，存在好与坏之分。如果说高效率就是"正确地去做事"，

Efficiency refers to do things right, while effectiveness refers to do right things.

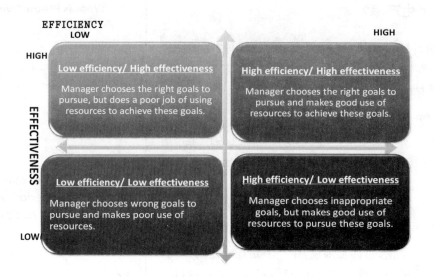

图 1-2　效率与效果矩阵

Figure 1-2　Matrix of Efficiency and Effectiveness

那么好效果就是"做正确的事"。根据效率的高与低,效果的好与坏,可将二者关系通过矩阵加以解释。如图 1-2 所示。

在此矩阵中,可以根据效率和效果的不同组合分为四种情况。

第一种情况:低效率、高效果。管理者在设定组织目标的时候是正确的,而且最终也实现了组织的目标,但是在目标实现过程中,效率低下,浪费了许多资源,没有为组织获得盈余。例如,有些企业在生产产品的时候,非常追求尽善尽美,生产出几乎无可挑剔的产品,但是因为精美,忽视了产品的成本,造成成本过高,消费者虽然喜欢,但是却没有购买能力,只能望洋兴叹。还有一些政府部门,经常受到公众的质疑,按道理说他们的工作是有效果的,最终事情还是得以解决了,但是解决的过程太过漫长,手续太过烦琐,效率低下,成本太高。很显然,这样的结果不利于组织的长期发展。

第二种情况:低效率、低效果。这是谁也不希望看到的一种糟糕的情况:整个组织工作效率低下,缺少凝聚力,而且也没有朝着正确的方向迈进。这样的组织很难求得发展,一方面缺少准确的发展战略和目标,另一方面组织所投入的人、物、财力利用率很低,组织如一盘散沙,整个组织处于低水平的管理状态。在组织经营过程中,有的组织会生产粗制滥造的产品,他们认为这样可以降低生产成本,但事实上这样的产品到了市场上根本销售不出去,因为顾客无需求,不仅造成库存积压,也丢掉了企业的声誉。

Low efficiency/High effectiveness

Results: A product that customers want, but that is too expensive for them to buy.

Low efficiency/Low effectiveness

Result: A low-quality product that customers do not want.

第三种情况：高效率、低效果。这种情况主要体现为管理者一开始就设定了错误的目标，但是在执行组织战略的过程中，效率很高，资源利用率很好，结果会南辕北辙。例如，生产牙刷的企业将牙刷质量作为企业的生存根本，不断提高牙刷质量，牙刷的成本增加，定价也较高。但是如果该企业的主要顾客为快捷型酒店，专供酒店用一次性牙刷，那么可能就会因为牙刷的高价格使顾客流失。这样的产品，效率越高，生产的产品越多，造成的库存积压也越多，给企业带来的损失也就越大。从这种意义上来说，高效率、低效果比低效率、低效果对组织的危害性更大一些。

第四种情况：高效率、高效果。这是所有组织都期待的一个情境，在效果好的情况下，高效率无疑会使组织的有效性增大。一个组织生产出消费者的确需要而且支付得起的产品，并通过管理不断提高工作效率，降低成本，增加收益，最终提高组织的有效性。

综上所述，效率和效果是衡量组织生产率的重要指标。效率强调方式，效果关注结果；效率强调资源利用率，效果关注目标达成情况。最终是为了实现高效率与高效果并存，使组织得到发展。如图 1-3 所示。

High efficiency/Low effectiveness

Result: A high-quality product that customers do not want.

High efficiency/High effectiveness

Result: A high-quality product that customers want and price that they can afford.

图 1-3　效率与效果的关系

Figure 1-3　Relationship between Efficiency and Effectiveness

（资料来源：Stephen P. Robbins and Mary Coulter. *Management* (13th edition). New York: Pearson, 2016, p. 40）

Do in China as the Chinese Do: An Overview of KFC's Localization Strategies in China

Kentucky Fried Chicken has been one of the most household international brands in urban China since it opened its first western-style quick service restaurant in Beijing in 1987. As the present largest fried chicken restaurant company in the world, KFC aims China as the most promising market and succeeds in its localization strategies in the huge China market. The prominent success of KFC in China's market can be attributed to its franchise policy and scientific managerial operations, well known as CHAMPS, which measures operational basics like Cleanliness, Hospitality, Accuracy, Maintenance, Product Quality and Speed. Moreover, the accomplishments are the reward towards KFC's comprehensive understanding of Chinese culture and its excellent localization strategies specifically manipulated to meet the characteristic requirements of the estimated 450 million urban Chinese consumers.

KFC devised an additional incentive scheme to encourage worker productivity. KFC's control mechanisms are designed to ensure standard levels of quality, service and cleanliness (QSC) at all of the restaurant's chain stores. This fits the positive image in Asia of American fast food restaurants as famous, air-conditioned, and hygienic. Moreover, KFC has adapted its advertising campaign to suit local preferences, including a Cantonese version of "We do chicken right" advertisements. As a country with the best culinary culture in the world, China was a big challenge for KFC's efforts to cater to the captious palate of Chinese consumers.

KFC's product strategies are categorized into two aspects. (1) To meet consumers' desire for novelty by introducing western style products like Mexican Chicken Warp and New Orleans Barbeque Wings. This means can satisfy young consumers who are more open and acceptable to the foreign flavors. (2) To cater to consumers' taste for traditional Chinese meal by offering Chinese style fast food from time to time, say, Old Beijing Chicken Roll, a wrap modeled after the way Beijing duck is served, but with fried chicken inside and accompanied with green onions and hoisin sauce. Chinese-style breakfast food, like porridge is also served since Oct 27, 2003 on the breakfast menu. The breakfast choices are a blend of East and West, ranging from Chinese seafood and chicken congee, Hong Kong milk tea to Western burgers, potato sticks and orange juice. Moreover, in purpose of maintaining its image of a U.S. brand and keeping consistent with its globalization strategy, most of KFC's Chinese side dishes are defined as short-term products and would be replaced by new products.

To represent the Chinese characteristics and increase the identification from Chinese consumers, KFC absorbs Chinese cultural elements into the arrangements and decorations of its outlets all over China. In 2003, KFC spent 900,000 US dollars to redecorate the flagship outlet in Beijing, which is also the world's largest KFC outlet, with the Great Wall, shadowgraph, Chinese kites and other traditional Chinese symbols. In the Chinese New Year of 2003, all the statues of Colonel Sanders in KFC outlets in China were put on the Chinese traditional suits which are known as "Tang suits".

One feature noticeable in KFC's commercials is its preference on the representation of an ancient art form of Beijing Opera. It is interesting to find a U.S. fast food brand presents a traditional art and attaches pop culture elements with it. One of the commercials depicts a Beijing Opera actor in costume and with make-ups still on his face is about to have his KFC meal. The second commercial exhibits the contradiction and later harmony of a father and son; the roles of father and son stand for two generations and serve as the distinct incarnations for traditional and pop cultures. The screen is divided into two parts: the father is singing Beijing Opera in the left room while the son is dancing with Hip hop music in the right room. They finally get to the reconcilement by eating the Old Beijing Chicken Roll served by the mother. The third commercial starts with a background music which merges the Beijing Opera and electronic midi. The three commercials exemplify KFC's efforts to integrate Chinese traditional culture into the modern pop culture.

（案例来源：改编自 Li, D. Do in China as the Chinese Do: An Overview of KFC's Localization Strategies in China. http://lidan.y3k.org/blog/en/2004/04/kfcs-localization-strategies-in-china/2004）

自 1987 年在中国开设第一家餐厅开始，肯德基在中国市场的扩张脚步势不可挡，无论是在收入、利润上，还是在餐厅数量上，都可以算得上中国最大的连锁快餐餐厅。其成功经验一方面依赖于切实可行的战略规划、成熟的快餐业运营模式、科学的管理方法，另一方面也依赖于肯德基成功的本土化战略。正如案例中所描述的那样，肯德基从产品种类、服务人员的选择、广告的设计、营销的方式等多个方面，融入中国本土文化，综合考虑中国消费者的独特需求，进而获得了消费者的青睐。其中，既有管理科学性的严谨，也有管理艺术性的灵活。本节将围绕管理的自然属性与社会属性、科学性与艺术性展开讨论。

一、管理二重性

管理的二重性是马克思主义关于管理问题的基本观点，它反映出管理的必要性和目的性。所谓必要性，是指管理是生产过程固有的属性，是有效地组织劳动所必需的；所谓目的性，是指管理直接或间接地同生产资料所有制有关，反映生产资料占有者组织劳动的基本目的。具体地说，管理的二重性是指管理既有自然属性，又有社会属性。其中，自然属性是与生产力、社会化生产相联系的，而社会属性是与生产关系、社会制度相联系的。任何生产活动都是在生产力与生产关系统一的条件下开展的，生产力与生产关系的统一性决定了管理的自然属性与社会属性的统一性。

（一）自然属性

管理的自然属性是指管理的生产力属性，强调管理是一种不随个人意识和社会意识的变化而变化的客观存在，是由一定的生产力状况决定的。

✍ **Two Attributes of Management**

The two attributes of management is decided by the twoness of laboring.

The natural attribute and the social attribute are the duality of management.

✧ Natural attribute

The natural attribute of management is related to the productive force, and means management exists in all kinds of society.

13

首先，管理是人类社会发展的客观要求。任何社会，只要有共同劳动，就需要管理。共同劳动最重要的一点是分工协作，要想保证劳动过程顺利进行，就必须在各个环节合理配置人、财、物等资源，协调各个环节之间的关系，保持各个环节之间的均衡和连续。而管理，正是对人、财、物等资源加以整合与协调的必不可少的过程。这种存在不会随着社会制度的变化而变化，在不同的社会制度下具有共同性，即自然属性。

Management is the objective need of social development.

其次，管理是一种职能，是社会分工的产物。正如前文所述，共同劳动的结果必然要产生分工协作，管理是保证共同劳动顺畅进行的一个必要职能。东方有帝王，统辖天下；西方有君主，统一指挥；古代有管理粮仓的岗位，现代有职业经理人，负责企业运营。这些管理职位的存在，不会因为社会制度或生产关系的变化而变化。管理的存在具有其客观必然性，是由一定的生产力状况决定的。

Management is the result of social division.

最后，管理活动必须尊重和利用客观规律。无论什么样的生产关系和社会制度，管理过程中都存在着很多客观规律。例如，管理中有一个"鲶鱼效应"，源自自然现象。以前，沙丁鱼在运输过程中存活率很低，后来有人发现，若在沙丁鱼中放一条鲶鱼，存活率会大大提高，原因就在于鲶鱼在陌生环境中，会变得性情急躁，四处乱游，而沙丁鱼发现多了一个"异己分子"，也会加速游动，这样沙丁鱼缺氧的问题就解决了。鲶鱼效应是企业领导层激发员工活力的有效措施，这个方法不仅在亚洲社会有效，在欧洲、非洲等其他地区的社会中也有效，是不会因社会制度的变化而变化的。管理活动要想行之有效，就必须尊重和利用这些规律。

Management should be in accordance with objective laws.

Global Perspective

Catfish Effect

In Norway, live sardines are several times more expensive than frozen ones, and are valued for better texture and flavor. It was said that only one ship could bring live sardine home, and the shipmaster kept his method a secret. After he died, people found that there was one catfish in the tank. The catfish keeps swimming, and the sardines try to avoid this predator. This increased level of activity keeps the sardines active instead of becoming sedentary.

In management, the catfish effect is the effect that a strong competitor has in causing the weak to better themselves. Actions done to actively apply this effect in an organization, are termed catfish management. It is a method used to motivate a team so that each member feels strong competition, thus keeping up the competitiveness of the whole team. This method is very popular in global merger and acquisition.

（资料来源：改编自维基百科，http://en.wikipedia.org/wiki/catfish_effect）

（二）社会属性

管理的社会属性是指管理的生产关系属性,强调管理只有在一定的生产关系和社会制度中才能进行,突出管理与生产关系、社会制度的关系。任何管理活动都是在特定的社会情境下进行的,反映了一定生产关系的性质和要求。管理活动必须考虑"为谁管理",即应为特定的社会生产关系服务,体现不同社会制度下管理的个性。

管理与生产关系和社会制度相联系,既是一定社会制度的体现,又反映和维护一定的社会制度,其性质取决于社会制度的性质,不同的社会制度有不同的社会属性。例如,在个人主义占主流的社会中,对员工的激励往往更多关注员工个性发展,强调个人成功;在集体主义占主流的社会中,管理则更多关注团结、目标一致,强调集体利益。这两种管理方案没有好坏之分,只是不同的社会制度下不同的解决办法。因为任何管理活动都是在特定的社会生产关系下进行的,都必然地要体现一定社会生产关系的特定要求,为特定的社会生产关系服务,从而实现其调节和维护社会生产关系的职能。在不同的社会制度条件下,谁来监督、监督的目的和方式都会不同,因而管理活动也必然具有不同的性质。表 1-1 列出了中国、日本和美国管理中的种种不同,体现了管理的不同社会属性。

◇　Social attribute

The social attribute of management is related to the production relations, and emphasizes the relationship between management and social systems.

表 1-1　中国、日本、美国：管理比较

Table 1-1　China, Japan, and the United States: A Management Comparison

United States Management	Japanese Management	Chinese Management
Planning ■ Primarily short-term orientation ■ Individual decision-making ■ Involvement of a few people in making and "selling" the decision to people with divergent values ■ Decisions are initiated at the top and flow down ■ Fast decision-making; slow implementation requiring compromise, often resulting in suboptimal decisions	■ Long-term orientation ■ Collective decision-making (ring) with consensus ■ Involvement of many people in preparing and making the decision ■ Decision flow from bottom-to-top and back ■ Slow decision-making; fast implementation of the decision	■ Long-term and short-term orientation (5-year plan and annual plan) ■ Decision-making by committees. At the top often individual ■ Top-down-participation at lower levels. ■ Top-down-initiated at the top ■ Slow decision-making / slow implementation. (Now changing)
Organizing ■ Individual responsibility and accountability ■ Clarity and specificity of decision responsibility ■ Formal bureaucratic organizational structure ■ Lack of common organization culture; identification with profession rather than with company	■ Collective responsibility and accountability ■ Ambiguity of decision responsibility ■ Informal organization structure ■ Well-known common organization culture and philosophy; competitive spirit toward other enterprises	■ Collective and individual responsibility ■ Attempts to introduce the "factory responsibility system" ■ Formal bureaucratic organization structure ■ Identification with the company but no competitive spirit
Staffing ■ People hired out of schools and from other companies; frequent company changes ■ Rapid advancement highly desired and demanded ■ Loyalty to the profession ■ Frequent performance evaluation for new employees ■ Appraisal of short-term results ■ Promotions based primarily on individual performance ■ Training and development undertaken with hesitation (employee may go to another firm) ■ Job insecurity prevails	■ Young people hired out of school; hardly any mobility of people among companies ■ Slow promotion through the ranks ■ Loyalty to the company ■ Very infrequent formal performance evaluations for new (young) employees ■ Appraisal of long-term performance ■ Training and development considered a long-term investment ■ Lifetime employment common in large companies	■ Most hired from school, fewer from other companies ■ Slow promotion, but regular salary increase ■ Lack of loyalty to both company and profession ■ Infrequent performance review (usually once a year) ■ 5-year plan, otherwise short-term targets ■ Promotions are supposed to be based on performance, potential ability, and education. But family ties and good relations with top managers are important ■ Training programs available. State exam administered for managers
Leading ■ Leader acts as decision-maker and head of group ■ Directive style (strong, firm, determined) ■ Often divergent values; individualism sometimes hinders cooperation ■ Face-to-face confrontation common; emphasis on clarity ■ Communication primarily top-down	■ Leader acting as social facilitator and group member ■ Paternalistic style ■ Common values facilitating cooperation ■ Avoidance of confrontation, sometimes leading to ambiguities; emphasis on harmony ■ Bottom-up communication	■ Leader as the head of the group (committees) ■ Directive. Parent-child relations (in TA terms) ■ Common values. Emphasis on harmony ■ Avoidance of confrontation ■ Communication top-down
Controlling ■ Control by superior ■ Control focus on individual performance ■ Fix blame ■ Limited use of quality control circles	■ Control by peers ■ Control focus on group performance ■ Saving face ■ Extensive use of quality control circles	■ Control by group leader (superior) ■ Primary control by groups-but also by individuals ■ Try to save face ■ Limited use of quality control

（资料来源：Heinz Weihrich, Management Practices in the United States, Japan, and the People's Republic of China. *Industrial Management*, 2012 (32): 3）

（三）二者的联系

1. 管理的自然属性离不开其社会属性，它总是存在于一定的生产关系和社会制度中，否则它就成了没有形式的内容；而管理的社会属性也离不开其自然属性，否则它就成了没有内容的形式。

◇ The relationship between natural and social attribute

Management is the unity of natural and social attributes.

2. 二者又是相互制约的。管理的自然属性要求社会具有一定的生产关系和社会制度与其相适应,而管理的社会属性的不断变化必然使管理活动具有不同的性质。正确地理解管理的自然属性和社会属性,有助于我们学习和借鉴外国先进管理经验,研究和总结我国管理经验的指导思想,真正做到"古为今用、洋为中用",既重视我国管理实际情况,又辩证地对待国外管理经验。

二、管理的科学性和艺术性

管理工作究竟是一门科学,还是一门艺术?这是多年来理论界和实业界一直在争论的问题。目前被普遍接受的一种看法认为,管理不仅具有科学性,也具有艺术性。管理作为一种实践活动,是一门艺术;而作为指导实践活动的知识,则是一门科学。作为科学的管理理论和作为艺术的管理实践是应当而且能够得到统一的。

（一）管理的科学性

一般认为,科学是人类认识自然、社会和思维的系统理论知识体系,它所反映的是世界的本质联系及其运动规律。科学是严格的、理性的和抽象的,可以指导人类实践活动。管理学是大量的学者和实践者在总结管理活动的客观规律的基础上形成的一系列基本的管理原则和管理理论,经过多年的研究、探索和总结,已经逐渐形成了一套比较完整的、反映客观规律的理论知识体系。管理人员如果运用这些管理理论作为工作指导,可以更好地完成管理工作,成为有效的管理者。

在全球化背景下,环境多变性是管理者不得不面对的一个现状。在这种多变的环境下,管理的科学性尤为重要。它不仅意味着管理是一种技术,更多则表现为遵守一种规范。管理理论为管理者们提供了一些重要的管理原则和管理程序,这些原则和程序越规范越好。例如,以顾客为中心的服务管理、全面质量管理等管理理念已成为诸多优秀公司成功不可或缺的要素。管理作为一门科学,是可以跨越国界的,无论是发达国家还是发展中国家,无论是东方还是西方,管理科学是贯通的,可以应用于各种情境。

（二）管理的艺术性

艺术是人类以情感和想象等形式来把握世界的一种特殊方式,即通过审美创造活动再现现实和表现情感或理想。艺术是融合人的创造性的方式和方法,是直觉而具体的,追求的是"美"。

✍ **Management: Science or Art**

Managing as practice is an art; the organized knowledge underlying the practice is a science.

✧ Management is a science.

Managers can work better by using the organized knowledge about management. It is this knowledge that constitutes science. Management knowledge can certainly improve managerial practice.

With the rapid development of economic globalization, management science not only provides knowledge and technology, but also implies obeying the management rules.

✧ Management is an art.

管理是一项很复杂的工作,面对复杂而多变的管理环境,管理者不可能找到一套固定公式来解决所有的管理问题,而是需要根据所处的宏观环境、微观环境的不同来随机应变。管理的艺术性就是指管理者在实践活动中对管理理论运用的灵活性和管理方法选择的技巧性。

管理工作是一种艺术性很强的工作,面对不同的管理对象,同样的管理方法可能产生大相径庭的结果。管理工作艺术性的特点要求管理人员在工作中能够做到随机应变,具有灵活性而且富于创新精神。在全球化背景下,管理者需要在多元化的环境下工作,不仅要面对多元化的外部环境,还要管理有着不同文化背景的员工,这对于 21 世纪的管理者来说具有更大的挑战性。成功的管理往往依赖于管理者对管理对象所处环境和形势的判断和理解,管理的艺术性也由此体现出来。

（三）科学性与艺术性的关系

管理的科学性与艺术性并非相互排斥,而是相互补充的。首先,管理的科学性是基础,脱离管理的科学性仅仅强调管理的艺术性,容易导致管理活动缺乏章法,随意性较强,让管理学习者和实践者无所适从。其次,管理的艺术性是管理科学不断前行的保证。脱离管理的艺术性,仅仅强调管理的科学性,容易导致管理活动失之于教条主义,纸上谈兵,只会束缚管理实践者的创新思维,阻挡管理科学的不断发展。同时,管理工作的科学性和艺术性互相促进,管理理论的不断繁荣会为管理者们提供更多行之有效的方法,将管理工作简单化；管理环境的日益复杂化催生了许多新的管理课题,需要不断尝试与探索,管理工作的科学性和艺术性成分不断增强、相互促进的过程提升了管理水平,推动了社会的发展。一句话,管理工作是科学性与艺术性的有机统一。

Management is doing things in light of the realities of a situation. Effective management is extracting voluntary cooperation from the staff. So it is definitely an art and it can be acquired only by practicing the theoretical knowledge skillfully and prudently.

Effective managers should adjust their management activities to adapt different management environments.

✧ The relationship between science and art

Science and art are not mutually exclusive but complementary to each other.

Management has got scientific principles which constitute the elements of science and skill and talent which are the attributes of art.

Management is the combination of art and science.

第四节　管理与环境

Johnson & Johnson and Tylenol Companies in Crisis

On this day in 1982, a sick 12-year-old girl in Elk Grove Village, Illinois, unwittingly took an Extra-Strength Tylenol capsule laced with cyanide poison and died later that day. She would be one of seven people to die suddenly after taking the popular over-the-counter medication, as the so-called Tylenol murders spread fear across America. The victims, all from the Chicago area, ranged in age from 12 to 35 and included three members of the same family. Johnson & Johnson, the maker of Tylenol, launched a massive recall of its product and offered a $100,000 reward for information leading to the arrest of the person or people responsible.

Investigators soon determined that the tainted Tylenol capsules hadn't been tampered with at the factories where they were produced. This meant that someone had taken the bottles from store shelves, laced them with poison and then returned them to grocery stores and pharmacies, where the victims later purchased the tampered bottles.

Johnson & Johnson reacted to the crisis swiftly and decisively, launching a massive public relations campaign urging the public not to use Tylenol. The company also ordered a national recall of 264,000 bottles of Tylenol and offered free replacement of the product in safer tablet form. At the time, it was unusual for companies to recall their products.

Before the "Tylenol Terrorist" struck, Tylenol was the nation's leading over-the-counter drug and Johnson & Johnson's best-selling product and some observers speculated that Tylenol would never be able to recover from the disaster. However, within months, Tylenol was back on store shelves with a new safety seal. The recall and re-launch cost Johnson & Johnson over $100 million, but in the end, Johnson & Johnson was praised for its handling of the crisis. Within a year, Tylenol's market share rebounded and its tarnished image was significantly repaired.

（案例来源：改编自 Marian C. Schultz and James J. Schultz. Corporate Strategy in Crisis Management: Johnson & Johnson and Tylenol. *Essays in Economic and Business History*, 1990 (7): 164-172；Johnson & Johnson and Tylenol, http://www.mallenbaker.net/csr/crisis02.php）

　　强生公司的"泰诺危机"是危机管理中非常成功而经典的案例。强生公司通过积极的行动和诚挚的承诺，重新获得顾客信任，最终挽回了公司的品牌形象。但是，事实上，强生公司的窘境，并不是自己造成的，产品质量本身并没有问题，公司运营过程也没有问题，但是却遭遇到了几乎将企业逼入绝境的危机。这就引发出一个问题：一个组织的成败，是否总是直接归因于企业的内部管理？组织在社会中运营，必然会受到组织环境的影响。任何组织都不是独立存在、自我封闭的。环境是组织赖以生存和发展的土壤，任何组织的任何决策都离不开对环境的认识和分析。本节将围绕着管理环境的构成以及对管理的影响展开讨论。

一、管理环境：不可忽视的力量

✍ **Organizational Environment**

全球化和网络化彻底改变了市场的游戏规则，组织所面临的环境对组织产生的影响越来越大。管理者必须时刻明智地对周围环境的变化做出反应，才可能在复杂多变的国际化环境中立足和生存。

（一）管理环境的概念

关于管理环境的定义，有两种不同的观点：一种观点以斯蒂芬·罗宾斯为代表，将管理环境界定为"对组织绩效有着潜在影响的外部机构或力量"，强调的是组织的外部环境；另一种观点是被我国许多学者所认可的，认为环境既包括组织的外部环境，也包括组织的内部环境，将管理环境界定为由相互依存、相互制约、不断变化的各种因素所组成的一个系统，是影响管理系统生存和发展的一切要素的总和。其中，外部环境是指存在于组织之外的、对组织管理过程产生影响的外界客观情况和条件的总和；内部环境是指存在于组织之内并对组织管理过程产生影响的内部客观情况和条件的总和。组织为了确保目标的实现，要综合考虑内部环境和外部环境的影响，通过管理来促进作业活动实现组织目标。如图 1-4 所示。

在国际化背景下，组织所面对的外部环境更为复杂，所涉及的方面更为广泛。本书采用斯蒂芬·罗宾斯的观点，重点围绕管理的外部环境进行阐述。

◇ The definition of organizational environment

Organizational Environment: all elements existing outside the organization's boundaries that have the potential to affect the organization.

External environment: The layer of the external environment that affects the organization indirectly.

Internal environment: The environment that includes the elements within the organization's boundaries.

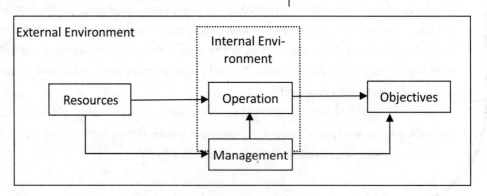

图 1-4　组织运营与管理环境

Figure 1-4　Relationship between Organization Operations and Management Environment

（二）管理环境的特征

随着经济全球化进程的日益加速，企业之间的竞争也越来越激烈，现代企业所面对的管理环境也愈加复杂。与以往的组织所面临的环境相比，现代组织所面临的环境具有以下三个特征。

◇ The feature of organizational environment

1. 动态性

动态性可以用环境因素不断发生变化的程度来衡量。动态性高的环境因素，变化速度较快，尤其对于同一个组织，当几种因素同时发生快速变化时，环境势必会发生激烈动荡，由此呈现出环境的不连续性。环境的动态性越高，不确定性就越高。

现代组织面对着国际化、信息爆炸、技术创新等复杂多变的管理环境。即使是看起来非常领先的时髦产品，也可能很快被市场所淘汰；即使是被许多企业视为经典的"质量至上"，在面对不同顾客群体需求的时候也可能失效。在国际化情境下，组织面临的环境将越来越动荡和变化多端，频繁且快速的环境变化令管理者们面临着严峻的考验。

2. 复杂性

复杂性可以用组织环境中影响因素的数量和种类来衡量。在一个复杂性环境中，有多个因素对组织同时产生影响。通常影响因素越少，环境的复杂性越低，不确定性越小；反之，影响因素越多，环境的复杂性越高，不确定性越高。

现代组织是在一个多元化的社会环境中生存的，组织的运营受到了经济、政治、文化、技术等多个要素的影响，而管理者对外在环境几乎无能为力，能够做的只是适应环境中的各个构成要素。这种情况在国际化情境下尤为突出。他们在管理过程中不得不应对来自不同社会制度、不同文化背景的竞争者、员工、顾客和社会群体，必须对构成环境的这些要素进行识别、评估，并做出反应。现代组织所面临的环境有越来越复杂的趋势。

3. 开放性

开放性可以用全球贸易壁垒和投资壁垒的减少来表示。近年来，全球环境从封闭走向开放。在封闭的全球环境中，各经济体之间的联系被国际贸易壁垒、投资壁垒及地理距离和文化差异所阻隔。随着开放的全球环境的出现，商品、服务和投资方面阻碍自由流动的壁垒在减少，这主要是基于以下环境因素的变化：一是一些全球贸易协定的诞生，如关贸总协定；二是国际社会对自由市场理念的接受程度不断提高。

全球化使组织管理者的工作更具有挑战性，要求他们必须立足于全球化视野去思考问题，必须认识到组织是在一个全球化的市场中存在和竞争的。因此，在开放的全球环境中，竞争更加激烈，不确定性程度将更高。

Dynamic environment: it can be measured by the extent to which the environmental factors change.

When external factors change rapidly, the organization experiences very high uncertainty. The environment is dynamic.

Complex environment: it can be measured by the number of factors that affect the organization.

When the organization has thousands of factors in the external environment, it creates uncertainty for managers. The environment is complex.

Open environment: it can be measured by the barriers to international trade and investment.

Globalization has increased the uncertainty of the management environment.

二、环境对管理工作的影响

本部分重点分析外部环境对管理工作的影响。外部环境包括组织外部存在的、对组织有潜在影响的所有因素。外部环境的变化影响到组织所需资源，特别是关键性资源的获取。离开外部环境要素，企业经营便会成为无源之水、无本之木。通过对外部环境的研究，可以发现可能利用的机遇，也可以尽力回避可能遭遇的威胁。具体说来，可以将外部环境归纳为政治及法律环境、经济环境、技术环境、自然环境、社会文化环境和伦理道德环境六个方面。如图 1-5 所示。

✍ **The Influence of Environment**

Managers operate in a pluralistic society, in which many organized groups represent various interests.

Environment elements include political and legal, economic, technological, natural, social and ethical environment.

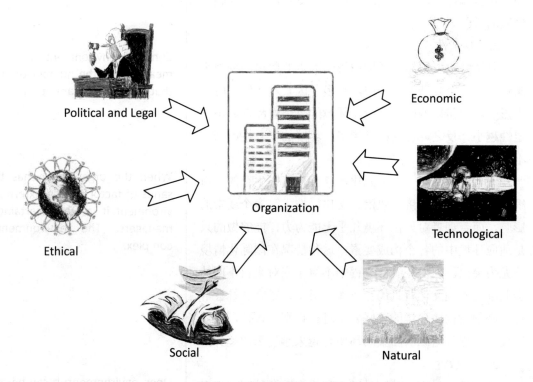

图 1-5　组织环境的构成
Figure 1-5　Environment Elements in the Organization

（一）政治及法律环境

政治及法律环境是由社会内部政治和法律的变化带来的，对管理者和组织有着重大的影响。政治及法律环境包括各级政府制定的规章制度及其他可能影响公司行为的政治活动。

政治环境包括一个国家的社会制度、政党制度、政府方针政策、政治团体及政治气氛。政治环境中有许多因素是以法律形式来制约组织活动的。

✧ Political and legal factors

Political and legal factors include federal, state, and local government regulations and political activities designed to influence company behavior.

组织必须了解国家和政府禁止企业做什么，允许企业做什么，以保证企业的经营活动既符合国家利益，又有利于自身发展。

大多数组织都喜欢在政局稳定的国家做生意，希望避免政治风险。对于跨国公司来说，必须了解和遵守东道国有关经济、消费者保护、就业、福利等方面的各种法律法规，及时调整自己的管理行为。

在全球化市场运营过程中，企业不得不面对其他国家政府和法律方面的问题。欧盟反倾销法规定，在进口商品来自"非市场经济国家"时，其正常价值的确定采取替代国制度，即根据一个市场经济国家相似产品的价格或其结构价值或者该国向共同体的出口价格来确定。欧盟一直没有承认中国的"市场经济国家"地位，因此中国出口欧盟的产品就受到不同于市场经济国家的特殊待遇，中国的出口企业由此也不断被提起反倾销诉讼。近十年来，中国企业在国际市场上不断遭遇反倾销制裁，已成为中国企业在进军国际市场时必须时刻警惕的一个重要问题。

Global Perspective

China to Combat Anti-dumping Cases

Since the initiation of the first anti-dumping investigation on imports from China in 1979, the EU has carried out over 140 anti-dumping investigations, according to the Xinhua News Agency. China has always been the victim of anti-dumping investigations as the nation is well known as a global factory. The EU has already imposed such tariffs on a range of Chinese products, from shoes to steel, amid increasing concerns that affordable Chinese products will threaten EU manufacturers. China has received the most complaints on anti-dumping from other countries since 1993.

（二）经济环境

经济环境是影响组织，特别是经济组织的重要环境因素，反映了公司经营所在的国家或地区一般的经济状况，包括经济结构、经济发展水平、经济体制和经济政策等。

在全球化的经营环境中，经济环境已经变得极为复杂，给管理者带来了更大的不确定性。世界各国的经济依存度越来越高。例如，21 世纪初期美国经济衰退和消费者信心削弱，影响了世界各国的经济和组织；同样，亚洲和欧洲的经济危机也给美国的公司和股票市场造成了重大的影响。

✧ Economic factors

Economic factors represent the overall economic health of the country or region in which the organization operates.

有利的经济环境会给组织的发展提供更为广阔的空间，成功的管理者必须意识到经济因素对组织的重大影响，并根据变化情况做出快速反应。随着中国经济发展水平的不断提高，中国已成为世界第二大经济体。同时，因为拥有足够多的人口、智能和活力，中国已成为全球企业关注的重要潜在市场。

China has become the world's second largest economy with the population, brain power, and dynamism.

（三）技术环境

◇　Technological factors

在管理环境中，技术环境是非常重要的一个构成要素，任何组织的生存与发展，其管理不可能脱离科学技术。概括而言，技术环境包括全社会的科学和技术进步，它直接作用于组织，影响组织对物质条件的获取，进而影响利用这些条件的组织活动的效率。具体说来，技术环境包括社会科技水平、社会科技力量、科技体制、科技政策等多个方面。

Technological factors include scientific and technological advancement in the society.

近年来，技术因素为各行各业的组织都带来了大规模的、意义深远的变革，互联网、掌上设备、手机、笔记本电脑等的出现，不仅为管理者们的工作提供了便捷的手段，同时也催生了新的经营模式。而移动电子商务（M-commerce）的出现，更是颠覆了传统的经营模式，向现代组织的管理者们提出了新的挑战。

M-commerce: Mobile or wireless commerce for buying and selling goods using for example cellular telephones or personal digital assistants.

Global Perspective

Mobile Wallets as Credit Card Killers

Google Wallet, bitcoin and other payment systems have spent years trying to oust the credit card as the be-all and end-all of payment methods. Publications and pundits everywhere have been quick to hail new technologies as "credit card-killers," and they're not without justification. As a payment method, the credit card has lost whatever futuristic luster it may have once had. Magnetic stripes wear out, plastic snaps in half, and the incessant manual inputting of 16-digit numbers eventually gets tiresome.

However, when it comes to new payment platforms like Apple Pay, are mobile wallets really that much more convenient than usual transaction methods? Sure, credit cards take up space in wallets, but scanning a fingerprint isn't really that much more convenient than swiping a card. So while they're definitely a bit more helpful, mobile wallets aren't doing enough in stores to really kick off a proper revolution.

One surprising aspect about Apple Pay isn't its application in the physical space, where it's been emphasized most. The potential for mobile wallets could have a profound impact on the world of online transactions—and while the technology is still evolving, mobile wallets are more than just credit card killers.

（案例来源：节选自 http://www.ecommercetimes.com/story/81788.html）

（四）自然环境

自然环境是制约组织经营活动的重要因素，是组织得以生存和发展所依赖的各种自然条件的总和，包括植物、动物、岩石以及其他自然资源。自然环境是一个国家或地区经济发展的基础，也为所在区域的组织提供了发展的机会。但是自然资源是不可再生的稀缺资源，对自然资源的利用一定要遵循可持续发展原则。

生态环境是近年来全社会重点关注的热点问题。所谓生态是指人与环境中存在的其他有生命的物体（如动、植物）及非生命物体（如土壤、水和空气）之间的关系。任何组织的发展都不能以破坏生态环境为代价，在资源日趋紧张的条件下，循环经济已成为现代经济发展的一种趋势。

◇ Natural environment

Natural environment encompasses all living and non-living things occurring naturally in some region.

Ecology is the relationship of people and other living things with their environment.

<u>Global Perspective</u>

The Circular Economy

The Circular Economy（CE）approach to resource-use efficiency integrates cleaner production and industrial ecology in a broader system encompassing industrial firms, networks or chains of firms, eco-industrial parks, and regional infrastructure to support resource optimization. State-owned and private enterprises, government and private infrastructure, and consumers all have a role in achieving the CE. The three basic levels of action are:

At the individual firm level, managers must seek much higher efficiency through the three Rs of CP (Reduce, Reuse, and Recycle), reduce consumption of resources and emission of pollutants and waste, reuse resources, and recycle by-products.

The second level is to reuse and recycle resources within industrial parks and clustered or chained industries, so that resources will circulate fully in the local production system.

The third level is to integrate different production and consumption systems in a region so the resources circulate among industries and urban systems. This level requires development of municipal or regional by-product collection, storage, processing, and distribution systems.

Efforts at all three levels include development of resource recovery and cleaner production enterprises and public facilities to support realization of the CE concept. This adds a strong economic development dimension through investment in new ventures and job creation. So the CE opens opportunities for both domestic and foreign enterprises.

A logical extension of the third regional level of action would be integrating management of flows among urban, suburban, and rural resource recovery systems. An example would be bio-refineries utilizing discarded biomass from rural and urban sources. Such refineries would operate with a range of technologies for converting these resources into bio-energy, bio-fuel, and bio-materials.

Consumers have a role at the household and neighborhood level in applying the CE concept. The majority of the Chinese people still fail to meet all of their basic material needs, including potable water for drinking and sanitation, affordable and good quality food, basic housing, and household equipment. The Circular Economy must support families in achieving these requirements of life. At the same time local initiatives must offer citizens education in the practices of reduce, reuse, and recycle at the home level.

（案例来源：节选自 http://www.indigodev.com/Circular1.html）

（五）社会文化环境

社会文化环境反映了一个区域中大众的规范、习惯、价值观和人口特征。重要的社会文化特性包括教育程度、文化水平、宗教信仰、审美观点、价值观念等。文化水平会影响居民的需求层次；宗教信仰和风俗习惯会禁止或抵制开展某些活动；价值观念会影响居民对组织目标、组织活动以及组织存在本身的认可；审美观点则会影响人们对组织活动内容、活动方式以及成果的态度。

随着消费者市场和劳动力供应日益趋于全球化，管理者们不得不面对越来越多元化的组织环境。员工的多民族化、教育水平的普遍提高、不断增加的移民趋势、"90后"新生代员工逐渐步入职场、家庭生活格局的变化、人口老龄化的日趋严重，都会向新时代的管理者提出严峻挑战。管理者们要做的，不是去消除不同社会文化之间的差异，而是了解社会文化之间的差异，并针对不同国家和地区的社会文化环境因素的变化和差异，相应调整自己的行为方式，使管理更加行之有效。

✧　Socio-cultural factors

Socio-cultural factors represent the demographic characteristics, norms, customs, and values of the population within which the organization operates.

"Post-90s" refers to the generation of Chinese born among 1990-1999.

"Post-90s employees" refers to post-90s workers directly or indirectly engaged in enterprises.

Global Perspective

Post-90s Employees in Labor-intensive Enterprises

People who were born after 1990 are a group of labors with a distinctive trait and large scale, concentrating on labor-intensive enterprises. They are now facing the pressure of job, life, and marriage. There were approximately 36.649 million "post-90s" employees in 2011 in China, accounting for 4.8% of national employment for the same period; in the future four years, 59.955 million college students are going to graduate and walk into the community as post-90s employees. With the continuous enlargement of the scale of post-90s employees, they increasingly play an important role in China's economic development.

Post-90s employees are in the early stage of their career; their job is unstable; they have a high turnover rate; their liquidity is frequent; they have no fixed abode, it is difficult to develop and maintain a stable relationship among colleagues, friends, and leaderships for them. Since they are away from family and friends, their original social relations support are gradually weakened. Therefore, social relation of post-90s employees is in a temporary shortage state; they lack of social support channel of talk, exchange thought and being cared.

Post-90s employees are psychological sensitive, their mood changes rapidly; they are easy to be anger and impulses. They are self-centered, critical to others and publicize themselves. They think that the whole world is paying attention to them; being self-centered and they are full of the spirit of criticism to authority, are not willing to accept the criticism, and easy to point out others' errors in behavior.

（案例来源：节选自 Li, P. L. and Lu, H. L. Research on Initiative Turnover Rate of the Post-90s Workforce—Taking Labor-Intensive Enterprises as an Example. *Journal of Human Resource and Sustainability Studies*, 2014(2): 12-25）

（六）伦理环境

伦理道德是一门探讨好与坏的是非问题以及道德责任与义务的学科。商业伦理关注的是真实与公正原则，包括经济活动中那些涉及对或错的道德准则或信念，如公平竞争、合法广告、社会责任等。这些准则或信念旨在帮助有关经济活动主体判断某种行为是正确的还是错误的，或者这种行为是否为组织所接受。

企业在经营过程中，常常要面对伦理选择的问题。是否该解雇一名效率低下的员工？他的家庭及孩子们是否会受到影响？如果企业在海外投资，而在当地使用童工合法，并且你的竞争对手已经这样做了，那么，你是否也该这么做？在当代社会中，许多企业把利益最大化作为企业发展的基本原则，却忽视了企业伦理方面的坚守。管理学者们为管理人员制定决策提供了三种伦理观，即功利主义伦理观（Utilitarian Theory）、权利主义伦理观（Theory Based on Rights）、公正主义伦理观（Theory of Justice）。如表 1-2 所示。

✧ Ethical environment

Ethics is the discipline dealing with what is good and bad and with moral duty and obligation

Business ethics is concerned with truth and justice.

表 1-2　三种伦理理论

Table 1-2　Three Ethical Theories

Ethical Theories	Key Points	Examples
Utilitarian theory	Plans and actions should be evaluated by their consequences.	economic good, pleasure rather than pain, happiness, security
Theory based on rights	All people have basic rights.	the rights to freedom of conscience, free speech, and due process
Theory of justice	Decision makers must be guided by fairness and equity, as well as by impartiality.	promotion on the basis of performance, not manager's subjective judgment

企业社会责任是组织伦理环境中一个非常重要的内容。企业社会责任并不是一个新的概念，它最早出现于 20 世纪 50 年代的美国，主要背景是经济增长伴生的环境问题、社会问题日益严重，人们逐渐意识到造成这些问题的主要原因是企业缺乏社会责任。要解决这些问题，不能仅仅靠传统的法律法规进行约束，还要通过提升企业社会责任来从内部解决问题。

Global Perspective

Coca-Cola's Happiness Machines

"Hello Happiness," a new video from Coca-Cola, opens with footage of migrant laborers in Dubai, standing before dawn in a patch of dirt as they wait for a van to pull up and shuttle them to work. Later, we cycle through shots of grim-faced men in work clothes—slouched on the bus as the sun rises, hunched on sagging bunk beds, crowded on the floor of a small room during mealtime with their elbows nearly touching. They tell us that they love and miss their families, and that they wish they could hear their children's voices more often. We learn that these workers make about six dollars per day, and that it costs nearly a dollar per minute to call home—so phone calls are rare. Then we are posed a question: "So what if every Coke came with a few extra minutes of happiness?"

In March, 2014, Coke installed five special phone booths in Dubai labor camps that accepted Coca-Cola bottle caps instead of coins. In exchange for the cap from a bottle of Coke—which costs about fifty-four cents—migrant workers could make a three-minute international call. The ad shows laborers in hard hats and reflective vests lining up to use the machine—and grinning, for the first time in the video, as they wait. "I've saved one more cap, so I can talk to my wife again tomorrow," one man tells the camera. More than forty thousand people made calls using the machines.

（案例来源：节选自 www.enwyorker.com/business/currency/coca-colas-happiness- machines）

所谓企业社会责任，就是企业在经营过程中认真考虑公司的行动措施对社会产生的影响。社会的构成是多维的，企业的社会责任感体现在不歧视员工、定期培训员工、善待员工等对员工的责任；体现在提供安全的产品、正确的产品信息、售后服务，给予顾客自主选择的权利等对顾客的责任；体现在不恶意竞争、企业联合等对竞争对手的责任；体现在为投资者带来有吸引力的投资回报，将财务情况及时、准确地报告给投资者等对投资者的责任；体现在提供就业机会、参与社区公益活动等对所在社区的责任。企业社会责任既是道德的要求，也是企业的理性选择，有利于企业经济管理活动的进行，有利于企业自身目标的实现。

Corporate social responsibility is the serious consideration of the impact of the company's actions on society.

Global Perspective

Johnson & Johnson's Credo

We believe our first responsibility is to the doctors, nurses and patients, to mothers and fathers and all others who use our products and services. In meeting their needs everything we do must be of high quality. We must constantly strive to reduce our costs in order to maintain reasonable prices. Customers' orders must be serviced promptly and accurately. Our supplies and distributors must have an opportunity to make a fair profit.

We are responsible to our employees, the men and women who work with us throughout the world. Everyone must be considered as an individual. We must respect their dignity and recognize their merit. They must have a sense of security in their jobs. Compensation must be fair and adequate, and working conditions clean, orderly and safe. We must be mindful of ways to help our employees fulfill their family responsibilities. Employees must feel free to make suggestions and complaints. There must be equal opportunity for employment, development and advancement for those qualified. We must provide competent management, and their actions must be just and ethical.

We are responsible to the communities in which we live and work and to the world community as well. We must be good citizens—support good works and charities and bear our fair share of taxes. We must encourage civic improvements and better health and education. We must maintain in good order the property we are privileged to use, protecting the environment and natural resources.

Our final responsibility is to our stockholders. Business must make a sound profit. We must experiment with new ideas. Research must be carried on, innovative programs developed and mistakes paid for. New equipment must be purchased, new facilities provided and new products launched. Reserves must be created to provide for adverse times. When we operate according to these principles, the stockholders should realize a fair return.

（案例来源：强生公司网站，http://www.jnj.com）

关键概念 KEY IDEAS AND CONCEPTS

Management

Organization

Managerial functions

Planning

Organizing

Staffing

Leading

Controlling

Ethnocentric orientation

Geocentric orientation

Productivity

Effectiveness

Efficiency

External environment

Internal environment

M-commerce

Ecology

Ethics

Business ethics

Corporate social responsibility

讨论问题 DISCUSSION QUESTIONS

1. How is management defined? Does your definition differ from the ones offered in this book? Explain why.

2. How to understand "Management applies to any kind of organization"? Give your ideas.

3. What are the primary functions of management and their contents?

4. What are the differences among productivity, effectiveness, and efficiency? Please explain the matrix of efficiency and effectiveness.

5. What are the two attributes of management? Please compare the management style in U.S., Japan and China.

6. Is management a science or an art? Could you give some examples to explain?

7. What are the characteristics of management environment?

8. Identify the elements of the external environment that are likely to be the most important to each of the following: a company president, a sales manager, a production manager, and a personnel manager.

9. Would the environment for a cell phone company contain the same elements as that for a government welfare agency? Discuss.

10. Contrast and compare the utilitarian theory, theory based on rights, and theory of justice.

综合案例 CLOSING CASE

E-Commerce Giants, Gov't Create New Markets in China's Rural Areas

China's major E-commerce giants and the government are following through on plans to turn the country's huge rural areas into new markets. The efforts are linking hundreds of millions of villagers to e-sales websites, while also creating sales channels to urbanites for everything from farm produce to tickets for lesser-known tourist spots.

E-commerce giants like Alibaba Group Holdings Ltd. and JD.com Inc. see China's large number of rural counties as a new possibility for growth after getting city dwellers hooked on buying goods from websites. Meanwhile, the government hopes the new business activity can lift some desperately poor areas out of poverty. Researchers at Alibaba, which owns the popular Taobao and Tmall shopping sites, estimate that the rural market was worth 180 billion Yuan in 2014 and that the figure will soar to 460 billion Yuan in 2016.

Alibaba and JD.com launched large campaigns last year to reach out to rural areas, where nearly half of China's 1.3 billion people lives. As a result of those campaigns, banners with large characters promoting E-commerce have started appearing on walls in villages around the country.

Alibaba's Strategy in China's Rural Areas

In July, Alibaba hosted a conference bringing together more than 170 officials from counties in 26 provinces and regions around the country to discuss E-commerce. The meeting near Alibaba's headquarters in Hangzhou, the capital of the eastern province of Zhejiang, allowed company representatives to meet some of the country's lower-level leaders, who expressed a desire to bring their areas' agricultural goods and tourism resources to the attention of the increasingly powerful urban consumers. Zhang Yong, Alibaba's COO, said in October that the firm will spend 10 billion Yuan over five years to set up 1,000 offices in counties and 100,000 more in villages to facilitate the new business. The hope is these offices will ease the flow of goods between urban and rural areas, and help residents of rural areas get used to online shopping, he said. The same month Alibaba signed an agreement with commerce officials in Zhejiang to start work on building logistics and training facilities in the counties and villages of the province. The facilities are intended to help farmers make online purchases that at least initially will have to be settled in cash because most villagers do not know how to make payments through the Internet. Alibaba employees are also going to help farmers take photographs of agricultural products such as radishes, cabbages and chestnuts that are put online, hopefully whetting the appetite of city dwellers.

There's some evidence that this effort is working. On November 11, a major promotional day for Alibaba, its e-sales websites took nearly 1,300 orders involving 210,000 Yuan worth of goods from a rural county in Zhejiang named Tonglu.

JD.com: Village Tour

JD.com started working to connect with villagers earlier than Alibaba. In May, the company cooperated with the Ministry of Agriculture to launch a campaign that invited villagers to shop on its website. The next month JD.com sent a team of employees on a six-month tour of more than 100 counties around the country. At each stop, locals were invited to events where they learned how to shop on the site for goods such as clothing, books and groceries, items of which China's urbanites buy with ease. To get the goods out to the new shoppers, the company has started building a distribution system to cover more than 1,000 counties, opening more than 500 distribution centers and training thousands of deliverymen.

Liu Qiangdong, JD.com's founder, said in February that his company's distribution centers also handed the installation of home appliances and other necessary services for more than 60,000 villages. To get these washing machines, refrigerators and televisions out, JD.com hired more than 2,000 deliverymen devoted to the home appliance business.

JD.com launched a pilot of its program in Zhaoxian County, in the northern province of Hebei. The company convinced Jin Xinlong, the owner of a small service shop for home appliances, to become JD.com's first distribution center in the county. Jin said this required him to follow stricter standards to run his business.

Business, Not Games

In July, the ministries of finance and commerce chose 55 poor counties to receive 20 million Yuan each to develop their E-commerce industry in a bid to reduce poverty. One of these counties was Tongshan, in the central province of Hubei, which had per capita GDP of 4,000 Yuan in 2014, compared to the national average about 46,000 Yuan.

The county head, Hu Juan, who attended Alibaba's meeting in July, said the central government's campaign has already boosted Tongshan's cooperation with E-commerce companies.

Tongshan has opened a Taobao shop to sell tickets for its main tourist attraction, the Jiulong Mountain scenic area. In the past, the area sold about 1,000 tickets a month, Hu said, but the online store has pushed that figure up to 10,000. Then local hotels got into the act, launching promotions on tourism websites such as Ctrip.com and Lvmama.com. Tongshan's government has also invited Yuantong E-commerce Services Co. to help local firms learn about online sales, and it also formed an association to guide and regulate E-commerce. Jiang Feng, the manager of Yuantong E-commerce, said his company mainly helped design and decorate shops on Taobao and Tmall. It also helped train locals, take the necessary photos and run promotions.

Tongshan then went a step further, setting up a service center led by Jiang that E-commerce companies in the county could turn to for help. The center helps the firms manage their presences on JD.com, Tmall and Yhd.com, another E-commerce site.

The county then trained the owners of Internet cafes to help villagers buy and sell products online, Hu said. In the past, the Internet cafes had made money by illegally allowing children to play video games, she said, but the new source of profits gave them a reason to turn the youngsters away.

（案例来源：Qu Yunxu and Wang Qionghui. E-commerce Giants, Gov't Create New Markets in China's Rural Areas. 财新网 http://english.caixin.com/2015-03-05/100788403.html，2015-3-5）

Discussion Questions

1. What opportunities and threats did E-commerce companies face in the rural market?
2. Before the E-commerce giants entered the rural market, few people believed that E-commerce could be accepted and successful in rural market. How did they push their ideas to the farmers? What strategies did they follow?
3. Compare and contrast the strategies in China's rural areas of Alibaba and JD.com.
4. What do you think about the future of E-commerce in China's rural areas?

第二章　管理思想的发展

学习目标

1. 考释管理思想史的主要发展
2. 阐释古典管理观的主要方式方法
3. 描述行为科学管理理论的主要内容
4. 解释现代管理理论的主要概念

主要内容

第一节　早期管理思想与实践
第二节　古典管理理论
第三节　行为科学理论
第四节　现代管理理论

Learning Outcomes

1. Identify and explain major developments in the history of management thought.
2. Explain the major approaches within the classical viewpoint of management.
3. Describe the major components of the behavioral science management perspectives.
4. Explain the major concepts in modern management theories.

Contents

2.1 Early Management Thought
2.2 Classical Perspectives
2.3 Behavioral Science Perspectives
2.4 Modern Management Theories

第一节 早期管理思想与实践

Robert's Rules Bring Order

During the late 1800s, when Henry Martyn Robert, a brigadier general in the U.S. Army, was pursuing his military career as a civil engineer, he frequently attended meetings with people from many backgrounds. Often he had to preside at these meetings.

He quickly learned about the challenge of running meetings when the first meeting over which he presided, involving a group of Baptist ministers, ended in total chaos. Robert was perplexed because nothing was settled or resolved. He had prepared his subject well and had even gathered advice on how to conduct a meeting. He decided that he would never again participate in such a disastrous encounter.

For the next 7 years, he collected information concerning how to conduct a meeting, and he subsequently produced a 176-page book titled *Pocket Manual of Rules of Order for Deliberative Assemblies*. The book provided a set of parliamentary rules for conducting meetings.

He promoted the book, which he had published on his own, by sending 1000 copies to the best parliamentarians in the United States, including governors, legislators, the vice president, and a few attorneys, and he asked the recipients for their comments. After receiving many enthusiastic responses and several very good suggestions, he modified the original text, changing the title to *Robert's Rules of Order*. The book has become a classic source of guidance for running large, formal meetings and is used by many legislative bodies, government councils, associations, and other organizations in which decisions are made by member vote. First published in 1876, the book has not been out of print since. More than 4 million copies have been sold throughout the English-speaking world. It has also been published in Braille.

（案例来源：Kathryn M. Bartol and David C. Martin. *Management* (3rd edition). 北京：机械工业出版社，1998，p. 40）

　　管理思想来源于管理实践。案例中 Robert 在工作中遇到了无法协调的问题之后，通过询问、整理、分析，归纳了一套大型会议运行准则。这就是早期管理思想的来源和体现。作为个体的人，限于体力等方面的原因，很难独立生存，在整个生产活动和其他活动过程中，都要以集体的方式与他人共同完成任务，这就需要一定的合作和组织，即管理工作。在管理工作中，管理者会同案例中的 Robert 一样，遇到这样或那样的管理问题，在摸索着寻找办法解决问题的过程中，人类的管理思想也逐渐形成和发展。这些思想虽然形成在许多年以前，但并不意味着是过时的或无用的理论。正如案例中的 Robert's Rules of Order 一样，几百年以后仍然不断演进，指导着现代人的管理工作。

　　本节将结合中外管理思想与实践，综合介绍早期的管理思想。

一、古代的管理实践

管理实践活动已经存在了上千年,几乎与人类有记载的历史一样悠久。早在原始社会,人们为了抵御恶劣的自然环境,就形成了以血缘关系为基础的氏族部落,共同生活,从事集体劳动,并选举部落首领负责组织狩猎等活动,部落成员之间进行简单的分工协作,狩猎来的食物按照一定的规则进行分配。这些维持共同生活的组织活动其实就是管理实践,其本质上与今天的管理并无显著差异。

奴隶社会中,出现了政府、军队、宗教团体、手工作坊等新的社会组织,在政府的治国施政、军队的指挥作战、宗教团体的日常运行、大型工程的修建等过程中,管理实践无处不在。埃及的金字塔、中国的万里长城、巴比伦古城都是举世闻名的古代建筑工程实践,在当时的技术条件下,修建这样的工程需要成千上万的人分工协作,共同劳动。以我国长城为例,长城是中国,也是世界上修建时间最长、规模最大的一项古代防御工程。当年秦始皇为了修筑长城动用了 30 万人,创造了人类建筑史上的奇迹。长城作为防御工程,翻山越岭,穿沙漠,过草原,越绝壁,跨河流,其所经之处地形之复杂,所用结构之奇特,在古代建筑工程史上可谓一大奇观。如此复杂浩大的工程,在当时的技术条件下能够完成,不仅体现了劳动人民的智慧和创造力,也是历史上卓越的管理实践。

在管理实践活动中,逐渐出现了管理思想的雏形。在埃及、中国、意大利等国的史籍和宗教文献中,都可以发现早期著名的管理思想。又如古巴比伦的《汉谟拉比法典》、古希腊哲学家柏拉图的《理想国》等都对当时的社会管理制度、管理思想进行了记录和阐述,说明早在数千年前人们就意识到了管理的重要性,并且存在一些朴素的管理思想。我国古代管理思想起源于《周礼》,该书第一次把中国官僚组织机构设计为 360 职,并规定了相应的级别和职数,层次、职责分明。古代管理思想中最有代表性的是中国著名的《孙子兵法》,距今已有 2500 多年,其"知己知彼,百战不殆"的战略思想,至今仍在企业和商务管理中被广泛使用。除此以外,《论语》中的"人治""礼治"的行政管理思想,《老子》中的"无为而治"的柔性管理思想等,都是我国人民管理经验和智慧的结晶,对于现代管理理论研究和管理实践工作仍有重要的借鉴价值。

☞ **Management Practice in Ancient Times**

Management practice has existed for thousands of years.

The Art of War is an ancient Chinese military treatise attributed to Sun Tzu, and is commonly known to be the definitive work on military strategy and tactics of its time.

总的来说,在中西方发展历史上都曾经有过丰富的管理思想与管理实践,但这些思想大多关注宏观层面的管理实践,同时,这些管理思想还比较零散,不够系统。直到18世纪工业革命时期,现代意义上的企业组织出现并得以迅速发展,对管理理论的产生起到极大的推动作用。

Much of the impetus for developing management theories and principles stemmed from the industrial revolution.

Global Perspective

Popular Chinese Business Book：The Art of War

When asking a dozen people to name the best business book ever and chances are, several of them will say, "*The Art of War*".

The Art of War was written by a Chinese general named Sun Tzu more than 2500 years ago. The text is composed of 13 chapters, each of which is devoted to one aspect of warfare. It has had an influence on Eastern and Western military thinking, business tactics, legal strategy and beyond. For the last two thousand years, it remained the most important military treatise in Asia, when even the common people knew it by name. Although it was meant to be a practical guide to warfare in the age of chariots, many corporate and government leaders have successfully applied its lessons to battles in the modern world.

Read widely in the east since its appearance 2500 years ago, *The Art of War* first came to the west with a French Jesuit in 1800s. The first annotated English language translation was completed and published by Lionel Giles in 1910. It's a smart book. Now it has been applied to many fields well outside of the military. It is very popular among Western business management, who have turned to it for inspiration and advice on how to succeed in competitive business situations.

二、工业革命后的企业管理实践

18世纪60年代兴起的工业革命开始于英国,在美国南北战争结束后又传到美国。工业革命是以机器取代人力,以大规模工厂化生产取代个体工场手工生产的一场生产与科技革命。通过工业革命,资本主义生产完成了从工场手工业向机器大工业的过渡,实现了从手工劳动向机器生产转变的重大飞跃。工业革命之后,出现了现代意义上的企业组织形式,也出现了对管理活动的客观需求。随着工业革命以及工厂制度的发展,不少对管理理论的建立和发展具有重大贡献的管理实践和思想应运而生。

✍ **A Very Important Influence on Management Is Industrial Revolution.**

The Industrial Revolution was the transition to new manufacturing processes in 1760s. This transition included going from hand production methods to machines, new chemical manufacturing and iron production processes, improved efficiency of water power, the increasing use of steam power, and the development of machine tools.

（一）小詹姆斯·瓦特与马修·鲁宾逊·博尔顿的管理思想与实践

在企业管理中最早使用科学管理方法的，当推小詹姆斯·瓦特（James Watt Jr., 1769—848）与马修·鲁宾逊·博尔顿（Mattew R. Boulton, 1770—1842），他们分别是蒸汽机发明者瓦特及其合作者博尔顿的儿子。他们于1800年接管了父辈创办的铸造工厂，开始进行管理改革。

小詹姆斯·瓦特与马修·鲁宾逊·博尔顿在工厂的生产和销售活动中运用了许多管理技术。例如：他们组织市场调查，向欧洲大陆派出许多代表，收集各项可能影响产品需求的资料，并据此确定企业的生产能力和编制生产计划；他们依据工作流程的需要，有计划地安排机器的空间布置，组织生产过程规范化，产品部件标准化；在会计与成本核算方面，他们建立了详尽的统计记录和控制系统，还采用了原料成本、人工费用、成品库存等分别记账的会计制度，从而能够计算工厂所制造的每台机器的成本和每个部门所获得的利润；在人事管理方面，他们进行了工作效率研究，制定了管理人员与员工的培训计划，实行按成果支付工资的方法，并试图改善员工福利，为员工建立了一套互助保险制度等。

（二）罗伯特·欧文的管理思想与实践

罗伯特·欧文（Robert Owen, 1771—1858）出生于英国北威尔士的一个手工业者家庭，1800年开始在苏格兰接办了一家工厂，是一名成功的企业家。他在企业经营中，开始了人事管理改革，效果显著。

当时的工厂中雇用了400～500名童工，每天工作13个小时。欧文认为必须对员工的工作条件进行改善，合理布局生产设备，缩短劳动时间，提高雇用童工的最低年龄限制，提高工资，在厂内免费为工人提供膳食，设立幼儿园和模范学校，创办互助储金会，通过建设工人住宅与修建街道来谋求改进厂区的整个状况。尽管他的合作伙伴对这些思想比较抵制，但是欧文仍坚持不懈地改善工人工作条件，他的改革得到了工人的大力支持，从而大大提高了工厂的利润。欧文最早注意到管理中人的因素的作用，这为以后行为科学的兴起奠定了重要基础。

（三）查尔斯·巴贝奇的管理思想与实践

查尔斯·巴贝奇（Charles Babbage, 1792—1871）出生于英国一个富有的银行家家庭，是一位著名的数学家。他对社会最大的贡献是生产出了世界上第一台分析机，即

❖ James Watt Jr. & Matthew R. Boulton

James Watt Jr. and Matthew R. Boulton used some new management tools in the process of production and sales, such as components standardize, cost kept, management of the factory improved, etc.

❖ Robert Owen

Robert Owen became interested in the working and living conditions of his employees, and tried to improve the living conditions of employees by upgrading streets, houses, sanitation, and the educational system.

Owen's ideas laid the groundwork for the human relations movement.

❖ Charles Babbage

Charles Babbage is widely known as the father of modern computer.

现代计算机的鼻祖，他也因此被誉为"计算机之父"。他把突出的数学贡献和卓越的数学思维应用到管理科学当中，运用技术性的方法作为解决企业经营管理方面的辅助手段，因而被公认为运筹学和管理科学的创始人，同时也是科学管理的倡导者、对管理问题进行定量化研究的先驱。巴贝奇对工业生产中的作业操作、工资、成本、均衡生产等多个方面都有贡献。

Babbage was enthralled with the idea of work specialization.

巴贝奇倡导工作分工，他全面地分析了分工所带来的劳动生产率提高的原因，认为不仅体力劳动需要工作分工，脑力劳动同样需要。同时，巴贝奇认为，工人和工厂所有者之间存在着某种共同利益，这种共同利益可以通过其利润加工资的分配制度体现出来。他提出，工人可以按照他对劳动生产率所做出的贡献分得工厂利润的一部分，他将工人的报酬分为两个部分：按照对劳动生产率所做出的贡献分得的利润和为增进生产率提出建议而应得的奖金。巴贝奇把工人的实际利益与企业效益及发展结合在一起，在调节劳资矛盾、发挥工人生产积极性方面无疑具有一定的贡献。

Babbage devised a profit-sharing plan that had two parts, a portion of wages that was dependent on factory profits and a bonus that was awarded for useful suggestions.

虽然小詹姆斯·瓦特与马修·鲁宾逊·博尔顿、罗伯特·欧文和查尔斯·巴贝奇等人早期的管理思想比较零散，多是管理思想先驱者们个人的尝试或设想，缺乏上升到理论层面的总结和传播。但他们的思想对后来的管理理论的创建和发展产生了不可忽视的重要影响。

第二节 古典管理理论

Management Philosophy in UPS

United Parcel Service, Inc., typically abbreviated to UPS, is the world's largest package delivery company and a provider of supply chain management solutions. The global logistics company is headquartered in Sandy Springs, Georgia, which is part of the Greater Atlanta metropolitan area. UPS delivers more than 15 million packages a day to more than 6.1 million customers in more than 220 countries and territories around the world. In addition, UPS is gaining market share in air service logistics.

Why has UPS been so successful? UPS is bound up in rules and regulations. It teaches drivers an astounding 340 steps for how to correctly deliver a package—such as how to load the truck, how to fasten their seat belts, how to walk, and how to carry their keys. There are safety rules for drivers, loaders, clerks, and managers. Strict dress codes are enforced—clean uniforms (called brown) every day, black or brown polished shoes with nonslip soles, no beards, no hair below the collar, and so on. Supervisors conduct three-minute inspections of drivers each day. The company also has rules specifying cleanliness standards for building, trucks, and other properties. No eating or drinking is permitted at employee desks. Every manager is given bound copies of policy books and is expected to use them regularly.

UPS has a well-defined division of labor. Each plant consists of specialized drivers, loader, clerks, washers, sorters, and maintenance personnel. UPS thrives on written records, and has been a leader in using new technology to enhance reliability and efficiency. Drivers use a computerized clipboard to track everything from miles per gallon to data on parcel delivery. All drivers have daily worksheets that specify performance goals and work output.

（案例来源：改编自 Richard L. Daft. *Management* (7th edition). 北京：清华大学出版社，2006，pp. 48-49）

美国联合包裹服务公司（UPS）成立于 1907 年，是世界上最大的快递承运商和包裹运送公司。它的成功来自它专业的运输、物流、资本与领先的电子商务服务，尤其是科学的运营管理方法。正如案例中描述的那样，UPS 要求当司机到达投送的地点时，他们会松开安全带，按喇叭，关发动机，拉紧手刹，将挡位置于停车挡，为送货完毕的启动离开做好准备。然后，司机从驾驶室出来，右臂夹着文件夹，左手拿着包裹，右手拿着车钥匙，看一眼包裹上的地址，以每秒钟 3 英尺（1 英尺≈0.305 米）的速度快步走到顾客的门前，敲门，不要去按门铃，以免在寻找门铃时浪费时间。送货完毕后，司机在回到汽车的路上完成登记工作。UPS 公司通过研究司机的动作，采取了合理的管理措施，提高了效率。生产率专家公认，UPS 是世界上效率最高的公司之一。它所采用的管理方法就是我们本节要讨论的古典管理理论之一——科学管理理论。

一、古典管理理论

管理理论得以比较系统地创建，是在 19 世纪末至 20 世纪初，其代表是美国人泰勒的科学管理理论、法国人法约尔的一般管理理论和德国人韦伯的行政组织理论。这些理论被统称为古典管理理论。

古典管理理论的产生是有客观依据的，当时这些工业先进国家经过产业革命后一定时间的发展，生产力已达到相当的高度，科学技术也有了较大的发展，许多新的发现也被应用于生产。但是，当时的管理还相当落后，多是建立在经验和臆断的基础上，缺乏科学依据。为了进一步发展生产，就必须在管理方面有一个较大的突破，这是当时社会的客观要求。早期的管理思想和管理实践为管理理论的突破提供了思想资料，在美、法、德等国家几乎同时出现了科学管理运动，形成了各有特色的古典管理理论。

各种古典管理理论强调管理研究方法的理性和科学性，致力于把组织建设成高效运转的机器。

二、科学管理理论

科学管理理论是 20 世纪初在西方工业国家影响最大、推广最普遍的一种管理思想理论。它包括一系列关于生产组织合理化和生产作业标准化的科学方法及理论依据，是由美国人泰勒首先提出并积极推广的，因此通常被称为"泰勒制"。

（一）泰勒生平

弗雷德里克·温斯洛·泰勒（Frederick Winslow Taylor, 1856—1915）出生于美国费城一个富裕的家庭，他的父亲是名律师，母亲是一位知识分子。泰勒从小就很爱好科学研究和实验，对任何事情都想找出一种最好的方法。父母希望他能够子承父业，成为一名律师，泰勒也不负其所望，考入了哈佛大学法学院，但是因为眼疾不得不中途辍学，1876 年进入小型水压厂，开始了他为期 4 年的学徒工生涯。在当学徒工的过程中，泰勒发现了资本家对工人们的剥削和压迫，对工人产生了同情，同时，也看到了工人们的"磨洋工"（Soldiering）现象和劳动生产率的低下。1878 年泰勒进入费城的米德维尔钢铁厂当工人，先后当过技工、工长、技师、总工程师。在不断升迁的过程中，他不得不面对管理工人的问题，这些经验催生出了科学管理理论的雏形。

✍ **Classical Theory**

Classical theory: A management perspective that emerged during the nineteenth and early twentieth centuries that emphasized a rational, scientific approach to the study of management and sought to make organizations efficient operating machines.

✍ **Scientific Management**

Scientific Management: the use of scientific methods to define the "one best way" for a job to be done.

✧ Frederick Winslow Taylor

Soldiering: Deliberately working at less than full capacity.

1890 年，泰勒跳槽到一家纸板投资公司任总经理。1893—1898 年，开始从事工厂的管理咨询工作，利用科学管理思想，帮助工厂提高生产率。1901 年泰勒宣布退休，开始无偿地为工厂进行咨询，并开始写作和演讲，推广其科学管理思想。1911 年泰勒出版了《科学管理原理》一书，在书中总结归纳了科学管理的重要原则。1915 年他因患肺炎去世，葬于一座能够俯瞰费城钢铁厂的小山上，墓碑上刻着"科学管理之父——弗雷德里克·温斯洛·泰勒"。

（二）科学管理理论的主要内容

1. 通过动作和实践研究法对工人操作的每一个环节进行科学的观察分析，开发出科学方法，用以替代传统的经验方法。

（1）铁锹实验

泰勒在钢铁公司工作时发现，不管搬运铁石还是搬运煤炭，都使用铁锹进行人工铲取，雇用的搬运工动不动达五六百名。不管他们铲运的是何种材料，工厂中的每个工人都使用同样大小的铁锹。这在泰勒看来是不合理的，如果能找到每锹铲运量的最佳重量，那将使工人们每天铲运的数量达到最大。在一次调查中，泰勒发现搬运工一次可铲起 3.5 磅的煤粉，而铁矿石则可铲起 3.8 磅。为了获得一天最大的搬运量，泰勒开始着手研究每一锹最合理的铲取量。他找了两名优秀的搬运工用不同大小的铁锹做实验，每次都使用秒表记录时间。最后发现：一锹铲取量为 21.5 磅时，一天的材料搬运量为最大。同时也得出一个结论，在搬运铁矿石和煤粉时，最好使用不同的铁锹。通过这种方式，工人的生产率得到了大幅度的提高。

（2）劳动标准化

通过铁锹实验，泰勒提出，必须用科学的方法对工人的操作方法、使用的劳动工具、工作时间的安排、作业环境的布置等进行全面的分析，消除不合理的因素，把各种最好的因素结合起来，形成一种最好的方法，决定每天最合理的产量。泰勒将其称为标准化原理。

2. 科学地挑选工人，并对他们进行培训、教育。

（1）生铁搬运实验

当时的工作要求工人们把 92 磅重的生铁块装到铁路的货车上。他们每天的平均生产率是 12.5 吨，泰勒则认为，通过科学分析装运生铁的操作以确定最佳方法，生产率应该能够提高到每天 48 吨左右。泰勒将工人分为头等工人和二等工人，认为既能干好而且又愿意干好的人才是头等工人。

◇ Main ideas of scientific management theory
Taylor's four principles of scientific management:
1. Develop a science for each element of an individual's work, which will replace the old rule-of-thumb method.

Time and Motion Study: A study of breaking down the work task into various elements, or motions, eliminating unnecessary motions, determining the best way to do the job, and then timing each motion to determine the amount of production that could be expected per day.

2. Scientifically select and then train, teach, and develop the workers.

他通过多次试验，从工人中找到了一位大个头、体格强壮的工人施米特，用金钱激励的方式，使施米特严格按照他说的去做。泰勒要求施米特按照规定的方法装运生铁，试着转换各种工作因素，以观察它们对施米特日生产率的影响。经过长时间对各种程序、方法和工具的组合进行科学实验，泰勒成功地达到了他认为可能达到的生产率水平。

（2）科学挑选与培训工人

泰勒认为，人有不同的禀赋才能，只要工作合适，都可能成为一流的工人。因此，要提高工人的劳动生产率，首先要根据工人的不同特长来分配工作，然后选择第一流的工人，并对其工作进行动作分解和优化使其达到最高效率，之后对其他工人进行培训，教会他们科学的工作方法，激励他们尽最大努力来工作。

3. 真诚地与工人们合作，确保工人们按照制定的科学原则进行工作。

为了鼓励工人努力工作，完成定额，泰勒建议实行"差别工资制"，其内容包括如下三点。

（1）通过动作和实践研究，制定出有科学依据的工作定额。

（2）采用差别计件的刺激性付酬制度（Piece Rate Compensation），即计件工资率随完成定额的程度而上下浮动。例如：对那些用最短的时间完成工作且质量高的工人，按一个较高的工资率计算，而对那些用时长且工作质量差的工人，则按一个较低的工资率来计算。

（3）工资支付的对方是工人，而不是职位，即根据工人的实际工作表现而不是根据工作类别来支付工资。通过金钱激励，克服工人消极怠工的现象，促使工人最大限度地提高生产效率。而随着生产率的提高，在生产率提高的幅度超过工资增加幅度的情况下，雇主也就从"做大的馅饼"中得到了更多的效益。劳资双方不再是你进我退、此消彼长的对立关系，通过相互协作、共同努力，雇主可以获得更多的利润，工人可以获得更高的工资，对双方都有利。

4. 明确管理者和工作人员各自的工作和责任，实现管理工作与操作工作的分工。

泰勒在企业的工作实践中，从工程技术人员的角度意识到改进和加强企业管理工作对提高劳动生产率的重要作用。

The success of any business organization depends on the selection of personnel to work in the organization. The organization should go to great lengths to ensure that only the best talent is selected and hired for a given job.

3. Cooperate fully with the workers so as to ensure that all work is done in accordance with the principles of the science that has been developed.

Piece rate compensation system is a system where compensation is based upon the number of units of work produced by an individual. It is associated with bonuses for extra efforts and aims to maximize employee's work effort.

4. Divide work and responsibility almost equally between management and workers.

首先，泰勒主张明确划分计划职能与执行职能，由专门的计划部门来从事调查研究，为定额和操作方法提供科学依据；制定科学的定额和标准化的操作方法及工具；拟订计划并发布指示和命令；比较"标准"和"实际情况"之间的差异，进行有效的控制。作业部门包括现场监督的工头和直接从事操作的工人，他们的任务是根据计划部门制定的标准和定额进行监督和生产作业。

其次，泰勒提出"职能工长制"，即将管理的工作予以细分，每个管理者只承担其中一两项管理工作。他设计出八个职能工长，代替原来的一个工长，其中四个在计划部门工作，四个在车间工作，每个职能工长只负责某一方面的工作，在其职责范围内可以直接向工人发布命令。通过职能工长制，可以提高管理工作的效率。

另外，泰勒还提出了"例外管理原则"，认为规模较大的企业组织和管理，必须应用"例外管理原则"。即企业的高级管理人员把一般日常事务授权给下级管理人员去处理，自己只保留对例外事项的决定和监督权。这一原则实际上为后来的管理分权化原则和事业部制管理体制提供了理论基础。

（三）科学管理理论的贡献和局限性

泰勒的科学管理理论在 20 世纪初得到了广泛的传播和应用，影响很大。他冲破了工业革命以来一直沿袭的传统经验管理方法，将科学引入了管理领域，提出系统的管理理论体系。在实践工作中，泰勒的科学管理理论取得了显著的效果，使企业的生产效率提高了两三倍，受到企业主的普遍欢迎。泰勒主张将管理职能从企业生产职能中独立出来，进一步促进了人们对管理实践的思考，从而有利于管理理论的发展。"科学管理"的概念已深入各行各业，直至今天依然很重要。

但是，科学管理理论也存在一定的局限性。它的研究范围比较小，内容比较窄，多局限于作业方法或现场监督，而对于企业中的其他活动，例如采购、销售、人事、财务等，则基本上没有涉足。另外，因为科学管理忽略了社会环境和员工需求，以机器为中心，对人的社会价值研究不足。虽然泰勒本意希望建立管理者和员工之间的和谐相处，但事实上许多企业管理人员严重忽视了人的尊严和人的主观能动作用，员工们常感觉被利用了，在管理者和员工间的冲突反而加剧。

关于科学管理原理的方法、贡献和局限，可以参考表 2-1。

Management by exception is a style of management that gives employees the responsibility to take decisions and to fulfill their work or projects by themselves. The managers should spend their time more effectively in areas where it will have the most impact.

✧ The contributions and limitations of scientific management theory

表 2-1　科学管理的特征

Table 2-1　Characteristics of Scientific Management

General Approach
● Developed standard method for performing each job.
● Selected workers with appropriate abilities for each job.
● Trained workers in standard methods.
● Supported workers by planning their work and eliminating interruptions.
● Provided wage incentives to workers for increased output.
Contributions
● Demonstrated the importance of compensation for performance
● Initiated the careful study of tasks and jobs.
● Demonstrated the importance of personnel selection and training.
Criticisms
● Did not appreciate the social context of work and higher needs of workers
● Did not acknowledge variance among individuals.
● Tended to regard workers as uninformed and ignored their ideas and suggestions.

（资料来源：Richard L. Daft. *Management* (7th edition). 北京：清华大学出版社，2006, p. 47）

Global Perspective

Taylorism and Economic Growth

Taylor took the lead in challenging the conventional system, theoretically proposing and practically implementing the qualitatively new approach to management and work organization. The key principles formulated by Taylor along with the other organizational engineers of his time, such as a focus on "rational economic man", normative approach to work organization and incentives, maximum division of labor, and rationalization of work and motion, emerged as fundamental pillars for technocratic, mechanistic management of the industrial age.

Overall, *The Principles of Scientific Management* served the urgent needs of its time—closing the gap between advancing technologies and obsolete organizational means, radically improving productivity, and providing the critical mass of managers with a science of effective work and administration. At the moment of publication of the book, the USA, Germany, and Imperial Russia served as fertile lands for the introduction of scientific management. Other countries that lagged behind economically, appealed to Taylorism historically at a later time.

The transition of the leading economic powers to the post-industrial era in the late twentieth century shifted focus in production systems to new dimensions of productivity and organizational efficiency such as innovation, creativity, networking, group organization, and value-based leadership. Those dimensions were not a part of Taylor's prescriptions and contradicted many of them. Hence, the authors assume that emergence of scientific management was historically predetermined by the specific economic environment and was most effective in the industries that defined the industrial type of growth. Even today, industries which created the backbone of the industrial age (machinery, steel, or textile) may still exploit Taylor's guidelines quite effectively; however, many of those principles and techniques (maximum division of labor, detailed monitoring of individual time and motions, focus on an individual, not a group, etc.) turned out to be much less applicable to innovative industries of the post-industrial era (like software or biotechnology).

（案例来源：节选自 Mikhail Grachev and Boris Rakitsky. Historic Horizons of Frederick Taylor's Scientific Management. *Journal of Management History*, 2013, 19(4): 512-527）

三、一般管理理论

当泰勒及其追随者正在美国研究和倡导生产作业现场的科学管理原理和方法时,法国诞生了关于整个组织的一般管理理论。科学管理理论注重每个工人的生产力,而一般管理理论关注的则是整个组织,致力于解释管理者的工作是什么,以及有效的管理由哪些因素构成,所以又被称为组织管理理论。一般管理理论的杰出代表是亨利·法约尔。

(一) 法约尔生平

亨利·法约尔(Henri Fayol, 1841—1925)出生于法国中部一个资产阶级家庭,1858 年按照父母意愿考上了圣·艾蒂安国立矿业学院,学习采矿工程专业。1860 年大学毕业,进入科芒特里富香博-德卡维尔矿业公司,并一直工作至 1918 年退休。他 25 岁的时候就已经是该公司的管理员,到了 1888 年,公司财政状况岌岌可危,法约尔临危受命,成为公司总经理。经过一系列的整顿和兼并重组,法约尔把公司经营得欣欣向荣。法约尔的名著《工业管理与一般管理》于 1916 年出版,它标志着一般管理理论的诞生,是古典管理理论的代表作,也是一部划时代的经典之作。1918 年从总经理的位置上退下来之后,法约尔将全部时间用于传播他的管理理论,他认为,他的理论还可以应用于商业之外的领域。法约尔由于长期从事企业高层管理工作,因此对全面管理有深刻的体会和理解,被后人称为"管理过程之父"。

(二) 一般管理理论的主要内容

1. 从经营活动中提炼出管理活动

法约尔区别了经营与管理,将管理包含在经营之中。认为经营的六大职能包括技术、商业、财务、安全、会计和管理等活动。其中,技术活动是指生产、制造、加工等活动;商业活动是指原材料及设备的采购、产品销售等活动;财务活动是指资金的筹集和运用等活动;安全活动是指设备维护和人员安全等活动;会计活动是指货物盘存、成本统计、核算等活动;管理活动是指计划、组织、指挥、协调和控制五项职能活动。在这六项活动中,管理活动处于核心地位,即企业本身需要管理,其他五项属于企业的活动也需要管理。

2. 提出管理的基本要素

法约尔首次把管理活动分为计划、组织、指挥、协调、控制五大职能,并对这些职能进行了详细的分析和研究。

✍ **Administrative Management**

Administrative Management: An approach that focuses on principles that can be used by managers to coordinate the internal activities of organizations.

✧ Henri Fayol

Fayol: *General and Industrial Management*

✧ The main ideas of administrative management theory
1. Isolate the main types of actives involved in industry or business: technical, commercial, financial, security, accounting, and management.

2. First outline five basic functions or elements of management: planning, organizing, commanding, coordinating, and controlling.

计划就是探索未来，制订行动计划；组织就是建立企业的物质和社会的双重结构；指挥就是使其人员发挥作用；协调就是连接、联合、调和所有的活动及力量；控制就是注意是否一切都按已制定的规章和下达的命令执行。

法约尔认为，这五个方面的活动，在任何组织的任何层次都会以这种或那种方式不同程度地存在着，因此组织中不同层次的工作人员都应根据任务的特点，拥有不同程度的五种职能活动的知识和能力。后来许多管理学者按照法约尔的研究思路对管理活动进行深入的理论研究，逐渐形成了管理过程学派。

3. 提出有效管理的十四条原则

法约尔在他的著作《工业管理与一般管理》中提出，管理的成功不完全取决于个人的管理能力，更重要的是管理者要能灵活地贯彻管理的一系列原则。他根据自己的经验总结了 14 条原则。这些原则是：劳动分工、权责对等、纪律严明、统一指挥、统一领导、个人利益服从整体利益、人员的报酬、集权、等级制度、秩序、公平、人员的稳定、首创精神、团结精神。如表 2-2 所示。

3. Identify 14 principles of management.

表 2-2　法约尔有效管理的十四条原则

Table 2-2　Fayol's General Principles of Management

1. **Division of work.** Work specialization can result in efficiencies and is applicable to both managerial and technical functions. Yet there are limitations to how much that work should be divided.

2. **Authority.** Authority is the right to give orders and the power to exact obedience. It derives from the formal authority of the office and from personal authority based on factors like intelligence and experience. With authority comes responsibility.

3. **Discipline.** Discipline is absolutely necessary for the smooth running of an organization, but the state of discipline depends essentially on the worthiness of its leaders.

4. **Unity of command.** An employee should receive orders from one superior only.

5. **Unity of direction.** Activities aimed at the same objective should be organized so that there is one plan and one person in charge.

6. **Subordination of individual interests to the general interest.** The interests of one employee or group should not prevail over the interests and goals of the organization.

7. **Remuneration.** Compensation should be fair to both the employee and the employer.

8. **Centralization.** The proper amount of centralization or decentralization depends on the situation. The objective is the optimum use of the capabilities of personnel.

9. **Scalar Chain.** A scalar (hierarchical) chain of authority extends from the top to the bottom of an organization and defines the communication path. However, horizontal communication is also encouraged as long as the managers in the chain are kept informed.

10. **Order.** Materials should be kept in well-chosen places that facilitate activities. Similarly, due to good organization and selection, the right person should be in the right place.

11. **Equity.** Employees should be treated with kindness and justice.

12. **Stability of personnel tenure.** Because time is required to become effective in new jobs, high turnover should be prevented.

13. **Initiative.** Managers should encourage and develop subordinate initiative to the fullest.

14. **Esprit de corps.** Since union is strength, harmony and teamwork are essential.

（资料来源：Kathryn M. Bartol and David C. Martin, *Management* (3rd edition). 北京：机械工业出版社，1998，p. 45）

法约尔指出，虽然他给出了 14 条原则，但是它们是灵活的，没有什么绝对准确的哲学信条。他认为，原则的应用是一门很难掌握的艺术，要求智慧、经验、判断和注意尺度。这些原则中的许多原则已经成为今天管理哲学的重要理论来源。

4. 提出管理教育的必要性和可能性

法约尔注意到，当时人们关注对知识的灌输和技术能力的培训，却普遍忽视了管理教育，其主要原因是对零散的管理知识和经验缺乏系统的认识。因此，法约尔指出，要适应企业经营的需要，必须加强管理教育。管理能力可以通过教育来获得，必须尽快建立一种管理理论。为此，他提出了一套比较全面的管理理论，首次指出管理理论具有普遍性，可以用于各种组织。法约尔提出，应在学校设置管理这门课程，传授管理知识，并在社会各个领域宣传、普及管理知识。

（三）一般管理理论的贡献和局限性

法约尔的管理理论起初并没有在国际上被广泛传播。但是，是金子总会发光。法约尔的一般管理理论以内容上的系统性、逻辑上的严密性、管理工作认识的普遍性，慢慢地得到了后人的普遍认可。一般管理理论被认为是西方古典管理理论的重要代表。法约尔对管理五大职能的分析为管理学提供了科学的理论框架，来源于长期实践经验的管理原则给管理者以巨大的帮助。虽然一般管理理论是以企业为研究对象建立起来的，但由于强调管理的一般性，这个理论也普遍适用于学校、政府、军队等其他类型的组织。法约尔为现代管理学理论的形成做出了卓越的贡献，他提出的许多概念、术语和原理在现代管理学中得到了普遍的继承和运用。如表 2-3 所示。

虽然法约尔的理论在当时有很强的先进性，但是在具体的实施过程中，仍然具有一定的局限性。法约尔虽然对管理职能和管理过程进行了系统的剖析，却回避了人性的问题；管理原则缺乏弹性，以至于有时实际管理工作者无法完全遵守管理原则。以统一指挥原则为例，法约尔认为，无论什么工作，下属只能接受唯一一个上级的命令，但事实上，当某一层次的管理人员制定决策时，他需要考虑来自各个专业部门的意见或指示，这与统一指挥原则是不相符的。

4. Convince that management could be taught to others and should be exploited.

✧ The contributions and limitations of administrative management

表 2-3　法约尔十四条原则在当代管理中的应用

Table 2-3　Fayol's General Principles of Management in Modern-Day Management

Principle	Current interpretation/application
Division of work	Specialization exists. Cross-training is used so that employees (and organizations) have more capabilities.
Authority	Empowerment and process ownership enable people at all levels to make decision. Fayol's ideas are still very relevant (e.g. authority and responsibility must be co-equal).
Discipline	Self discipline. Respect based on knowledge.
Unity of command	With matrix organizations and teams, people receive instructions from multiple people which can cause problems. Functionally employees may report to one boss who evaluates the employees.
Unity of direction	Strategic management involves bottom up, top down and cross functional input to integrated plans.
Subordination of individual interests to the general interest	Team members align individual and team, personal, and work goals. Those goals still have to support the general interest/organization.
Remuneration	Pay for knowledge and core competencies. Obey the rule of team rewards and profit sharing.
Centralization	Role of employee is increased. Local decisions and process ownership are preferred.
Scalar chain	Horizontal or cross functional authority. Team structure.
Order	Chaos, creativity, and innovation.
Equity	Equity is demanded by workers based on performance.
Stability of personnel tenure	It is better to have best managers for a while than mediocre managers for a longer time.
Initiative	Respecting and caring for customers is an impetus for initiative. Managers who encourage initiative are valued. The principle of initiative is relevant to today's concepts of empowerment and process ownership.
Esprit de Corps	Only dysfunctional conflict is bad. Diversity and differences are necessary if creativity and innovation are to flourish. The concept of esprit de corps is still relevant in terms of strength of teams to accomplish objectives.

（资料来源：节选自 Midred Golden Pryor and Sonia Taneja, Henri Fayol, Practitioner and Theoretician—Revered and Reviled. *Journal of Management History*, 2010,16(4): 489-503）

四、行政组织理论

行政组织理论是古典管理理论的另一个重要的组成部分，它强调组织活动要通过职务或职位，而不是个人或世袭地位来设计和运作。这一理论的创立者是德国学者马克斯·韦伯，他从社会学研究中提出了所谓"理想的"行政性组织，为 20 世纪初的欧洲企业从不正规的业主式管理向正规化的职业性管理过渡提供了一种纯理性化的组织模式，对当时新兴的资本主义企业制度的完善起着划时代的作用。

（一）韦伯生平

马克斯·韦伯（Max Weber, 1864—1920）出生于德国图林根的一个中产阶级家庭，父亲是法学家和政界人

✍ **Bureaucratic Management**

Bureaucratic Management: An approach that emphasizes the need for organizations to operate in a rational manner rather than relying on the arbitrary whims of owners and managers.

✧　Max Weber

士，母亲是加尔文教派教徒，有深厚的文化修养和政治责任感。家庭对韦伯的影响很大，使韦伯一生的命运与政治相连。

1882年韦伯考入海德堡大学法律系，1889年获得博士学位，1891年在柏林大学任教，可以说早年的韦伯事业上是一帆风顺的。然而到了1897年，韦伯竞选国会议员失败，父子因为政治问题发生了激烈的争执，而两个月后父亲去世了，这场没有和解的争吵成为韦伯毕生的遗憾，对韦伯打击异常沉重。1898—1902年，他不得不靠到欧洲四处旅游来治疗心灵的创伤。直到1902年，韦伯才回到海德堡，开始恢复写作，从此进入了学术研究的鼎盛时期，出版了大量的学术论文和著作，其中包括最为典型代表的"行为组织理论"。

由于当时德国经济并不发达，时局不很稳定，因此韦伯的理论当时并没有得到重视。直至其去世后的若干年，他的理论才广为流传，他也被后人称为"组织理论之父"。

（二）行政组织理论的主要内容

1. 权力的类型

韦伯认为，等级、权力和科层制度（官僚组织体系）是一切社会组织的基础。社会或组织与其构成部分的关系，主要不是通过契约关系或道德一致来维持的，而是通过权力的行使来凝聚的。韦伯将权力定义为一种引起服从的命令结构，任何组织都必须以某种形式的权力作为基础。人类社会存在三种权力：传统型的权力、个人魅力型的权力和法定的权力。

其中，传统型的权力由传统惯例或者世袭得来，这种权力建立在对习惯和古老传统神圣不可侵犯性的要求之上，对这种权力的服从是绝对服从于统治者，因为他具有沿袭下来的神圣不可侵犯的地位和权力。

个人魅力型的权力是建立在对某个英雄人物或者某个具有优良品质的人的个人崇拜基础之上的权力，对这种权力的服从通常可以溯源于对领袖人物的权力信仰和信任。所谓的救世主、先知、政治领袖等，往往被认定具有超自然的、超人的权力。韦伯认为，个人魅力型的权力产生于动乱和危机之中，崩溃于稳定秩序条件下的日常事务管理以及使这种权力制度化的尝试之中，所以个人魅力型的权力不能作为政治统治稳固制度的基础。

法定的权力是由社会公认的法律规定的，对这种权力的服从是绝对的，没有普通老百姓和领袖官员之分。法定的权力是按照一定法律而建立的，对这种权力的服从就等

◆ The main ideas of bureau-cratic management theory

1. Identify the right of managers: traditional authority, charismatic authority and legal-rational authority.

Traditional Authority: past customs; personal loyalty

Charismatic Authority: personal trust in character and skills

Legal-Rational Authority: rational application of rules or laws

于对确认的职务或地位的权力的服从。只有合理合法的权力才能作为行政组织体系的基础,其最根本的特征在于其提供了慎重的公正。

2. 理想的行政组织体系

韦伯提出,理想的官僚组织体系需具备以下六个特征。如图 2-1 所示。

(1)劳动分工:工作应当分解成为简单的、例行的和明确定义的任务。

(2)职权等级:公职和职位应当按等级来组织,每个下级应当接受上级的控制和监督。

(3)正式的选拔:所有组织成员都是依据经过培训、教育,或正式考试取得的技术资格选拔的。

(4)正式的规则和制度:为了确保一贯性和全体雇员的活动,管理者必须使用书面形式的规则和标准的操作程序。

(5)非人格性:规则和控制的实施具有一致性,避免掺杂雇员的人格特性和个人偏好。

(6)职业定向:管理者是职业化的雇员,而不是所管理单位的所有者,他们领取固定的工资,并在组织中追求他们职业生涯的成就。

2. Describe an ideal form of organization—the bureaucracy: division of labor, authority hierarchy, formal selection, formal rules and regulations, impersonality, and career orientation.

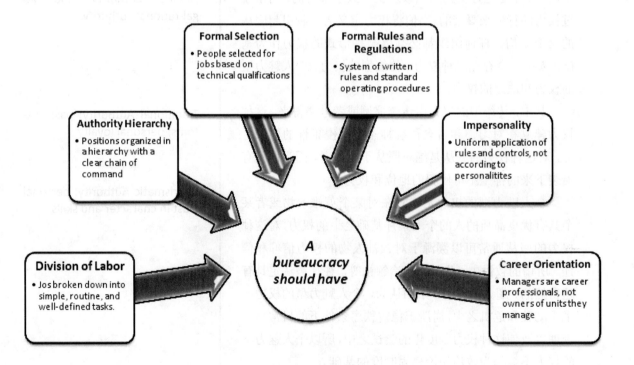

图 2-1　理想的官僚组织体系特征

Figure 2-1　Characteristics of Ideal Bureaucracy

(资料来源:改编自 Stephen P. Robbins and Mary Coulter, *Management* (11th edition). 北京:清华大学出版社, 2013, p. 32)

Global Perspective

Modern-day Bureaucracy

Weber's theory of bureaucracy is still appropriate for modern-day businesses but it is better to do some changes and improvements.

In this rapid development society, to some degree, bureaucracy seems to affect the efficiency of modern-day business. Most top-heavy bureaucracies have so many layers of management, which leads to that it is impossible for them to communicate with each other. Nowadays, most staffs have been well educated and they have their own ideas. Sometimes they have new and good ideas that can improve their products or some suggestions about management. Because of too many layers, it is difficult to pass these ideas and suggestions to higher level management and almost impossible to the highest management. Even through the highest level of management knows and adopts these good ideas and suggestions, it will spend a long time. Nowadays more and more things are time-sensitive and a long time later, they maybe lose their function. The phenomenon needs to be changed today.

The other aspect which needs to be changed is that although speciation leads to some efficiency with the bureaucracy, it also creates barriers between different departments. Many times there is a lack of cooperation between the departments because managers are protecting their own turf. Within department mangers' authority, they all want to make more benefit to their own department and more welfare to their lower level staffs, which may cause low cooperation in one enterprise, especially in today's big enterprises. What's more, speciation limits potential of employees because jobs are narrow and employees cannot work across departments. This is bureaucracy brings to the modern-day business. If there are some coordinators to link up different departments, the problem will be solved.

（案例来源：作者根据相关内容整理）

韦伯认为，这样高度结构化的、正式的、非人格化的科层组织体系是达到目标、提高效率最有效的形式。它在精确性、稳定性、纪律性和可靠性等方面都优于其他组织形式，能适用于所有的管理工作及日益增多的各种大型组织，如教会、政府机构、企业和各种团体。尽管这种"理想的官僚行政组织"在现实中是不存在的，但它代表了一种可供选择的现实世界的重构方式。

（三）行政组织理论的贡献和局限性

韦伯对理想的行政组织体系的描绘，为行政组织指明了一条制度化的组织准则，这是他在管理思想史上的最大贡献。韦伯提出的行政组织体系为资本主义提供了一种高效率的、合乎理性的管理体系。韦伯的这一理论，对泰勒、

◇ The contributions and limitations of bureaucratic management

法约尔的理论是一种补充，对后来的管理学家，特别是组织理论家产生了很大的影响。同时，韦伯强调以知识和技能进行管理的必要，抨击了旧的传统以及阻碍经济发展的政治控制，把组织形态与权威性质结合起来进行分析，为后人研究组织问题指出了重要的方向。

同时，韦伯的理论也存在着许多的不足。首先，韦伯的理论是一种高度理想化的纯理论描述，现实中几乎不存在这样的理想官僚组织，因而无法对韦伯的理论进行实证性论证。其次，韦伯过于强调了机械式正式组织的功能，忽视了组织运作过程中的实际状态，过分强调了层级官僚制体制，忽视了下级人员的主动性和积极性，过于强调遵守组织规则和各项制度，使组织陷于僵化，缺乏应变能力和弹性。

另外，韦伯的理论过分强调专业分工和职能权限划分的意义，忽视了组织与环境之间的相互协调关系，过于强调组织利益和组织效率，忽视了组织成员多方面的心理需求。这与科学管理理论和一般管理理论是非常类似的，因此，人们将其与泰勒的科学管理理论、法约尔的一般管理理论并称为古典管理理论。

第三节　行为科学理论

Panda Express

Panda Express is the pioneer in the quick-service Chinese food market and quickly becomes the Chinese food of choice for consumers and developers. It has more than 1700 restaurants throughout the United States and Puerto Rico and is America's fastest growing Chinese restaurant.

Scientific management ideas are always used in the quick-service food market to increase the productivity. Panda Express also operates like that. Andrew Cherng, the founder and chairman of Panda Express, believes the quality meals made with fresh and premium ingredients served fast and hot would win over the hears and stomachs of hungry guests. However, Cherng doesn't agree the "rational economic man" hypothesis, and believes that a company can be successful only when the employees who comprise it are good enough as itself. "You can't expect people to do a good job at work if their lives are a mess." That's the philosophy of Cherng. In fact, he says that his company's success doesn't come just from the meals prepared in the kitchen, but because "he cares about the emotional well-being or his employees." With five guiding values—being proactive, showing respect/having a win-win attitude, pursuing growth, having great operations, and being giving—and a caring and strong management team, this company has prospered.

（案例来源：根据 Panda Express 官网资料整理，www.pandaexpress.com）

以泰勒、法约尔、韦伯的理论为代表的古典管理理论直至今天仍然被广泛传播和应用，这些理论对于提高生产效率的确非常有效。但是，古典管理理论多侧重于生产过程、组织控制，强调管理的科学性、合理性和纪律性，却很少关注人的因素和作用。古典管理理论的假设前提是"经济人"假设，即社会是由一群无组织的个人组成，他们在思想上、行动上力争获得个人利益、追求最大限度的经济收入。基于这种认识，工人被称为机器的附属品，成为像机器一样的"工具人"。事实上，在组织的管理实践中，管理者们发现古典管理理论在提高生产率的同时，也使得工人的劳动变得异常紧张、单调和疲劳，容易引起工人的不满，进而影响整个组织的效益。正如案例中 Cherng 所说的那样，只有组织中的员工表现好，顾客才会对组织满意。在同样的组织环境中，不同的员工，即使体力和技能大致相当，也可能产生不同的结果。20世纪 20 年代中期以后，人们开始将管理的注意力从生产现场的机器转向生产过程中操作机器的人，出现了人际关系学说和行为管理理论。

本节将围绕"社会人"的概念讨论行为科学理论的具体内容。

一、霍桑实验

（一）实验背景

20 世纪初，企业普遍奉行科学管理理论和方法，认为工作环境的物质条件以及工人的技术和体质与生产率之间存在着明确的因果关系，如果工作环境理想，温度和照明度适当，工作任务经过科学的测定，同时采用某种合理的工资制度，那么工人便能达到较高的工作效率。当时的美国西方电气公司的霍桑电话机厂，有 25000 多名员工，生产电话机、电气设备，工作环境和物质条件都很好，员工的工资、奖金、福利都不错，具有较完善的娱乐设施、医疗制度和养老金制度，但是工人的劳动热情并不高，而且还常有怨言，因此生产效率也不理想。为了探究其中的原因，1924 年 11 月，由美国国家科学院赞助开展了工作条件与生产效率关系的研究，即霍桑实验。

（二）实验的第一阶段（照明实验）

实验的第一阶段为期 3 年，从 1924 年一直到 1927 年，主要目的是通过照明的强度变化，来检验照明水平对工人生产率的影响。研究人员将工人们分为两组，一组是控制组，一组是实验组。实验组的照明强度不断变化，而控制组的照明强度保持不变。研究人员原来估计个人的产量会与光线亮度有直接关系，但是，实验结果让他们非常惊讶。随着照明亮度的增加，实验组和控制组的生产率都增加了；而且，当实验组亮度水平下降时，两个组的生产率仍然继续提高。研究人员得出结论，照明强度与生产率没有直接关系，还有许多其他因素对实验结果产生影响。但是到底是哪些因素产生了影响，研究人员无法解释。

（三）实验的第二阶段

1927 年，研究人员邀请哈佛大学的乔治·埃尔顿·梅奥（George Elton Mayo）教授作为顾问加入研究，重新开始实验。他们选择了继电器装配和云母片装配两个小组进行实验，探讨究竟是什么原因导致产量的增加。在试验中他们改变了传统的严格命令和控制的方法，就各种项目的实验向工人提出建议、征询意见，力图创造一种"更为自由愉快的工作环境"。结果发现，管理方式的改变带来了士气的提高和人际关系的改善。这种可以自由发表意见、得到关心的工作环境使工人感到受到了重视，士气和态度也随之改变，从而促进了产量的变化。在此研究基础上，研究小组进行了为期两年的大规模访谈，涉及两万多人次，结果发现，影响工作效率最重要的因素不是待遇和

✍ **Hawthorne Studies**

✧ The background

Hawthorne studies: A series of experiments on worker productivity begun in 1924 at the Hawthorne plant of Western Electric Company in Illinois.

✧ First set of studies: Illumination Studies

Conclusions: Productivity almost always increased after any change in illumination. Factors other than lighting were at work.

✧ Second set of studies: Relay Assembly Test

Conclusions: The possibility that individuals singled out for a study may improve their performance simply because of the added attention they receive from the researchers, rather than because of any specific factors being tested.

工作环境，而是工作中发展起来的人际关系。

（四）实验的第三阶段（配线观察室实验）

梅奥在第二阶段的访谈中发现，员工的工作绩效，不仅取决于他们自身的情况，还要受到其所在群体中其他人的影响。这一发现使得研究小组继续关注员工在工作中的群体行为。在实验的第三阶段，研究小组挑选了 14 名男工，除了 2 名检验工之外，其余 12 名员工被分成了 3 组，构成"正式组织"，工人的报酬采用集体计件工资制。研究发现，工人们对于"合理的日工作量"有明确的概念，而且这个工作量低于管理当局估计的水平和他们的实际能力。他们在产量水平上达到了某种默契，并运用团体的压力来加以维护，使人们共同遵守。这些压力包括冷遇、讽刺、嘲笑等，人们不愿意被团体抛弃，所以自觉维持着非正式的定额。

二、人际关系学派

梅奥在参加霍桑实验的过程中，不断发现"人"在生产率提高中的作用，认为人的心理因素和社会因素对生产效率有极大的影响。1933 年，梅奥出版了《工业文明中人的问题》，对霍桑实验的结果进行了系统总结，阐述了与古典管理理论不同的新观点，提出人际关系学说。

（一）梅奥生平

乔治·埃尔顿·梅奥（George Elton Mayo，1880—1949）是美国著名的行为科学家，人际关系理论创始人。他出生于澳大利亚一个幸福家庭，先后在圣彼得学院和阿德雷德大学接受教育，1899 年获得逻辑和哲学硕士学位，后来又到英国的爱丁堡学习医学，并进行精神病理学研究。1911—1919 年在澳大利亚的昆士兰大学任逻辑学、伦理学和哲学讲师。第一次世界大战期间，他利用业余时间，用心理疗法治疗被炸弹震伤的士兵，成效显著。1922 年在洛克菲勒基金会的帮助下，梅奥移居美国。1923—1926 年期间他作为宾夕法尼亚大学的研究人员为洛克菲勒基金会进行工业研究。1926 年，梅奥进入哈佛大学工商管理学院从事工业研究，任哈佛大学工商管理研究院工业研究室副教授。1927 年冬，梅奥应邀参加了始于 1924 年但中途遇到困难的霍桑实验，断断续续进行了 9 年的两阶段实验研究，并在实验的基础上，于 1933 年出版了《工业文明中人的问题》一书，正式创立了人际关系学派。

◆ Third set of studies: The Bank-wiring Observation Room Study

Conclusions: There are informal social relations within groups and group norms are used to restrict output when doing so seems advantageous to the group.

✍ **Human Resources Perspective**

◆ George Elton Mayo

George Elton Mayo: *The Human Problems of an Industrial Civilization*

（二）人际关系学派

人际关系学派的主要观点包括以下三个内容。

1. 员工是"社会人"

这是人际关系学派最大的贡献。当时流行的科学管理理论把人当作"经济人"来看待，认为金钱是刺激人的积极性的唯一动力。而人际关系学派则提出，人是"社会人"，具有社会心理方面的需要，而不是单纯地追求金钱收入和物质条件的满足。每个人都有各自的特点，个体的观点和个性都会影响个人对上级命令的反应和在工作中的表现。因此，应该将员工当作"社会人"来看待，帮助他们满足友谊、安定、归属等心理需求。

2. 正式组织中存在着非正式组织

人际关系学派根据霍桑实验的结果提出，在正式组织之外，还存在一些小的团体。这些小的团队是人们在自然接触过程中自发形成的，即非正式组织。正式组织中人的行为遵循效率的逻辑，而非正式组织中人的行为往往遵循感情的逻辑，合得来的就在一起，合不来的或不愿交往的就会被排除在组织外。在非正式组织中有着不成文的规定：工作不能太认真，否则可能会被认为是出风头；不能过于懒惰，否则会被当作懒汉；不能告密，否则会认为是拍马屁；不能耀武扬威，要和平相处等。

3. 新的企业领导能力在于通过提高员工的满意度来激发士气，从而达到提高生产率的目的

科学管理原理认为，生产效率的高低主要取决于作业方法、工作条件、工资制度，因此，管理者应致力于寻找恰当的工资制度，改善工作条件，制定科学的作业方法，以提高工人的劳动生产率。人际关系学派则提出不同的观点，认为生产效率的高低主要取决于工人士气的高低，而工人的士气取决于他们感受的各种需要得到满足的程度。这些需要中，不仅仅包括金钱等物质需要，还包括尊重或安全等社会需要。因此，新型的管理者应该认真分析员工需要的特点，不仅要解决工人生产技术或物质生活等方面的问题，还要掌握他们的心理状况及思想情绪，适时、合理、充分地激励工人，达到提高生产率的目的。

（三）人际关系学派的贡献和局限性

人际关系学派对管理学发展的最大贡献在于：实现了管理学研究从关注工作到关注人的转变，改变了当时那种认为人与机器没有差别的流行观点，激起了人们重新认识组织中人的因素的愿望，使西方管理思想经历了科学管理

✧ Human resources perspective

The main contributions of Human resources perspective theory:

1. Workers are also social men, not just economic men.

Social norms, group standards and attitudes more strongly influence individual output and work behavior than do monetary incentives.

2. Emphasizing that alongside the formal organization of an industrial workplace there exists an informal organizational structure as well.

Informal groups within the work plant exercise strong social controls over the work habits and attitudes of the individual worker.

3. Studying human motivation and the managerial styles that lead to more productivity.

Human resources perspective: A management perspective that suggests jobs should be designed to meet higher-level needs by allowing workers to use their full potential.

✧ The contributions and limitations of human resources perspective theory

理论阶段后进入行为科学理论阶段。另外，非正式组织的发现为正式组织理论的诞生奠定了基础。

然而，人际关系学派也存在一定的局限性：过于强调社会需要，忽视经济需要；过于强调非正式组织的作用；过于强调"心里满足"对工作效率的影响，忽视经济报酬、外部监督、工作条件、作业标准等因素的影响。

Global Perspective

The Cure for Stress in Foxconn

Foxconn was the world's largest contract electronics manufacturer. From 2000 to 2013, the 18 attempted suicides by Foxconn employees resulted in 14 deaths. The suicides drew media attention, and employment practices at Foxconn were investigated by several of its customers, including Apple and HP.

One main reason for the suicides is workplace stress. Foxconn began to implement a number of wide-ranging reforms to motivate employees, including reducing workers' hours and significantly boosting wages. Because of severe labor shortages in China, Foxconn's factory employees work long days and are under extreme pressure to produce products. Many employees are young migrant workers living away from their families and other support groups. Foxconn provided a frustration venting room where factory workers can slam inflatable punching bags in one way that management of the company is helping its employees in China reduce personal and work-related stress. Foxconn has also set up a help line and hired psychiatrists to assist lonely and depressed workers and has recruited singers, dancers, and gym trainers to teach all employees how to relax and relieve stress.

（案例来源：根据富士康网站及相关新闻报道整理，www.foxconn.com.cn）

三、行为科学理论

✍ **Behavioral Science**

梅奥等人的研究结论带来了人们对组织中的人的一种全新的认识，在此之后，致力于人的因素研究的行为科学家也不断涌现。越来越多的心理学家从研究个体需要的角度出发，关注管理中的激励问题，行为科学研究在 20 世纪五六十年代迎来鼎盛时期，并产生了一门新的交叉学科——组织行为学。

Behavioral science: An approach that emphasizes scientific research as the basis for developing theories about human behavior in organizations that can be used to establish practical guidelines for managers.

行为科学学派当中，研究人员大致分为三大类：一类关注个体行为；一类关注组织行为；一类关注领导行为。

（一）关注个体行为的研究

❖ Research on individual behaviors

在行为科学理论的研究中，个体行为是主要的研究内容。行为科学家们认为，人的行为是由动机导向的，而动机则是由需要引起的，在人们的某种需要未得到满足之前，就会产生对某件事的驱动力，就会寻找能够满足需要的目标，进而从事某种行为。

关于个体行为研究的代表性成果包括：麦克雷戈（Douglas McGregor）的 X-Y 理论、马斯洛（Abraham Maslow）的需要层次理论、赫茨伯格（Fredrick Herzberg）的双因素理论、弗鲁姆（Victor Vroom）的期望理论、麦克莱兰（David C. McClelland）的成就需要理论、亚当斯（J. Stacy Adams）的公平理论等。

（二）关注组织行为的研究

如果将组织看成一个系统，则组织中的各种团体就是其子系统，个体则是构成子系统的具体要素。因此，组织行为有其自己的特征和规律，并不是个体行为的简单总和。所以有必要对组织行为进行研究，以便发现它对个体的影响和在组织中发挥的作用。目前有关组织行为的研究中，德国心理学家勒温（Kurt Lewin）的"场理论"、巴维拉斯（Alex Bavelas）的信息交流理论等是比较主流的研究内容。

✧ Research on organization behaviors

（三）关注领导行为的研究

员工与管理者构成了组织的人员主体，管理者的领导方式必然会对员工的工作产生一定的影响。有一些行为科学家们关注领导行为的研究，其中比较有代表性的成果包括坦南鲍姆的连续统一体理论、布莱克等人的管理方格理论、威廉·大内提出的 Z 理论等。

行为科学理论的具体内容，将在后面有关章节中具体介绍。

✧ Research on leadership

第四节　现代管理理论

The Management Theory Jungle

Although students of management would readily agree that there have been problems of management since the dawn of organized life, most would also agree that systematic examination of management, with few exceptions, is the product of the present century and more especially of the past two decades. Moreover, until recent years almost all of those who have attempted to analyze the management process and look for some theoretical underpinnings to help improve research, teaching, and practice were alert and perceptive practitioners of the art who reflected on many years of experience. Thus, at least in looking at general management as an intellectually based art, the earliest meaningful writing came from such experienced practitioners as Fayol, Mooney, Alvin Brown, Sheldon, Barnard, and Urwick. Certainly not even the most academic worshipper of empirical research can overlook the empiricism involved in distilling fundamentals from decades of experience by such discerning practitioners as these. Admittedly done without questionnaires, controlled interviews, or mathematics, observations by such men can hardly be accurately regarded as a priori or "armchair."

The noteworthy absence of academic writing and research in the formative years of modern management theory is now more than atoned for by a deluge of research and writing from the academic halls. What is interesting and perhaps nothing more than a sign of the unsophisticated adolescence of management theory is how the current flood has brought with it a wave of great differences and apparent confusion. From the orderly analysis of management at the shop-room level by Frederick Taylor and the reflective distillation of experience from the general management point of view by Henri Fayol, we now see these and other early beginnings overgrown and entangled by a jungle of approaches and approaches to management theory.

（案例来源：Harold Koontz. The Management Theory Jungle. *The Journal of the Academy of Management*, 1961, 4(3): 174-188）

20 世纪 60 年代以后，随着科学技术的迅速发展，企业规模的不断扩大，企业在经营过程中不得不面对日益复杂的环境，企业不仅要考虑自身条件的限制，还要研究环境的特点及要求，提高适应外部环境的能力。与此同时，人类在科学技术方面的新发展，如系统论、控制论和信息论的广泛研究与应用，为管理理论的发展提供了基础和条件。许多学者从不同的角度、用不同的方法对管理问题进行了研究。这一现象带来了管理理论研究的空前繁荣，形成了众多的管理理论学派。1961 年 12 月，美国著名管理学家哈罗德·孔茨（Harold Koontz）教授发表了一篇论文，详细地阐述了管理研究的各种方法，并认为存在着"管理理论的丛林"。本节将对主要的现代管理理论学派进行详尽的介绍。

一、管理科学学派

管理科学理论的基础是定量管理理论。定量管理理论是在第二次世界大战中产生和发展起来的。当时，英美军队为了解决战争中的一些问题，建立了由各种专家组成的运筹研究小组，取得了巨大的成效。例如，英国通过数学家建立的资源最优分配模型，有效地解决了如何以有限的皇家空军力量来抵抗强大的德国空军的问题。定量研究所取得的成效，在"二战"后引起了企业界的关注，特别是当运筹学研究专家在"二战"后纷纷到公司就业以后，定量研究方法日益在企业管理中得到了推广应用。

（一）定量管理理论的核心内容

定量管理理论的核心思想是将运筹学、统计学、计算机技术以及其他定量研究技术应用于管理活动当中，来支持管理决策，提高组织效率。它的特点是通过建立一套决策程序和数学模型来寻求决策的科学化，尽量减少决策中的个人主观判断成分；各种可行方案均以效益高低作为评价依据，力求实现决策方案的最优化；广泛使用电子计算机作为辅助决策的手段，对复杂问题能迅速找到优化的解决方案。这种方法在合理分配资源、安排工作进度、优化产品结构、选择运输路线等方面的应用效果最为显著。

✍ **Quantitative Management**

Quantitative management viewpoint emerged as a major force during World War II.

✧ The main ideas of quantitative management

The quantitative management viewpoint focuses on the use of mathematics, statistics, computer simulations, and other quantitative techniques to support managerial decision making and organizational effectiveness.

Global Perspective

How Today's Managers Use the Quantitative Approach

No one likes long lines, especially residents of New York City. If they see a long checkout line, they often go somewhere else. However, at Whole Foods' first gourmet supermarkets in Manhattan, customers found something different—that is, the longer the line, the shorter the wait. When ready to check out, customers are guided into serpentine single lines that feed into numerous checkout lanes. Whole Foods, widely known for its organic food selections, can charge premium prices, which allow it the luxury of staffing all those checkout lanes. And customers are finding that their wait times are shorter than expected. The science of keeping lines moving is known as queue management. And for Whole Foods, this quantitative technique has translated into strong sales at its Manhattan stores.

The quantitative approach contributes directly to management decision making in the areas of planning and control. For instance, when managers make budgeting, queuing, scheduling, quality control, and similar decisions, they typically rely on quantitative techniques. Specialized software has made the use of these techniques less intimidating for managers, although many still feel anxious about using them.

（案例来源：Stephen P. Robbins and Mary Coulter. *Management* (11th edition). 北京：清华大学出版社, 2013, p. 35）

（二）管理科学理论

随着定量管理理论的普及和推广,越来越多的学者认识到科学决策的重要性,通过将科学的知识和方法应用于研究复杂的管理问题,可以帮助组织确定正确的目标和合理的行动方案。一些学者将数量方案在管理中的应用称为"管理科学",提出了管理科学理论,形成了管理科学学派。

1. 代表人物

管理科学学派也称为管理数理学派,主要代表人物是美国的埃尔伍德·斯潘赛·伯法 (Elwood Spencer Buffa)。伯法 1923 年出生于威斯康星州的毕洛伊特市,从小家境贫寒,经常需要打工,通过勤工俭学来完成学业。打工的经历,让他懂得了要尊重体力劳动,同时也让他对大型机器车间和工程部门的工作比较熟悉,为他后来获得机械工程学学士学位奠定了基础。1942 年,伯法参加了海军的电子技术程序设计工作,在那里,他学会了电子技术,负责维修雷达和声呐系统等设备。1948 年,他成为伊斯特曼·柯达公司的经营分析员。1958 年,伯法获得加利福尼亚大学的博士学位。

在伯法生活的时代,企业间的竞争日益加剧,对管理也提出了更高的要求。依赖于管理者的主观分析和经验判断的定性管理,已不再能满足企业管理工作的需要,而更加标准化的定量管理技术则越来越被管理学界所重视,如何通过量化的数学模型,利用计算机的处理能力来加强对企业的管理,减少管理者由于自身局限性而难以避免的失误,提高管理效率,成为管理学界亟待解决的问题。伯法 1961 年出版了《现代生产管理》一书,采用科学的计量方法,将管理问题的研究由定性化转向定量化。由此,管理科学学派成为管理学中不可忽视的一个重要分支。

2. 主要思想

管理科学理论的主要思想是通过复杂的数学模型和统计方法,提高决策效率,主要包括如下几个特点。

（1）以经济效果作为评价标准。生产和经营管理各个领域的各项活动,都以经济效果好坏作为评价标准,要求行动方案能以较少的消耗获得总体的最大经济效益。

（2）依靠量化方法进行决策。强调使用先进的科学理论和管理方法,如系统论、信息论、控制论、运筹学等数学方法及数学模型,找出最优的实施方案,描述事物的现状及发展规律,力求减少决策的个人艺术成分,增加决策的科学性。

◇ Management Science Theory

Management science is an approach aimed at increasing decision effectiveness through the use of sophisticated mathematical models and statistical methods.
(1) Evaluate the management activities by their economic outcomes.
(2) Use quantitative methods to make decisions.

（3）依靠计算机技术进行各项管理。为了应对企业决策与日俱增的复杂性问题，应借助计算机的力量，及时处理大量数据，提供准确信息。

3. 主要贡献及局限性

管理科学学派是泰勒科学管理学派的继续和发展，其最大贡献就是将管理从定性研究推向了定量研究。该理论的主导思想是使用先进的数学方法和计算机技术研究管理问题，强调量化研究，使生产力得到最为合理的组织，减少了决策的随意性，增加了决策的科学性，提高了决策的效率。

但是，完全采用管理科学的定量研究方法来解决组织中的管理问题，在实际中面临着许多困难，目前管理科学理论多数应用于生产管理和运营管理领域，主要研究操作方法、作业过程方面的管理问题，而解决复杂环境下的组织问题还不能完全依赖管理科学的定量方法。另外，管理科学理论强调在管理活动中应用先进的工具和科学的方法，但不太注意管理中人的作用，较少考虑人的行为因素，不能很好地解释和预测组织中成员的行为。

二、管理过程学派

管理过程学派又称为管理职能学派、经营管理学派。这个学派的理论实际上是法约尔管理思想的延伸和扩展，以管理职能及其发挥作用的过程为研究对象，认为管理就是通过别人或同别人一起完成工作的过程。在现代管理理论丛林中它是一个公认的主流学派，其主要代表人物是美国的管理学家哈罗德·孔茨。

（一）孔茨生平

哈罗德·孔茨（Harold Koontz，1908—1984）是美国著名的管理学家，管理过程学派的主要代表人物之一。他出生于美国俄亥俄州，获得美国西北大学管理学硕士、耶鲁大学哲学博士学位。孔茨担任过企业和政府的高级管理人员、大学教授、公司董事长和董事、管理顾问等多个职位，曾多次为世界各地的高层管理人员举办管理学讲座。自 1941 年以来，孔茨完成了大量有关管理理论的 20 多本著作和近百篇论文，其中在《管理学原理》及《管理理论的丛林》等代表作中提出了管理过程理论的思想，奠定了孔茨作为管理过程学派主要代表人物之一的学术地位，在西方管理学界产生了很大的影响。

（3）Use information technology to support management.

✍ **Management Process**

✧ Harold Koontz

（二）管理过程学派的主要思想

管理过程理论是在法约尔的一般管理理论基础上发展而来的。法约尔将管理活动分为计划、组织、指挥、协调和控制等五大管理职能，孔茨等人在仔细研究这些管理职能的基础上，将管理职能分为计划、组织、人员配备、领导和控制五项，将协调看作管理的本职，是五项职能有效综合运用的结果。

管理过程学派强调了管理的重要性和普遍性，认为管理中存在着一些普遍通用的原则，这些原则是可以通过科学的方法发现的，这些管理原则如同灯塔一样，能使人们在管理活动中辨明方向。另外，该学派将管理理论同管理人员所执行的管理职能，也就是管理人员所从事的工作联系起来。他们认为，无论组织的性质多么不同，组织所处的环境有多么不同，管理人员所从事的管理职能都是相同的，管理活动的过程就是管理的职能逐步展开和实现的过程。因此，管理过程学派把管理的职能作为研究的对象，他们先把管理的工作划分为若干职能，然后对这些职能进行研究，阐明每项职能的性质、特点和重要性，论述实现这些职能的原则和方法。

管理过程理论尝试整合和吸收管理工作中的各种概念、原理和管理技术，详见图 2-2。

✧ The main ideas of management process theories

The management process or operational approach draws together the pertinent knowledge of management by relating it to the managerial job.

The management process approach mentions 5 managerial functions: planning, organizing, staffing, leading, and controlling.

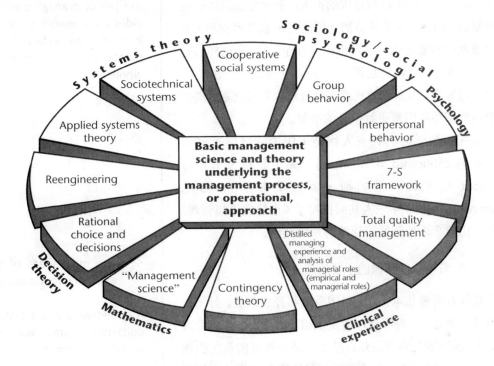

图 2-2　管理过程理论的基本管理思想

Figure 2-2　Basic Management Science and Theory underlying the Management Process or Operational Approach
（资料来源：Heinz Weihrich, Mark V. Cannice and Harold Koontz. *Management: A Global and Entrepreneurial Perspective* (13th edition)，北京：经济科学出版社，2011, p. 22）

（三）管理过程学派的贡献和局限性

管理过程学派是最为系统的一个学派，它为经营管理实践的理解和理论研究提供了一个由管理职能构成的理论框架，这个框架包括的内容广泛，容易理解，可扩展性强。管理学的新概念、新思想、新理论几乎都可以纳入这个框架。组织的经营管理事务纷繁，头绪众多，有了这种框架之后，就可以从几个主要方面对管理进行深刻的理解和有条不紊的分析。许多管理学教材都是按这一框架来安排，对管理学的发展和传播影响很大。同时，管理过程学派强调了管理理论的普遍性，这对于纷繁的管理理论从差异走向统一提供了一种思路。在管理理论的发展过程中，过程学派一直在探求走向统一的途径。

但是，管理过程学派所归纳的管理职能并不适用于所有组织，所归纳出的管理职能对静态的、稳定的生产环境较为合适，而对动态多变的生产环境则难以应用，需要随着发展对各项职能的内涵不断地进行修正和更新。

三、系统管理学派

第二次世界大战之后，随着资本和生产的进一步集中，企业规模的进一步扩大，企业内部关系变得更加复杂。与此同时，随着企业经营范围的扩大，企业面临的环境也更加复杂。因此，需要从更加开放的视角来理解管理，并从企业整体的要求出发实现组织的有序运转。在这样的背景下，系统管理学派应运而生，它基于一般系统理论、控制论和运筹学，用系统的观点来分析研究管理问题，提供了把内外部环境因素进行整合的框架。

系统管理学派的代表人物是美国的管理学家理查德·约翰逊(Richard A. Johnson)、弗里蒙特·卡斯特(Fremont E. Kast)和詹姆斯·罗森茨韦克(James E. Rosenzweig)。1963年三人共同撰写了《系统理论与管理》一书，比较全面地阐述了管理的系统理论。

（一）系统管理学派的主要思想

系统有两种基本类型：封闭系统和开放系统。封闭系统不受环境影响，也不与环境发生相互作用。在古典管理理论中，泰勒等人的理论观点基本上是一种封闭系统的观点。相反，开放系统则存在着系统与环境之间的动态相互作用，因此系统与外部是有着物质、能量和信息流动的。

✧ The contributions and limitations of management process theories

✍ **Systems Approach to Management**

Systems Approach to Management is a way of thinking about the job of managing which provides a framework for visualizing internal and external environmental factors as an integrated whole.

✧ The main ideas of systems approach to management

A closed system is a system that does not interact with the external environment.

An open system is a system that interacts with the external environment.

图 2-3 描述了作为一个开放系统的组织。对于组织来说，输入包括材料、劳动力、资本、技术、信息等多个要素，通过转换过程，将这些输入转化成产品和服务、财政、信息、人力等多个输出结果。系统的成功取决于与环境之间的成功的交互作用。

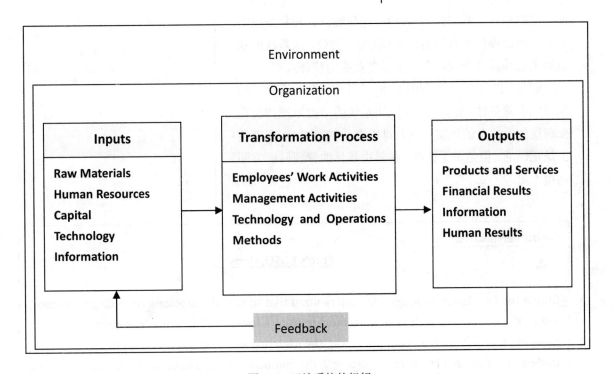

图 2-3　开放系统的组织
Figure 2-3　Organization as an Open System
（资料来源：改编自 Stephen P. Robbins and Mary Coulter. *Management* (11th edition)，北京：清华大学出版社, 2013, p. 36）

系统管理学派的主要思想类似于解决"盲人摸象"问题的原理：单纯地考虑某个方面，都可能造成结论的片面性，只有整合在一起系统地考虑，才可能得到准确的答案。其主要观点可以概括为以下两个方面。

1. 企业是一个由多个子系统组成的开放的有机系统，具有开放性和整体性的特点。开放性是指系统本身和外部环境因素存在相互联系、相互作用和相互影响的关系；整体性是指作为整体的系统不仅仅是各构成部分的单纯加总，而是存在协同。各个子系统相互作用，不可分割，构成了一个整体。

1. Subsystems are parts of a system that depend on one another. The organization must be managed as a coordinated whole.

2. 由于组织还是社会大系统中的一个子系统，因此组织预定目标的实现，不仅取决于内部条件，还取决于其外部条件，如资源、社会技术水平、法律制度等。管理人员应该力求在与外部条件的相互作用中，使各部分之间保持动态平衡。

2. The factors outside the organization can affect the organization's operations. In order to consider the environment adequately, an organization needs to operate as an open system.

（二）系统管理学派的贡献和局限性

系统管理理论通过对组织的研究来分析管理行为，体现了管理哲学的改变，使人们从整体的观点出发，对组织的各个子系统的地位和作用，以及它们之间的相互关系，有了更清楚的了解。同时，系统管理理论强调了组织与外部环境的相互关系问题，为人们处理和解决各种复杂组织的管理问题提供了有用的思路和方法。另外，从系统的观点来考察和管理企业，有助于提高企业的整体效率。

但是，也有不少学者指出，面对当代复杂的管理环境和组织运营条件，系统理论企图用系统的一般原理和模式来解决如此复杂的现实问题是难以奏效的，它虽然在理论上是正确的，但是过于笼统，在解决具体的管理问题方面显得不足。

✧ The contributions and limitations of systems approach to management

---

Global Perspective

Ford's EDSEL Flops

During the late 1940s, managers at Ford realized that they had a problem. According to studies, 1 out of 5 car buyers each year were moving from a low-priced to a medium-priced car. Ford, however, had only one medium-priced car, the Mercury, and only 26 percent of the Ford owners trading up selected a Mercury. Accordingly, the company began a decade of elaborate planning and preparation aimed at creating a successful new midpriced car geared to young executives and professionals—Edsel.

To build and distribute the new car, Ford conducted extensive marketing research and set up a separate division at headquarters and separate Edsel dealers. The executives felt that they were being conservative in estimating that 200,000 cars would be sold the first year. However, in 1958, only 35,000 Edsels were sold, far short of the conservative target. Two years later, production of the Edsel was scrapped. Losses reached about $200 million.

What went wrong? First, there was a stock market collapse in August, 1957 that had a severe negative impact on purchases of medium-size cars. Second, Ford relied heavily on initial marketing data in planning the car. It failed to alter the plans in the face of the growing impact of smaller, more fuel-efficient foreign cars, which were beginning to capture portions of the U.S. market. Third, the first Edsels were prone to oil leaks, mysterious rattles, faulty brakes, and starting difficulties. Because of these maladies, the car was quickly labeled a "lemon" and became the source of jokes. Fourth, Ford relied on a network of inexperienced new dealers to woo prospective customers. Fifth, the car was introduced while other car makers were offering discounts on their previous year's models, making the new Edsel seem expensive. Perhaps the Edsel could have survived one of these difficulties, but in combination, the problems were lethal. The situation illustrates the need to pay close attention to things going on outside that can affect system functioning and success.

（案例来源：改编自 Kathryn M. Bartol and David C. Martin. *Management* (3rd edition). 北京：机械工业出版社，1998，p. 56）

四、权变管理学派

权变管理学派是 20 世纪 70 年代在经验主义学派基础上进一步发展起来的一种管理理论。70 年代的美国，社会动荡，经济衰退，政治不稳，企业经营环境的复杂性和不确定性不断增强，企业管理者不得不面对比以往更加复杂的外部环境，传统的管理方法、企业的组织形式已经难以适应环境的巨变，很难找到一种最好的、适合所有组织的管理方案。人们不再相信会有一种最好的管理方式，而是必须因地制宜，因时制宜，随机应变地处理管理问题，于是形成了一种管理取决于所处环境状况的理论，即权变理论。权变管理学派认为，在管理中要根据企业所处的内外部条件随机应变，没有什么一成不变、适用于所有情境的最好的管理理论和方法。

权变管理学派的代表人物是美国的弗雷德·卢桑斯、弗雷德·菲德勒和琼·伍德沃德。

（一）代表人物简介

弗雷德·卢桑斯（Fred Luthans），美国尼勃拉斯加大学教授，权变学派的主要代表人物，在 1973 年发表了《权变管理理论：走出丛林的道路》一文，1976 年又出版了《管理导论：一种权变学说》一书，系统地介绍了权变管理理论，提出了用权变理论可以统一各种管理理论的观点。

弗雷德·菲德勒（Fred E. Fiedler），美国西雅图华盛顿大学心理学与管理学教授，兼任荷兰阿姆斯特丹大学和比利时卢万大学客座教授。从 1951 年起，他从管理心理学和实证环境分析两方面研究领导学，提出"权变领导理论"。菲德勒的理论对领导学和管理学的发展产生了重要影响。主要著作和论文包括《一种领导效能理论》（1967）、《让工作适应管理者》（1965）、《权变模型——领导效用的新方向》（1974），以及《领导游戏：人与环境的匹配》等。

琼·伍德沃德（Joan Woodward），英国女管理学家，不列颠大学教授，组织设计权变理论主要代表人物之一，开创了公司生产过程类型的技术型模式，著有《经营管理和工艺技术》《工业组织：理论和实践》《工业组织：行为和控制》，认为技术类型和公司之间存在着明显的相关性，即"结构因技术的变化而变化"，组织的绩效与技术和结构之间的"适应度"密切相关。她的研究揭示了技术系统与社会系统之间的复杂关系，在管理学领域独树一帜。

✍ **Contingency Approach**

Contingency approach: a management approach that recognizes organizations as different, which means they face different situations and require different ways of managing.

✧ Fred Luthans, Fred E. Fiedler and Joan Woodward

（二）权变管理学派的主要思想

所谓权变，就是相机而变、随机应变。权变管理思想强调，管理者在采取管理行动时，需要根据具体环境条件的不同而相应采取不同的管理方式，组织的管理应根据其所处的内外部环境条件的变化而变化。权变理论学派的成果丰富，观点、主张和侧重点不同，但主要集中在计划、结构和领导等三个领域。其主要有如下三个观点。

1. 管理并不是一些适用于所有情境的简单原理，管理实践必须与管理环境紧密结合，没有所谓最好的管理方法。

2. 环境是自变量，管理观念和管理方法是因变量。组织所处的环境决定着哪一种管理观念和管理方法更适合组织。

3. 环境变量与管理变量之间存在着函数关系，即权变关系。两者之间的关系可以解释为"如果-那么"的关系，即：如果我所处的环境是这样的，那么对我来说最好的管理方法是那样的。企业管理要随着环境的变化而变化。

权变理论学派的研究者们通过分析比较，发现了100多个权变变量，其中比较常见的权变变量包括组织规模、任务结构性、环境不确定性、个体差异等要素。如表2-4所示。

✧ The main ideas of contingency approach

1. Management is not based on simplistic principles to be applied in all situations. Managerial practice depends on circumstances. There is no one best way to do things.

2. Circumstances are independent factors. Management ideas and models are dependent factors. Managers must understand the environment very well. The management style depends on its circumstances.

3. A good way to describe contingency is "if-then". If this is the way my situation is, then this is the best way for me to manage in this situation. There are no simplistic or universal rules for managers to follow.

表 2-4　常用的权变变量

Table 2-4　Popular Contingency Variables

Organization Size	As size increases, so do the problems of coordination. For instance, the type of organization structure appropriate for an organization of 50000 employees is likely to be inefficient for an organization of 50 employees.
Routineness of Task Technology	To achieve its purpose, an organization uses technology. Routine technologies require organizational structures, leadership styles, and control systems that differ from those required by customized or nonroutine technologies.
Environmental Uncertainty	The degree of uncertainty caused by environmental changes influences the management process. What works best in a stable and predictable environment may be totally inappropriate in a rapidly changing and unpredictable environment.
Individual Differences	Individuals differ in terms of their desire for growth, autonomy, tolerance of ambiguity, and expectations. These and other individual differences are particularly important when managers select motivation techniques, leadership styles, and job designs.

（资料来源：Stephen P. Robbins and Mary Coulter. *Management* (11th edition). 北京：清华大学出版社, 2013, p. 38）

（三）权变管理学派的贡献和局限性

权变管理理论希望通过观察和分析大量实际案例，找出管理思想、技术和方法与环境之间的关系，在管理理论和管理实践之间成功架起一座桥梁，使管理理论更好地服务于管理实践。同时，权变管理理论重视组织与环境之间的关系，加强了学术界对组织开放性的认识。权变管理理论否定了一味追求最好的管理方法和寻求万能模式的教条主义，指出管理职能不是一成不变的，使人们对管理的动态性有了新的认识，对管理理论的发展形成了有效的补充。

但是，权变管理理论也存在一定的局限性。权变理论过于强调变化，缺乏统一的概念和标准，过于强调特殊性，忽视了普遍性，过于强调个性，否定了共性。每个管理学者都根据自己的标准来确定自己的理想模式，未能形成普遍的管理职能。另外，由于权变理论多是采用案例分析的方法来发现问题和解决问题，这种研究方法的科学性和规范性受到了一些学者的质疑。

◇ The contributions and limitations of contingency approach

Global Perspective

Trying to Change the Corporate Culture of a Multinational Enterprise: General Semiconductor

When Ronald Ostertag took over the management of General Semiconductor, he realized quickly that he would have to change the $500 million company's culture for the firm to survive.

The first step Ostertag took toward changing General Semiconductor's corporate culture was to replace nearly every member of the company's senior management team. Job insecurity rapidly spread throughout the ranks. "I realized we needed to do something to develop a sense of teamwork," says Ostertag suggesting that laying people off was not enough, "we needed to develop a culture of mutual respect that fostered cooperation and innovation."

However, changing General Semiconductor's culture was a significant challenge because the New York-based manufacturer of electronics parts had 60000 workers around the world who spoke five different languages. Only 200 of those workers were employed in the United States. Its facilities outside the United States were in China mainland, France, Germany, Ireland, and Taiwan Island of China.

After taking over as CEO, Ostertag decided to schedule a team-building meeting in which the new management team would decide on the company's guiding principles. "Our task," he says in retrospect, "was to put down on paper what our core values were and then make sure everyone was on the same page." A cohesive mission statement and a list of eight company values, which are called General Semiconductor's "culture points," came out of that meeting and were centered around goals like "quality," "integrity," "good customer service," and "on-time delivery."

Soon, everyone in the company knew the culture points and even carried them around on small cards. "They knew when they saw me coming, whether it was in the factory in France or Ireland or here, that I might come up to anyone and ask them to rattle off four or five of those values," says Ostertag, "I didn't mean it as a test, but more to show that that is what everyone here is striving for."

Unfortunately, Ostertag's changes did not occur quickly enough for General Semiconductor to fend off a hostile takeover. Believing that more improvements could be made and greater value extracted from General Semiconductor, Vishay Inter-technology purchased the company in 2001. Today, General Semiconductor is a subsidiary of the Pennsylvania-based firm. Vishay Inter-technology has grown considerably and broadened its product line through acquisitions. It also has a global presence with manufacturing facilities in six Asian countries, including China, Europe, Israel, and the United States, and sales offices in many other countries around the globe. Vishay uses the international expertise in developing new technologies. This is exemplified in the continued success of the subsidiary now named Vishay General Semiconductor LLC which had two patents issued in May. These new technologies were developed by researchers working in the unit's R&D labs in Tianjin and Taipei, China.

（案例来源：改编自 Michael A. Hitt，J. Stewart Black, and Lyman W. Porter. *Management* (3rd edition). 北京：中国人民大学出版社，2013, pp. 71-72）

关键概念 **KEY IDEAS AND CONCEPTS**

Classical theory

Scientific management

Soldiering

Time and motion study

Piece rate compensation system

Management by exception

Administrative management

Bureaucratic management

Traditional authority

Charismatic authority

Legal-rational authority

Human resources perspective

Behavioral science

Quantitative management

Management science

Management process approach

Systems approach

Open system

Contingency approach

讨论问题 **DISCUSSION QUESTIONS**

1. Please describe briefly the major developments in the history of management thought.

2. Contrast the three major approaches within the classical viewpoint: scientific management, bureaucratic management, and administrative management. Give some examples of how these approaches are reflected in an organization with which you are familiar.

3. What is scientific management? Discuss the four main principles of scientific management. What might be some disadvantages of this approach?

4. What were Henri Fayol's major contributions to the management movement?

5. What were main ideas of bureaucratic management?

6. Why were the Hawthorne Studies so critical to management history?

7. Explain the main contributions of human resources perspective theory.

8. Explain what the quantitative approach has contributed to the field of management.

9. Explain the major ideas underlying the systems viewpoint. Use this viewpoint to analyze your college or university.

10. Explain the basic ideas underlying the contingency view and give an example.

Starbucks Coffee's Operations Management: 10 Decisions Areas

Starbucks Coffee's business fulfills the 10 decisions of operations management through varying strategic initiatives for productivity and management in different areas of the organization.

1. Design of Goods and Services. Starbucks emphasizes premium design for its goods and services. The premium character is linked to the company's broad differentiation generic strategy, along with its premium pricing strategy. Other firms, such as manufacturers, are also involved in the design of some goods like Starbucks mugs. In this decision area of operations management, Starbucks ensures that its goods and services reflect the firm's high-end brand image.

2. Quality Management. Starbucks also uses the premium character in quality management. For instance, the company carefully sources its coffee beans from coffee farmers who comply with Starbucks quality standards. The firm also prefers to buy coffee from farmers certified under the Starbucks Coffee and Farmer Equity (CAFE) program. Premium quality service is ensured through servant leadership and a warm friendly culture. In this decision area of operations management, Starbucks implements high quality to align with the firm's premium brand image.

3. Process and Capacity Design. Process and capacity efficiency is one of the contributors to Starbucks' success. The company's processes are highly efficient, as observable in its cafés. Also, Starbucks optimizes capacity and capacity utilization by designing processes to meet fluctuations in demand. For example, processes at the firm's cafés are flexible to adjust personnel to a sudden increase in demand during peak hours. In this decision area of operations management, Starbucks aims to maximize cost-effectiveness through efficiency of workflows and processes.

4. Location Strategy. Starbucks' location strategy focuses on urban centers, especially those with large middle and upper class populations. Most of its cafés are in densely populated areas. Also, Starbucks occasionally uses strategic clustering of cafés in the same geographic area to gain market share and drive competitors away. This decision area of operations management shows that Starbucks emphasizes areas with affluent consumers who could afford its premium priced products.

5. Layout Design and Strategy. The layout design of Starbucks cafés maximizes workflow efficiency. It also supports a warm and friendly ambiance to match the company's organizational culture. This layout strategy does not maximize space utilization for tables and seats because Starbucks' focus is on premium customer experience, which involves higher prices for more leg

space in the cafés. In this decision area of operations management, Starbucks prioritizes customer experience over space utilization.

6. Job Design and Human Resources. Starbucks' human resource management integrates organizational culture in all areas of the business. This organizational culture involves the employees' first attitude that cares for Starbucks workers. Also, at the cafés, the company uses work teams of baristas. In other parts of the organization, Starbucks uses functional positions, such as HRM positions and inventory management positions, with less emphasis on work teams. In this decision area of operations management, the focus is on ensuring that the Starbucks culture is woven into every job, while satisfying basics on technical specifics of tasks.

7. Supply Chain Management. Starbucks Coffee's supply chain is global, although majority of the company's coffee beans come from farmers in developing countries. The company's strategy for its supply chain involves diversification of suppliers to ensure stability of supply. Starbucks also uses its Coffee and Farmer Equity (CAFE) program to select and prioritize suppliers. This program uses criteria for ethical practices, including emphasis on sustainability. Thus, in this decision area of operations management, Starbucks integrates ethics and corporate social responsibility with supply chain efficiency.

8. Inventory Management. Inventory management at Starbucks is linked with the firm's supply chain and various facilities. At the cafés, inventory management involves office automation and manual monitoring. In Starbucks' supply hubs, automation is more comprehensively used. The company aims to minimize stockout and ensure continuous supply of coffee beans to its cafés. Starbucks addresses this decision area of operations management by focusing on supply adequacy and automation.

9. Scheduling. Starbucks uses automated and manual scheduling approaches for its various business activities. The company also applies flexible schedules for management personnel. This decision area of operations management relates with Starbucks in terms of the firm's objective of streamlining processes, while allowing some degree of flexibility among management positions in the organization.

10. Maintenance. Starbucks maintains its physical assets through dedicated teams of employees trained for maintaining facilities and equipment, as well as third parties that offer maintenance services. These third parties include local businesses that provide equipment tune-ups for Starbucks cafés. In addition, the company maintains its human resource capacity through training and retention strategies that include relatively high compensation. Thus, Starbucks addresses this decision area of operations management through the involvement of café personnel, dedicated maintenance teams, and third-party service providers.

（案例来源：Lawrence Gregory. Starbucks Coffee's Operations Management: 10 Decisions, *Productivity*, http://panmore.com/starbucks-coffee-operations-management-10-decisions-areas-productivity, 2015-9-15）

Discussion Questions

1. Modern management thoughts are different from earlier approaches, and they focus on the external environment outside the boundaries of the organization. Please analyze the Starbucks' operations management with modern management theories.

2. What are Starbucks' core competencies and how does it keep its competitive advantages?

3. Should Starbucks change its operations management strategies in other countries around the world? If you say no, then explain why. If you say yes, what kinds of strategies should it change?

4. What other challenges may Starbucks encounter in the future?

第三章　管理者与优秀的企业

学习目标

1. 解释管理者的概念
2. 界定管理者的角色与技能
3. 辨析管理者与企业家的差异
4. 描述优秀企业的竞争优势

主要内容

第一节　管理者与企业家精神
第二节　管理者的角色与技能
第三节　优秀企业及其竞争优势

Learning Outcomes

1. Explain the nature of managers.
2. Define the roles and skills of managers.
3. Differentiate managers and entrepreneurs.
4. Describe the competitive advantage for an excellent company.

Contents

3.1 Manager and Entrepreneurship
3.2 Manager's Roles and Skills
3.3 Excellent Company and Its Competitive Advantages

第一节 管理者与企业家精神

How Managers Keep Tesla Motoring

What does it take to turn a vision into an ongoing, productive reality? If your vision is to lead an automotive revolution by selling all-electric cars that deliver a comfortable, convenient ride while cutting dependence on fossil fuels, it takes engineering genius, quality-driven workers, marketing know-how, and cash. And then it takes people who can harness all these resources, figure out the best way to direct them, and get the whole organization to outperform the competition. In other words, achieving the vision requires talented managers.

For a picture of what this means, think about how the managers of Tesla Motors have pulled together a host of resources aimed at achieving an ambitious goal: selling the world's first marketable all-electric car. As envisioned, Tesla car would run on a battery with enough power to carry the car 300 miles on a single charge. So far, the company has begun selling its $109,000 battery-powered Roadster, which is a high-performance vehicle but doesn't fulfill the affordability part of the Tesla equation. The company planned to begin making a sedan, the Model S, targeted to sell for $54,700, beginning in 2012.

A project like that requires sizable fund-raising-millions of dollars, in fact, Tesla's chief executive, Elon Musk, has come up with some creative financing ideas and persuaded investors with deep pockets to buy in. Musk also negotiated with Toyota's president, Akio Toyota, to set up a joint venture in which Tesla helped Toyota develop an electric version of Toyota' RAV4 sport utility vehicle. The deal called for Toyota to invest $50 million for an ownership share of Tesla. It might seem strange to share technology with a potential competitor, but the deal gives Tesla much-needed cash and makes it more attractive to other potential investors. For example, Panasonic, which has been a leader in developing powerful lithium ion batteries and hopes to supply electric vehicles, invested $30 million in Tesla in exchange for an ownership share. The deal gives Tesla not only cash but also access to expertise in designing one of the trickiest parts of an electric car.

Building an innovative automobile also requires a great design and factory located near the right kind of talent to bring a new design to market. The responsibility for design a battery that is safe yet delivers enough power and costs less than $10,000 to make falls to Wes Hermann, manager of Tesla's engineering in college and then worked for a foundation that studies the environmental impact of energy use. Working for Tesla was a chance to put theory into practice. Of course Hermann can't achieve those goals on his own; he has to hire and direct a team of engineers.

The hit to the auto industry from the recent financial crisis brought Tesla an opportunity in the form of an empty factory. General Motors closed a plant it had jointly operated Toyota in Fremont, California, not far from Tesla's Palo Alto headquarters in the heart of Silicon Valley. Tesla bought the plant and set up a temporary office in the parking lot.

Preparing the plant to make the Model S is the responsibility of Gilbert Passion, Tesla's vice president of manufacturing. Passion is aiming to meet the ambitious goal of assembling Model S cars within two years. The people who report to him are busy preparing diagrams and schedules to set up workstations for building high-tech automobiles. Meanwhile, Tesla's vice president of human resources, Arnnon Geshrui, is overseeing the task of hiring hundreds of new workers. Geshuri has the background for a challenge; before working at Tesla, he managed human resources at Google when that company's head count was rising exponentially.

（案例来源：托马斯·S. 贝特曼，斯科特·A. 斯奈尔著. 于淼等评注. 管理学：全球竞争中的领导与合作（英文注释版·第 10 版）. 北京：电子工业出版社，2014，pp. 2-3）

特斯拉（Tesla）的诞生可谓是汽车领域一次卓越的技术创新，该创新佳绩的取得与首席执行官伊隆·马斯克（Elon Musk）密不可分，他是当今商业世界最不可思议的人物之一。他集强大的创造技术与敏锐的前瞻力于一身，并在创建组织中取得显著成就，无论外界质疑声多么大，马斯克总能平息这些质疑声，将所谓不可能实现的事情变成现实。当然，并不是每一个管理者或组织都会成功，如果缺少了卓有成效的管理，那么就可能影响企业的长期发展。特别是在全球化、技术革新、知识和创意越发重要的当前经济环境下，没有卓越的管理者、没有高效的管理工作，企业要想实现基业长青是几乎不可能的。

本章将通过多种视角来阐述在当前全球经济环境下，成为一名卓有成效的管理者所必备的素质，并介绍管理者是如何充分运用管理技巧，发挥管理角色，使企业良好的运作，蓬勃发展的。本节将围绕管理者基本内涵、管理者角色及技能展开讨论。

一、谁是管理者？

Who Is the Manager?

管理者在组织中工作，但不是每一个在组织工作的人都是管理者。在不同的组织中，有各种各样以及不同称谓的组织成员。我们可以简单地将所有成员分为两类：非管理类员工与管理者。非管理类员工（Nonmanagerial Employees）只关注工作本身而无须去监管其他人的工作，从而也没有必要对其他人的工作负责。例如在沃尔玛超市负责结算的收银员；在 KFC 快餐连锁店里负责卫生的保洁人员；在王府井新天地某家国际知名品牌服装店里的导购人员等，都叫作非管理类员工。他 / 她们之间通常相互称为同事、团队成员，一般处于组织的最底层（作业层），不具有监督他人工作的职责。另一方面，管理者（Manager）是指那些直接监督组织中其他人工作的一群人。简单地说，管理者是组织中那些指挥别人工作并对这些人的工作负有责任的人。换言之，管理者是组织中有下属的那些人，他们需要从事一些指挥工作。但这并不意味着他们就不需要承担具体事务。有的时候，管理者所从事的工作任务与监督他人工作并没有直接关系，例如医院里医术精湛的院长既要负责管理整个医院的日常工作，同时也有责任为某些病人亲自服务或做手术。

Nonmanagerial employees are people who work directly on a job or task and have no responsibility for overseeing the work of others.

Managers are individuals in an organization who direct and oversee the activities of other people in the organization so that organizational goals can be accomplished.

二、管理者的层级

所有的组织，小到私人经营的个体企业，大到巨型的全球化公司，都需要管理者。但是，企业规模不同，需要的管理者人数与层级也不一样。小企业也许只要一位或几位管理者就足够了，大中型企业可能就需要很多层级的管理者来管理企业，以提高整个企业的运行效率和效益。一般而言，可以将组织中的管理者按照管理工作的内容性质以及位置，将其分为高层管理者、中层管理者、基层（或一线）管理者。如图 3-1 所示。

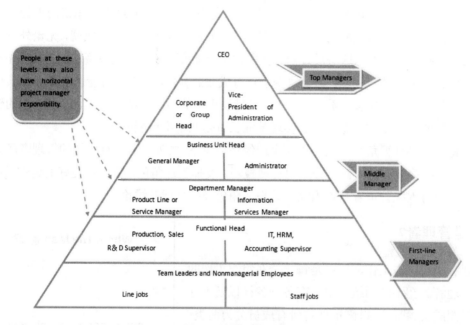

图 3-1　管理者的层级

Figure 3-1　Management Hierarchy

（资料来源：改编自 Thomas V. Bonoma and Joseph C. Lawler. Chutes and Ladders: Growing the General Manager. *Sloan Management Review*, 1989, Spring: 27–37）

高层管理者（Top-level Manager）是一个组织的高级执行官，他对组织的所有管理活动负责。高层管理者通常也是战略家，即着眼于长远问题，并关注生产、发展和整个组织的有效运营。他们通常是处在组织最高层或接近最高层的人员，他们需要对组织发展的方向做出判断，并且建立能够规范所有组织成员的制度和组织文化。企业高层管理者包括董事长、总经理、副总经理等，例如阿里巴巴董事局主席马云。

对于全球性的企业而言，高层管理者有时是以一个团队的形式出现的。Hambrick 和 Mason 提出的高层梯队理论（Upper Echelons Theory）就指出，高层管理团队的特征会影响到组织绩效与战略选择，团队成员不同的认知基

Top-level managers are the senior executives of an organization and are responsible for its overall management. Top-level managers, often referred to as strategic managers, are supposed to focus on long-term issues and emphasize the survival, growth, and overall effectiveness of the organization.

础、价值观、洞察力以及这些特质的作用过程会影响到组织的竞争行为。特别是面对 21 世纪全球经济日新月异的高速发展以及瞬息万变的国内外经济环境,高层管理者前瞻性行为对于企业应对危机乃至长远发展具有决定性作用。

中层管理者(Middle Manager)是处在组织最高层和最底层之间,负责组织目标的实施、制定部门目标及行动方案的那些人,包括部门或机构主管、项目经理、业务主管、地区经理、部门经理或门店经理等。中层管理者是组织序列中上下级关系的"夹心饼干",既肩负着领导下属的重任,又要协调好同级部门之间的分工合作,还承担着辅助上级的责任,兼有管理者和被管理者的双重身份。在传统的战略管理理论中,中层管理者一直被认为是战略执行者。但最新的研究认为,面临复杂动态竞争环境的企业应该注重培养中层管理者的战略意识,鼓励中层管理者参与战略决策,这有助于提升决策质量和战略绩效。

基层管理者(First-line Manager)是直接负责非管理类员工日常活动的人,即管理一线员工,通常被认为是最初级的管理层次。通常情况下,基层管理者与一线员工一起工作,例如工厂中的领班或组长、商场中的销售主管、学校里的系主任、医院里的护士长等。

大企业通常拥有基层、中层和高层三个层次的管理人员。例如,苏宁是一家大型商业企业,在中国和日本拥有两家上市公司,年销售规模超过 3000 亿元,员工 18 万人,位列中国民营企业前三。其基层管理者负责管理商店的各个部门,他们必须确保这些商店日常的正常运营。中层管理者的管理业务是区域业务,主要任务是确保管辖区域内所有商店的基层管理者能够进行有效的工作,同时,他们也可以提出增加辖区内销售额、改进服务或降低成本等方面的建议。高层管理人员包括苏宁公司的董事长和总裁等决策层人员,他们负责制定公司政策、产品和组织战略等方面的决策。

Middle managers are those managers found between the lowest and top levels of the organization. This level of managers sets goals of the organization and decides what the employees in each area must do to meet those goals.

First-line managers are those individuals who are responsible for directing the day-to-day activities of nonmanagerial employees.

Global Perspective

New Manager Self-Test

Managing Your Time

Instructions: Think about how you normally handle tasks during a typical day at work or school. Read each item and check whether it is Mostly True or Mostly False for you.

1. I frequently take on too many tasks.

2. I spend too much time on enjoyable but unimportant activities.

3. I feel that I am in excellent control of my time.

4. Frequently during the day, I am not sure what to do next.

5. There is little room for improvement in the way I manage my time.

6. I keep a schedule for events, meetings, and deadlines.

7. My workspace and paperwork are well organized.

8. I am good at record keeping.

9. I make good use of waiting time.

10. I am always looking for ways to increase task efficiency.

Scoring and Interpretation: For questions 3 and 5–10, give yourself one point for each Mostly True answer. For questions 1, 2, and 4, give yourself one point for each Mostly False answer. Your total score pertains to the overall way that you use time. Items 1–5 relate to taking mental control over how you spend your time. Items 6–10 pertain to some mechanics of good time management. Good mental and physical habits make effective time management much easier. Busy managers have to learn to control their time. If you score 8 or higher, your time-management ability is good. If your score is 4 or lower, you may want to reevaluate your time-management practices if you aspire to be a manager.

（案例来源：Richard L. Daft. *Management* (12th edition). Boston: Cengage Learning, 2014, p. 22）

三、企业家精神

在成立时间较久的企业中，高层、中层和基层管理者一般都是职业经理人（Professional Manager）。职业经理人是在一家公司领取薪金、执行管理职能的专职人员，像其他员工一样，他们因工作而得到薪金。研究发现，在 1880 年至 1920 年之间，美国的职业经理人数量从 16.1 万人增加到超过 100 万人。据中国企业联合会课题组发布的《2013 中国职业经理人年度报告》显示，我国职业经理人规模正逐步增加，并且中青年已成为职业经理人队伍的主体，截至 2013 年，31 岁至 40 岁的职业经理人已占到 52.3%。

企业家（Entrepreneur）是创建和经营自己公司的人，有时也称为创业者。企业家并不等同于我们通常所说的老板、总经理，更多的是指那些善于把握机会，勇于创新、尝试和冒险的创业者和开拓者。在创建企业时，他们执行应该由职业经理人执行的基本管理职能，当企业规模扩大时他们就有可能聘用职业经理人。

✍ **Entrepreneurship**

Professional managers are paid to perform management functions with a company. Like other employees, they receive salaries for the work they do.

Entrepreneurs are people who launch and run their own business.

这些人在创业之初未必拥有多少资源,他们更擅长的是发现机会并调动和整合资源开发这些机会。例如中国阿里巴巴的马云、京东的刘强东、海尔的张瑞敏、联想的柳传志等,美国微软的比尔·盖茨、脸书的扎克伯格、苹果的乔布斯等。

据中国企业家调查系统 20 年的问卷追踪调查显示,企业家大多具有比较强的创新意识和企业家精神(Entrepreneurship),对人性、对员工有积极正面的看法,重视企业的持续发展、员工成长和自身精神境界的提升,同时,比较重视企业文化建设,关注整个社会的商业文明进程。企业家作为企业文化的塑造者、企业发展的引领者、社会资源的组织者,承受着来自各个方面的较大压力,需要应对复杂环境,不断学习、不断超越、不断迎接挑战,其精神追求与创新动力至关重要。

企业家精神是在不考虑现有可控资源下寻求机会的过程。企业家比职业经理人更具有冒险精神。实际上,当企业家预见到新的机会时,总要超越当前资源约束,因而企业家总是专注于"如何"而不是"为什么不",他们以创新和独特的方式追求机会、创造价值和谋求增长。所以,企业家精神的内涵,首先是对机会的追求和把握,具有企业家精神的人都善于把握环境的趋势和变化,而且往往是尚未被普通人注意到的趋势和变化;其次是创新,创新意味着变革、革新、转换和引入新方法,即新产品、新服务或者新商业模式;最后是增长,企业家不满足于停留在小规模或现有规模上,希望其事业能够尽可能地增长,他们致力于不断寻找新的趋势和机会,不断创新,不断推出新产品和新的经营方式。

企业家常常有着与普通的管理者不同的个性特征。企业家比普通的管理者更独立,他们可能更乐于冒险,接受挑战,有些企业家在开始创业或拥有自己的企业之前,干过许多种工作。如表 3-1 所示。

According to experts on the subject, entrepreneurship is the process by which individuals—either on their own or inside organizations—pursue opportunities without regard to these sources they currently control. In effect, entrepreneurs look beyond current resource constraints when they envision new possibilities. Entrepreneurs are preoccupied with "how to" rather than "why not".

表 3-1 企业家与管理者特征对比

Table 3-1 Contrasting Trait Profiles for Entrepreneurs and Administrators

ENTREPRENEURS TEND TO	ADMINISTRATORS TEND TO
Focus on envisioned futures	Focus on the established present
Emphasize external/market dimensions	Emphasize internal/cost dimensions
Display medium-to-high tolerance for ambiguity	Display a low-to-medium tolerance for ambiguity
Exhibit moderate-to-high risk-taking behavior	Exhibit low-to-moderate risk-taking behavior
Obtain motivation from a need to achieve	Obtain motivation from a need to lead others (i.e., social power)
Possess technical knowledge and experience in the innovative area	Possess managerial knowledge and experience

(资料来源:Philip D. Olson. Choices for Innovation-Minded Corporations. *The Journal of Business Strategy*, 1990, 11(1): 42-46)

Jack Ma

Jack was born in 1964, in Hangzhou, Zhejiang province. He graduated in 1988 with a bachelor's degree in English from Hangzhou Teacher's Institute (now Hangzhou Normal University), and initially worked as an English teacher at the Hangzhou Electronics and Engineering Institute (now Hangzhou Dianzi University).

Jack worked as an interpreter. It was during a trip to the United States in 1995 that Jack was introduced to the Internet. On his return, he borrowed US$2,000 and founded China-pages.com, reputedly one of China's first online commercial directories. Between 1997 and 1999, Jack used this experience in his role as Head of Information at the China International Electronic Commerce Centre of the Ministry of Foreign Trade and Economic Cooperation (MOFTEC). Jack developed some of MOFTEC's most high profile Internet projects, including the China Market website. It was reportedly during this period that Jack realized the potential of the business-to-business e-commerce model and established a key friendship with Yahoo co-founder Jerry Yang.

In 1999, Jack became the lead founder of Alibaba Group. He serves as Chairman and CEO.

Under Jack's entrepreneurial leadership, Alibaba rapidly expanded into a conglomeration of various e-commerce businesses and affiliated entities. The company formed with an initial investment of US$60,000 and operated out of Jack's Hangzhou apartment, but within the year Jack had raised an additional US$25 million from investors. In 2000, he said, "In circumstances like this, one must run as fast as a rabbit but be as patient as a turtle." Alibaba.com, the flagship online business-to-business platform had reached a profit by 2002. In 2003, Jack launched both Taobao.com, a consumer-to-consumer online marketplace, and Alipay, a third-party online payment platform. In 2005, Jack took Alibaba into a strategic partnership with Yahoo. Yahoo invested US$1 billion for a 40% stake, while Alibaba assumed control over China Yahoo. Alibaba.com listed on the Hong Kong Stock Exchange in 2007, becoming the second largest Internet company IPO to date, after Google. Jack expanded the portfolio of e-commerce ventures again in 2008 with Tmall.com, a business-to-consumer online shopping platform focused on brand-name goods.

However, Alibaba's rise to become the dominant e-commerce player in China has not been without a number of high profile setbacks. In 2011, customers' trust in Alibaba.com was damaged when in a drive to expand the user base, 2,236 dealers were granted trusted "gold" status only to subsequently defraud buyers. In the same year, the US government named Taobao.com for enabling the sale of counterfeit goods. In his defence, Jack argued that, "We have done our best to fight against fake products. I want to tell everyone that no matter online or offline, the good guys outnumber bad guys and good commodities outnumber bad commodities." Jack has always maintained that his primary mission is to champion small enterprises, but his decision to raise prices in an effort to tackle piracy angered these very same customers. In reference to this period, Jack has said, "I was so lonely at that time," and that "Nobody wanted to believe Jack Ma." In 2011, it emerged that Jack had reportedly transferred ownership of Alipay to a private firm under his control. This controversial move caused further reputational damage.

Ironically, in June 2012 Jack said, "This is not a business that belongs to Jack Ma." And yet, he has continued to tighten his grip on the group though a process of organizational restructuring. In 2012, he negotiated a much-desired deal with Yahoo to buy back half of their 40% stake for US$7.1 billion.

This values Alibaba at around US$35 billion. Remarking on the deal, Jack said, "We are grateful for Yahoo's support of our growth over the past seven years, and we are pleased to be able to deliver meaningful returns to our shareholders including Yahoo." Shareholders also approved plans to privatize the Hong Kong-listed Alibaba.com. Moreover, Jack refocused Alibaba around seven major business groups. He wrote, "We must accelerate the implementation of the 'One Company' strategy and effectively integrate B2B's system with Taobao's market system so as to truly create a mechanism for openness, synergy and sharing."

The impressive expansion of Jack's company has been fuelled by the phenomenal growth in online spending in China. Jack has acknowledged this, stating "Of course, the rapid rise of both Alibaba and Taobao owe more to the need of the country at this time than to our power." Alibaba businesses currently account for 71% of consumers' online purchases. Between January and November 2012, Taobao Marketplace and Tmall.com reached a combined gross merchandise volume (GMV) of RMB 1 trillion. This surpassed Amazon and eBay to make Alibaba the largest e-commerce company in the world by annual GMV. Jack said, "It's very likely that next year, our transaction volume will be bigger than all the American e-commerce companies combined." On the downside, the group has already experimented with a variety of growth strategies. Moreover, with a personal stake in Alibaba already worth an estimated US$2.6 billion, some have seen signs that he may be losing focus. Jack himself has said, "I am going to enjoy some other things apart from business." Consequently, one of the greatest leadership challenges now facing Jack is the need to maintain his company's momentum in the face of growing competition in the e-commerce market from the likes of Tencent and Wal-Mart.

（案例来源：World of CEOs. Jack Ma: Executive Chairman, Alibaba Group. http://www. worldof-ceos.com/dossiers/jack-ma, 2015-10-27）

企业家精神对组织的生存和发展起着重要作用。随着竞争格局的变化，企业家精神不应只是大企业进行"创造性破坏"式的改变现状来适应环境变化的"专利"。日益激烈的全球竞争以及日新月异的技术进步使得所有企业（当然包括新兴企业）都必须重视企业家精神，用来提高竞争地位和获得竞争优势。自 20 世纪 80 年代以来，人们发现虽然大公司拥有的资源和享有的声望足以抵消偶尔的决策失误所造成的损失，能够承担更大的风险，拥有更完备的商业知识，但在与小企业的竞争中却并不是能够一直占据优势。迅速发展的创新型小企业利用市场环境巨变的时机，侵蚀着大公司的市场份额和利润。于是一些大中型企业提出了内部企业家精神（Intrapreneurship），并在实践中推广。所谓内部企业家精神，就是企业家精神在大中型企业内部的一种应用和体现，它更强调的是在组织内部的既定环境下将创新思想转变为企业的实际产品、技术或服务。这种创新精神对于提高大中型企业的市场竞争力有一定的推动作用。

Entrepreneurship within a large or medium-size company is sometimes called intrapreneurship.

Global Perspective

Intrapreneurship in Haier

Entrepreneurship within a large or medium-size company is sometimes called intrapreneurship. It's used frequently in the companies such as the Haier.

March 10, 2015, "Haier Star Box" home debut Shanghai Expo, cool looks, powerful, and sometimes attracted many visitors to the eye. "Haier Star Box" is not only a field of intelligent control air breakthrough products, it is taking the Internet Haier thinking, make a new open innovation model.

Star Box is central air-conditioning system "smart thermostat". On the product itself, the star has a message box to display and touch screen operation, you can directly control each room's temperature and wind speed. It also has a smart home products. An important feature: Connecting to the network via Wi-Fi, and APP dedicated smart phone adapting, enabling remote temperature control in addition to the product itself, Haier Star Box also opened API and SDK, not only allow Haier product access, any intelligent hardware, products, and developers can access this product.

Haier intrapreneurship Star Box product is in line with long-term accumulation of Haier's product development capabilities, manufacturing capacity and Haier product line. In fact, Haier current and future products will be based on an open and cooperative modes, either creative production, or R & D management and technology, Haier has in creating an open innovation ecosystem.

（案例来源：节选自 The New Model of Open Innovation "Haier Star Box" to Create Intelligent Home First Entry. http://www.fireinews.com/news-9523347.html, 2015-3-12）

另一方面，企业家精神在经济运行与经济发展中的作用越来越大，对企业家精神的研究也从个体层面扩展到企业层面和宏观层面，越来越多的研究开始关注企业家精神与经济增长的关系。具体来看，企业家精神主要通过两个渠道影响经济增长。一是企业家精神与创业：企业家勇于承担风险的特点有助于促进创立企业从而影响经济增长。二是企业家精神与创新：企业家精神不仅与新企业建立有关，而且在某种意义上，内部企业家精神对企业的战略更新起着重要的作用，它有助于企业推出新的产品，挖掘新的市场，推动企业创新。

Entrepreneurship is benefit for launching new companies and promoting innovations.

第二节　管理者的角色与技能

Organizations and Managers in Today's World

Around the globe, the job of managers in the past has been to give orders, see that the orders are followed and hold employees accountable if they do not comply. All have been changed now. Although organizations still need managers to coordinate the work activities of their employees, the manager's role has changed. The reason for this is that as organizations are becoming more open and flexible, and less bureaucratic and hierarchical, managers are required to take on the role of a team leader and team member, rather than being the "person in charge". Managers are now being asked to act more like coaches than bosses.

What does it take to be a successful manager in today's organizations? According to the knowledgeable management observers, successful managers will need four characteristics: be a specialist or expert in something; be a team player; know enough about different disciplines to be a generalist; and be self-reliant by thinking of yourself as a marketable bundle of skills. Although these characteristics may seem contradictory, they are a reflection of the importance of being flexible and knowing your own personal skills, values and interests. Knowing yourself (what we call self-knowledge) is an important characteristic you can develop. You will also need to develop your people skills. Today and in the future, managers will be continually dealing with people both inside and outside the organization. To do so successfully, you need to be able to listen, motivate, lead, inspire and communicate effectively—all important people skills.

What managers (particularly top managers) also have to do is to find new and novel ways to achieve a higher level of collaboration with their employees, suppliers, customers and other stakeholders. Organizations that can master this collaboration are more likely to be able to deal with today's challenges, such as employee engagement, globalization, the need for innovation, effective use and integration of new technologies, and the need to find more sustainable business practices that also take into account environmental and social aspects in relation to the organization's long-term financial benefits. In today's world, organizations that can develop strong connections with their various stakeholders, employees, customers or the wider society, are more likely to be successful both today and in the future. And that is where some new leadership is required, which is based on ethical, sustainable and inclusive principles.

（案例来源: D. Argus. It's Human Nature. *AFR Boss*, 2010 (3): 32–33; and R. Turner. You'll Never Make it On Your Own. *The Australian Deal*, 2009 (8): 38–39）

随着环境的变化以及企业竞争的加剧，管理者面临的任务更加复杂多变，为了更好地履行管理者的职责，管理者像演员一样扮演不同的角色，并为了解决企业经营中的问题而不断提高自己的各项技能。那么，一个管理者应该承担哪些角色，并具备怎样的管理技能才能胜任作为管理者的角色？本节将围绕管理者的角色与技能展开论述。

一、管理者的角色

The Roles of Manager

如果观察管理者某一天的工作或某一阶段的工作，就会发现，尽管不同层次的管理者都在忙于计划、组织、领导及控制方面的工作，但是在一定程度上很难用精确的词汇来描述他们真正在做什么。更准确地说，你会看到管理者们在组织中扮演着不同的角色。角色定位不同，管理者的工作内容和工作重点也不同，并因此形成管理效果上的差异。合理的角色定位是有效管理的必要条件之一，为了提高管理绩效，研究者们从不同的角度对管理者的角色进行了大量研究。

在研究管理者的角色时，著名的管理学家彼得·德鲁克（Peter Drucker）认为，管理者的角色可分为三类，即管理一个组织，求得组织的生存和发展；管理管理者；管理工人和工作。到 20 世纪 60 年代后期，亨利·明茨伯格（Henry Mintzberg）通过对五位在任总经理进行实地调研，有了新的发现。过去人们通常认为管理者在决策之前都会仔细地、系统地对相关信息进行处理，但是明茨伯格却发现，他所研究的管理者从事的都是大量变动的、没有固定模式的短期性活动，这些管理者鲜有时间仔细思考，因为他们经常被各种事务打断，管理者的活动持续时间通常不会超过 9 分钟。除了这些发现以外，明茨伯格还在这些经理角色的实际工作基础上提出了一个分类体系来定义管理者的工作。他认为管理者角色（Managerial Roles）是管理者应该具备的行动或行为所组成的各种特定类型，这和日常生活中一个人可能同时担当不同的角色类似，例如一个人可以同时是学生、雇员、志愿者、篮球队员、男女朋友、兄弟姐妹等多种身份，在扮演这些不同身份时所做的事情也会不同。

Mintzberg's categorization approach defines what managers do based on managerial roles—specific categories of managerial actions or behaviors expected of a manager. Think of the different roles you play—such as student, employee, volunteer, basketball team member, boyfriend/girlfriend, sibling, and so forth—and the different things you're expected to do in those roles.

明茨伯格认为，管理者扮演着 10 种不同的但又高度相关的角色。这 10 种角色可以分为三类（见表 3-2）：人际角色（Interpersonal Role）、信息角色（Informational Role）、决策角色（Decisional Role）。换句话说，管理者们会与人交谈，收集和传递信息，做出决策。

（一）人际角色

Interpersonal roles

管理的本质是对人的协调，因而管理工作是人员密集型工作，尽管不同层次管理者表现各异，但大部分管理者要花费三分之二到四分之三的时间用于各种形式（面对面、书面、电话等）的沟通。如果你是一个不合群的人，或者性格内向、厌烦与人打交道，那么可能就不适合从事管理工作。

表 3-2　10 种基本管理角色

Table 3-2　Ten Basic Managerial Roles

Category	Role	Sample Activities
Interpersonal	Figurehead	Attending ribbon-cutting ceremony for new plant
	Leader	Encouraging employees to improve productivity
	Liaison	Coordinating activities of two project groups
Informational	Monitor	Scanning industry reports to stay abreast of developments
	Disseminator	Sending memos outlining new organizational initiatives
	Spokesperson	Making a speech to discuss growth plans
Decisional	Entrepreneur	Developing new ideas for innovation
	Disturbance Handler	Resolving conflict between two subordinates
	Resource Allocator	Reviewing and revising budget requests
	Negotiator	Reaching agreement with a key supplier or labor union

（资料来源：Ricky W. Griffin. *Management* (11th edition). Boston: Cengage Learning, 2012, p. 12）

在扮演人际角色的过程中，管理者还有三种从属角色：名义首脑（Figurehead Role）、领导者角色（Leader Role）和联络者角色（Liaison Role）。

名义首脑角色方面，管理者要履行一些礼仪性质的职责，如接见来访的参观者，在新工厂的开工仪式或新店开业仪式上讲话，或者代表企业出现在社区午餐会上支持当地的慈善活动等。这一角色在很多国家的政府组织中一直被保持着，例如日本的天皇、英国的女王等。2015 年习近平主席访英期间，英国女王夫妇在皇家骑兵检阅场为习近平举行了盛大的欢迎仪式，并一同乘坐英国王室的马车前往白金汉宫下榻。这些活动一般具有较强的象征意义，而非实质内容。

领导者角色方面，管理者要激励员工实现组织目标，例如招聘、培训与激励员工等工作。领导者在形成组织特有的经营风范、管理风格和鼓舞士气等方面起着决定性作用，而领导者的经营风范、管理风格和对士气的激励方式是领导者本身价值观的一种体现。

联络者角色方面，管理者需要与所在群组的外部人员打交道。现有研究证实，管理者花在与外界打交道上的时间，与他们跟自己的下属、老板打交道的时间差不多。调查表明，中高层管理者花 47%的时间与同等职位的人联络，41%的时间与本部门人员联络，12%的时间与上级联络。管理者们所接触的人是多种多样的，包括下属、客户、商业伙伴、供应商、其他公司领导、政府官员、其他董事会成员、与机构无关的个人等。即便是基层管理者，也会有广泛的人际关系，需要与不同的人经常接触。

The roles of figurehead, leader, and liaison which involve dealing with other people.

The manager is often expected to serve as a figurehead: taking visitors to dinner, attending ribbon-cutting ceremonies, and the like. These activities are typically more ceremonial and symbolic than substantive.

The manager is also expected to serve as a leader: hiring, training, and motivating employees.

The liaison role often involves serving as a coordinator or link among people, groups, or organizations.

（二）信息角色

管理者不仅要花费大量的时间与各种人进行的面对面接触，还需要花费足够多的时间来获取和共享信息。明茨伯格在他的研究中发现，管理者要花费40%的时间用于获取和传递信息，因而处理信息是管理者的重要工作。从这方面来看，管理可以看作处理信息的过程，即管理者通过敏锐的眼光审视组织所在的宏微观环境，在面对面交谈中倾听他人以获取信息，加工处理获取的信息，并与组织内外部共享信息，以便掌握组织发展的有利与不利因素，使组织的各层管理者能根据这些信息与因素做出合理判断。明茨伯格认为，信息角色有 3 种从属角色：监督者角色（Monitor Role）、传播者角色（Disseminator Role）、发言人角色（Spokesperson Role）。

所谓监督者角色，是指管理者通过广泛的信息搜集，获知组织与其工作相关的最新发展，甚至借助私人接触获得相关信息。他们关注环境变化，注重实际调查，能深入企业或社会实践中获取相关资讯。除了这些第一手信息之外，管理者还可以通过阅读报纸、观看财经类新闻、查看新闻资讯客户端、关注微信公众号等持续关注环境中那些可能影响客户、竞争对手、技术变革等方面的变化。

管理工作过程中，管理者有较多的时间和机会与下属接触，管理者承担着关键信息分配枢纽的作用。在传播者角色方面，管理者与组织内部的下属或其他人分享获取的信息，让他们能够了解到组织发展的战略、目标以及外部经营环境发展的挑战与机会。随着科学技术的发展，管理者作为信息传播者的角色正悄然发生着改变，信息共享和获取的方式也发生着改变，面对面的信息传播逐步被组织内高速的网络沟通方式所取代，信息的分享或获取越来越依赖于组织对信息管理系统的投入，办公信息沟通可以借助办公自动化（Office Automation，简称 OA）来完成，企业的生产、财务等信息可以通过 ERP 系统来实现共享，甚至以前常用的公司电子邮件或语音邮件也逐渐被更加私人化的微信所替代。正如思科公司 CEO 约翰·钱伯斯（John Chambers）所说的那样："如果不具备与客户、员工及供应商交流的能力，那么你就无法管理好自己的企业。"

与管理者作为信息传播者向组织内部员工传递信息的角色不同，发言人角色强调的是管理者与部门和组织外部的人共享信息。例如，为了公司的事业发展，公司总裁对外进行宣传，采购经理向供应商提出一个产品的行政建议，CEO 向所在社区的公众发表企业公益演说等。

◇ Informational roles

The roles of monitor, disseminator, and spokesperson, which involve the processing of information.

The monitor role involves seeking current information from many sources. The manager acquires information from others and scans written materials to stay well informed.

The disseminator role involves transmitting information received from outsiders or from other employees to members of the organization.

The spokesperson formally relays information to people outside the unit or outside the organization. When they represent the organization to outsiders, managers perform a spokesperson role.

作为发言人,管理者必须向可能对部门有影响的人告知相关信息,如作为工长,他就需要让厂长知道他负责工段的运营情况。通常情况下大公司的 CEO 每年都要向董事和股东报告和解释财务情况,要向消费者报告公司完成了它的社会责任,要向政府部门和官员报告公司遵守了各种法律以及依法纳税等。

Global Perspective

Jim McNerney

Boeing CEO Jim McNerney struggled with the spokesperson role after the 787 Dream liner passenger plane was grounded around the world in early 2013 due to problems with the electrical system that led to battery fires. As soon as it became apparent that the first fire wasn't an isolated incident, McNerney orchestrated an intense internal investigation, but he left the job of communicating with investors, analysts, the media, and the general public to other executives, including chief engineer Mike Sinnett. A few weeks after the first fire, during a conference call to discuss fourth-quarter financial results, McNerney deflected questions from investors and analysts, saying "I can't predict the outcome and I'm not going to. We're in the middle of an investigation." Although McNerney has been harshly criticized for not being more forthcoming with investors and analysts, some customers have praised Boeing for its overall communications strategy during the crisis. Explaining his decision to stay behind the scenes, McNerney said, "I'm the one who has to stand up with absolute confidence when Boeing proposes a solution .... And the only way I know how is to dive in deeply with the people doing the scientific and technical work."

（案例来源：Richard L. Daft. *Management* (12th edition). Boston: Cengage Learning, 2014, p. 26）

（三）决策角色

获取和分享信息并不是信息的结束,它是决策的初步基础。获取信息并在企业内、外部与人共享的目的,是有助于管理者做出决策。明茨伯格认为,管理者扮演着 4 种决策从属角色:企业家角色（Entrepreneur Role）、干扰对付者（Disturbance Role）、资源分配者（Resource Allocator Role）以及谈判者（Negotiator Role）。

在企业家角色方面,管理者需要改进自己的部门或企业,并使它适应环境的变化。当一个 CEO 寻找到新的点子,并且调研发现可能效果不错时,他就会启动一个好项目,可能由他自己亲自管理,也可能授权给下属。例如,如今消费者网络购物高速增长,2015 年阿里巴巴双十一销售额当天达到了 143 亿美元,巨大的网上销售催生了对物流的需求,马云意识到物流对电商发展的制约,于是开始组建社会化物流网络"菜鸟",而另一个电商巨头京东的 CEO 刘强东则选择自建物流,两者的主要目的都是通过部门改进来适应环境的变化。

◇ Decisional roles

Decisional roles pertain to those events about which the manager must make a choice and take action. Mintzberg identified four decisional roles: entrepreneur, disturbance handler, resource allocator, and negotiator.

As entrepreneurs, managers initiate and oversee new projects that will improve their organization's performance.

在干扰对付者角色方面,管理者应该对那些需要立刻得到重视并采取行动的紧急问题做出反应。如果说企业家角色强调管理者是企业中引起变化的主动力量,那么干扰对付者角色强调的则是管理者应付外界压力的相对被动的特性。当一个衰败企业的董事会雇用一位新任 CEO 以使企业起死回生时,管理者经常扮演着干扰对付者的角色。泰科国际(Tyco International)是一家全球性制造巨头,自 1991 年起该公司开始长达 10 年的疯狂收购,收购了 12 家公司,大肆收购使泰科国际长期债务高达逾 800 亿美元,并承担数亿美元损失;2002 年,爱德华·布林(Edward Breen)出任 CEO 后,推动泰科剥离资产,甩掉债务,2006 年,泰科净利润同比增长 40%,达 8.17 亿美元,2009 年营收逾 170 亿美元。另外一个例子是 2015 年德国大众公司"排气门"事件对大众汽车销售的影响,乘用车品牌首席执行官赫伯特·迪斯(Herbert Diess)10 月 28 日在日本东京车展为"排放门"道歉,迪斯说:"大众做了错事,我代表全公司道歉……我们正在竭尽所能,重新为品牌赢得信任。"他说,当务之急是解决问题,查找实情并确保此类丑闻永远不再发生。他承诺,将打造一个"全新的,甚至更好的大众"。

As disturbance handlers, managers take corrective action in response to unforeseen problems.

在资源分配者角色方面,管理者要决定谁会得到哪些资源以及获得多少资源。组织的资源都是有限的,在资源有限的条件下如何让这些资源得到合理配置,充分发挥资源的价值为组织带来更大的利润,需要管理者对这些资源进行分配。例如,企业的营销经理每年要决定企业产品的推广费用应该有多少用在广告上,有多少用在促销活动上,有多少用在公共关系上。

As resource allocators, managers are responsible for allocating human, physical and monetary resources.

在谈判者角色方面,在与其他组织沟通以争取本组织的利益时,管理者便以组织代表的身份与其他组织进行谈判。例如足球俱乐部的老板需要与转会球星谈判合同,公司总裁必须与工会谈判解决诸如罢工等问题。2008 年 10 月法国航空公司空乘人员举行为期 5 天的罢工,公司总裁让·西里尔·斯皮内达(Jean Cyril Spinetta)10 月 30 日回应工会代表,并同意在 11 月 7 日举行合同谈判。

Managers also perform as negotiators when they discuss and bargain with other groups to gain advantages for their own units.

Global Perspective

New York City Police Department

In the first 178 days of 2013, New York City averaged less than a murder a day. The drop from 202 murders during the first half of 2012 to 154 during the first half of 2013 surprised even police administrators.

Analyzing the findings, Police Commissioner Raymond W. Kelly attributed the decrease partly to changes in how resources are allocated. For example, Kelly increased the number of cops assigned to high-crime neighborhoods and poured resources into a new anti-gang strategy aimed at preventing retaliatory violence among neighborhood gangs. The strategy relies heavily on closely tracking the activities of gangs and trying to prevent shootings before they happen. Kelly said the initiative led to a 52 percent decline in shootings in one precinct. Another program receiving additional resources is aimed at identifying and monitoring abusive husbands whose behavior seems likely to turn lethal.

Deciding how to allocate resources in the country's biggest police force is similar to the job of a CEO in a midsize Fortune 500 company—except that the stakes are much higher because the metrics by which performance is measured have to do with life and death. In addition to fighting everyday crime, the New York Police Department (NYPD) has to battle terrorism. Kelly has put an emphasis on hiring native speakers of languages such as Farsi, Arabic, Urdu, Pashto, and Hindi, and set up a counterterrorism bureau and intelligence division that deploys NYPD cops in foreign cities. He has also invested $100 million in a surveillance network that oversees wide portions of Manhattan and the outer boroughs.

（案例来源：Richard L. Daft. *Management* (12th edition). Boston: Cengage Learning, 2014, p. 27）

　　值得注意的是，这 10 种角色是不可分割的，没有任何一个角色可以缺失同时又使管理者的职能保持完整。例如一个管理者没有与外界同僚的联系，就会缺乏外部信息，结果管理者既不能传播下属需要的信息，也不能做出符合环境要求的决策。另一方面，管理者角色理论认为，现实中由于组织类型不同，管理者在组织内所处的层次不同，其扮演这十种角色的侧重点是不同的，甚至同一组织、同一层次管理者在组织的不同时期扮演的角色也是变动的。

　　决定管理者角色变动的因素主要有：①环境方面的变数，包括周围环境、产业部门以及组织的特点；②职务方面的变数，包括职务的级别及所负担的职能；③个人方面的变数，包括担任该项职务者的个性和风格上的特点；④情绪方面的变数，包括许多与时间有关的因素。管理者组织环境越是富有动态性（竞争性、变化率、成长、生产的压力），他花在非正式信息交流上的时间就越多，他的工作就越多变而琐碎，他的行动就越活跃，他的口头联系就越多。

二、管理者的技能

从上文的分析可以看出，管理者的工作复杂多样，除了要扮演不同的角色之外，还需要一些特殊的技能以确保工作的顺利进行。根据罗伯特·卡茨（Robert L. Katz）的研究，管理者需要三种技能：技术技能、人际技能和概念技能。而且他还发现，这些技能在不同管理层具有不同的重要性。

技术技能（Technical Skill）是指那些完成工作所需要的专业程序、技术和知识。技术技能对基层管理者和团队领导者尤为重要，这些管理者需要花费较多的时间用于培训下属以及解决与工作相关的问题。特别是与工程、生产制造或财务等具体职能相关的方法、技术和设备等。例如面对市场的发展变化，销售经理应该掌握的技能就是发现市场前景，运用基于客户需求的合理促销手段做成生意的能力；车间主任应该掌握的就是生产设备运行情况、维修情况，解答一线工人生产疑难问题的能力。对于高层管理者而言，技术技能通常是指管理者对该行业的认识，以及对组织运作流程和产品的整体把握。

人际技能（Interpersonal Skill）是指管理者与其他个体和群体良好合作的能力，简而言之，就是成功与人打交道的能力。管理的工作就是指挥他人，通过他人的努力，合作完成工作或任务，他们必须具备良好的人际技能以沟通、激励、指导和委派任务。拥有人际技能的管理者能够在群体中有效地工作，鼓励他人发表见解和感受，对他人的需要和观点敏感，是很好的倾听者和沟通者。

概念技能（Conceptual Skill）是分析和判断复杂形势，为组织的未来做出合理决策的能力，包括把组织视为一个整体的能力，了解组织不同部门相互之间如何影响的能力，理解组织如何适应社区、社会和经济因素、客户以及竞争状况之类的外部环境要素，以及这些要素如何影响企业的能力。概念技能较其他两种技能更抽象一些，更多的是管理者对管理工作方向性的分析与把握，一般情况下高层管理者需要较高的概念技能，以便为企业的使命、愿景及战略提出更符合实际需要的决策，因而概念技能的重要性随着管理者层级的增加而增加。

但是，这并不是说高层管理者不需要其他两种技能，作为财务总监或企业 CEO，即使自己不懂会计是如何处理具体的财务问题，也应该具备看懂财务报表的能力，例如对企业现金流量表、资产负债表及损益表中所包含信息的理解等。

✍ **The Skills of Manager**

Technical skill: Job-specific knowledge, expertise, and techniques needed to perform work tasks.

Interpersonal skill: Working well with other people both individually and in groups by communicating, motivating, mentoring, and delegating.

Conceptual skill: Analyzing and diagnosing complex situations to see how things fit together and to facilitate making good decisions.

自 20 世纪 90 年代以来，组织政治逐渐成为国内外组织管理实务界和理论界关注的热点，于是在卡茨提出的三大技能之外，也有学者提出对于中层管理者与基层管理者还需要具备政治技能。所谓政治技能（Political Skill）是指建立权力基础并构建合适的社会关系的能力。事实上，"政治技能"一词最早出现在 1981 年杰弗瑞·菲佛（Jeffrey Pfeffer）关于组织权力角逐的文献中。菲佛认为，个体的政治技能关系到组织有限资源的获取与有效运用，是个体在组织中获得成功的必要要素之一。一般而言，高政治技能的管理者往往有突出的社交敏锐性、人际影响力、关系网络能力和真诚表现力，这些有助于他们抓住职场机会，赢得职业发展。中国人民大学教授刘军等人的研究也发现，高政治技能的员工往往能在华人组织情境中与领导建立和维系良好的关系，成为领导的"圈内人"，而领导往往愿意将晋升或职业发展的机会提供给处于"圈内人"地位的员工。

管理者技能分析显示，概念技能处理的是观点、思想，人际技能关心的是人，技术技能涉及的是事，政治技能则是资源的整合。管理层越高，技术技能所占比例越低，概念技能所占比例越大。这就可以解释为什么有的优秀部门管理者却无法胜任诸如副总裁那样的职位，是因为他们的管理者技能结构不适合更高的管理职位的要求。

Political skill: Building a power base and establishing the right connections so they can get needed resources for their groups.

Global Perspective

Management Skill Builder: Political Skill

Forget, for a moment, the ethics of politicking and any negative impressions you might have of people who engage in organizational politics. If you want to be more politically adept in your organization, follow these eight suggestions:

● Frame arguments in terms of organizational goals. Effective politicking requires camouflaging your self-interest. No matter that your objective is self-serving; all the arguments you marshal in support of it must be framed in terms of the benefits that will accrue to the organization. People whose actions appear to blatantly further their own interests at the expense of the organization are almost universally denounced, are likely to lose influence, and often suffer the ultimate penalty of being expelled from the organization.

● Develop the right image. If you know your organization's culture, you understand what the organization wants and values from its employees—in terms of dress, associates to cultivate and those to avoid, whether to appear to be a risk taker or risk-aversive, the preferred leadership style, the importance placed on getting along well with others, and so forth. Then you are equipped to project the appropriate image. Because the assessment of your performance isn't always a fully objective process, you need to pay attention to style as well as substance. In addition, studies consistently show that people who can successfully project sincerity are perceived in a positive image.

- Gain control of organizational resources. The control of organizational resources that are scarce and important is a source of power. Knowledge and expertise are particularly effective resources to control. They make you more valuable to the organization and, therefore, more likely to gain security, advancement, and a receptive audience for your ideas.

- Make yourself appear indispensable. Because we're dealing with appearances rather than objective facts, you can enhance your power by appearing to be indispensable. You don't really have to be indispensable as long as key people in the organization believe that you are. If the organization's prime decision makers believe there is no ready substitute for what you are giving the organization, they are likely to go to great lengths to ensure that your desires are satisfied.

- Be visible. If you have a job that brings your accomplishments to the attention of others, that's great. However, if you don't have such a job, you'll want to find ways to let others in the organization know what you're doing by highlighting successes in routine reports, having satisfied customers relay their appreciation to senior executives, being seen at social functions, being active in your professional associations, and developing powerful allies who speak positively about your accomplishments. Of course, the skilled politician actively and successfully lobbies to get the projects that will increase his or her visibility.

- Develop powerful allies. It helps to have powerful people on your side. Network by cultivating contacts with potentially influential people above you, at your own level, and in the lower ranks. These allies often can provide you with information that's otherwise not readily available. In addition, decisions are sometimes made in favor of those with the greatest support. Having powerful allies can provide you with a coalition of support if and when you need it.

- Avoid "tainted" members. In almost every organization, there are fringe members whose status is questionable. Their performance and loyalty are suspect. Keep your distance from such individuals. Given the reality that effectiveness has a large subjective component, your own effectiveness might be called into question if you're perceived as being too closely associated with tainted members.

- Support your boss. Your immediate future is in the hands of your current boss. Because that person evaluates your performance, you'll typically want to do whatever is necessary to have your boss on your side. You should make every effort to help your boss succeed, make her look good, support him if he is under siege, and spend the time to find out the criteria she will use to assess your effectiveness. Don't undermine your boss. And don't speak negatively of him to others

（案例来源：Stephen P. Robbins, David A. DeCenzo and Mary Coulter. *Fundamentals of Management: Essential Concepts and Applications* (9th edition). New York: Pearson, 2013, pp. 21-22）

第三节　优秀企业及其竞争优势

ASSESSING OUTCOMES AND SEIZING OPPORTUNITIES

The technology marketplace is littered with lost opportunities, even by companies that are competitive and successful. Several years ago, Microsoft was on the verge of losing a major opportunity to its competitors, who were already providing new products to its customers via the Web. These firms, including Google and Yahoo, had proven that they could make money through advertising revenues attached to their services, which ranged from Internet search engines to photo sharing.

Ray Ozzie, installed as the chief software architect at Microsoft, had to find a way to guide his firm in the right direction. Microsoft, well known for offering stand-alone software products, has begun to integrate them so that they have a broader range of capabilities. Ozzie and his team believe that customers want Internet search capabilities literally built in to the programs they regularly use—from the Microsoft Outlook e-mail and calendar program to video gaming community sites. Under CEO Steve Ballmer's and Ray Ozzie's leadership, Microsoft has acquired Medstory Inc., a health search engine. Microsoft is offering space to advertisers, in turn providing those advertisers with an interested audience. "Advertisers do want a targeted audience," observes one industry analyst. If Microsoft can provide captive viewers, "I don't see a reason why advertisers won't move from the competition."

On another front, Microsoft is focusing on security, based on its Trustworthy Computing Initiative, which began several years ago. Ozzie must ensure that security technology evolves ahead of hackers—as well as competitors. Despite skepticism from some observers, many industry analysts believe that Ozzie has Microsoft moving forward in a rapidly changing environment. "The world of online services and software-as service has been passing Microsoft by, and I credit Ozzie with getting the company more fully in the game," notes observer Dwight Davis of Summit Strategies.

（案例来源：Thomas S. Bateman and Scott A. Snell. *Management: Leading & Collaborating in a Competitive World* (9th edition). New York: McGraw-Hill Irwin, 2014, p. 80）

像 IT 行业中的微软、苹果、IBM、阿里巴巴以及制造行业中的通用，零售业的沃尔玛，餐饮业的星巴克以及肯德基、麦当劳等，这些管理得比较好的优秀企业，它们发展并拥有许多忠实的客户群，即使在经济环境充满挑战的时代，这些企业也能够想到继续成长壮大的办法；而那些管理较差的企业，其客户却正在减少，营业收入也在不断下降，甚至最终结果是寻求破产保护，例如金宝汤、安然、雷曼兄弟等公司都曾经辉煌一时，这些公司雇用数万员工，每天为数以万计的客户提供商品和服务。然而，今天这些公司都已不复存在了。糟糕的管理葬送了它们的前程。通过本节的学习，可以了解世界上优秀的企业如何不断改善自己的管理，增强企业的动态能力，以持续获得竞争优势。

一、优秀的企业

美国《财富》杂志每年都会根据企业在创新、管理质量、产品质量及服务质量四方面内容的表现，对全球企业进行排名。在"2015 年全球最受尊敬公司排行榜"中，苹果公司连续八年高居榜首，谷歌晋升排行榜第二位，取代 2014 年榜单第二名亚马逊，而巴菲特麾下的伯克希尔-哈撒韦公司（Berkshire Hathaway Cooperation）则上升一位，位居第三。中国的联想集团、华硕电脑、国泰航空及宝钢集团等也榜上有名。

纵观这些上榜企业，在以下三个方面具有相同特征。

第一，全面发展。凡是上榜企业都是业绩非凡的国际化公司，这些公司的共性是全面发展，从各项考核指标分析都有行业领先的特点。如苹果，在创新、人员管理、企业资产利用、社会责任、管理质量、财务稳健性、长期投资价值、产品质量和长期投资价值等 9 个类别全部获得了最高评价。

第二，百花齐放，各有所长。被评为"全球最受尊敬公司"的这些企业不仅仅在各项考核指标上具有明显的整体比较优势，而且在某些方面表现非凡，具有差异性领先的特点。换句话说，要胜出，就得与众不同。如微软成长性最好且盈利水平最高，索尼产品质量领先，谷歌创新力最强。

第三，创新是全球化的主流价值观。创新作为考核评价全球最受尊敬企业的第一指标，本身就说明对创新能力的重视。事实也的确如此，唯有创新才能不断增强企业发展的推动力，使企业具有长远的发展前景。以苹果为例，在乔布斯带领下形成了注重创新、完美设计、严格保密等创新氛围。这种氛围能够激励员工不断地学习和思考来寻找创新机会，鼓励员工使用新的方法完成工作，产生新颖的、有创造性的想法并进行实践检验，进而促进企业创新能力和创新绩效的提升。

优秀企业不是利润最大化的企业，而是价值最大化的企业。企业要做到优秀，必须全方位发展，各方面业绩显著。21 世纪是一个快速巨变的时代，人类世界的变化从来没有像今天这样快，管理者每天都要和变化着的工作职场、道德与信任问题、全球经济不确定性以及日新月异的技术打交道。不了解和适应全球环境变化的管理者，会发现自己的企业将是逆潮流而动，企业很可能失掉竞争力，并由此衰落下去。

✍ **Excellent Companies**

Characteristics of excellent companies:

1. Comprehensive development

2. Differentiation strategy

3. Strong innovation capability

所以，任何地方的管理者都有可能面对变革的管理环境，管理者的管理方式也必然会发生变化。资源、能力等企业赖以生存的基础在遭遇环境变化以后往往就不再是企业竞争优势的来源，甚至有可能成为阻遏企业进一步成长的障碍。在动荡的外部环境中，企业如何才能获得持续成长，成为摆在企业和研究者面前的一个重要课题。

Global Perspective

Is It Still Managing When What You're Managing Are Robots?

The office of tomorrow is likely to include workers that are faster, smarter, more responsible—and who just happen to be robots. Are you at all surprised by this statement? Although robots have been used in factory and industrial settings for a long time, it's becoming more common to find robots in the office and it's bringing about new ways of looking at how work is done and at what and how managers manage. So what would the manager's job be like managing robots? And even more intriguing is how these "workers" might affect how human coworkers interact with them.

As machines have become smarter and smarter—did any of you watch Watson take on the human Jeopardy challengers—researchers have been looking at human-machine interaction and "how people relate to the increasingly smart devices that surround them." One conclusion is that people find it easy to bond with a robot, even one that doesn't look or sound anything like a real person. In a workplace setting, if a robot moves around in a "purposeful way", people tend to view it, in some ways, as a coworker. People will give their robots names and even can describe the robot's moods and tendencies.

As telepresence robots become more common, the humanness becomes even more evident. For example, when Erwin Deininger, the electrical engineer at Reimers Electra Steam, a small company in Clear Brook, Virginia, moved to the Dominican Republic when his wife's job transferred her there, he was able to still be "present" at the company via his VGo robot. Now Deininger "wheels easily from desk to desk and around the shop floor, answering questions and inspecting designs." The company's president was "pleasantly surprised at how useful the robot has proven" and even more surprised at how he acts around it. He finds it hard to not think of the robots, in a very real sense, Deininger himself. "After a while," he says, "it's not a robot anymore."

There's no doubt that robot technology will continue to be incorporated into organizational settings. The manager's job will become even more exciting and challenging as humans and machines work together to accomplish the organization's goals.

（案例来源：Stephen P. Robbins, David A. DeCenzo and Mary Coulter. *Fundamentals of Management: Essential Concepts and Applications* (9th edition). New York: Pearson, 2013, p. 16）

二、建立竞争优势

竞争优势（Competitive Advantage）是一个组织因为能够比竞争者更有效率地生产或提供社会需要的产品或服务，从而在绩效上胜出对手的能力。竞争优势包括四个组成部分，分别是对顾客的响应、创新、质量及效率。如图3-2所示。

✍ Build Competitive Advantage

Competitive advantage is the ability of an organization to produce goods or services more effectively than competitors do, thereby outperforming them. This means an organization must stay ahead in four areas: (1) being responsive to customers, (2) innovation, (3) quality, and (4) efficiency.

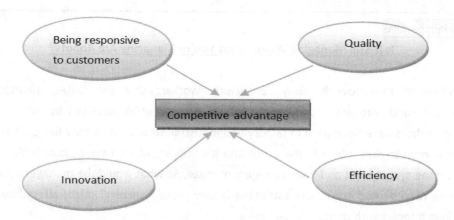

图 3-2　竞争优势的基础

Figure 3-2　Sources of Competitive Advantages

（一）快速响应顾客需要

约翰·钱伯斯（John Chambers）作为思科公司的CEO，喜欢听那些不满意的顾客发给他的语音邮件。他说道："用文字电子邮件的效率可能更高，但是我更想听到的是他们的抱怨，想听到留言的人对我们所实施战略的满意度，而用普通电子邮件我是无法感知这些内容的。"这才是一个真正了解顾客重要性的管理者。一切企业品牌的背后是市场中的顾客，没有他们，多数组织将不复存在。关注顾客长期以来被看作市场部门相关人员的责任，其他部门的管理者往往忽视顾客的意见或抱怨，"让市场人员去担心顾客吧"是许多管理者的想法，然而研究发现，员工的态度和行为在顾客满意度方面起着非常重要的作用。

管理者们已经意识到，组织若想在当今竞争激烈的环境中生存，获得成功，必须能够为顾客提供持续的高质量服务。而员工是这个过程中重要的一部分。斯坦福大学商学院教授杰弗瑞·菲佛（Jeffrey Pfeffer）认为，优秀企业与竞争对手的区别之处在于它们对待员工方面的差异，投资员工的企业能够创造出别的企业难以复制的持续竞争优势，这些企业的管理者会使用诸如就业保障、选择性聘

✧ Being responsive to customers

The first law of business is: take care of the customer. Without customers—buyers, clients, consumers, shoppers, users, patrons, guests, investors, or whatever they're called—sooner or later there will be no organization.

用、自我管理的团队和分权、基于企业绩效的高额报酬、广泛的培训、缩小地位差别（管理者和员工之间）以及广泛分享财务信息之类的理念来提升公司的整体财务绩效。

（二）创新让你永超对手

企业必须持续创新。创新（Innovation）就是引入新产品或新服务，或寻找传递新的产品或服务方式。再也没有比不创新更具风险的了。创新意味着用不同的方法做事情，探索新的领域，承担风险。创新不仅是高技术公司或者其他技术复杂组织的事情，几乎在所有类型的公司中，都需要创新。

在当前这个充满挑战的环境中，创新是关键。公司能否在竞争中胜出，取决于它们的反应速度和灵活性，即及时地改进或调整应对竞争者行动的工作方法。拥有快速反应能力和灵活性的公司便是机敏的竞争者，其管理者具有良好的计划和组织能力，能够谋划在先，然后迅速集中有关资源对正在变化的环境做出反应。

（三）质量必须持续改进

一般而言，质量（Quality）是指卓越的产品。近几年来，质量的重要性越来越受到重视，可接受的质量标准显著提升。因此，许多组织将为市场不断提供优质产品和服务作为组织的生命线来抓。20 世纪 60 年代，许多组织开始从日本学习和引进全面质量管理（TQM）。在全面质量管理活动中，员工被分到不同的质量控制小组中去，负责探寻有助于完成自身工作的新的、更好的方法，并对自己生产的产品的质量加以监督和评价。今天许多组织学习 ISO 9000 质量管理标准，建立和完善质量保证体系，并将其作为建立组织竞争优势的重要方面。

（四）提高效率

凡能在生产产品或提供服务上减少资源（如：劳动力和原材料）的消耗，组织就可以提高其效率。几个世纪前，企业以员工服务的时间长度来奖励他们，然而今天，组织激励的重点是效率，即尽可能快地以尽可能少的资源（如劳动力和原材料）生产产品或提供服务。谷歌公司不断地以较快速度持续改善其搜索引擎。事实上，谷歌的整体企业文化就是以快速创新为基础的。谷歌前副总裁雪莉·桑德伯格（Sheryl Sandberg）曾经因为计划太快而犯错，导致公司损失几百万美元，谷歌联合创始人拉里·佩奇（Larry Page）回应她的解释和道歉时说，他实际很喜欢她所犯的错误，因为这表明桑德伯格非常赞同谷歌的价值

✧ Companies must continually innovate.

Innovation is the introduction of new goods and services.

✧ Quality must be improved

In general, quality is the excellence of your product. The importance of quality and the standards for acceptable quality have increased dramatically in recent years.

✧ Increasing efficiency

How fast can you develop and get a new product to market? How quickly can you respond to customers' requests? You are far better off if you are faster than the competition—and if you can respond quickly to your competitors' actions.

观。佩奇告诉桑德伯格："我想经营的公司是一个能反应更迅速、做得更多的公司，而不是过于谨慎而做得太少的公司。如果我们没有这些错误，我们就不能承担足够的风险。"

Global Perspective

How Bezos Built a Business

Amazon CEO Jeff Bezos has quantitative skills, computer expertise, and formal training in management. After earning a bachelor's degree in computer science and a master's in business administration, he worked as a hedge fund manager. As he pursued that career during the 1990s, he observed some of the early changes the Internet was making in the way people did business.

Bezos decided that this new technology offered an opportunity to sell books in a new way, offering a far bigger selection than any bricks-and-mortar store could hold. In 1994, he wrote a business plan for a company he wanted to launch. He would call it Amazon, and it would be the world's largest bookstore, serving U.S. customers from its website. In his plan, he estimated that the company could achieve sales of $100 million a year within a decade. As it turned out, Bezos was wrong. He started Amazon and was selling that much in just a few years. In 1997, he took the company public, raising funds by selling shares to investors. And his idea for a U.S. bookstore became a global enterprise employing 70,000 people and selling music, games, tools, kitchen gadgets, and far more.

Bezos sets clear priorities. He insists on excellent services but at a low cost. That requires seeking efficiency and avoiding frills in the company's operations. He seizes new opportunities when they offer a chance to meet customer needs. For example, when hardware makers began to create e-readers, Bezos saw a way for readers to have access to even more titles. Initially, consumers were reluctant to try the new technology, so Amazon got involved in developing a more enticing model. From the start, the Kindle was priced so low it just covered the cost. The goal wasn't to make money on the hardware but to make it available to consumers so they could buy electronic books, magazines, and more. Incidentally, the low-price strategy also makes it harder for computer companies to beat Amazon at the e-reader game.

（案例来源：Thomas S. Bateman and Scott A. Snell. *Management: Leading & Collaborating in a Competitive World* (11th edition). New York: McGraw-Hill Irwin, 2015, p. 15）

Nonmanagerial employee

Manager

Top-level manager

Middle manager

First-line manager

Professional manager

Entrepreneur

Entrepreneurship

Intrapreneur

Intrapreneurship

Interpersonal role

Informational role

Decisional role

Figurehead role

Leader role

Liaison role

Monitor role

Disseminator role

Spokesperson role

Disturbance handler

Resource allocator

Negotiator

Technical skill

Interpersonal skill

Conceptual skill

Political skill

Competitive advantage

Innovation

讨论问题 DISCUSSION QUESTIONS

1. Identify and describe a great manager. What makes him or her stand out from the crowd?

2. Describe a typical manager's day. What are some of the expected consequences of this type of daily experience?

3. Mintzberg defines what managers do based on managerial roles. Please give your understandings about the 10 roles.

4. Which would you rather be—a manager or an entrepreneur/intrapreneur? And why?

5. Explain the meanings of technical, conceptual, interpersonal skills and political skills. Discuss the importance of each skill at school and in jobs you have held.

6. What are your strengths and weaknesses as you contemplate your career? How do they correlate with the skills and behaviors identified in this chapter?

7. Devise a plan for developing yourself and making yourself attractive to potential employers. How would you go about improving your managerial skills?

8. Recall a recent group project or task in which you have participated. Describe how members of the group displayed each of the managerial skills.

9. Watch a movie or television program that involves an organization of some type. One of the newer *The Last Ship* or *James Bond* movies would be good choices (or perhaps Citizen Kane for classic movie buffs). For television, options like *The Office*, *30 Rock*, or *The Good* Wife would be ideal. Identify as many management activities, skills, and roles as you can.

10. Discuss some of the ways that organizations and jobs have changed over the past ten years. What changes do you anticipate over the next ten years? How might these changes affect the manager's job and the skills that a manager needs to be successful?

Managing McDonald's Australia

Worldwide, the McDonald's Corporation has more than 30,000 restaurants in over 120 countries. Every day, the company has more than 50 million customers coming through its doors or drive-throughs. While McDonald's restaurants around the world follow a set of basic rules, each country is given a good amount of freedom to innovate. In Australia, it operates through McDonald's Australia Limited as an unlisted Australian public company limited by shares. It opened its first restaurant in 1971, in the Sydney suburb of Yagoona. From there it has grown rapidly to where it has more than 85,000 employees across more than 820 McDonald's restaurants and cafes serving more than 1.7 million customers every day with an annual turnover of $3 billion. While some of the restaurants and cafes are company run, more than two-thirds of them are franchise businesses operated by individual businessmen and women. The Australian business is among the most successful arms of the Chicago-based fast-food empire. Australia is also acknowledged as a leader within the McDonald's Corporation. For example, the McCafes, launched in Melbourne's Swanston Street in 1993, have been adopted in other parts of the world. McDonald's Australia has also been a leader in the introduction of nutritional labeling—a move that has now been copied by other McDonald's operations around the world.

Catriona Noble became the managing director/CEO for McDonald's Australia in May 2010. Like so many other senior managers within the McDonald's Corporation, Noble started working for the company early in her life as a 14-year-old casual crew member cooking French fries and serving customers. After finishing high school, Noble travelled for a while before starting a Bachelor of Business (Marketing) degree at University of Technology Sydney (UTS) and then transferred to Macquarie University to do a Bachelor of Economics (Law). While she was studying at university she also accepted a position as part-time manager at a McDonald's restaurant. While it meant a lot of hard work to balance her studies and a part-time job, Noble found it very stimulating to get hands-on experience of management and leadership skills in her job at McDonald's in addition to what she was studying at university. She quickly moved from being first assistant to becoming one of McDonald's youngest restaurant managers at age 19, overseeing 100 staff and an operation with a turnover in excess of $4 million. This was the beginning of a rapidly developing career path at McDonald's. Before long, she moved into a training role for two years, which was followed by a transfer to a Newcastle-based role as operations consultant to help with the revamping of five company-owned stores.

Over the following years, Catriona Noble spent time in various roles within the McDonald's Australian operations, as well as some time at McDonald's Hamburger University in Illinois, before becoming the national training manager for Australia. During her time in this role, the National Training Centre in Sydney was recognized as a centre of excellence for the Asia, Pacific, Middle East and Africa (APMEA) region. This was followed by a promotion to director of operations in NSW McOpCo, where she was responsible for 127 restaurants. She then became national marketing manager in 2003 and was an important force behind the development of a fully integrated crew campaign, with crew advertisements, as well as the research and development of deli choices and potential dinner solutions. Noble moved to Melbourne in 2005 as the regional manager for the Southern Region of Australia. In this role, she was responsible for all aspects of McDonald's business in Victoria, Tasmania, South Australia and Western Australia, including franchising, operations, advertising, marketing and sponsorship.

After a stint as senior vice-president of corporate strategy and business planning back in Sydney, Noble then became McDonald's Australia's chief operating officer and a member of the board in 2007, before being elevated to managing director of the Australian operation in 2008 and the ultimate top job of CEO for Australia in 2010. Becoming the managing director/CEO at age 40 also meant that Catriona Noble became the first female managing director of one of McDonald's top ten subsidiaries in the world. As the CEO, she is now responsible for marketing, public affairs, operations, supply chain, the Pacific Islands and business planning, taking on a leadership role for the ongoing development and integration of McDonald's business plan in Australia.

What stands out in Catriona Noble's rapid career within McDonald's Australia has been her willingness to work hard, learn and grow, as well as being ambitious in taking on new responsibilities and challenges which she has tackled with enthusiasm and willingness to implement changes to achieve improvements. She has also been able to build strong relationships with customers, team members and suppliers, and she is regarded as an inspirational leader with a great understanding of the business from the bottom to the top. She has even jokingly suggested she has "ketchup in her veins." She is very focused on creating a culture where teamwork is central in how all staff at McDonald's, as well as 300 franchisees and more than 4,000 suppliers, work together in looking after their customers.

Noble has been an important driving force behind a range of new items on the McDonald's menu, including healthy options such as salads and wraps. "That is a really important part of our five-year plan—to understand what our consumers want and to respond to that." She also sees a lot of growth options, despite the Australian operation having performed very well since 2003. It has raised its sales by over 50 percent, due in large part to the introduction of the McCafe outlets, the refurbishment of its restaurants, the inclusion of healthier products on the menu, and the introduction of the premium Angus burgers, which have been a huge success. Through the

McCafe-only stores, McDonald's has also been able to take on the other coffee chains such as Starbucks and Gloria Jean's. Noble is also very aware of changing consumer tastes, and of the criticisms that have been directed towards some of McDonald's fattier menu items, and she is currently leading a push to investigate alternative cooking platforms where McDonald's aims to use a lower-fat, healthier way to cook. Other changes she has implemented are the extended trading hours, with more 24-hour operations. And these changes seem to have really paid off, or as Noble puts it, "Our business results have been pretty spectacular .... We are one of the leading countries globally in terms of top-line growth and operating income growth and we are recognized as an innovator within the McDonald's world."

An important influence on Catriona Noble's development has been the mentors that have guided her throughout her career. People like Charlie Bell, who also started at "Maccas" at age 15 and worked his way up to become the managing director of McDonald's Australia in 1993 at age 33 and who in 2002 moved on to McDonald's global headquarters in Chicago where he became CEO for the worldwide McDonald's Corporation in 2004, before tragically dying of cancer a year later. "Charlie was a great mentor," says Noble, who first met Bell when she was 17. "He had an unbelievable energy. He was a terrific motivator. He could light up a room. He taught me a lot about connecting with people and getting them to aspire to do more and be better." Another mentor was Bell's successor, Guy Russo, who ran the chain's Australian operations from 1999 until 2005. According to Noble, it was Russo who changed the culture in the company in 2000 by introducing changes that allowed more talented women to be identified and promoted, as well as implementing more flexible working arrangements. These changes have now resulted in the senior management team at McDonald's Australia being made up of six women and six men.

Noble also had the opportunity to learn alongside Peter Bush, "the architect of healthy choices" range at McDonald's. "Bushy was very embracing of me and let me be part of the team and that is where I learnt the value of adapting to change. Now I need to lead change .... I have to be an architect of change. One of the most important skills business leaders need today is change management skills, not just to lead change but to embrace it and initiate it." After all, Noble knows it is a challenging market out there with hungry competitors such as KFC, Subway, Red Rooster, Pizza Hut and Sumo Salad, all competing for the customer's dollar!

What lies ahead for Catriona Noble? Could a role even higher in the global McDonald's empire be on the cards? Possibly even the head office of McDonald's in Chicago? Well, Noble seems to be willing to entertain the thought, or as she diplomatically puts it: "There's a lot of recognition in the US about the great job Australia has done in terms of leading the business, which is helpful."

（案例来源：Stephen Robbins, Rolf Bergman, Ian Stagg and Mary Coulter. *Management* (6th edition). Melbourne: Pearson Australia Group Pty Ltd., 2012, pp. 34-35）

Discussion Questions

1. Using the ten roles as a guide, what is Catriona Noble's role as the CEO of McDonald's Australia? What activities does she need to undertake in playing these roles?

2. In what ways do Catriona Noble's technical, human, conceptual skills and political skills help her overcome the managerial difficulties and assist her to maintain McDonald's advantage in Australia? Be specific in your description.

3. What do you learn from Catriona Noble and how do you improve your managerial skills?

第四章　管理决策

学习目标

1. 理解管理决策的内涵及其理论
2. 描述管理决策的步骤
3. 掌握决策制定的方法
4. 描述决策的类型及管理者面临的决策情境
5. 理解管理者偏见对管理者决策的影响

主要内容

第一节　管理决策相关理论
第二节　决策类型及方法
第三节　管理者偏见与新挑战

Learning Outcomes

1. Understand the nature of managerial decision making and its theory.
2. Describe the steps of decision-making.
3. Learn the approaches of decision-making.
4. Describe the types of decisions and decision-making conditions managers face.
5. Understand the impact of managers' bias on decision-making.

Contents

4.1 Related Theories of Decision-making
4.2 The Types and Approaches of Decision-making
4.3 Managers' Bias and New Challenges

第一节　管理决策相关理论

Citi ODs on CDOs

When the closing bell tolled at the New York Stock Exchange on Friday, November 21, 2008, shares of Citigroup closed at $3.77, making the country's largest financial institution worth about $20.5 billion. Two years earlier, Citigroup's stock price had put its value at $244 billion. It was, to say the least, a significant loss in shareholder value.

Obviously, the reasons behind such a monumental collapse are extremely complex, but in order to see what happened, let's focus on just a few factors—in particular, some miscalculated strategy initiatives and some mismanaged tactical policies.

When Charles O. Prince III took over as Citigroup CEO in October 2003, he targeted the bank's trading operations as a source of increased earnings. Now, one of the specialties of traders in the financial industry was creating collateralized debt obligations, or CDOs: securities that pool various forms or classes of debt—or fixed income assets—into bundles for resale to investors. A financial institution like Citi might buy mortgages from original lenders, pool the projected revenue, and sell securities backed by the pooled revenue. In return for the promise to redeem the securities at interest, the bank that issues them takes fees of up to 2.5 percent of the amount of the securities sold.

In the heady days of the housing boom that lasted from about 1995 to mid 2006, there was a lot of money to be made in CDOs, and between 2003 and 2005 Citi tripled the volume of CDOs that it issued. In 2005, its trading operations generated $500 million in fees, and in that year Prince made a concerted effort to produce even more revenue from the group responsible for trading CDOs and similar instruments. He bulked up the unit, recruited key personnel from competitors, and doubled and tripled bonuses for traders. Randall H. Barker, who oversaw the build up in the department, received $20 million a year in compensation, and Thomas G. Maheras, who headed it, took home $30 million.

CDOs may be profitable, but they can also be tricky. Mortgages became a popular component of CDOs because of the housing boom, but CDOs typically contain several different classes of fixed income assets—from mortgages and credit card loans to junk bonds to aircraft leases and movie revenues. Because the risk entailed by each class of assets may depend on very different factors, overall risk can be quite difficult to determine. Charles Prince was aware of the risks entailed by investment in fixed asset securities, but as one former Citigroup executive puts it, "he didn't know a CDO from a grocery list." Like any responsible manager, he thus sought advice, turning to Robert E. Rubin, a onetime Wall Street executive and Secretary of the Treasury in the Clinton administration who had chaired Citi's executive committee since 1999. As Treasury secretary, Rubin had helped relax federal oversight of such exotic financial instruments as CDOs, and according to the same former executive, Rubin "had always been an advocate of being more aggressive in the trading arena. He would say, 'You have to take more risk if you want to earn more.'" Prince and Rubin endorsed a strategy that called for taking greater risks in the interest of expanding business and generating higher profits.

Unfortunately, housing prices started to drop in 2006. Refinancing became more difficult, initial terms on adjustable rate mortgages (ARMs) were expiring, higher interest rates were taking effect, and before long, 16 percent of all subprime ARMs were delinquent or in foreclosure proceedings. In September 2007, Prince learned that Citi was sitting on $43 billion in mortgage related assets. To be on the safe side, however, Prince dispatched a risk management team to take a closer look at Citi's mortgage related holdings. What they discovered was that it was too late to be on the safe side. Four months later, Citi announced a fourth quarter loss of nearly $10 billion.

By the end of 2008, losses would total $65 billion more than half of which stemmed from the mortgage related securities for which Maheras had vouched back in September 2007. At Citi, the problem was made worse by a breakdown in internal risk management practices. Normally, risk managers carefully monitor the activities of managers in lending and trading units in order to guard against excessive risk taking. Clearly, Thomas Maheras's trading unit had taken huge risks in saddling the bank with $43 billion in mortgage related assets, but as we've seen, when CEO Prince wanted to know if those risks were excessive, he asked Maheras. Maheras, whose unit was generating immense profits (and hefty bonuses) from CDO trading, said no.

Apparently, Prince was no better served by David C. Bushnell, his senior risk officer and the manager responsible for putting the brakes on potentially dangerous trading activities. Maheras and Bushnell were longtime friends, having climbed the Citi corporate ladder together, and some insiders at the bank report that the boundaries between their two units weren't as rigorous as they should have been. Risk management, says one former employee, "has to be independent, and it wasn't independent at Citigroup, at least when it came to trading."

In fact, at one point, risk managers responsible for overseeing trading activities reported to Maheras as well as Bushnell, thus giving the trading unit leverage over the very same managers who were supposed to be keeping an eye on the activities of traders.

Maheras and Bushnell were eventually fired, Prince resigned, and Citigroup received $45 billion in cash infusions from the federal government. The bank has a new CEO, Vikram S. Pandit, who has promised to see that Citi "takes the lessons learned from recent events and makes critical enhancements to its risk management framework. A change in culture," Leach adds, "is also required at Citi."

（案例来源：Ricky W. Griffin. *Management* (11th edition). Boston: Cengage Learning, 2012, pp. 238-239）

案例中查尔斯·普林斯（Charles O. Prince）作为首席执行官接掌花旗银行之后，对银行经营业务进行了调整，将银行间交易业务作为花旗银行收入的主要来源，并一头扎进债务抵押证券（CDOs）业务当中，他向分析家们保证说该业务没有任何问题。作为银行智囊及董事会成员的鲁宾（Robert E. Rubin）则鼓励普林斯要更勇于承担风险。银行收入的增长使他们的分红滚滚而来，但却给银行带来了致命的经营风险，最后不得不通过美联储注资及更换管理者解决由次贷引发的危机。实际上，管理者常常也被称为决策者，他们需要做出许多重要的战略性决策，同时，也要为组织的其他方面做出决策，包括组织结构、控制系统、对环境系统的反应等，他们发现问题、制定解决问题的方案，并对结果进行监测。商业领域既有像案例中那样失败的决策，也不乏优秀的决策例子。那么管理者做决策时都要做哪些工作？怎样才能做出正确的决策从而降低企业的经营风险？优秀的管理决策具有哪些特征？本节将围绕决策的相关内容展开讨论。

一、管理决策概念与特点

（一）管理决策概念

管理决策是现代管理活动中十分重要的一项工作。决策是管理的核心，整个管理过程都是围绕着决策的制定和实施而展开的。关于管理决策的定义，目前学术界并没有给出一个统一的概念界定，可以指特定的行为，也可以指一般过程。世界著名经济学家、美国科学家赫伯特·西蒙（Herbert Alexander Simon）认为"管理就是决策"。简单地说，决策（Decision-Making）指的是从可行的备选方案中选择解决方案的过程。决策本身是一种选择的行为，从一组备选方案中选择其一，但决策过程远非如此简单。例如有学者将其定义为"以合适的方式在替代方案中识别并选择行动以满足形势需要的过程"。更为具体的定义是："所谓决策，是组织或个人为了实现某种目标面对未来一定时期内有关活动的方向、内容及方式的选择或调整过程。"

正如本书前三章内容所讲，管理者的一项重要任务就是管理组织环境。外部环境力量会给管理者及其组织带来许多机会或威胁，为了应对这些机会和威胁，管理者必须做出决定，从一组替代方案中选择一个解决方案。因而，从这个意义上说，管理者决策（Managerial Decision-Making）是管理者通过分析备选方案、并选择最终方案，来应对机会和挑战的过程，以实现特定的组织目标，确定具体的行动方向。因此好的决策是那些选择了恰当的目标及行动方向，进而能够提高组织绩效的决策；相反，不理想的决策可能会降低组织绩效。应对机会的决策发生在管理者寻找提高组织绩效的方法以造福顾客、员工及其他利益相关者群体时，而应对威胁的决策发生在组织内外事件不利于组织绩效或不利于管理者寻找提高组织绩效的方法时。但无论何时，决策都是管理者的核心工作，可以说在一切社会组织的管理活动中，决策都处于重要地位。

值得注意的是，"决策者"（Decision-Maker）不等同于管理者。所有的管理者都是决策者，但并不是所有的决策者都是管理者。例如，一个挑选衣服或鞋帽的消费者也需要做出决策，但他不是管理者。而所有的管理者，无论他在组织中的地位如何，都必须为实现组织目标而制定决策。尽管每一种职能要求的决策类型可能不同，但是决策仍然贯穿于管理的所有基本职能当中。因此，一名好的管理者必须能够准确做出各种决策。

✍ **The Concept and Features of Decision-Making**

✧ The concept of decision-making

Decision-making is the process of identifying and choosing among alternative courses of action in a manner appropriate to the demands of the situation.

Managerial decision-making is the process by which managers respond to opportunities and threats by analyzing the options and making determinations, or *decisions*, about specific organizational goals and courses of action.

Global Perspective

Detroit Bankruptcy

"This was bad decisions piled on top of each other," said Gary Brown, the Detroit City Council president pro tem in March 2013, a few months before Detroit became the largest U.S. city ever to file for bankruptcy. True, city managers didn't have much control over the loss of jobs in the auto industry, which had once made Detroit one of the nation's largest and most vibrant cities. However, an in-depth analysis of the mess in Detroit reveals a pattern of bad decisions extending back decades. For example, when Detroit's population and property values declined in the 1960s, city leaders decided to keep adding workers to the payroll. The city didn't make the decision to start seriously downsizing and cutting expenses until the last decade before the bankruptcy. In addition, when temporary prosperity returned after a decline in the 1960s, leaders failed to take advantage of it by investing in new technology that could improve efficiency and productivity. For instance, the team reviewing the city's problems found that in some departments, the records were "basically stuff written on index cards." No one could tell the team how many police officers were patrolling the streets or what the details of the department's budget were. The crisis for Detroit has been years of poor decision making, and there will be no easy fixes. However, leaders and demoralized residents hope that bankruptcy and emergency management will finally lead to the right decisions that can overhaul the out-of-control city systems and services, pay off the overwhelming debts, and give Detroit a fresh start.

（案例来源：Richard L. Daft. *Management* (12th edition). Boston: Cengage Learning, 2014, pp. 283-284）

（二）管理决策的特点

✦ Characteristics of managerial decisions

正如前文所述，管理者一直面临较多的问题及机会，有些情境下需要一个简单快速的决策，而某些情境下的决策则较为复杂，但管理者往往因为一些原因而忽视决策问题。这些原因包括：第一，当管理者开始着手解决问题时，他们不能确定解决该问题需要多少时间、精力，甚至不知道有多少麻烦在等着他们；第二，参与决策可能会带来一些风险，例如，参与一个问题的解决，但如果最后未能圆满解决，可能会影响管理者的优秀工作经历；第三，由于问题过于复杂，很容易被拖延或忙于其他非紧急事务活动中。为了更好地做出决策，解决问题，管理者需要洞察力、勇气及勇于承担决策后果的能力。

图 4-1 说明了管理决策的几个特点，这有助于解释管理者所面临的困难与压力。

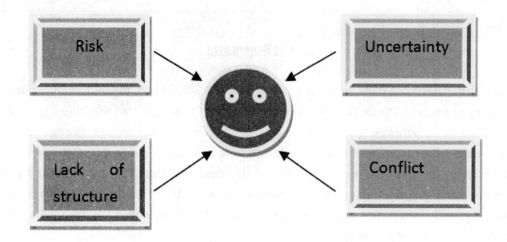

图 4-1　管理决策的特点

Figure 4-1　Characteristics of Managerial Decisions

1. 非结构化（Lack of Structure）

非结构化是管理决策制定过程中的常态。对于大多数决策而言，没有现成的程序可以遵循。很多问题都是新的、非结构化的，对决策者而言，该如何处理及处理后的结果，都具有较强的不确定性。当然，也有一些决策是常规的、程序化的决策。依据决策的结构化程度，我们可以将决策分为程序化决策和非程序化决策。

程序化决策（Programmed Decisions）是先前遇到过并做出的、有客观正确的答案，因而使用简单的规则、政策或计算就可以解决问题的决策。在面对程序性化决策时，管理者很容易遵循明确的程序或结构以做出正确的决策。例如作为一家小企业的老板，每个月要做出给员工发多少工资的决策，他很容易根据企业的绩效考核指标及公式算出员工的工资金额。

Programmed Decisions are decisions encountered and made before, having objectively correct answers, and solvable by using simple rules, policies, or numerical computations.

表 4-1 给出了程序化决策的一些其他例子。

如果公司所有重要的事情都如上面的决策一样被编程了，那么管理者的工作将会变得非常容易。但事实上管理者们经常面临着非程序化决策（Nonprogrammed Decisions），即新的、异常的、复杂的决策，这些决策一般没有明确的答案。它们可能有多种解决方案，每种方案各有优缺点，因为没有一个预先确定的结构可以借鉴，决策者必须仔细思考、比较，并从中选择一个好的决策方法。正如表 4-1 中展示的那样，重要的、困难的决策往往是非程序化的，它们需要创造性的方法加以解决。

Nonprogrammed Decisions are new, novel, complex decisions having no proven answers.

表 4-1　程序化决策与非程序化决策对比

Table 4-1　Comparison between Programmed Decisions and Nonprogrammed Decisions

	Programmed Decisions	Nonprogrammed Decisions
Problem	Frequent, repetitive, routine. Much certainty regarding cause-and-effect relationships.	Novel, unstructured. Much uncertainty regarding cause-and-effect relationships.
Procedure	Dependence on policies, rules, and definite procedures.	Necessity for creativity, intuition, tolerance for ambiguity, creative problem solving.
Examples		
Business firm	Periodic reorders of inventory.	Diversification into new products and markets.
University	Necessary grade-point average for good academic standing.	Construction of new classroom facilities.
Health care	Procedure for admitting patients.	Purchase of experimental equipment.
Government	Merit system for promotion of state employees.	Reorganization of state government agencies.

（资料来源：Thomas S. Bateman and Scott A. Snell. *Management: Leading & Collaborating in a Competitive World* (11th edition). New York: McGraw-Hill Irwin, 2015, p. 81）

2. 不确定性（Uncertainty）

如果拥有做出决策所需要的所有信息，并且能够准确预测该行为的结果，那么就是在确定性的情况下做出的决策。对于管理者来说，当然希望能够在确定性的情况下做出决策，但是完全确定的情况是极少存在的，对于重要的、非程序化决策，不确定性（Uncertainty）是常态。所谓不确定性，是指管理者没有充足的信息来预测不同行动方案的结果。决策者可能自认为他们自己有确定的把握进行决策，但实际上他们仍然是在不确定条件下做出决策的，因为他们缺乏相关信息并且不能准确估计与预测他们行动之后不同结果的可能性。

Uncertainty means the manager has insufficient information to know the consequences of different actions.

3. 风险（Risk）

尽管管理者不能确定未来将会发生什么，但当他们能估计或预测各种行动结果的可能性时，我们称之为风险决策，即行为结果成功出现的可能性小于100%时，损失可能发生，决策失误就会造成金钱、时间、名誉或其他重要资产的损失。如同不确定性一样，风险是管理者决策中必须面对的，但并不意味着每个管理者都愿意承担风险，虽然有时冒险者很受人钦佩，但现实情况是好的决策者更倾向于管理风险，即他们更愿意接受这样一个事实：决策的后果是要承担风险的，但他们会尽其所能以预见风险，减少风险并控制风险。

Risk exists when the probability of an action being successful is less than 100 percent and losses may occur.

The managers accept the fact that decisions have consequences entailing risk, but they do everything they can to anticipate the risk, minimize it, and control it.

4. 冲突（Conflict）

在决策制定过程中，管理者需要面对很多的冲突，因此一些重要的决策很难顺利地做出。当管理者必须考虑来自不同方面的相反压力时，冲突（Conflict）就会表现出来，并表现在两个层次上。

Conflict, which exists when a manager must consider opposing pressures from different sources, occurs at two levels.

113

第一，冲突来自决策者自身。决策者需要在多种可替代方案中进行选择，选择本身就是一个不断放弃的过程，在放弃的过程中，决策者会感受到来自内心的心理冲突。例如，管理者有时会在不想解雇任何人时而被迫解雇某些人，或者在三个申请人同时申请某一个职位时，需要选择其中之一，而拒绝其他两个。

第二，冲突来自人与人之间。在支付一项并购案时，首席财务官倾向于通过增加长期贷款来完成，但首席执行官却可能倾向于最小化长期贷款而从其他来源寻找资金；营销部门想要更丰富的产品线，以销售更多的产品，设计人员想设计出高质量的产品，生产人员则想通过长期生产单一产品以降低成本，当企业的资源有限时，同时实现这三种需求就会有一定难度，也就会产生决策冲突。

二、管理决策理论

决策是人类的高级思维活动，在管理中决策占据着极为重要的地位。决策时，管理者使用的决策理论有三种：古典模型、行政模型和政治模型。决策制定时究竟选择哪个理论主要取决于管理者个人偏好、决策程序化程度以及决策的风险性程度。

（一）古典模型

古典决策理论（Classical Model）又称规范决策理论或"最优"决策理论，它是以"经济人"假设为前提的。古典决策理论认为决策者应该从经济的角度去看待问题，在决策中应该谋求最大利益。古典决策理论认为决策应该是理性的，理性的决策应有以下几个前提（见表4-2）：

● 决策者已经了解问题，并已达成共识的目标，问题已经被准确地阐明和详细地界定清楚；

● 决策者可以收集完整的信息，为创造具有确定性的条件努力，所有方案以及每个方案的所有潜在结果都已经考虑到了；

● 备选方案的评价标准是已知的，决策者选择使组织实现经济回报最大的方案；

● 决策者是理性的，并运用逻辑来赋值，安排优先顺序，评价方案，并做出使组织目标的实现概率最大化的决策。

古典模型理论被认为是主观规范性（Normative）的理论，即它详细说明了决策者"应该"如何做决策。虽然古典模型为组织如何取得理想的结果提供了指南，但是该理论并没有说明管理者实际上是如何做出决策的。

1. Conflict is caused by decision-makers.

2. Conflict occurs among managers.

✍ **The Theories of Decision-Making**

✧ Classical model

The classical model of decision making is based on rational economic assumptions and managers' beliefs about what ideal decision-making should be.

The classical model of decision-making is considered to be normative, which means that it defines how a decision-maker should make decisions.

表 4-2 古典模型的假设条件
Table 4-2 Assumptions Underlying Classical Model

1. The decision-maker operates to accomplish goals that are known and agree on. Problems are precisely formulated and defined.
2. The decision-maker strives for conditions of certainty, gathering complete information. All alternatives and the potential results of each are calculated.
3. Criteria for evaluating alternatives are unknown. The decision-maker selects the alternative that will maximize the economic return to the organization.
4. The decision-maker is rational and uses logic to assign values, order preferences, evaluate alternatives, and make the decision that will maximize the attainment of organizational goals.

古典模型理论的价值在于，它能够帮助决策者更加理性地做出决策。

在许多方面，古典模型理论代表了"理想的"决策模型。当把古典模型理论应用于程序化决策和确定性或风险性决策时，它可以获得最优价值，因为决策者可以收集到相关信息，也可以计算出事件发生的概率。

但是，"完全理性"虽然是比较方便简洁的一种假定，但它并不一定同实际的选择过程一致，在现实组织中的管理者很难做出"理想的"决策。首先，完全理性要求决策者对任何一个选择结果有完全的了解和预见，但在现实经济活动中，它们却总是片面和不完全、无法预知的，决策者自身也存在知识和计算能力等方面的局限性。因此，决策者往往需要在缺乏完全信息的情况下进行决策。其次，"完全理性"要求决策者在所有可能的决策中进行选择，但实际情况往往是，决策者由于不可能具备完全的知识，因而不可能充分了解全部的决策。最后，决策者所面对的环境因素往往是随时变化的，影响决策的各种因素具有很大的不确定性。因此，人们在现实经济活动中做出"完全理性"的决策基本是不可能的。

鉴于古典决策理论所具有的缺陷，在实际的决策中，常常使用一些其他的决策理论，以弥补该理论的不足。

（二）行政模型

决策的行政模型（Administrative Model）描述了管理者在艰难情境下是如何决策的，这些管理决策难以以固定的程序来进行，无法实现任何程度的量化，不能做出在经济上理性的决策。它解释了为什么决策制定本质上是不确定的，以及管理者决策为何通常是令人满意的决策，而不是最优决策。

✧ Administrative model

The administrative model of decision-making explains how managers make decisions; they assume that decision-making is nearly always uncertain and risky, making it difficult for managers to make optimal decisions.

该模型是基于赫伯特·A. 西蒙（Herbert Alexander Simon）和詹姆斯·玛氏（James March）的研究提出的，他们反对古典决策理论的假设，认为管理者在现实工作中无法获得做出决策所需的所有信息，更为重要的是，即使所有决策信息都是可以获取的，一些管理者也因缺少足够的能力，而无法对所有决策信息给出准确的评价。

西蒙认为现实经济生活中的决策者应该是介于完全理性和非理性之间的"有限理性"（Bounded Rationality）"管理人"。有限理性是指人们由于受个人价值观、无意识反射、技能及习惯的限制而保持理性的程度是有局限性的，这种局限性也受到信息及知识不完整的限制。而"管理人"应该是社会的、感情的、道德的综合，"管理人"具有有限的认知能力，但是也具有实际的解决问题的能力。

Bounded rationality suggests that decision-makers are limited by their values and unconscious reflexes, skills, and habits. They are also limited by less-than-complete information and knowledge.

在管理决策中，应该以"管理人"代替传统的"经济人"假设。"管理人"与"经济人"最大的区别在于，"经济人"是完全理性的，在决策中"经济人"追求"最优"的方案；"管理人"可以意识到自己的理性是有限的，认为不可能找到"最优"的方案或寻找"最优"方案需要花费大量的成本，因此在决策过程中只要找到"满意"方案就可以。满意性（Satisficing）的意思是，决策者选择一个足够好的解决方案。管理者不会为了追求使经济效益最大化的最好方案而努力去寻求所有可能的备选方案，他们会选取看上去似乎能够解决问题的足够好的方案，即使在理论上假设还有更好的方案存在。决策者不能证明获取全部信息所需要的时间和费用的合理性。西蒙的"满意决策"原则，让决策理论更接近于现实生活。

Satisficing means the acceptance of solutions that are good enough. Rather than pursuing all alternatives to identify the single solution that will maximize economic returns, managers will opt for the solution that appears to solve the problem, even if better solutions are presumed to exist. The decision-maker cannot justify the time and expense of obtaining complete information.

行政模型的假设与古典模型的假设不同，它强调影响个人决策的组织因素。行政模型应该有如下几个前提（见表 4-3）：

● 决策目标往往是模糊的和互相矛盾的，还缺乏管理者之间的共识，管理者常常没有意识到组织里存在的问题或机会；

● 并非总是运用理性程序，就算启用理性程序，也仅仅局限于对问题的简单认识，不能抓住真实组织事件的复杂性；

● 因为人力、信息和资源的局限，管理者对备选方案的搜寻是有限的；

● 大多数管理者满足于满意的而非最优的解决方案，其中一部分原因是由于管理者掌握的信息有限，另一部分原因是对于最优方案的构成要素，他们仅有的评价标准也是模糊的。

表 4-3　行政模型的假设条件
Table 4-3　Assumptions Underlying Administrative Model

1.	Decision goals often are vague, conflicting, and lack consensus among managers. Managers are often unaware of problems or opportunities that exist in the organization.
2.	Rational procedures are not always used, and, when they are, they are confined to a simplistic view of the problem that does not capture the complexity of real organizational events.
3.	Managers' searches for alternatives are limited because of human, information, and resource constraints.
4.	Most managers select for a satisficing rather than a maximizing solution, partly because they have limited information and partly because they have only vague criteria for what constitutes a maximizing solutions.

行政模型中的另一个重要要素是直觉（Intuition），它反映了根据过去的经验但不经过有意识的思考而迅速做出决策。直觉决策并不是随意性的或者非理性的，它是基于多年的实践和代代相传的经验做出的，这些实践经验使得管理者能够迅速确定解决方案，而不需要经过艰辛的计算过程。在今天快节奏、动荡不安的商务环境里，直觉在决策中起着越来越大的作用。有研究发现，将近半数的商务人士在工作时的决策常常是依据直觉做出的。

Another aspect of administrative decision-making is intuition. Intuition represents a quick apprehension of a decision situation based on past experience without conscious thought.

钱学森先生指出，任何有人介入的系统都是复杂系统。管理决策涉及人的因素，因此具有明显的复杂性特征。同时，决策主体所处的生存与发展环境正变得日益复杂，并充满高度的动态不确定性，这也使管理决策者不得不更加关注决策问题内在的非线性以及环境开放性等复杂系统的本质特征。鉴于管理决策的复杂性以及建立在人类"完全理性"假设基础上的传统规范性决策理论（如期望效用理论）无法合理解释"阿莱悖论"（Allais Paradox）、"埃尔斯伯格悖论"（Ellsberg Paradox）等决策现象，决策科学家越来越接受西蒙关于决策的"满意准则"和人类"有限理性"原则以及建构在该原则基础上由丹尼尔·卡尼曼（Daniel Kahneman）提出的更关注人类实际如何做出决策的前景理论。

前景理论（Prospect Theory）表明，决策者们发现，实际发生的损失要比放弃可能得到的收益会给他们带来更大的痛苦。其基本思想是对最大期望效用理论内部的各个因子进行改造，可以更加真实地描述决策行为。它假设风险决策过程包括编辑和评价两个阶段，在决策的编辑阶段，决策者通过"框架""参照点"等对信息进行加工处理；在决策的评价阶段，决策者依赖价值函数和主观概率的权重函数，以最大期望效用值为依据做出决策。但价值函数是经验型的，它有三个特征：一是大多数人在面临获得时是风险规避的；二是大多数人在面临损失时是风险偏

Prospect theory suggests that decision-makers find the notion of an actual loss more painful than giving up the possibility of a gain.

This theory is descriptive. It tries to model real-life choices, rather than optimal decisions.

爱的；三是人们对损失比对获得更敏感，因此，人们在面临获得时往往是小心翼翼，不愿冒风险，而在面对失去时会很不甘心，容易冒险。人们对损失和获得的敏感程度是不同的，损失时的痛苦感要大大超过获得时的快乐感。

Global Perspective

Hard Facts and Half Truths

Stanford University professors Jeffrey Pfeffer and Bob Sutton, the authors of *Hard Facts*, *Dangerous Half-Truths*, and *Total Nonsense*, have put out a call for a renewed reliance on rationality in managerial decision-making—an approach that they call evidence based management (EBM). "Management decisions," they argue, "should be based on the best evidence, managers should systematically learn from experience, and organizational practices should reflect sound principles of thought and analysis." They define evidence based management as "a commitment to finding and using the best theory and data available at the time to make decisions," but their "Five Principles of Evidence Based Management" make it clear that EBM means more than just sifting through data and crunching numbers. Here's what they recommend:

1. Face the hard facts and build a culture in which people are encouraged to tell the truth, even if it's unpleasant.

2. Be committed to "fact based" decision-making—which means being committed to getting the best evidence and using it to guide actions.

3. Treat your organization as an unfinished prototype—encourage experimentation and learning by doing.

4. Look for the risks and drawbacks in what people recommend (even the best medicine has side effects).

5. Avoid basing decisions on untested but strongly held beliefs, what you have done in the past, or on uncritical "benchmarking" of what winners do.

Pfeffer and Sutton's research shows that pay for performance policies get good results when employees work solo or independently. But it's another matter altogether when it comes to collaborative teams—the kind of teams that make so many organizational decisions today. Under these circumstances, the greater the gap between highest and lowest paid executives, the weaker the firm's financial performance. Why? According to Pfeffer and Sutton, wide disparities in pay often weaken both trust among team members and the social connectivity that contributes to strong team based decision-making. Or consider another increasingly prevalent policy for evaluating and rewarding talent. Pioneered at General Electric by the legendary Jack Welch, the practice of "forced ranking" divides employees into three groups based on performance—the top 20 percent, middle 70 percent, and bottom 10 percent and terminates those at the bottom. Pfeffer and Sutton found that, according to many HR managers, forced ranking impaired morale and collaboration and ultimately reduced productivity.

They also concluded that automatically firing the bottom 10 percent resulted too often in the unnecessary disruption of otherwise effective teamwork. That's how they found out that 73 percent of the errors committed by commercial airline pilots occur on the first day that reconfigured crews work together.

（案例来源: Ricky W. Griffin. *Management* (11th edition). Boston: Cengage Learning, 2012, p. 248）

（三）政治模型

决策的政治模型（Political Model）理论用于当条件不确定、信息有限、管理者对追求什么目标或采取什么行动计划有异议时制定的非程序化决策。大多数组织决策都涉及众多追求不同目标的管理者，他们不得不相互交谈以分享信息和达成协议。结盟（Coalition）是支持某一特定目标的管理者之间非正式的一种联盟，即共同支持某一特定方案。例如，通过收购另一家公司促进公司发展的管理者，与其他高级主管进行非正式的交谈，努力劝说他们支持该决策。当结果不可预见时，管理者就通过讨论、谈判和讨价还价来赢得支持。没有结盟，强权的个人或团体就会使决策过程脱离正轨。结成联盟就意味着给予其他几位管理者以机会，可以为决策出力，增强对最终选定方案的责任感。

政治模型与大多数管理者和决策者所在的现实经营环境非常类似。决策模型有 **4** 个假设：

● 组织是由具有不同利益、目标和价值观的群体组成的，管理者对问题的轻重缓急看法不一，因而可能不会理解其他管理者的目标与利益；

● 信息是含糊的、不完整的。保持理性的努力是有限度的，其原因在于众多问题的复杂性和个人及组织自身的局限性；

● 管理者没有时间、资源或者智力去识别问题的各个维度并处理所有的相关信息，为了收集信息和减少含混性，管理者需要进行沟通，交换意见；

● 为了决定目标和探讨方案，管理者要求进行辩论，决策是联盟成员之间讨价还价和辩论的结果。

古典模型、行政模型和政治模型的特点如表 4-4 所示。近几年来有关决策程序方面的研究发现，在稳定的环境里，理性的、古典的决策程序与组织的高绩效水平联系在一起；但在不确定的环境里，必须快速做出决策，而且决策需要在艰难的条件下做出，因而与高绩效水平相关联的是行政决策程序和政治决策程序。

✧ **Political model**

The political model of decision-making is useful for making nonprogrammed decisions when conditions are uncertain, information is limited, and there are manager conflicts about what goals to pursue or what course of action to take.

A coalition is an informal alliance among managers who support a specific goal.

The assumptions underlying political model.

1. Organizations are made up of groups with diverse interests, goals, and values. Managers disagree about problem priorities and may not understand or share the goals and interests of other managers.

2. Information is ambiguous and incomplete. The attempt to be rational is limited by the complexity of many problems, as well as personal and organizational constraints.

3. Managers do not have the time, resources, or mental capacity to identify all dimension of the problem and process all relevant information. Managers talk to each other and exchange viewpoints to gather information and reduce ambiguity.

4. Managers engage in the push and pull of debate to decide goals and discuss alternatives. Decisions are the result of bargaining and discussion among coalition members.

表 4-4　古典决策模型、行政决策模型和政治决策模型的特点
Table 4-4　Characteristics of Classical, Administrative, and Political Decision-Making Models

Classical Model	Administrative Model	Political Model
Clear-cut problem and goals	Vague problem and goals	Pluralistic; conflicting goals
Condition of certainty	Condition of uncertainty	Condition of uncertainty or ambiguity
Full information about alternatives and their outcomes	Limited information about alternatives and their outcomes	Inconsistent viewpoints; ambiguous information
Rational choice by individual for maximizing outcomes	Satisficing choice for resolving problem using intuition	Bargaining and discussion among coalition members

（资料来源：Richard L. Daft. *Management* (12th edition). Boston: Cengage Learning, 2014, p. 295）

三、管理决策的步骤

✍ **Decision-making Process**

无论是程序化决策还是非程序化决策，也不论管理者选择哪种决策理论，决策绝不是在不同方案中进行选择那么简单，因为决策是一个过程，从识别问题开始，到选择能解决问题的方案，最后要对决策效果进行评价。一般来说，这样的一个过程往往要包括 6 个步骤，图 4.2 详细列出了这一过程。

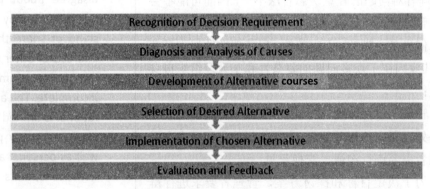

图 4-2　管理决策过程的 6 个步骤
Figure4-2　Six Steps in the Managerial Decision-Making Process

（一）识别决策需求

管理者面临的需求有两种表现方式：问题或机遇。每一项决策都始于一个问题（Problem），即现有状况（事情现存方式）和预期状况（事情应该如何）之间的不一致。这种不一致具体体现为：在与过去绩效相比，或与其他组织或部门现在绩效相比，或与未来计划或预测的绩效相比时，发现现有状况是不令人满意的。

◇ **Recognition of Decision Requirement**

The decision-making process begins with the existence of a problem or, more specifically, a discrepancy between an existing and a desired state of affairs. Such discrepancies—say, in organizational or unit performance—may be detected by comparing current performance against past performance, the current performance of other organizations or units, or future expected performance as determined by plans and forecasts.

例如，作为某家食品公司的部门经理，前几年已累计花了近 5 万元用于所乘汽车的维修。现在汽车的发动机又坏了，4S 店的工作人员经过估算，修车是相当不划算的。于是现在就出现了一个问题：经理出去谈业务需要一辆能正常行驶的车，但是目前这辆车却不能满足需求，在需求和现实之间出现了不一致。如何解决这个问题，就需要经理做出决策。此例中的决策比较简单，但在现实世界中，大多数问题并不像本例那样有明显的解决方案。而且，问题的识别是主观的，那些无法正确识别问题且未采取任何措施的管理者，与那些错误地解决某一问题的管理者同样糟糕。

同样，当管理者看到了超过当前预期目标的潜在成就时，就存在机遇（Opportunity）。此时，管理者意识到了在目前基础上进一步提高绩效水平的可能性。例如，各餐馆之间的竞争非常激烈，许多经营者重点关注光顾饭店客人的满意度。但是，有些经营者发现，有外卖需求的顾客越来越多，是否具有外卖业务以及外卖的送餐速度和服务态度，已经成为许多顾客评价餐馆的一个重要指标。如果能够成功开展外卖业务，可能会为餐馆带来更高的利润和顾客满意度。那么这个时候，机遇就产生了。

An opportunity exists when managers see potential accomplishment that exceeds specified current goals. Managers see the possibility of enhancing performance beyond current levels.

感知到问题或机遇的存在是决策过程的第一步，这就要求管理者能监视组织内外部环境，以发现值得高级管理者关注的问题或机遇，这类似于军事上的"收集情报"，以此来判断组织是否在令人满意地朝着它既定目标前进。例如，谷歌公司的办公室里一直向员工供应免费的零食和水果，其中包括巧克力豆等糖果。但是，一些管理者发现，公司内部员工喜欢吃非常多的糖果作为工作之余的零食，他们觉得这与公司"保持员工幸福与健康"的目标是相悖的，于是公司决定分析这一问题，找寻一种方法，既可以使员工吃到免费的糖果，又可以让员工们意识到健康的重要性，食用其他的零食或饮品。

Recognizing that a problem or opportunity exists is only the beginning of this stage. The decision-maker also must want to do something about it and must believe that the resources and abilities necessary for solving the problem exist. Then the decision-maker must dig in deeper and attempt to diagnose the situation.

（二）原因诊断与分析

一旦某个问题或机遇引起了管理者的注意，管理者们就应该对现状展开深入的分析和理解。识别问题或机遇的存在仅仅是管理决策步骤的开始，决策者必须做一些努力，并确信有足够的资源和能力解决该问题，因而决策者就需要更加深入地挖掘问题或机遇存在的原因，诊断具体情况。

◇ Diagnosis and analysis of causes

诊断（Diagnosis）是决策过程的一个步骤，它是指管理者分析潜在的、与决策形势有因果关系的要素。如果管理者不首先比较深入地探讨问题的原因而直接去制订解决问题的方案，就很容易犯错误。

Diagnosis is the step in the decision-making process in which managers analyze underlying causal factors associated with the decision situation.

例如，一个销售经理发现销售额大幅度下降，如果他认为销量下降是由于经济形势不佳（因而他无能为力），那他就不会采取行动。但如果他尝试去解决这个问题，就不会仅仅是训斥他的销售人员或增加广告预算，而是必须分析销售额为什么下降，通过适当的分析，然后制订一个解决方案。

这一阶段管理者可能需要思考如下问题：

- 影响我们的不稳定因素是什么？
- 它是何时出现的？
- 它出现在哪里？
- 它是怎么出现的？
- 它针对的对象是谁？
- 该问题的紧迫性如何？
- 事件之间的相互关系是什么？
- 何种行为产生了何种结果？

这些问题能帮助我们弄清楚究竟发生了什么，以及为什么会发生这些事情。

（三）拟订备选方案

一旦问题或者机遇的识别和分析工作已经完成，决策者就开始考虑采取行动以应对机会或威胁。管理专家认为，管理者之所以做出不好的决策，其中一个原因就是他们不能拟订和考虑不同的备选方案。一项研究也发现，限制对备选方案的搜索是组织决策失败的首要原因。

但是管理者可能发现很难想出创造性的备选方案来解决某一具体问题，或许每个管理者都从自身的角度看世界，从而有一定的"管理思想集"，他们都囿于自己的心智模式，所以发现从一个全新的角度看问题很难，提出创造性的备选方案解决问题或利用机会可能需要我们放弃现有的思想而发展新的思想，这往往很难做到。

对于程序化决策，备选方案很容易识别，而且事实上这些方案常常是根据组织的规则和程序制定的，决策起来比较简单。但是，非程序化决策往往要求制定能够满足公司需要的新行动方案，管理者可能要开发一两种新的方案，然后选择最满意的方案。这往往是比较难的。虽然管理者应该寻求创造性解决方案，但也必须认识到，现实中的各种约束往往会限制他们的选择，这些制约因素包括：法律约束、道德与伦理规范、权利制约、管理者权力及权威的制约、可用技术、经济因素及非官方的社会规范等。

Managers should ask a series of questions:
- What is the state of disequilibrium affecting us?
- When did it occur?
- Where did it occur?
- How did it occur?
- To whom did it occur?
- What is the urgency of the problem?
- What is the interconnectedness of events?
- What result came from each activity?

❖ Development of alternative courses

Having recognized the need to make a decision, a manager must generate a set of feasible alternative courses of action to take in response to the opportunity or threat. Management experts cite failure to properly generate and consider different alternatives as one reason why managers sometimes make bad decisions.

Common constraints include legal restrictions, moral and ethical norms, authority constraints, and constraints imposed by the power and authority of the manager, available technology, economic considerations, and unofficial social norms.

（四）选择理想方案

当管理者制订了可行的备选方案之后，就必须从其中选择某个方案。选择方案时首先要对这些方案进行评价（见图4-3），分析每个方案的利弊得失。

⟡　Selection of desired alternative

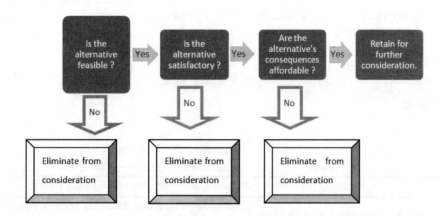

图 4-3　管理决策步骤中评价备选方案
Figure 4-3　Evaluating Alternatives in the Decision-Making Process

图 4-3 表明，由于前文提到的一些现实约束，管理者需要对每一个备选方案的可行性、令人满意性及其后果进行评估。首先要问的问题是该备选方案是否可行，其实现概率是否较高？例如，对于一个小型的、在生存线上挣扎的公司，实行一个需要庞大财政支出的备选方案几乎是不可能的。再如，一些方案虽然很好，但是可能因为法律上的障碍也不可行。在现实工作中，有限的人力、物力和信息资源，可能会使一些备选方案变得不切实际。

在可行性评估通过之后，还要进行下一步的评价，看它在多大程度上能满足决策的目的。例如，当某经理在寻找使产能翻倍的方案时，可能一开始就考虑从现有的一家公司并购一个工厂。但详细分析之后发现，并购的新工厂只能增加生产能力 35%，那么，这种备选方案就不能令人满意。

最后，即使备选方案证明是可行的和令人满意的，仍然需要对其可能的后果进行评估。一个备选方案对组织的其他部门会产生怎样的影响？这些具体影响会带来哪些财务性与非财务性成本？例如，通过削减价格来刺激销售的计划可能会破坏现金流，或者需要一个新的广告计划以及一个新的佣金结构来提升销售额，如果其结果对于整个系统而言过于昂贵，那么也必须舍弃。

在评估之后，可能最后仍有两个或更多的备选方案被保留。于是，在这些备选方案中选择最优决策就成为了真正的症结所在。一般而言，最佳的方案应该能够更好地适合组织的总体目标和价值观，并运用最少的资源获取预期的成果。

The best alternative solution is the one that best fits the overall goals and values of the organization and achieves the desired results using the fewest resources.

123

备选方案的选择取决于管理者的个性因素和接受风险性与不确定性的意愿。风险倾向（Risk Propensity）是指在有机会获得更大回报的情况下甘愿冒险的意愿。管理者愿意承受的风险水平影响到决策评价。以表 4-5 列举的各种情形为例，在每种情况下，你愿意选择哪个方案？低风险倾向的人愿意接受有把握的中等回报，他们选择努力打成平局、在国内修建工厂、选择当医生这样的职业。但风险偏好者却愿意努力赢得胜利、去外国兴建工厂或者从事表演性职业。

Risk propensity is the willingness to undertake risk with the opportunity of gaining an increased pay-off.

表 4-5　不同风险水平的决策方案
Table 4-5　Decision Alternatives with Different Levels of Risk

In each of the following situations, which alternative would you choose?	
You're the coach of a college football team, and in the final seconds of a game with the team's archrival, you face a choice:	1. Choose a play that has a 95 percent chance of producing a tie score; OR 2. Go for a play that has a 30 percent chance of victory but will lead to certain defeat if it fails.
As president of a Canadian manufacturing company, you face a decision about building a new factory. You can:	1. Build a plant in Canada that has a 90 percent chance of producing a modest return on investment; OR 2. Build a plant in a foreign country that has an unstable political history. This alternative has a 40 percent chance of failing, but there turns will be enormous if it succeeds.
It's your senior year, and it is time to decide your next move. Here are the alternatives you're considering:	1. Go to medical school and become a physician, a career in which you are 80 percent likely to succeed; OR 2. Follow your dreams and be an actor, even though the opportunity for success is only around 20 percent.

（资料来源：Richard L. Daft. *Management* (12th edition). Boston: Cengage Learning, 2014, p. 298）

（五）实施选择方案

实施（Implementation）阶段包括运用管理能力、行政能力和劝说他人能力确保选定方案的落实。

确定一个备选方案之后，管理者需要将其付诸实施。有些决策执行比较容易，但有些执行起来可能会比较困难。例如在并购决策中，管理者必须决定如何整合包括采购、人力资源、分销等所有新业务进入现有组织框架内。选定方案的最终成功取决于它是否能够转化为行动。有时，选定方案一直没能变成现实，因为管理者缺乏实施方案所需要的资源或能力。方案的实施可能要求与受决策影响的人员商讨，必须运用沟通技能、激励技能和领导技能以确保决策的贯彻落实。当员工们看到管理者通过追踪了解实施情况来不断扩大决策战果时，他们更容易产生积极的行动。如果管理者缺乏实施决策的能力或愿望，选定的方案就不能得到落实，组织也不会受益。

✧　Implementation of chosen alternative

The implementation stage involves the use of managerial, administrative, and persuasive abilities to ensure that the chosen alternative is carried out.

The ultimate success of the chosen alternative depends on whether it can be translated into action.

When employees see that managers follow up on their decisions by tracking implementation success, they are more committed to positive action.

（六）评价与反馈

决策过程的最后一步要求管理者评价其决策的有效性，即决策者需要收集信息，了解决策的实施情况和决策对于实现目标的有效性，他们应该确保所选方案已经达到了最初的目的。如果执行的方案未达到目标，管理者可以有以下选择：可以选择先前确定的可以替代的备选方案（例如可以是次优或第三选择），或管理者认识到在决策开始阶段未能正确界定问题因而可以重新开始，或管理者可以确认原来的执行方案实际是合适的，只是尚需时日才会发挥作用，或需要改变不同的方式来实施。

反馈（Feedback）非常重要，因为决策是个连续的、永无止境的过程。当管理者或董事会投票做出最终决策时，决策过程并没有完全结束。决策执行之后的反馈仍然是决策的一个重要环节。反馈向决策者提供了信息，他们可以借此开始新一轮的决策，或者对现有决策进行必要的调整。决策可能失败，也可能效果不太理想，因此又需要重新分析问题、评价方案并选定新方案。许多重大问题的解决都是连续尝试几个解决方案的结果，反馈就是监督决策结果，并为管理者提供必要信息的环节。管理者可以依据决策反馈，决定是否需要做出新的决策，或对现有决策进行修订。

◇ Evaluation and feedback

In the evaluation stage of the decision process, decision-makers gather information that tells them how well the decision was implemented and whether it was effective in achieving its goals.

Feedback is important because decision-making is an ongoing process. Decision-making is not completed when a manager or board of directors votes yes or no.

Global Perspective

Replacing Google with Apple Maps

The first versions of the Apple iPhone included Google Maps as a default app—a logical choice, given that people often use their mobile devices to get directions and Google Maps was the most popular mapping software. However, Google became more of a competitor after it financially backed and later purchased the Android operating system for smart phones.

That created a tough decision for Apple when it prepared to launch iOS 6, its operating system for mobile phones. Apple terminated its agreement with Google and replaced Google Maps with its own Apple Maps. Unfortunately, Apple Maps was far from ready for the big time. Information was missing and incorrect. For example, Apple Maps users posted photos of places such as the Washington Monument tagged blocks from the satellite image of it and creepy 3D images of roads surging into the air or bridges dipping into the river. The Australian government even warned people not to use Apple Maps after police were called to rescue people misdirected into arid wilderness. Consumers also complained about the lack of directions for public transit systems.

Why did Apple release its mapping application? Managers evidently concluded that competing with Google outweighed the technical problems. Some believe that Google was unwilling to share data needed for the app to offer turn-by-turn directions, a feature Apple considered essential. Yet state-of-the-art mapping software requires so much data, so many functions, and so many licensing agreements on a global scale that creating a fully functional product would have taken years longer. In the end, Apple added Google Maps to its App Store.

（案例来源: Thomas S. Bateman and Scott A. Snell. *Management: Leading & Collaborating in a Competitive World* (11th edition). New York: McGraw-Hill Irwin, 2015, p. 87）

第二节 决策类型及方法

How Do You Make Decisions?

Instructions: Most of us make decisions automatically, without realizing that people have diverse decision-making behaviors, which they bring to management positions. Think back to how you make decisions in your personal, student, or work life, especially where other people are involved. Please answer whether each of the following items is Mostly True or Mostly False for you.

	Mostly True	Mostly False
1. I like to decide quickly and move on to the next thing.		
2. I would use my authority to make a decision if I'm certain I am right.		
3. I appreciate decisiveness.		
4. There is usually one correct solution to a problem.		
5. I identify everyone who needs to be involved in the decision.		
6. I explicitly seek conflicting perspectives.		
7. I use discussion strategies to reach a solution.		
8. I look for different meanings when faced with a great deal of data.		
9. I take time to reason things through and use systematic logic.		

Scoring and Interpretation: All nine items in the list reflect appropriate decision-making behavior, but items 1–4 are more typical of new managers. Items 5–8 are typical of successful senior-manager decision-making. Item 9 is considered part of good decision-making at all levels. If you checked Mostly True for three or four of items 1–4 and 9, consider yourself typical of a new manager. If you checked Mostly True for three or four of items 5–8 and 9, you are using behavior consistent with top managers. If you checked a similar number of both sets of items, your behavior is probably flexible and balanced. New managers typically use a different decision behavior than seasoned executives. The decision behavior of a successful CEO may be almost the opposite of a first-level supervisor. The difference is due partly to the types of decisions and partly to learning what works at each level. New managers often start out with a more directive, decisive, command-oriented behavior to establish their standing and decisiveness and gradually move toward more openness, diversity of viewpoints, and interactions with others as they move up the hierarchy.

（案例来源：Richard L. Daft. *Management* (12th edition). Boston: Cengage Learning, 2014, p. 283）

作为管理者，由于面临的决策情境不同，针对的业务不同，在做出决策时使用的方法存在很大的差异。由于企业活动非常复杂，因而管理者的决策也是多种多样的。在实际决策时，管理者应该了解各种决策类型的特点，以便更好地做出决策。本节将详细介绍管理者遇到的决策类型以及使用的决策方法。

一、决策的基本类型

（一）程序化决策和非程序化决策

决策，从不同的角度来看，有不同的分类。按照问题类型、组织层次可以将决策分为程序化决策和非程序化决策（见表4-1）。图4-4和表4-6描述了问题类型、组织层次与决策之间的关系与区别。结构性问题与程序化决策相对应，非结构性问题需要非程序化决策。中低层管理者主要处理熟悉的、重复的发生的问题，因此，他们主要依靠像标准操作程序那样的程序化决策。组织层级中管理者层次越高，他们面临的问题越有可能是非结构性问题，越需要进行非程序化决策。因此，高层管理者将例行性决策权授予下级，以便将自己的时间用于解决更为棘手的问题。

✍ **The Types of Decisions**

✧ Programmed and non-programmed decisions

Lower-level managers essentially confront familiar and repetitive problems so they most typically rely on programmed decisions such as standard operating procedures. However, as managers move up in the organizational hierarchy, the problems they confront are likely to become less structured, and they most typically rely on non-programmed decisionns.

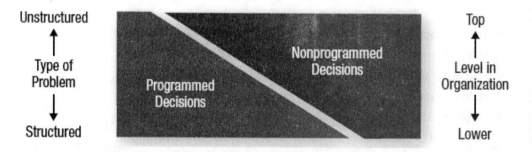

图4-4　问题类型、决策类型和组织层次

Figure 4-4　Types of Problems, Types of Decisions, and Organizational Level

（资料来源：Stephen P. Robbins, David A. DeCenzo and Mary Coulter. *Fundamentals of Management: Essential Concepts and Applications* (9th edition). New York: Pearson, 2013, p. 94）

表4-6　程序化决策与非程序化决策的区别

Table 4-6　Programmed versus non-programmed decisions

Characteristics	Programmed Decisions	Non-programmed Decisions
Type of problem	Structure	Unstructured
Managerial level	Lower levels	Upper levels
Frequency	Repetitive, routine	New, unusual
Information	Readily available	Ambiguous or incomplete
Goals	Clear, specific	Vague
Time frame for solution	Short	Relatively long
Solution relies on …	Procedures, rules, policies	Judgment and creativity

（资料来源: Stephen P. Robbins and Mary Coulter. *Management* (11th edition). New Jersey: Prentice Hall, 2012, p. 187）

在现实世界中，只有极少数的管理决策是完全程序化的或是完全非程序化的，大多数决策介于两者之间。一方面，极少有程序化决策完全排除个人判断；另一方面，在处理大多数非常规事件时，程序化决策也有助于非程序化决策过程的推进。

Programmed Decision-Making at UPS

UPS is unrivaled in its use of programmed decision-making. Practically all the motions, behaviors, and actions that its drivers perform each day have been carefully honed to maximize efficiency and minimize strain and injuries while delivering high-quality customer service. For example, a 12-step process prescribes how drivers should park their trucks, locate the package they are about to deliver, and step off the truck in 15.5 seconds (a process called "selection" at UPS). Rules and routines such as these are carefully detailed in UPS's "340 Methods" manual (UPS actually has far more than 340 methods). Programmed decision-making dictates where drivers should stop to get gas, how they should hold their keys in their hands, and how to lift and lower packages.

When programmed decision-making is so heavily relied on, ensuring that new employees learn tried-and-true routines is essential. UPS has traditionally taught new employees with a two-week period of lectures followed by practice. In the 2000s, however, managers began to wonder if they needed to alter their training methods to suit their new Generation Y trainees (Generation Y typically refers to people born after 1980), who were not so keen on memorization and drills. Generation Y trainee esteemed to require more training time to become effective drivers (90–180 days compared to a typical average of 30–45 days), and quit rates for new drivers had increased.

Given the fundamental importance of performance programs for UPS operations, managers decided to try to alter the training new hires receive so it would be better received by Generation Y trainees. In the late 2000s, UPS opened an innovative Landover, Maryland, training center called UPS Integrad, which has over 11,000 square feet and cost over $30 million to build and equip. Integrad was developed over a three-year period through a collaborative effort of over 170 people, including UPS top managers (many of whom started their careers with UPS as drivers), teams from Virginia Tech and MIT, animators from the Indian company Brainvisa, and forecasters from the Institute for the Future with the support of a grant from the Department of Labor for $1.8 million. Results thus far suggest that Integrad training results in greater driver proficiency and fewer first-year accidents and injuries.

Training at Integrad emphasizes hands-on learning. For example, at Integrad a UPS truck with transparent sides is used to teach trainees selection so they can actually see the instructor performing the steps and then practice the steps themselves rather than trying to absorb the material in a lecture. Trainees can try different movements and see, with the help of computer diagrams and simulations, how following UPS routines will help protect them from injury and how debilitating work as a driver can be if they do not follow routines. Video recorders track and document what trainees do correctly and incorrectly so they can see it for themselves rather than relying on feedback from an instructor, which they might question. As Stephen Jones, Director of International Training & Development at UPS, indicates, "Tell them what they did incorrectly, and they'll tell you, 'I didn't do that. You saw wrong.' This way we've got it on tape and they can see it for themselves."

At Integrad, trainees get practice driving in a pseudo town that has been constructed in a parking lot. They also watch animated demonstrations on computer screens, participate in simulations, take electronic quizzes, and receive scores on various components that are retained in a database to track learning and performance. Recognizing that Generation Y trainees have a lot of respect for expertise and reputation, older employees also are brought in to facilitate learning at Integrad. For example, long-time UPS employee Don Petersik, who has since retired from UPS, trained facilitators at Integrad and shared stories with them to reinforce the UPS culture—such as the time he was just starting out as a preloader and, unknown to him, the founder of UPS, Jim Casey, approached him and said, "Hi, I'm Jim. I work for UPS." As Petersik indicated, "What's new about the company now is that our teaching style matches your learning styles." Clearly, when learning programmed decision-making is of utmost importance, as it is at UPS, it is essential to take into account diversity in learning styles and approaches.

（案例来源: Gareth R. Jones and Jennifer M. George. *Contemporary Management* (9th edition). New York: McGraw-Hill Education, 2014, pp. 188-189）

（二）战略决策、战术决策和业务决策

按照决策涉及业务的具体程度，可以将其分为战略决策、战术决策和业务决策。

战略决策是指直接关系到组织的生存发展的全局性、长期性、战略性问题的决策，如企业方针、目标与计划的制订、产品转向、技术改造和引进、组织结构的变革等。战略决策的特点是：影响的时间长、范围广，决策的重点在于解决组织与外部环境问题，注重组织整体绩效的提高。战略决策属于组织的高层决策，是组织高层领导者的一项主要职责。战略决策大多是定性决策。

战术决策又称策略决策，是指组织在执行战略决策过程中，在合理选择和使用人力、物力和财力等方面的决策。如企业的销售、生产等专业计划的制订，产品开发方案的制订，员工招聘与工资水平，资源和能源的合理使用等方面的决策。战术决策是为了保证战略决策的实现所做的决策，它具有局部性、中期性、具体性等特点。这类决策大多由中层管理人员来进行，决策的重点是对组织内部资源进行有效的组织和利用，以提高管理效能。战术决策所要解决的问题大多可以定量化。

业务决策是指在日常业务活动中为了提高效率所做的决策。如基层组织中任务的日常分配、劳动力调配、个别工作程序和方法的变动等。业务决策具有日常性、短期性、琐碎性等特点，属单纯执行性决策。这类决策所要解决的问题常常是具体而明确的，一般由基层管理者进行。

（三）确定型决策、风险型决策与不确定型决策

正如第一节所言，管理者面对的决策情境包括确定性、风险性与不确定性，由此根据决策情境可以将决策分为确定型决策、风险型决策和不确定型决策。

确定型决策是指各种可行方案的条件都是已知的，结果只有一个，是易于分析、比较和抉择的决策。

风险型决策是指各种可行方案的条件大部分是已知的，结果有多个，且每个结果发生的可能性即概率为已知的一种决策。这类决策的结果通常要按概率法则加以确定，因此存在着一定的风险。

非确定型决策是指各种可行方案的条件大多未知，结果有多个，且每个结果发生的可能性即概率为未知的一种决策。因为已知的条件太少，且无概率可言，因此这类决策的决策结果更多取决于决策者个人的经验、直觉和性格等。

◇ Strategic decisions, tactical decisions and operational decisions

Strategic decisions are decisions that apply to the entire organization, establish the organization's overall goals and seek to position the organization in terms of its environment.
Most strategic decisions are qualitative decision.

Tactical decisions are decisions to help execute the major strategic plans and to accomplish a specific part of the strategy.

Operational decisions are decisions that are developed at the lower levels of the organization and specify the details of how the tactical plans are to be achieved.

◇ Decisions under certainty, decisions under risk and decisions under uncertainty

Decisions under certainty mean the situation is certainty and people are reasonably sure about what will happen when they make a decision.
Decisions under risk mean the decision-maker is able to estimate the likelihood of certain outcomes.

Decisions under uncertainty mean decision-maker has neither certainty nor reasonable probability estimates available.

组织的业务决策常属于确定型决策,而战略性决策一般属于风险型决策或非确定型决策,战术性决策则三者兼而有之。

(四)个人决策和集体决策

按照决策主体的数量,可以将决策分为个人决策和集体决策。

个人决策是指在决策过程中,最终方案的选择仅仅由一个人决定,即决策的主体是一个人。在个人决策中,常常要运用直觉决策,管理者运用专业知识和过去已习得的与情境相关的经验,在信息非常有限的条件下迅速做出决策。

管理者在何种情况下最有可能使用个人决策的方法?研究者确定了七种情况:(1)时间有限,但又有压力要做出正确决策时;(2)不确定性水平很高时;(3)几乎没有先例可参考时;(4)难以科学地预测变量时;(5)事实有限,不足以明确指明前进道路时;(6)分析性资料用途不大时;(7)当需要从几个可行方案中选择一个,而每一个方案的评价都较好时。

集体决策是指决策过程由两个人以上的群体完成,即决策的主体是两个人以上的群体。群体通常能比个人做出质量更高的决策,因为它具有更完整的信息和更多的备选方案;同时,以群体方式做出决策,易于增加有关人员对决策方案的接受性。因此,大多数重要的组织决策都是由团队成员或管理者团队共同做出的。

集体决策的效果受群体大小、成员从众现象等因素的影响。群体越大,异质性的可能性就越大,需要更多的协调和更多的时间促使所有的成员取得一致或达成妥协。因此,群体不宜过大,小到 5 人,大到 15 人即可。有证据表明,5～7 个人的群体在一定程度上是最有效的决策群体规模。

与个人决策相比,群体决策的效率相对较低。在决定是否采用群体决策时,主要的考虑是效果的提高是否足以抵消效率的损失。群体决策的优缺点可以参看表 4-7。

(五)其他分类

决策还可以根据时间的长短分为长期决策、中期决策和短期决策;根据决策性质的不同,决策可以分为定性决策和定量决策;根据决策层次的不同,决策可以分为高层决策、中层决策和基层决策;根据决策目标的多少,决策可以分为单目标决策和多目标决策。

✧ Individual decisions-making and group decision-making

Individual decision-making means final decision depends on an individual opinion, not a group's opinion.

Group decision-making means the processes of decision-making go on within a work group.

✧ Other decisions

Many (or perhaps most) important organizational decisions are made by groups or teams of managers rather than by individuals.

表 4-7　群体决策的优劣势
Table 4-7　Advantages and Disadvantages of Group Decision-Making

ADVANTAGES	DISADVANTAGES
1. Greater pool of knowledge. A group can bring much more information and experience to bear on a decision or problem than can an individual acting alone.	1. Social pressure. Unwillingness to "rock the boat" and pressure to conform may combine to stifle the creativity of individual contributors.
2. Different perspectives. Individuals with varied experience and interests help the group see decision situations and problems from different angles.	2. Domination by a vocal few. Sometimes the quality of group action is reduced when the group gives into those who talk the loud stand longest.
3. Greater comprehension. Those who personally experience the give-and-take of group discussion about alternative courses of action tend to understand the rationale behind the final decision.	3. Log rolling. Political wheeling and dealing can displace sound thinking when an individual's pet project or vested interest is at stake.
4. Increased acceptance. Those who play an active role in group decision-making and problem solving tend to view the outcome as "ours" rather than "theirs."	4. Goal displacement. Sometimes secondary considerations such as winning an argument, making a point, or getting back at a rival displace the primary task of making a sound decision or solving a problem.
5. Training ground. Less experienced participants in group action learn how to cope with group dynamics by actually being involved.	5. "Groupthink." Sometimes cohesive "in groups" let the desire for unanimity override sound judgment when generating and evaluating alternative courses of action.

（资料来源：Robert Kreitner. *Management* (11th edition). New York: Houghton Mifflin Harcourt Publishing Company, 2009, p. 221）

二、决策方法

决策方法包括定性决策方法和定量决策方法两大类。

定性决策方法又称决策的"软"方法，是指决策者在系统调查研究分析的基础上，根据所掌握的信息，通过对事物运动规律的分析，在把握事物内在本质联系的基础上进行决策的方法，主要包括头脑风暴法、德尔菲法以及名义小组法等。定量决策方法又称决策的"硬"方法，是指在建立数学模型的基础上，运用统计学、运筹学和电子计算机技术来对决策对象进行计算和量化研究以解决决策问题的方法。

（一）定性决策方法

1. 头脑风暴法

头脑风暴法（Brainstorming）由面对面的互动小组自发地提出尽可能多的解决问题的方案，是非常有效的快速产生广泛备选方案的方法。即通过有关专家之间面对面的信息交流，引起思维共振，产生组合效应，从而产生创造性思维。头脑风暴法又可分为直接头脑风暴法（通常简称为头脑风暴法）和质疑头脑风暴法（也称反头脑风暴法）。前者是在专家群体决策时尽可能激发创造性，产生尽可能多的设想的方法；后者则是对前者提出的设想、方案逐一质疑，分析其现实可行性的方法。采用头脑风暴法组织群体决策时，要集中有关专家召开专题会议，由主持者以明确的方式向所有参与者阐明问题，说明会议的规则，在融

✍ **The Methods of Decision-Making**

Qualitative decision-making methods include brainstorming, Delphi technique and nominal group techniques, etc.

Quantitative decision-making methods include decisions under certainty, decisions under risk and decisions under uncertainty.

✧ **Qualitative decision-making methods**

1. **Brainstorming**

Brainstorming uses a face-to-face interactive group to spontaneously suggest as many ideas as possible for solving a problem. Brainstorming has been found to be highly effective for quickly generating a wide range of alternatives, but it does have some drawbacks.

洽轻松的会议气氛中，由专家们自由提出尽可能多的方案。

为便于提供一个良好的创造性思维环境，应该确定专家会议的最佳人数和会议进行的时间。经验证明，专家小组规模以 10～15 人为宜，会议时间一般以 20～60 分钟效果最佳。

实践表明，头脑风暴法可以排除折中方案，对所讨论问题通过客观、连续的分析，找到一组切实可行的方案，因而头脑风暴法在工作中得到了较广泛的应用。

头脑风暴法的过程如下（参看表 4-8）：

- 管理者在最大范围内说明小组面临的主要问题；
- 小组成员分享他们各自的想法及行动备选方案；
- 不允许小组成员对备选方案进行评判，直到所有的备选方案都被展示出来；
- 尽可能地鼓励小组成员创新与脑力激荡，提出的想法越多越好；此外，小组成员被鼓励"捎带"或在其他人的想法的基础上提出更多建议；
- 当所有的备选方案都产生后，小组成员讨论每个备选方案的利弊，并制订出最佳备选方案。

表 4-8　头脑风暴法的实施过程
Table 4-8　Steps of Brainstorming

	Steps
1	One manager describes in broad outline the problem the group is to address.
2	Group members share their ideas and generate alternative courses of action.
3	As each alternative is described, group members are not allowed to criticize it; everyone withholds judgment until all alternatives have been heard. One member of the group records the alternatives on a flip chart.
4	Group members are encouraged to be as innovative and radical as possible. Anything goes; and the greater the number of ideas put forth, the better. Moreover, group members are encouraged to "piggyback" or build on each other's suggestions.
5	When all alternatives have been generated, group members debate the pros and cons of each and develop a short list of the best alternatives.

2. 德尔菲法

德尔菲法（Delphi Technique）的实质是利用专家的主观判断，通过信息沟通与循环反馈，使预测意见趋于一致，逼近实际值。与头脑风暴法不同的是，德尔菲小组成员不是面对面，而是通过匿名书面通信方式进行决策的方法。

德尔菲法以匿名的方式，轮番征求一组专家各自的预测意见，具有反馈性、匿名性和统计性的特点，其常用工作程序如下（参看表 4-9）：

- 小组组长首先写出问题陈述及一系列要解决的问题，请参与的管理者或专家回复；

2. Delphi technique

Delphi technique is a written approach to creative problem-solving, in which group members do not meet face-to-face but respond in writing to questions posed by the group leader.

133

- 调查问卷发给最了解该问题的管理者或专家，要求这些管理者或专家提出解决方案，并将问卷寄回；
- 高层管理者记录和总结这些方案，然后将这些方案反馈给参与者，同时增加要做出决策的另外一些问题；
- 重复这个过程，直到参与者达成共识。

  这时，最合适的行动方案就产生了。

表 4-9　德尔菲法的实施步骤
Table 4-9　Steps of Delphi Technique

Steps	
1	The group leader writes a statement of the problem and a series of questions to which participating managers are to respond.
2	The questionnaire is sent to the managers and departmental experts who are most knowledgeable about the problem. They are asked to generate solutions and mail the questionnaires back to the group leader.
3	A team of top managers records and summarizes the responses. The results are then sent back to the participants, with additional questions to be answered before a decision can be made.
4	The process is repeated until a consensus is reached and the most suitable course of action is apparent.

德尔菲法的优点：① 便于独立思考和判断；② 低成本实现集思广益；③ 有利于探索性解决问题；④ 应用范围广泛。

德尔菲法的不足：① 缺少思想沟通交流；② 易忽视少数人的意见；③ 存在组织者主观影响。

3. 名义小组法

在集体决策中，如果对问题的性质不完全了解且意见分歧严重，则可采用名义小组法（Nominal Group Technique）。使用该决策方法时，小组成员先写下各自的想法及解决方案，并将他们的建议读给整个小组，然后讨论并对所有备选方案进行排序。名义小组法为提出备选方案提供了一种更为结构化的方法，通过书写自己的观点，给每一位管理者更多的时间和机会来思考潜在的解决方案。名义小组法的具体操作步骤如下（参看表 4-10）：

- 管理者先概述要解决的问题，然后给小组成员 30 到 40 分钟的时间单独工作，写下他们的想法和解决方案，鼓励各成员对解决方案创新；
- 小组成员轮流向小组表述各自的建议，管理者写下所有建议的备选方案，在所有的备选方案提出前不能有任何批评或评价；

3. Nominal group technique

Nominal growp techniqne is a decision-making technique in which group members write down ideas and solutions, read their suggestions to the whole group, and discuss and then rank the alternatives.

The nominal group technique provides a more structured way of generating alternatives in writing and gives each manager more time and opportunities to come up with potential solutions.

- 逐一讨论所有的备选方案,要求小组成员解释方案中的信息,并评价每个备选方案,以确定其优缺点;
- 在对所有备选方案讨论时,每个小组成员都将备选方案从最喜欢到最不喜欢进行排序,然后选择排序最好的备选方案。

表 4-10 名义小组法的实施步骤

Table 4-10 Steps of Nominal Group Technique

	Steps
1	One manager outlines the problem to be addressed, and 30 or 40 minutes are allocated for group members, working individually, to write down their ideas and solutions. Group members are encouraged to be innovative.
2	Members take turns reading their suggestions to the group. One manager writes all the alternatives on a flip chart. No criticism or evaluation of alternatives is allowed until all alternatives have been read.
3	The alternatives are then discussed, one by one, in the sequence in which they were proposed. Group members can ask for clarifying information and critique each alternative to identify its pros and cons.
4	When all alternatives have been discussed, each group member ranks all the alternatives from most preferred to least preferred, and the alternative that receives the highest ranking is chosen.

名义小组法的主要优点在于,群体成员正式开会但不限制每个人的独立思考,可以有效地激发个人的创造力和想象力。而传统的会议方式往往做不到这一点。在名义小组法中,小组的成员并不互相通气,也不在一起讨论、协商,因此小组只是名义上的。

常见的定性决策方法还有淘汰法、环比法等。淘汰法是根据一定的条件和标准,对全部备选的方案筛选一遍,淘汰达不到要求的方案,缩小选择的范围。环比法是在所有方案中进行两两比较,优者得 1 分,劣者得 0 分,最后以各方案得分多少为标准选择方案。

定性决策方法具有灵活简便、费用较少的特点,特别适用于非规范化的综合决策问题,还有利于调动专家、员工的积极性,提高他们的创造力。此外,吸收员工和专家参与决策,便于统一思想,也预先为决策的实施创造了有利条件。但是,定性决策方法是建立在个人主观意见的基础上,缺乏严格论证,主观成分强,有一定的主观倾向性。

Global Perspective

The Power of Collaboration

How do you make the right decisions for 15,000 employees? Allan Bradshaw, head of Weyerhaeuser, was faced with this task as he and his team evaluated their company's future. Weyerhaeuser is an international forest products company with interests in construction, real estate, and lumber. As the firm made acquisitions and the market for home construction shifted, Weyerhaeuser's managers needed to make some major changes to its residential wood products division, which employed 15,000 workers. The division was fragmented, literally and figuratively. Five businesses operated under the same division, confusing customers about brands. Workers were located in four different time zones, and the home-building industry was consolidating. Bradshaw and his team decided it was time for a complete—extreme—makeover.

In a bold move, the group dissolved the old organization and created a new one, called iLevel. Teams made up of 10 experts, each from different areas of the company, worked to redesign sales, manufacturing, marketing, and other business functions. They develop adoptions for the organization. "Then we evaluated each option against a set of criteria to determine which option provided the best return for the company," says Bradshaw. "There was a lot of discussions and debates," he recalls.

In the end, a new organization emerged that focuses on finding solutions for customers and providing one-stop shopping for all aspects of home building and improvement—for builders as well as homeowners. As a sponsor of ABC's Extreme Makeover: Home Edition, Weyerhaeuser prides itself on its ability to tear down the old and put up the new. Its new iLevel division is intended to do the same. "A level is a No. 1 tool for a builder," explains Bradshaw. "Level means quality. It means honesty. That we're going to level with you."

（案例来源：Thomas S. Bateman. *Management: Leading & Collaborating in a Competitive World* (8th edition). New York: McGraw-Hill Education, 2009, p. 107）

（二）定量决策方法

定量决策方法,是指利用数学模型进行决策方案优选的决策方法。根据数学模型涉及的问题的性质（或者说根据所选方案结果的可靠性）,定量决策方法一般分为确定型决策方法、风险型决策方法和不确定决策方法三种。

1. 确定型决策方法

确定型决策方法的特点是只有一种选择,决策没有风险,只要满足数学模型的前提条件,数学模型就会给出特定结果。确定型决策方法主要包括盈亏平衡分析模型和经济批量模型。这里主要介绍盈亏平衡分析模型。

盈亏平衡分析（Break-Even Analysis）模型是通过考察产量（或销售量）、成本和利润的关系以及盈亏变化的规律来为决策提供依据,是一种广泛帮助管理者预测获利的技术,尽管简单,但对管理者很有价值,因为它指出了收入、成本和利润之间的关系。

要计算盈亏平衡点（BE）,管理者需要知道出售产品

✧ Quantitative decision-making methods

1. The method for certainty situation

Break-even analysis, a technique for identifying the point at which total revenue is just sufficient to cover total costs, is a widely used technique for helping managers make profit projections.
Break-even analysis is a simplistic formulation, yet it is valuable to managers because it points out the relationship among revenues, costs, and profits.

的单位价格（P）、单位变动成本（VC）和总固定成本（TFC）。一个项目的盈亏平衡点是总收入刚好等于总成本时的情形，但总成本由两部分组成：固定成本和变动成本，固定成本是无论产量如何变化都不变的费用，例如保险费、财产费，当然这个固定成本是短期内不变，长期内成本都是可以变化的。可变成本与产量成比例变化，包括原材料、劳动力成本和能源成本。盈亏平衡点的计算公式如下：

$$BE = \frac{TFC}{P - VC}$$

这个公式告诉我们：①当我们以涵盖所有单位可变成本的价格卖掉所有的成品时，总收入等于总成本；②价格与可变成本的差额与销售产量的乘积等于固定成本。

例如，假设一家早餐店，一杯咖啡售价 1.75 美元，如果它的固定成本（包括房租、保险费等）是每年 47000 美元，而变动成本是每杯 0.40 美元，则该早餐店咖啡的盈亏平衡点就是：$\frac{47000}{1.75 - 0.40}$ =34815（大约每周卖 670 杯），或者说每年年收入达到近 60926 美元，这一关系如图 4-5 所示。

This formula tells us that (1) total revenue will equal total cost when we sell enough units at a price that covers all variable unit costs, and (2) the difference between price and variable costs, when multiplied by the number of units sold, equals the fixed costs.

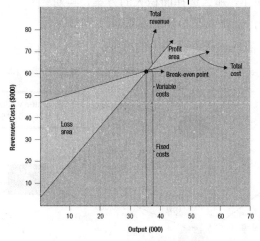

图 4-5　盈亏平衡分析

Figure 4-5　Break-Even Analysis

（资料来源：Stephen P. Robbins, David A. DeCenzo and Mary Coulter. *Fundamentals of Management: Essential Concepts and Applications* (9th edition). New York: Pearson, 2013, p. 112）

2. 风险型决策方法（决策树）

有时我们会碰到这样的情况，一个决策方案对应几个相互排斥的可能状态，每一种状态都以一定的可能性（概率 0-1）出现，并对应特定结果，这时的决策就被称为风险型决策。风险型决策的目的是如何使收益期望值最大，或者损失期望值最小。期望值是一种方案的损益值与相应概率的乘积之和。下面我们用决策树来说明风险型决策方法。

2. The method for risk situation (decision trees)

决策树（Decision Trees）是用于分析雇佣、营销、投资、设备购买、定价及类似过程决策的常用方法，之所以称之为决策树，是因为画出的图很像有许多树枝的树，就是用树枝分叉形态表示各种方案的期望值，剪掉期望值小的方案枝，剩下的最后的方案即是最佳方案。

决策树由决策结点、方案枝、状态结点、概率枝四个要素组成。方块结点代表决策结点，由决策结点引出的若干条树枝称为方案枝。圆圈结点代表状态结点，由状态结点引出的若干条树枝称为状态枝，状态枝上标明状态的情况和可能的概率。

如图 4-6 所示，这是一家咖啡店进行选址时的决策。这家咖啡店通过调查发现，有两个选择方案：第一个有100 平方米，第二个是 250 平方米。一大一小两个方案，其中如果选择面积大的方案，并且在经济繁荣时期，估计每年能盈利 30 万元，但在经济衰退的情况下，场地过大带来的高昂经营成本意味着公司只能盈利 5 万元；如果选择面积小的方案，估计在经济繁荣情况下会盈利 24 万元，而在衰退情况下也能盈利 12 万元。经济繁荣或衰退出现的概率如图 4-6 所示，那么选择面积大的方案，其期望利润是 225,000 元，选择面积小的方案的期望利润是204,000 元，从这点上看应该选择面积大的方案。

The method of decision trees is a useful way to analyze hiring, marketing, investment, equipment purchases, pricing, and similar decisions that involve a progression of decisions. It's called the method of decision trees because, when diagrammed, it looks a lot like a tree with branches. Typical decision trees encompass expected value analysis by assigning probabilities to each possible outcome and calculating payoffs for each decision path.

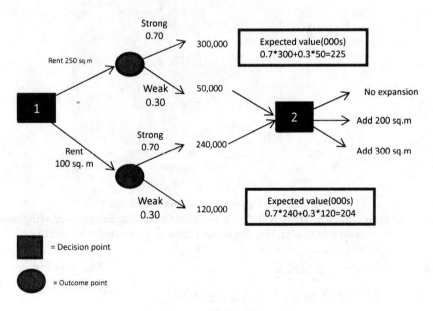

图 4-6　决策树分析
Figure 4-6　Decision Trees Analysis

如果一开始决定租用面积小的咖啡店，而等到经济繁荣再扩租，结果又会如何呢？这时决策树将延伸至第二个决策点，这里有三种选择：不扩租、扩租 200 平方米或扩租 300 平方米。沿用之前的方法，管理者可以计算出扩租决策之后各方案的潜在利润以及各种选择的期望值。

3. 不确定型决策方法

我们看到，在风险型决策方法中，计算期望值的前提是能够判断各种状况出现的概率。如果出现的概率不清楚，就要用不确定型决策方法。常用的不确定型决策方法主要有四种，即冒险法、保守法、折中法和后悔值准则。具体采用何种方法，取决于决策者对待风险的态度。例如，乐观主义者倾向于采用最大最大化（Maximax）选择决策，即冒险法，在各种可能的最大收益值中选取最大收益值的方法；悲观主义者通常遵循一种最大最小化（Maximin）选择决策，即保守法，从每个方案出现的最坏结果中选择一个最小收益值最大的方案作为决策；持折中态度的管理者们喜欢采用乐观系数法（a），首先对乐观程度和悲观态势有一个基本的估计（即 a 系数），然后以 a 系数为权，对每一方案的最大收益值和最小收益值进行加权平均，得出每个方案可能的折中收益值，然后取各个方案的折中收益值最大的方案为最终决策；那些期望"后悔"值最小的管理者喜欢采用最小最大化（Minimax）选择决策，即后悔值准则，在每个方案的最大后悔值中选取最小的后悔值，以使得方案实施后对原先所选取的方案的后悔程度达到最低的方案作为决策。

3. The method for uncertainty situation

The optimistic manager will follow a maximax choice (maximizing the maximum possible payoff), the pessimist will follow a maximin choice (maximizing the minimum possible payoff).

A Compromise decision-making means choosing a proper alternative according to optimistic coefficient "a".

The manager who desires to minimise his or her maximum "regret" will opt for a minimax choice.

Global Perspective

Visa International in New York

Tom is a marketing manager at Visa International in New York. He has determined four possible strategies (we'll label these S1, S2, S3, and S4) for promoting the Visa card throughout the northeastern United States. However, he is also aware that one of his major competitors, American Express, has three competitive strategies (CA1, CA2, and CA3) for promoting its own card in the same region. In this case, we'll assume that the Visa executive has no previous knowledge that would allow him to place probabilities on the success of any of his four strategies. With these facts, the Visa card manager formulates the matrix in Table 1 to show the various Visa strategies and the resulting profit to Visa, depending on the competitive action chosen by American Express.

In this example, if Tom is an optimist, he'll choose S4 because that could produce the largest possible gain ($28 million). Note that this choice maximizes the maximum possible gain (maximax choice). If Tom is a pessimist, he'll assume only the worst can occur. The worst outcome for each strategy is as follows: S1 =$11 million; S2 = $9 million; S3 = $15 million; and S4 = $14 million. Following the maximin choice, the pessimistic manager would maximize the minimum payoff—in other words, he'd select S3.

In the third approach, Tom recognizes that once a decision is made it will not necessarily result in the most profitable payoff. What could occur is a "regret" of profits forgone (given up)—regret referring to the amount of money that could have been made had a different strategy been used. Managers calculate regret by subtracting all possible payoffs in each category from the maximum possible payoff for each given—in this case, for each competitive action. For Tom, the highest payoff, given that American Express engages in CA1, CA2, or CA3, is $24 million, $21 million, or $28 million, respectively (the highest number in each column). Subtracting the payoffs in Table 1 from these figures produces the results in Table 2.

The maximum regrets are S1 = $17 million; S2 = $15 million; S3 = $13 million; and S4 = $7 million. The minimax choice minimizes the maximum regret, so Tom would choose S4. By making this choice, he'll never have a regret of profits forgone of more than $7 million. This result contrasts, for example, with a regret of $15 million had he chosen S2 and American Express had taken CA1.

Table 1   Payoff Matrix for Visa

Visa Marketing Strategy	American Express's Response (in $millions)		
	CA1	CA2	CA3
S1	13	14	11
S2	9	15	18
S3	24	21	15
S4	18	14	28

Table 2   Regret Matrix for Visa

Visa Marketing Strategy	American Express's Response (in $millions)		
	CA1	CA2	CA3
S1	11	7	17
S2	15	6	10
S3	0	0	13
S4	6	7	0

（案例来源：Stephen P. Robbins, David A. DeCenzo and Mary Coulter. *Fundamentals of Management: Essential Concepts and Applications* (9th edition). New York: Pearson, 2013, pp. 109-110）

第三节　管理者偏见与新挑战

Boeing's Decision to Innovate

For Alan Mulally, getting the approval from Boeing's board of directors to build the 787 Dreamliner was far from a sure thing. Boeing had made cutbacks in new-product investments, and Mulally's previous project, development of the 777, had run far over budget (although it did make money for the company). However, the Dreamliner's design was so impressive that the directors believed the project would succeed even if Mulally's projections turned out to be too rosy.

Mulally recognized, however, that he must address concerns about cost overruns. He had an idea to minimize that risk: Design and construction wouldn't be centralized within Boeing. Rather, the company would work with a global network of suppliers. They would share in the costs and use their own investments in factories and equipment to build components of the aircraft. With this arrangement, Boeing hoped to keep the costs of developing the aircraft around $5 billion. With the average jetliner selling for around $100 million, the program could cost far more and still make money.

Implementing the decision was both difficult and rewarding. Coordinating the work of a network of suppliers proved to be far more difficult to manage than anyone seems to have anticipated. Meanwhile, leadership at the top changed: Boeing hired James McNerney, aboard member with broad business experience, to be its new CEO, rather than Mulally, whose background was in aircraft engineering. Shortly afterward, Mulally left Boeing to run Ford. Without Mulally, who pushed hard to keep work on schedule, the plane's development fell further and further behind. McNerney struggled to find a successful replacement at the head of the commercial-aircraft division, appointing three managers to that post.

Nevertheless, airline customers loved the idea of a plane that would please passengers while saving money. Robert Milton was CEO of Air Canada's parent company when it ordered 60 Dreamliners. Milton noted that "issues" are bound to arise whenever a company introduces "an airplane so radically different." Customers placed orders totaling 848, a record for a new jetliner.

（案例来源: Thomas S. Bateman and Scott A. Snell. *Management: Leading & Collaborating in a Competitive World* (11th edition). New York: McGraw-Hill Irwin, 2015, p. 90）

管理过程不仅是一个管理物的过程，更重要的是管理人的过程。同时，管理活动又都是通过交流和沟通来实现对下属的影响的，在此过程中，领导者对下属及其行为或下属对领导者进行认知时，必然会受到社会知觉偏差的影响。管理者在进行管理活动时，必须对认知偏差的影响有足够的了解，才能做出有效的管理决策，才能进行科学的管理。案例中波音公司的管理者决策时在信息收集、评价及应用这些信息所做出选择时，远远偏离了客观性，在做出判断时受到了较多偏见的影响。

本节将介绍管理者决策中常见的几种认知偏差及其影响，以及新常态下管理决策面临着的新的挑战。

一、管理者认知偏差

✍ **Cognitive Bias of Managers**

当管理者制定决策时，他们不仅具有自己特定的风格，而且可能利用经验法则或直观判断法（Heuristics）来简化决策制定过程。经验法则是有用的，因为它能够帮助决策者更好地理解复杂的、不确定的、模糊的信息。虽然管理者可以使用经验法则，但这并不意味着其决策结果都是可靠的。因为它们可能会导致决策者在处理和评估信息时产生错误和偏见。图 4-7 展示了管理者可能会犯下的常见的决策错误和偏见。

Heuristics means judgemental shortcuts or "rules of thumb" used to simplify decision-making.

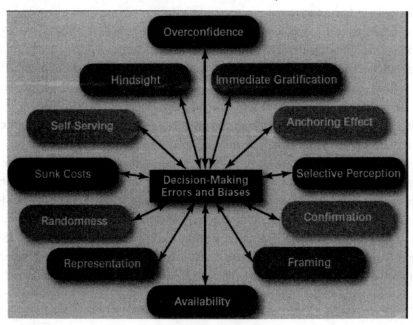

图 4-7 决策时常见错误和偏见

Figure 4-7 Common Decision-Making Errors and Biases

（一）过度自信

◇ Overconfidence bias

当决策者时常高估自己的知识和能力，或者对自己以及自己的表现持有一种不切实际的肯定时，他们就表现出过度自信偏见（Overconfidence Bias）。行为心理学家丹尼尔·卡林曼（Daniel Kahneman）指出，"过度自信的产生是因为往往看不到自己的盲目性"。例如，有一些经验丰富的投资顾问，其成功的投资案例可能多来源于运气，而并非高超的投资技能。但是投资成功的结果会让这些投资顾问过度自信，认为自己拥有卓越的投资技能。这种现象并非个案，它存在于各个行业当中。因此，一般情况下，我们不应该轻易相信过于果断和自信的人对他们自己的评价，除非我们有足够的理由相信，他们对自我的判断比较准确。

The overconfidence bias is the bias in which people's subjective confidence in their decision-making is greater than their objective accuracy. Most people overestimate their ability to predict uncertain outcomes.

过度自信在做风险型决策时特别危险。例如一家快餐连锁店的管理人员确信，低员工离职率是顾客满意和企业营利能力的关键驱动因素，于是他们决定投资保持员工快乐的项目以留住员工，但事实上，当他们分析企业经营数据时却发现，那些高离职率的店铺利润反而更高，而低离职率的店铺却在苦苦挣扎。

Overconfidence can be particularly dangerous when making risky decisions.

（二）即时满足偏见

即时满足偏见（Immediate Gratification Bias）是指决策者倾向于获得即时回报，避免即时成本。对于这些人来说，能迅速获得回报的决策比将来获得回报的决策更具吸引力。于是，在这种偏见影响下，管理者决策时往往关注的仅仅是当下的收益，而忽视未来的收益，从而使决策变得短视，不利于企业基业常青。

✧ Immediate gratification bias

The immediate gratification bias describes decision-makers who tend to want immediate rewards and to avoid immediate costs.

（三）锚定效应偏见

锚定效应（Anchoring Effect Bias）偏见是指管理者过分看重初始信息，而忽略了后续信息，不能及时做出调整。即第一印象、想法、价格和预测比后续得到的信息更重要。例如，管理者往往根据员工过去一年的表现提供一个标准百分比的加薪，即使这种加薪完全超出了其他公司支付给相同技能员工的薪资。该现象有时会出现在房地产销售中，例如在房地产市场繁荣时期，很多房主倾向于给他们要出售的房子定一个非常高的价格，即使后来房地产市场萧条，这些卖房者也不愿意大幅度降低房价以迎合整个市场情况。

✧ Anchoring effect bias

The anchoring effect describes when decision-makers fixate on initial information as a starting point and then, once set, fail to adequately adjust for subsequent information.

（四）选择认知偏见

当管理者根据他们带有偏见的感知有选择地组织和阐述事件时，他们就是在运用选择性认知偏见（Selective Perception Bias）。这对他们关注信息、确定问题以及形成备选方案都会产生影响。

例如，有些人事经理在招聘人才时，会以自身的兴趣、背景、经验及态度选择员工，常会误认为与他具有类似背景的候选人，将来可以与自己一样在工作上表现良好。

✧ Selective perception bias

When decision-makers selectively organize and interpret events based on their biased perceptions, they're using the selective perception bias.

（五）证实偏见

当管理者努力寻找那些能够证实其以往选择的信息，并忽视那些与其以往判断相左的信息时，他们就表现出证实偏见（Confirmation Bias）。这些人往往会接受那些肯定其所持观点的信息，却抱着一种吹毛求疵的态度来对待那些质疑其所持观点的信息。

✧ Confirmation bias

Decision-makers who seek out information that reaffirm their past choices and discount information that contradicts past judgments exhibit the confirmation bias.

（六）框架偏见

框架偏见（Framing Bias）是指管理者选择和强调一种情况的某些方面，而不考虑其他方面。当他们过分关注和强调一种情境的特定方面而同时轻视或排除其他方面时，他们看到的现象就不够真实全面，往往会产生不正确的参考标准。例如，研究发现，与标明"15%肥肉"的肉相比，顾客更喜欢标明"85%的瘦肉"的肉。

◇ Framing bias

The framing bias happens when decision-makers select and high-light certain aspects of a situation while excluding others.

（七）易获得性偏见

易获得性偏见（Availability Bias）是指管理者倾向于记住那些记忆中最近发生的和生动的事件。结果它弱化了管理者客观地回忆事件的能力，并影响了管理者对事件的判断和对可能性的估计。例如，某员工在 2015 年前 9 个月有完美的工作考勤记录，但在过去 2 个月由于交通拥堵有 4 天迟到，当考虑是否给其加薪时，领导应该根据其整个的出勤记录来做判断，然而事实上管理者倾向于给最近行为赋予更多的权重，这就是因为易获得性偏见——管理者使用从记忆中容易获得的信息来做出判断。这种偏见会造成现有的可获得信息无法展示实际情况的全貌。

◇ Availability bias

The availability bias occurs when decision-makers tend to remember events that are the most recent and vivid in their memory.

（八）典型性偏见

当管理者根据其熟悉的其他事件推断某事发生的可能性时，就发生了典型性偏见（Representation Bias）。存在这种偏见的管理者将过去和现在的情况类比，并认为情境是相同的（实际上并不是）。举例来说，公司从某个大学招聘了一名学生，该学生逐渐成长为出色的销售代表，这并不意味着出自同一所大学的大学生都是同样合格的候选人。但事实上，管理者一直在做类似的招聘决策。

◇ Representation bias

When decision-makers assess the likelihood of an event based on how closely it resembles other events or sets of events, that's the representation bias.

（九）随机偏见

随机偏见（Randomness Bias）是决策者试图从随机事件中归纳出某个结论。他们之所以会这样做，是因为大多数决策者难以确定决策结果的可能性，他们希望对随机发生的事件进行总结，并以总结的经验去解决未来的问题。但在总结归纳过程中，管理者很难剔除事件随机性的影响。

◇ Randomness bias

The randomness bias describes when decision-makers try to create meaning out of random events.

（十）沉没成本

沉没成本偏见（Sunk-cost Bias）是指决策者忘记当前的行动无法影响过去的事件。当管理者将花在某个项目上的所有资金汇总后得出结论：该项目过于昂贵，于是就简单地放弃，这时就出现了沉没成本偏见。管理者在评估备选方案时，不是从将来的结果出发，而是错误地依据以

◇ Sunk-cost bias
The sunk-cost bias takes place when decision-makers forget that current choices can't correct the past.

往所投入的时间、金钱或精力，即他们无法忽略和忘记沉没成本，是沉没成本偏见的常见表现。

（十一）自利偏见

当管理者将成功归因于自己而把失败归因于外部因素时，这就是所谓的自利偏见（Self-serving Bias）。例如，当一名员工迟到时，他常常会更多地将其归因于交通堵塞，而不是他的懒散；管理者在对员工进行绩效考评时，对于未完成任务的员工，倾向于认为是员工自身能力因素的影响，与他们的领导无关；而当取得好的绩效时，管理者往往夸大行动者的个人因素，低估环境因素。

（十二）后视偏见

后视偏见（Hindsight Bias）是指当结果已众所周知时，决策者还错误地认为他们本来可以恰当地预测事件的后果。也就是人们常说的"事后聪明"。这种现象通常发生在我们回首过去的决策并重构当初为何选择这个决策时。有后视偏见的人在事后总觉得自己早就可以预测事件的发生，因此难以用公平的眼光评价他人。当下属成功地完成某个任务时，有后视偏见的管理者会告诉下属，他早就知道这件事是可以成功的，因此不会给下属充分的肯定和奖励。

管理者可以通过认识和避免这些决策错误和偏见，来回避其带来的负面影响。而且，随着学者们对认知偏差的深入研究，逐渐认识到在某些情况下，偏差并不一定都是有害的。所以，武断地认为认知偏差就是有害的，凡是认知偏差就应该纠正，是不客观也是不现实的。适当地在决策过程中运用认知偏差，反而会起到事半功倍的效果。

二、管理者决策遇到的新挑战：大数据时代

研究表明，全世界的信息到 2020 年将达到 40 ZB，其数量相当于全世界海滩上沙粒总和的 57 倍。这导致"大数据"（Big Data）概念的产生，其存储数据如此巨大以至于传统的数据库管理系统无法处理，需要更加复杂的分析软件及超级计算机。大数据不仅包括已经存在于企业中的数据，还包括网络浏览器痕迹数据、社交网络通信、传感器数据和监视数据。大数据在科学、商业、医药、科技等领域引起了大量关注，该概念被称为"创新、竞争力和生产力的下一个前沿"。

◇ Self-serving bias

Decision-makers who are quick to take credit for their successes and to blame failure on outside factors are exhibiting the self-serving bias.

◇ Hindsight bias

The hindsight bias is the tendency for decision-makers to falsely believe that they would have accurately predicted the outcome of an event once that outcome is actually known.

✎ **New Challenge: Big Data**

Big Data includes not only data in corporate databases but also web-browsing data trails, social network communications, sensor data, and surveillance data.

大数据对决策制定会产生什么样的影响？答案非常多。有了这类数据在手，决策者就相当于拥有了非常强大的工具，以帮助他们做出决策，即利用大数据分析（Big Data Analytics）来优化决策。大数据分析是通过研究各种类型的数据以发现隐藏的模式、未知的关系或其他有用信息的过程。然而，一些专家也提出了不同的看法，他们认为，为进行大数据分析而收集和分析数据是浪费精力的一种做法，因为企业将会变成信息的"沼泽地"，员工将会被大量的信息所淹没，以至于不能够把有价值的信息和无用的信息区分开。

大数据下决策的技术含量、知识含量大幅度提高，对大数据的有效利用成为企业决策的关键，因此管理大量的数据是个挑战，如果不能找到有效数据，企业就无法进行有效的数据分析，这些数据就会被浪费掉。大数据时代不仅要求企业具有搜集和分析数据的能力，更需要企业具有处理和利用这些数据的能力。

Big Data analytics is the process of examining large amounts of data of a variety of types to uncover hidden patterns, unknown correlations, and other useful information.

关键概念 KEY IDEAS AND CONCEPTS

Decision-making

Managerial decision-making

Programmed decisions

Nonprogrammed decisions

Uncertainty

Risk

Conflict

The classical model of decision-making

The administrative model of decision-making

Bounded rationality

Satisficing

Intuition

Prospect theory

The political model of decision-making

Diagnosis

Brainstorming

Delphi technique

Nominal group technique

Break-even analysis

Decision trees

Overconfidence

Immediate gratification bias

Anchoring effect

Confirmation bias

Framing bias

Availability bias

Representation bias

Randomness bias

Sunk-cost bias

Self-serving bias

Hindsight bias

Big Data

Big Data analytics

讨论问题 DISCUSSION QUESTIONS

1. Why is decision-making often described as the essence of a manager's job?

2. Describe the six steps in the decision-making process.

3. What are the main differences between programmed decisions and nonprogrammed decisions?

4. In what ways do the classical and administrative models of decision-making help managers appreciate the complexities of real-world decision-making?

5. All of us bring biases to the decisions we make. What would be the drawbacks of having biases? Could there be any advantages to having biases? Explain why. What are the implications for managerial decision-making?

6. "Because managers have so many powerful decisionmaking tools to use, they should be able to make more rational decisions." Do you agree or disagree with this statement? Why?

7. Explain how a manager might deal with making decisions under conditions of uncertainty.

8. Why do you think organizations have increased the use of groups for making decisions? When would you recommend using groups to make decisions?

9. Identify some problems you want to solve. Brainstorm with others a variety of creative solutions.

10. Explain the differences between three common methods of group decision-making — brainstorming, Delphi technique, and nominal groups.

11. All of us bring biases to the decisions we make. What would be the drawbacks of having biases? Explain.

Designing for Dollars

Great product design is absolutely critical for most consumer products companies. But how do these companies know when a design feature will pay off, especially when every dollar counts? How do they make those tough decisions?

Suppose you are the product development manager for a whitegoods manufacturer who is considering manufacture of a front-loader washing machine. To date, the company has only manufactured top-loader washing machines, as the majority of washing machines sold in Australia have been top loaders. However, you have increasingly become aware of the growing trend towards front loaders in some sectors of the market, and you have decided to get together with the company's industrial designer to review what you know about the pros and cons of the two different types of washing machine. Below is a list of your first brainstorming session.

Points in favor of front-loader washing machines:

- Lower water usage.
- Suitable for under-counter usage in kitchens or bathrooms.
- More fashionable.
- Usually physically smaller than top-loaders.
- Can add a drying element to completely wash and dry in the same appliance.
- Tumble dryers can be placed directly on top, saving space.
- Probably more attractive for retirement villages and apartment living.
- Could be made with a stainless steel case to match other appliances. (But so could a top-loader.)

Points against front-loader washing machines:

- Smaller loads than most top-loaders.
- Cannot add clothes after washing cycle starts.
- Cycle times are usually much longer due to pauses between direction of rotation of washing action.
- Most front-loaders on the market have up to a three-minute pause at the end of a washing cycle before the door of the machine can be opened. This seems to annoy many people.
- Usually only have a cold water connection, hence the need for a water heating element for hot and warm washes.

The decision you are faced with is a tough one. You know that your company has vast experience in making top-loaders. It would also be simpler and less costly to continue making top-loaders because a changeover to making front-loaders would result in higher tooling and design work in making the transition. Certainly, initial costs will be higher, which will mean that the purchase price will need to be higher than for a similar top-loader. On the other hand, you cannot deny that there is a strong market trend towards front-loaders.

You know that your CEO would want to know what the return on investment would be—that is, would it pay off financially—in manufacturing front-loaders. However, both you and the industrial designers who have been asked to investigate this business opportunity are not in a position to answer that question. All you have is a gut-feeling that you ought to get into this segment of the market.

In an endeavor to answer this question you decide to research the field and see whether you can find some information to help you build a case that you can take to your CEO. As you search for information, you learn that when one of your competitors, Whirlpool, faced a similar problem, they looked at what other "design-centric" companies such as BMW, Nike and Nokia did. Surprisingly, only a few of them had a system for forecasting return on design. Most of them simply based future investments on past performance.

Delving further into the overseas literature, you discover that, when confronted with a similar problem, Whirlpool had found that a focus on customer preferences worked much better than a focus on bottom-line returns. If the product development department could objectively measure what customers want in a product and then meet those needs, the company could realize financial returns. The design group at Whirlpool had created a standardized company-wide process that puts design prototypes in front of customer focus groups and then gets detailed measurements of their preferences about aesthetics, craftsmanship, technical performance, ergonomics and usability. Whirlpool then charts the results against competing products and the company's own products. This metrics-based approach gives decision-makers a baseline of objective evidence from which to make investment decisions. This meant that design investment decisions at Whirlpool could be based on fact, not opinion. This "new" decision-making approach at Whirlpool had also transformed the company's culture, and led to bolder designs since the designers could now make a strong case for making those investments.

Having found this information about how Whirlpool went about transforming its decision-making process, you now think you can begin to build a convincing case for the introduction of front-loaders that you can take to your CEO.

（案例来源：Stephen Robbins, Rolf Bergman, Ian Stagg and Mary Coulter. *Management* (6th edition). Melbourne: Pearson Australia Group Pty Ltd., 2012, pp. 286-287）

Discussion Questions

1. Would you characterize product design decisions as structured or unstructured problems?

2. Describe and evaluate the process Whirlpool went through to change the way design decisions were made. Describe and evaluate Whirlpool's new design decision process.

3. What criteria do the washing machine design group use in design decisions? What do you think each of these criteria involves?

第五章　计划

学习目标

1. 界定目标与计划的内涵及关系
2. 明确各种不同类型的组织计划
3. 总结计划工作的编制步骤
4. 界定有效目标的特征
5. 概述目标管理的四个基本步骤

主要内容

第一节　计划的本质与内容
第二节　计划过程与方法
第三节　目标管理

Learning Outcomes

1. Define goals and plans and explain the relationship between them.
2. Identify different kinds of organizational plans.
3. Summarize the basic steps in the planning process
4. Define the characteristics of effective goals.
5. Outline the four essential steps in the management-by-objectives (MBO) process.

Contents

5.1 The Nature and Purposes of Planning
5.2 The Planning Process and Approaches
5.3 Management-by-Objectives （MBO）

第一节 计划的本质与内容

Toys "R" Us is Not Playing Around When It Comes to Planning

Toys "R" Us, Inc., with its mascot Geoffrey the Giraffe, is a well-known brand. The toy retailer was founded in 1948 as Children's Supermart and later rebranded as Toys "R" Us after adding toys to its baby furniture business. By 2014 the company had grown to 872 stores in the United States, and more than 700 stores outside the United States.

Despite its growth, 2013 was not a good year for Toys "R" Us. Net sales in stores were down, and the company's net loss was $1 billion. Chairman and CEO Antonio Urcelay and President Hank Mullany announced Toy "R" Us' "TRU Transformation" plan.

"Our 'TRU Transformation' strategy is grounded in consumer research and customer insights, and is anchored by three guiding principles—Easy, Expert, Fair," Mullany said. "Among our highest priorities will be to deepen our focus on the customer, build meaningful relationships through loyalty and targeted marketing programs, and improve the shopping experience both in-store and online."

First, Urcelay and Mullany recognize that external factors affect sales at Toys "R" Us. The factors identified by Urcelay and Mullany are opportunities and threats, over which Toys "R" Us has no control. They include falling birthrates, changes in the play patterns of children, and the growth of online shopping. While it might be easy for Urcelay and Mullany to blame falling sales on these factors, the two company leaders also looked at internal factors that hurt the business. They are the factors over which the company does have control. "We are encouraged that all of these issues are firmly within our own control to fix," Urcelay said. "And our strategy will address these to improve the business over the short-term and put the company on track for the future."

Urcelay and Mullany described four categories of weaknesses at Toys "R" Us and discussed how they could be turned into strengths. First, the retailer said it has provided a weak customer experience in-store and online. Customers complain that the checkout process in stores is slow and that the stores are cluttered and disorganized. The apps for Toys "R" Us' online stores are out of date and frustrating to customers. When customers do buy a product online, they often encounter shipping problems. Toys "R" Us would like to turn this weakness into a strength by making its stores easy, uncluttered places at which to shop with sales associates who have been trained and are perceived as experts on the products. It also plans to better staff its store and to expedite its checkout process.

Second, there is a perception that prices at Toys "R" Us are higher than at other retailers. Toys "R" Us would like to turn this weakness into a strength by making sure its prices are perceived as fair and by reducing the many exclusions to its price-matching policy. The company also plans to better use data from its loyalty program to send targeted offers to customers and to communicate more simplified offers to customers.

Third, the retailer has struggled with inventory management. Customers often find that sought-after items are out of stock. Toys "R" Us had already begun to work on this before the 2013 financial returns were in. The company expanded its ability to ship online orders from stores and distribution centers, resulting in a much more flexible inventory system. It also is using a "product life cycle management" system to get the right goods into stores at the right times. Further, clearance events will move out merchandise that has been around the store for too long.

Finally, the retailer plans to right-size its cost structure. The company is working on an assessment of its business structure and operations to increase efficiency and effectiveness. As a part of this assessment, the company found 500 positions to eliminate. "As we look to the future, our strategy will establish a path to sustainable business growth, building upon the company's unique strengths," Urcelay said. "Toys 'R' Us is one of the most recognized brands in the world with a strong international presence and a large and loyal customer base."

Having identified the organization's strengths, weaknesses, opportunities, and threats is an important step in the planning process discussed in this chapter. This analysis gives Toys "R" Us the information it needs to turn weaknesses into strengths, to take advantage of opportunities, and to avoid damage from threats. Such planning will help Toys "R" Us hold onto and improve its market position.

As Mullany said: "We are committed to delivering on our mission to bring joy into the lives of our customers by being the toy and juvenile products authority and definitive destination for kid fun, gift-giving solutions, and parenting services."

（案例来源：Gareth R. Jones and Jennifer M. George. *Contemporary Management* (9th edition). New York: McGraw-Hill Education, 2014, pp. 215-216）

玩具反斗城（Toys "R" Us, Inc.）是美国一家大型跨国玩具连锁店，在全球拥有 1572 家零售商店，但 2013 年该企业的经营却表现不佳，全球商店净销售额下降了 1 亿美元。为了应对这一困境，公司高层决定实施"TRU 变革计划"，来改善销售额下滑的状况。事实上，企业管理者在工作中常常会遇到案例中所讲述的挑战或威胁，为此他们不得不采用多种方法来分析环境、制定战略，以实现企业的目标，满足顾客的需要。也就是说，需要在面临机遇或挑战的时候，不断地为企业做出各种战略选择，即实施计划职能。计划是所有管理者都需要去做的事情，那么计划有哪些类型？管理者怎样才能制订出正确的计划？如何通过计划实现企业的目标？将是本节主要讨论的内容。

一、计划及其重要性

（一）计划的概念

在日常生活、工作、学习中，我们常常会听到、看到或用到"计划"这个词，大到阿波罗登月计划，小到班级的春游计划甚至个人的学习计划，计划可谓无处不在。古人"运筹帷幄、决胜千里""未雨绸缪"等指的就是计划。"凡事预则立，不预则废"，这个"预"字指的也是计划。在组织的管理工作中，计划更是与每一个人息息相关。营销部门要有营销计划，生产部门要有生产计划，管理高层也要为组织的发展做好战略计划。

在管理学发展的历史过程中，许多专家、学者、管理大师在不同的背景下，从不同角度对"计划"这个词进行了诠释。对计划的概念认知总体上有两种观点。一种是名词性质的理解，也是狭义上的计划（Plan），主要是指为实现组织既定目标所制订的具体行动方案。另外一种则是动词性质的理解，也是广义的计划（Planning），指的是定义组织目标，确定战略以实现这些目标，以及制订方案以整合和协调工作活动。它同时涉及结果（做什么）和手段（如何做）。

在本章使用"计划"这个术语时，我们指的是广义的计划，这一定义意味着：① 计划界定了特殊时期的特定目标；② 写下目标并告知所有组织成员；③ 通过这些目标制订具体的方案，以明确组织将向何处发展，进而实现组织目标。正如哈罗德·孔茨（Harold Koontz）所言："计划工作是一座桥梁，它把我们所处的此岸和我们要去的彼岸连接起来，以克服这一天堑。"计划，就是针对明确的工作目标，配置实现目标所必需的各种资源，排除各种不确定性因素，选择一条适合自身特点的实现工作目标的路径。

（二）计划的重要性

一般认为，计划是管理最基本的职能，其他每一个职能都要围绕计划来展开，然而计划也是最有争议的管理职能，许多学者和企业家们认为，"计划赶不上变化"，计划不能预测不确定的未来，计划只能适应环境的变化，却无法改变动荡不安的环境。那么管理者为何还需要计划？可以从以下四个方面来解释（见图 5-1）。

✍ **The Definition and Importance of Planning**

✧ The definition of planning

Planning involves defining the organization's objectives or goals, establishing an overall strategy for achieving those goals, and developing a comprehensive hierarchy of plans to integrate and coordinate activities. It's concerned with ends (what is to be done) as well as with means (how it's to be done).

✧ Why do managers plan?

155

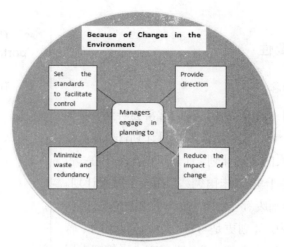

图 5-1 计划的缘由
Figure 5-1   Reasons for Planning

（资料来源：Stephen P. Robbins, David A. DeCenzo and Mary Coulter. *Fundamentals of Management: Essential Concepts and Applications* (9th edition). New York: Pearson, 2013, p. 124）

1. 为管理者和非管理者提供指导

当员工知道组织或工作部门正在努力实现什么目标以及他们必须为这些目标做出哪些贡献时，才能够协调行动，彼此展开合作，并且从事必要的工作以实现这些目标。如果没有计划，各部门和个体可能会各自为战，从而妨碍组织有效率地实现其目标。

另一方面，计划表明了一个组织将要达到的目标以及为实现目标采取的战略。没有了计划的指导，管理者很难明确最适合其自身发展的具体任务和工作方式，结果可能就会因同时追求多个相互冲突的目标而使管理者无法协调各方面资源。因而，通过计划可以保证管理者在组织目标及战略指导下有效地控制资源的使用。

2. 降低不确定性

计划的制订过程是管理者展望未来、预测变化、考虑变化的影响以及制定妥善的应对措施的过程，它可以降低决策的不确定性。虽然计划无法消除不确定性，但是管理者可通过计划来做出有效应对。

未来的不确定性和管理环境的瞬息万变使得计划成为管理者必不可少的一项管理活动，为了实现预期目标，管理人员必须对未来的变化进行预测，必须推测和估计这些变化对于实现组织目标可能造成的各种影响，必须了解变化发生时可能有哪些解决的备选方案，以及打算采取哪种方案应对环境变化。一旦出现变化，便可以及时采取措施，而不至于手足无措，无所适从。尽管有些变化不可预测，而且计划期越长，不确定性可能越大，但这并不能说明计划无用。相反，周密的计划和科学的预测将使未来的不确定性和风险降到最低限度。

1. Planning provides direction to managers and non-managers alike.

2. Planning reduces uncertainty by forcing managers to look ahead, anticipate change, consider the impact of change, and develop appropriate responses.

3. 尽量减少浪费和冗余

当根据计划来协调各种工作活动时,会更容易发现一些低效率的行为或活动,进而可以迅速对其进行纠正或消除。计划活动旨在以目标明确的共同努力代替互不协作的分散活动,以均匀一致的工作流程来代替缺乏协调的随意行动,以深思熟虑的决策来代替仓促草率的判断。这将大大有利于减少组织活动中的浪费,提高资源的使用率,从而可以更加经济合理地完成组织及其他各种组织的活动。

4. 为控制的实施提供标准

当管理者制订计划时他们会设定目标和标准,以便在完成任务之后,通过考察这些目标的执行情况来评判计划完成效果。如果没有计划,就没有既定目标来衡量人们的工作努力程度。计划工作具有承上启下的作用。一方面,计划工作是决策的逻辑延续,为决策所选择的目标活动的实施提供了保证;另一方面,计划工作又是组织、领导和控制等管理活动的基础,是组织内不同部门、不同成员行动的依据。因此计划在管理活动中具有十分重要的地位,它是最基本的一项管理职能。

（三）有效计划的四个特征

管理大师亨利·法约尔（Henri Fayol）认为,有效的计划应该具备四个方面的特征:统一性、连续性、精确性和灵活性。

统一性（Unity）意味着无论在任何时候,一个组织都应该有且只有一个核心的指导性计划起作用,以实现组织的目标,同时运行多个实现组织目标的计划可能会造成组织的混乱或无序。但这并不意味着一个组织只允许执行一个计划,而是指针对某一活动的所有计划的目的必须统一,步调必须一致,且它们之间的关系是相互促进、相互配合的。事实上,一项复杂的活动除了一个总计划外,往往有许多分计划或辅助计划,分派给不同部门去执行,如果各个计划之间是协调统一的,那么计划的实施有助于组织准确高效地完成任务,达到目标。相反,若计划不统一不协调、相互矛盾、重叠,就会分散管理者的精力,浪费人、财、物、时等资源,结果可能导致计划实施过程混乱,与组织既定目标南辕北辙。

连续性（Continuity）意味着计划是一个持续的过程,在这个过程中,管理者建立和完善以前的计划,并持续修正各层级计划——公司计划、业务计划和职能计划等,使它们整合成一个更大的计划框架。计划不是静态的,而是一个持续动态的过程。计划活动需要管理者不断地根据企

3. Planning reduces overlapping and wasteful activities.

4. Planning establishes the goals or standards that facilitate control.

❖ Four characteristics of effective planning

Unity means that at any time only one central, guiding plan is put into operation to achieve an organizational goal.

Continuity means that planning is an ongoing process in which managers build and refine previous plans and continually modify plans at all levels—corporate, business, and functional—so they fit together into one broad framework.

业外部环境变化以及企业内部要素的改变，不断加以修正，以保证组织目标能按照预期实现。

精确性（Accuracy）意味着管理者在计划过程中必须尽全力收集和使用所有有用信息。当然，管理者必须认识到不确定性的存在，而且信息几乎总是不完整的。但这不是说计划可以模糊或不准确，精确的计划能很好地指导和控制未来活动的依次展开，可以避免管理人员猜测、误解、随意决断，保证计划自身得到准确的执行。科学的决策方法和客观的分析推理是提高计划精确性的手段。

Accuracy means that managers need to make every attempt to collect and use all available information in the planning process.

尽管计划需要连续性和精确性，但需要强调的是，法约尔认为计划过程应该足够灵活（Flexible），这样计划可以根据环境因素的变化而变化，管理者不应被一个静态的计划所束缚，去学"刻舟求剑"的楚国人。精确性是指计划目标与未来实际状况接近的程度，而灵活性则是指计划适应变化的能力。计划的灵活性体现在计划本身具有改变方向的能力，即制订计划时需要依据未来可能发生的各种偶然事件，事先拟出若干套可供选择的替代方案。这样，不管环境发生什么变化，都能使计划有回旋的余地，甚至原有计划失误时，仍能使组织朝着既定的目标前进。一个不容改变的僵硬的计划，极大程度上会导致计划的失败。

Fayol emphasized that the planning process should be flexible enough so that plans can be altered and changed if the situation changes; managers must not be bound to a static plan.

二、计划的内容及类型

✍ The Contents of Planning and Types of Plans

（一）计划的内容

✧ The contents of planning

企业面临环境的复杂性以及管理工作的多样性，使得计划的内容更加丰富。但无论如何复杂多样，计划的内容都可以用"5W2H"来表示。

(1) What：要做什么或完成什么，明确工作任务。

(2) Who：由哪些人执行，明确工作任务的担当者。

(3) When：什么时候执行到何种程度，明确工作任务进度。

(4) Where：在什么地方进行工作，明确工作开展地点、区域。

(5) Why：为什么要这样做，明确工作起因、动机。

(6) How：怎么开展工作，明确工作方式方法。

(7) How many：完成多少工作，明确工作量。

5W2H: what, who, when, where, why, how, and how many

（二）计划的类型

✧ Types of plans

计划活动的结果表现为各种具体的计划形式，如新工厂的建设计划、新产品的开发计划。在实际工作中，计划有许多表现形式和层次。

Global Perspective

Is Planning Necessary？

Brian Allman of Reno, Nevada, was 17 years old when he bought a simple vending machine at Sam's Club for $425 and used it to start Bear Snax Vending, stocking the machine and four others he added later with Skittles, M&Ms, and Snickers to serve several small to midsize businesses, such as banks. Allman did this without apparently drawing up a business plan. Nine years after founding Bear Snax Vending without a formal business plan, Brian Allman was still running it. (Allman was also working as a financial advisor for financial services firm Edward Jones.)

Why Plan?

Almost everyone starting a new business is advised to write a business plan. The reasons: Creating such a plan helps you get financing. ("If you want us to invest our money, show us your plan.") It helps you think through important details. ("Don't rush things; it's best to get the strategy right.") Finally, it better guarantees your firm will succeed. (A study of 396 entrepreneurs in Sweden found that a greater number of firms that failed never had a formal business plan.)

"Going with What You've Got."

Even so, sometimes major decisions, including starting up companies, are made without much planning. Indeed, one study found that 41% of Inc. magazine's 1989 list of fastest-growing private firms didn't have a business plan and 26% had only rudimentary plans, percentages essentially unchanged in 2002. Planning of any sort, of course, requires time, and sometimes you need to make a quick decision and "go with what you've got"—with or without a plan.

（案例来源：Angelo Kinicki and Brian Williams. *Management: A Practical Introduction* (7th edition). New York: McGraw-Hill Education, 2015, p. 136）

1. 公司层、业务层、职能层计划

在大型组织中，计划可能是多层次的，一般包括公司层、事业或部门层和职能层。如果组织只生产单一产品或提供单一服务，那么任何组织的管理者都只需要进行单一的计划，就可以囊括所有的事情。但是许多组织的业务是多元化的，例如美国的通用电气公司（General Electric）是世界上最大的全球化公司之一，其公司业务涉及 150 多个行业，公司层由首席执行官杰弗瑞·梅尔特（Jeffrey Immelt）、高层管理团队及其公司层的支持人员构成，他们共同负责为整个组织制订计划和战略决策（图 5-2）。

1. Corporate-level plans, business-level plans and functional-level plans

In large organizations planning usually takes place at three levels of management: corporate, business or division, and department or functional.

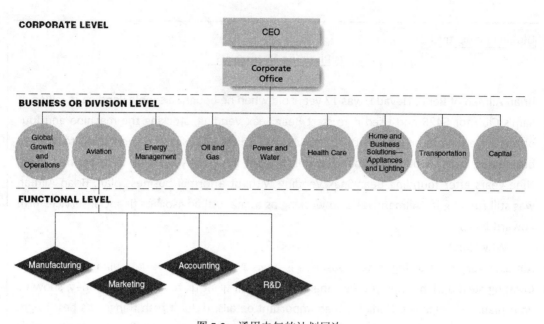

图 5-2　通用电气的计划层次
Figure 5-2　Levels of Planning at General Electric

公司层面的计划（Corporate-level Plan）是高层管理者做出的关于本组织使命、整体战略以及结构的决策。公司层面的战略决策决定了组织在哪个行业或哪个国家的市场进行竞争。例如，通用电气公司层的计划就是在所涉足的所有行业中应该保持市场份额第一或第二，无法达到这个目标的部门或子公司将会被卖掉，通用电气医疗系统出售给法国汤普森公司（Thomson）就是这个原因。

Corporate-level plan is the top management's decisions pertaining to the organization's mission, overall strategy, and structure.

公司层计划之下是业务层计划（Business-level Plan），在该层面上公司的不同子公司或业务单位在不同行业中竞争，例如通用电气就拥有 150 多个业务单位，包括航空、能源管理、石油和天然气、电力和水、医疗保健、交通运输等。每个子公司或业务单位都有自己的部门经理，他们在各自的子公司或业务单位中，负责根据公司层计划，来制定本单位的战略和计划。

公司层计划为分公司或业务单位经理创建业务层计划提供了框架。在组织中的业务层，每个业务单位的管理者都要围绕公司层目标来创建一个业务层计划，详细说明本业务单位的长期目标及实现该目标的战略和结构。业务层计划应提供业务单位或组织在行业内与竞争者有效竞争的具体方法。例如，通用的家电和照明事业部为实现公司的企业目标，即成为行业排名第一或第二的企业，制定了本部门的发展战略：降低成本。通过降低各部门的成本来降低价格，进而与主要竞争对手飞利浦公司（Philips）竞争，争夺市场份额。

Business-level plan is the divisional managers' decisions pertaining to divisions' long term goals, overall strategy, and structure.

在业务层计划之下是职能层计划（Functional-level Plan），即每个业务单位内都有自己的职能部门，如生产、营销、人力资源管理、研发等，例如通用航空与通用能源和医疗保健都有其自身的营销职能部门。各职能部门经理负责职能计划和战略的制定与实施，以提高管理工作效率，有效发挥该职能层的作用。职能层计划陈述了每个职能部门为达到业务层目标的职能目标，这反过来又促进了整个公司目标的实现。职能层战略是具体的行动计划，职能管理者可以按照提高每个职能部门执行力的具体活动方式来工作，以增加企业的商品和服务价值，从而提高顾客的价值。例如，与通用照明事业部的成本驱动计划一致，其生产职能部门采用的计划也是"在接下来的三年中减少20%的成本"，通过改进生产设施、开发全球电子商务网络等方式，来减少生产和库存成本。

Functional-level plan is the functional managers' decisions pertaining to the goals that they propose to pursue to help the division attain its business-level goals.

2. 战略计划、战术计划与作业计划

与上述分类方法相似，根据计划制订者的层次可以将计划分为战略计划、战术计划以及作业计划（见图5-3）。

2. Strategic plans, tactical plans and operational plans

图 5-3　计划金字塔

Figure 5-3　Planning Hierarchy

（资料来源：Richard L. Daft. *Management* (12th edition). Boston: Cengage Learning, 2014, p. 219）

战略计划的制订起于使命陈述，每一个组织都有一项使命（Mission），即它的宗旨（Purpose）或存在的意义，回答的是"我们为什么成为企业"的问题。管理者首先要界定公司所追求的价值是什么。任何一个组织只有确定了自己的使命，其行动才能位于正确的轨道上。因此，使命陈述对企业至关重要。例如柯达公司（Kodak）的使命陈述是"为消费者提供各种有效方法，使他们无论何时何地都能够拍摄、保存、处理、打印和传递图像"，脸书公司（Facebook）的使命是"一项联系你和周围人群的社会公共服务事业"，阿里巴巴集团（Alibaba）的使命是"让天下没有难做的生意"。一个典型的使命陈述应该包括的内容见表5-1。

An organization's mission is its purpose or reason for being. Mission statements answer the question, "What is our reason for being?" or "Why are we here?"

表 5-1　组织使命陈述包括的内容
Table 5-1　What a Mission Statement Includes

Customers: Who are the firm's customers?
Markets: Where does the firm compete geographically?
Concern for survival, growth, and profitability: Is the firm committed to growth and financial stability?
Philosophy: What are the firm's basic beliefs, values, and ethical priorities?
Concern for public image: How responsive is the firm to societal and environmental concerns?
Products or services: What are the firm's major products or services?
Technology: Is the firm technologically current?
Self-concept: What are the firm's major competitive advantage and core competencies?
Concern for employees: Are employee a valuable asset of the firm?

（资料来源：Fred R. David. *Strategic Management, Concepts and Applications* (11th edition). New Jersey: Prentice Hall, 2006, p. 70）

使命陈述的思想起源于彼得·德鲁克（Peter Drucker）。20 世纪 70 年代，他在《管理：任务、责任和实践》一书中首先提出了企业使命的概念，指出企业必须有本企业的宗旨和使命的明确界定，必须弄清楚"本企业是个什么样的企业""应该是个什么样的企业""将来应该是个什么样的企业" 3 个经典问题。20 世纪 90 年代以来，对使命陈述的研究越来越受到学术界的重视，学者们建议每个组织都应当有一个规范完整的使命陈述，一个优秀的使命陈述是有效的战略计划过程的关键要素，使命陈述表明了企业的目标和雄心，是公司行为的向导，而且还可以作为公司文化的象征，是其他一切规划行动的基础。使命陈述已经得到了我国学术界和企业界的重视，但在实践中，许多企业仍存在着自身定位不清、不明白企业存在的目的和意义的问题。有调查数据发现，目前我国企业的使命陈述普遍不规范，包含表 5-1 中 7～9 项使命要素的企业仅占 8%，多数企业使命陈述仅包含 3～4 项要素，这说明我国企业使命陈述包含要素数目偏低，准确性仍有待提高。

Global Perspective

<u>Mission Statements for Three Different Companies: Hilton, Amazon, & Patagonia</u>

Here are the mission statements for three companies, drawn from their websites. The mission statement for Hilton Hotels, a large company, reads: "To be the prominent global hospitality company—the first choice of guests, team members and owners alike." Amazon's mission statement is "Use the Internet to offer products that educate, inform, and inspire. We decided to build an online store that would be customer friendly and easy to navigate and would offer the broadest possible selection...."Clothing maker Patagonia's mission statement is to "Build the best product, cause no unnecessary harm, and use business to inspire and implement solutions to the environmental crisis."

（资料来源：根据相关网站信息整理，www.patagonia.com，www.retailindustry.about.com，www. hilton-worldwide.com）

企业确定了清晰的使命陈述之后,就可以制订战略计划。战略计划(Strategic Plans)指应用于整个组织、为组织未来较长时期设立总体目标和寻求组织在环境中的地位的计划。战略计划一般由组织的高层管理人员来制订。战略计划倾向于长远打算,可能会规划组织未来1~5年的行动步骤。战略计划的目的是在规定的时间期限内将组织目标转化为现实。通常表现为一个总的行动方案,指明了为实现目标而做的重点部署和资源安排。例如,一家小公司的目标设定为在 3 年内将市场占有率从 15%提高到20%。为实现该目标,可以采取下列战略计划:

(1)分配资源,开发竞争力强、增长潜力大的新产品;

(2)改进生产方式,以更低的成本获取更大的产出;

(3)开展研究,为现有产品和服务开发新用途。

为了确保组织能实现战略计划,组织还需要制订战术计划(Tactical Plans),主要适用于中层管理人员,战术计划说明了主要的子单位必须做什么,选择为实现战略计划而采取的措施,比战略计划具有更大的灵活性,时间长度一般是 6~24 个月。

作业计划(Operational Plans)是指制订总体目标如何实现的细节的计划,是根据战略计划和战术计划而制订的执行性计划。作业计划一般由低层管理人员制订。一般时间跨度较短,为 1~52 周。作业计划是部门管理者经常使用的工具,通过制订作业计划,可以明确基层主管、部门管理者和员工的个人计划,通常用时间表来规范作业计划。时间表为基层管理者完成每一个作业目标规定了精确的时限。当然,因为组织的资源是有限的,管理者需要为所有实现目标的行动方案分配资源,因此,作业计划还必须考虑成本与收益,与公司的预算计划相协调。

战略计划、战术计划与作业计划的关系如表 5-2 所示。总之,战略计划、战术计划和作业计划强调组织纵向层次的指导和衔接,它们应在统一计划、分级管理的原则下,合理划分管理权限,既要充分发挥战略计划对战术计划和作业计划的指导作用,又要通过战术计划和作业计划的实施保证战略计划目标的实现。

Strategic plans are plans that apply to the entire organization, establish the organization's overall goals, and seek to position the organization in terms of its environment.

The strategic priorities and policies are passed down to middle managers, who must do tactical planning—that is, they determine what contributions their departments or similar work units can make with their given resources during the next 6-24 months.

Operational plans are made by first-line management. Middle managers then pass these plans along to first-line managers to do operational planning—that is, they determine how to accomplish specific tasks with available resources within the next 1-52 weeks.

表 5-2 三种计划与三个管理层

Table 5-2 Three Levels of Management, Three Types of Planning

Management Level	Member	Types of Planning	Responsibility	Time
Top management	Chief executive officer, president, vice president, general managers, division heads	Strategic planning	Make long-term decisions about overall direction of organization. Managers need to pay attention to environment outside the organization, be future oriented, deal with uncertain and highly competitive conditions.	1-5 years
Middle management	Functional managers, product-line managers, department managers	Tactical planning	Implement policies and plans of top management, supervise and coordinate activities of first-line managers below, make decisions often without base of clearly defined information procedures.	6-24 months
First-line management	Unit manager, team leaders, first-line supervisors	Operational planning	Direct daily tasks of nonmanagerial personnel; decisions often predictable; following well-defined set of routine procedures.	1-52 weeks

Global Perspective

Strategic, Tactical, & Operational Plans: Southwest Airlines

Ranking No. 9 on Fortune's 2014 Most Admired Companies list, Dallas-based Southwest Airlines has inspired a host of low-fare imitators—big ones like Alaska and JetBlue and small ones like Allegiant, Frontier, Spirit, Sun Country, and Virgin America—which have grown rapidly in recent years compared to mainline carriers such as United, Delta, American, and US Airways. It has continually achieved its strategic goals and as of 2014 had been profitable for 41 consecutive years.

Strategic Plans. The goal of Southwest's top managers is to ensure that the airline is highly profitable, following the general strategy of (a) keeping costs and fares down, (b) offering a superior on-time arrival record, and (c) keeping passengers happy. One of the most important strategic decisions Southwest made was to fly just one type of airplane—Boeing 737s. (Several dozen Boeing 717s, inherited when the company acquired AirTran, were leased to Delta. Southwest has about 680 jets overall.) Thus, it is able to hold down training, maintenance, and operating expenses.

Another strategic decision was to create a strong corporate culture that, according to one former CEO, allows people to "feel like they're using their brains, they're using their creativity, they're allowed to be themselves and have a sense of humor, and they understand what the mission of the company is."

Tactical Plans. Cutting costs and keeping fares low has traditionally been a key tactical goal for Southwest's middle managers. For example, the organization cut costs in its maintenance program by doing more work on a plane when it's in for a check instead of bringing it in three different times. In addition, it has tried to get more use out of its planes every day by limiting the turnaround time between flights to 20 minutes, compared to up to an hour for other airlines.

Although now it flies longer flights between bigger cities, which uses fuel more efficiently but is more subject to delays, until recently Southwest flew short-haul flights to midsize cities to save time and money by avoiding traffic. There is just one class of seating, doing away with the distinction between coach and first class. Originally, even the boarding passes were reusable, being made of plastic (most passengers print out their own passes now). Finally, the airline saves by not feeding passengers: it serves mostly peanuts, no in-flight meals.

How do you make arrival times more reliable? To achieve this second tactical goal, middle managers did away with guaranteed seat reservations before ticketing, so that no-shows wouldn't complicate (and therefore delay) the boarding process. (It changed that policy slightly in 2007 to ensure that passengers paying extra for "business select" fares would be placed at the front of the line.)

In addition, as mentioned, the airline has tried to turn planes around in exactly 20 minutes, so that on-time departures are more apt to produce on-time arrivals. Although the airline is about 83% unionized, turnaround was helped by looser work rules, so that workers could pitch in to do tasks outside their normal jobs. "If you saw something that needed to be done," said one former employee, "and you thought you could do it, you did."

Unfortunately, in 2013, in an attempt to offer more convenient flight schedules, the airline instituted a new system to reduce times it allowed for flights and compressed its turnaround times even further—the result of which sent its on-time performance reeling to last place among U.S. carriers. Its involuntarily denied–boarding rate and mishandled-baggage rate also increased slightly.

Despite the delays, Southwest still retained its top ranking for having the lowest customer complaints. The difference lies in small things: the free peanuts (an emotional subject among travelers), switching of flights without charge, and no charge for checked-in luggage up to two pieces. (The airline does, however, charge for checking a third bag.)

Operational Plans. Consider how Southwest's first-line managers can enhance productivity in the unloading, refueling, and cleaning of arriving planes. "One example of productivity customers mention all the time," said former chairman Herb Kelleher, "if you look out the window when the airplane is taxiing toward the jetway, you see our ground crews charging before the airplane has even come to rest. Customers tell me that with other airlines nobody moves until the airplane has turned off its engines."

The New Southwest. In January 2014, Southwest began venturing into the international market, marking a significant shift. Its initial flights are to the Caribbean, but other international routes may be attempted later. Some operations, such as fast turnaround times, may be difficult to implement because of departure restrictions. Southwest also faces costly upgrades to its computer systems and an antiquated phone system, its traditionally low fares are not so low anymore, and it is negotiating with workers to try to achieve more productivity and flexibility.

（案例来源：Angelo Kinicki and Brian Williams. *Management: A Practical Introduction* (7th edition). New York: McGraw-Hill Education, 2015, pp. 144-145）

第二节 计划过程与方法

Garmin's Change in Direction

As the global leader in satellite navigation equipment, Garmin Ltd. recently hit a milestone number. It has sold more than 100 million of its products to customers—from motorists to runners to geocachers and more—who depend on the company's equipment to help "show them the way." Despite this milestone, the company's core business is in decline due to changing circumstances. In response, managers at Garmin, the biggest maker of personal navigation devices, are shifting direction. Many of you probably have a dashboard-mounted navigation device in your car and chances are it might be a Garmin. However, a number of cars now have "dashboard command centers which combine smartphone docking stations with navigation systems." Sales of Garmin devices have declined as consumers increasingly use their smartphones for directions and maps. However, have you ever tried to use your smartphone navigation system while holding a phone to look at its display? It's dangerous to hold a phone and steer. Also, GPS apps can "crash" if multiple apps are running. That's why the Olathe, Kansas-based company is taking action to "aggressively partner" with automakers to embed its GPS systems in car dashboards. Right now, its biggest in-dash contract is with Chrysler and its Uconnect dashboard system found in several models of Jeep, Dodge, and Chrysler vehicles. Garmin also is working with Honda and Toyota for dashboard systems in the Asian market.

Despite these new market shifts, customers have gotten used to the GPS devices and they have become an essential part of their lives. That's why Garmin's executive team still believes there's a market for dedicated navigation systems. It's trying to breathe some life into the product with new features, better designs, and more value for the consumer's money. For instance, some of the new features include faster searching for addresses or points of interest, voice activated navigation, and highlighting exit services such as gas stations and restaurants.

（案例来源：Stephen P. Robbins, David A. DeCenzo and Mary Coulter. *Fundamentals of Management: Essential Concepts and Applications* (9th edition). New York: Pearson, 2013, pp. 146-147）

　　管理者面对市场环境的不断变化，有时不得不进行业务转型，就像案例中佳明有限公司（Garmin Ltd.）一样，最后需要根据顾客市场的变化识别发展方向，并落实制订的方案。在不断变化的市场环境中，组织若想能适应环境发展的趋势，必须保证组织的转型方向准确。组织为实现这一目标需要做哪些工作，又该如何做呢？本节将重点围绕计划的过程和方法展开讨论。

一、计划制订过程

制订计划虽然会因层次或对象的不同而有所差异,但管理者在制订任何完整计划时,实质上都将遵循同样的步骤。小型的计划制订通常比较简单,实际操作中可能会省略或跳过其中的某些步骤,但对管理者来说,制订计划时思考的过程是类似的。图 5-4 列出了常用的计划制订过程。

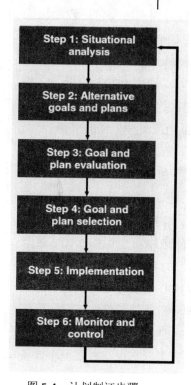

图 5-4 计划制订步骤

Figure 5.4 Formal Planning Steps

(一)步骤一:环境分析

计划制订以环境分析为起点,在组织有限的时间和资源内,计划制订者应收集、解释并总结与计划制订相关的信息。他们需要研究过去已经发生的事件,分析现状并预测未来趋势。所有的管理者都应当清楚而全面地了解未来可能出现的机会和威胁,知道其有利与不利之处,明晰需要解决的问题,以及为什么要解决这些问题,并预期可能会得到的结果。因此,分析挖掘和识别外界环境中和组织内的机会是制订计划的真正起点。

环境分析的重点是,聚焦于组织或业务单元内部,系统地分析内部环境的变化,同时剖析外部环境的影响,根据环境分析的结果,识别机会,提出计划假设。通过环境分析可以为制定计划的各种决策提供必要信息。

✧ Situational analysis

A process planners use, within time and resource constraints, to gather, interpret, and summarize all information relevant to the planning issue under consideration.

例如，一家杂志社打算向青少年市场推出一份足球类杂志。作为杂志社的管理者，应对如下内容进行分析：目前整个中国足球市场特别是青少年足球市场的宏观环境，该杂志对青少年的吸引力，该杂志对广告主的吸引力，本公司在足球杂志领域内是否有能力有效地服务这个市场，目前的经济条件下其他体育杂志在这个市场的销售情况等。这样分析之后将有助于公司决定是否继续下一步。

环境分析可以从宏观与微观两个方面进行。宏观主要是分析组织外部环境，外部环境因素主要包括政治法律（Political/Legal）、经济（Economic）、社会文化（Sociocultural）、技术（Technological）及自然环境（Environment）（简称 PESTE），即通过 PESTE 分析知晓外部环境发展的趋势与变化。通过这些分析，管理者就可以确定组织可以利用的机会，抵消或缓冲外在的威胁。

除了外部环境分析，组织还需要进行内部环境分析（Internal Analysis），主要聚焦于组织内在资源与能力。资源主要是组织拥有的资产、财务、实物、人力及无形资产等，这些可以用于研发、制造顾客所需要的产品。能力则是在上述业务活动中所需要的技能，即组织如何完成这些业务。组织主要的价值创造能力被称为核心竞争力（Core Competencies）。组织资源及核心竞争力是组织竞争的主要武器。内部分析之后，管理者应该能够确定组织的优势和劣势。前者是指组织做得好的方面或所拥有的独特资源；后者则是指组织做得不好方面或它现在需要但不具备的资源。

将内外部分析结合在一起就称为 SWOT 分析，因为它明确了组织的优势（Strengths）、劣势（Weaknesses）、机会（Opportunities）与威胁（Threats）。完成 SWOT 分析之后，管理者就可以制定相应的战略：①利用企业的优势与外部机遇；②缓冲或保护组织免受外部威胁；③改正致命的弱点。

（二）步骤二：确定备选目标与方案

在环境分析结果基础上，计划制订过程的第二步是产生组织可以追求的替代性目标以及为实现这些目标而制订的替代计划。这一步骤强调创造性，一旦该步骤产生了一系列替代方案，那么就需要对这些方案的优点和可行性进行评估。继续上一步骤中出版杂志的例子。作为管理者，可能会考虑是该选择年轻男性还是年轻女性作为目标顾客，或者将年轻男女都作为目标顾客；可能会考虑是选择通过网上订阅的渠道还是报摊售卖的方式进行销售等。

Opportunities are positive trends in the external environment; threats are negative trends.

The internal analysis provides important information about an organization's specific resources and capabilities.

The major value-creating capabilities of the organization are known as its core competencies.

Any activities the organization does well or any unique resources that it has are called strengths. Weaknesses are activities the organization doesn't do well or resources it needs but doesn't possess.

After completing the SWOT analysis, managers are ready to formulate appropriate strategies: (1) exploit an organization's strengths and external opportunities, (2) buffer or protect the organization from external threats, or (3) correct critical weaknesses.

✧ Confirm alternative goals and plans

Once a range of alternatives has been developed, their merits and feasibility will be evaluated.

目标（Goals）是管理者要达到的状态或终点，为了指导行为，提高效率，目标应该具体明确，且富有挑战性。例如，决定"增加今年的销售额"不如"决定未来 6 个月内将使华北市场的销售额增加 4 个百分点"更能指引和激励员工。具体且富有挑战性的目标表明了要达到的方向以及衡量目标获得成功的标准。

为了使目标制定更加有效，管理者可以利用 SMART 准则作为指导。SMART 准则是指：

- 具体性（Specific）：目标必须是精确的，员工应该知道未来需要做什么才算完成任务。

- 可衡量性（Measurable）：目标应尽可能地量化其预期的成果，这样可以很清晰地评价组织最终是否实现了目标。

- 可实现性但富有挑战性（Attainable but challenging）：制定的目标应该让员工意识到是可以实现的，这样不至于使其面对较高的目标时感到沮丧；但也不能过低，要让他们感到工作具有挑战性，这样他们会努力工作，且有创新意识。

- 相关性（Relevant）：每一个目标都应该有助于组织总体使命的实现，并与企业的价值观、道德标准一致。

- 时间约束性（Time-bound）：为完成目标制定一个日期规划，使组织的目标在规定日期内达成。

以格力集团的业务为例，看如何使用 SMART 准则制定目标。格力集团的空调业务是具有周期性的，夏天或冬天往往是销售或维修的旺季，每到这个时候，格力集团的各分公司就会发现业务量超出了公司正常的处理能力；而其他季节是淡季，业务量很少。因此，公司可以提出具体的目标，要求业务量较少的秋季和春季销售额增长 50%。这一目标可以通过跟踪与消费者签订的年度维修和更换合同的数量来衡量。淡季增加销售额的目标是可以实现的，因为消费者希望每年天一热（冷）空调就能够正常工作，如果各分公司能够考虑到这个需求，做到未雨绸缪，春天或秋天就开始宣传或开展市场促进活动，设计良好的维修或更换方案，那么就可能会吸引消费者在淡季签订服务合同，保证旺季来临时可以正常使用空调。该目标的实现对于企业提升年度销售额是非常有帮助的，同时，也可能因产品宣传和市场推广，提升公司的专业化形象，与公司使命相匹配。最后，通过让公司员工在淡季时开始推销维修和更换业务，明确计划开始的时间，使得该目标具有时间约束性。这就是 SMART 准则在制定目标时的具体应用。

Goals are the targets or ends the manager wants to reach.

- Specific: When goals are precise, employees know what they need to do to accomplish them.

- Measurable: As much as possible, the goal should quantify the desired results, so that there is no doubt whether it has been achieved.

- Attainable (but challenging): Employees need to recognize that they can attain their goals, so they won't become discouraged. However, they also should feel challenged to work hard and be creative.

- Relevant: Each goal should contribute to the organization's overall mission and be consistent with its values, including ethical standards.

- Time-bound: Effective goals specify a target date for completion.

（三）步骤三：评估备选目标与计划

接下来，管理者要评价每一个备选目标和计划的优势、劣势和潜在影响，考虑目标的优先级别，有时可能会取消其中的一些目标。此外，管理者还要考虑备选计划在多大程度上能满足较高优先级的目标，以及考虑每一个备选计划的成本和可能的投资回报。在前面关于杂志社出版发行足球类杂志的例子中，管理者需要对备选目标进行评价，可能会认为单独在报摊销售杂志不足以赢利来保证发行，还需要通过其他在线方式（如：博客）提高利润。

✧ Evaluate alternative goals and plans

Managers evaluate the advantages, disadvantages, and potential effects of each alternative goal and plan.

（四）步骤四：选择目标和计划

一旦管理者评估了目标和计划，他们就需要从中选择最适合的可行性方案。评估过程识别了目标和计划的优先级并在它们之间进行了权衡。例如，假如杂志社计划推出一系列新出版物，而管理者仅想选择其中的一些，这时他就需要在每种出版物所需的前期投资、每个市场的大小以及哪一个最适合公司现有的生产线或公司形象等要素之间进行权衡。这一过程中，经验判断往往起到了重要的作用，管理者还可以使用实证分析、数据调查等其他方式帮助他进行权衡和选择。

✧ Choose goal and plan

Once managers have assessed the goals and plans, they select the most appropriate and feasible alternative.

一般情况下，一个正规的计划制订过程最终会产生一组目标和计划，它们对应着一组特定的情境是适当且可行的。在一些组织中，备选方案的产生、评估及选择步骤同样会生成计划情境。不同的应急计划与不同的情境相对应，管理者往往会首先选择与最有可能出现的情境相匹配的目标和计划。但是，管理者也要做好准备，一旦环境发生变化，转换到另一种情境下时，应迅速转换到与之相配的计划上面。这种方法有助于组织做好对危机的预测和管理，使组织有更大的灵活性和响应性。

（五）步骤五：执行目标和计划

管理者选择了目标和计划之后必须实现它。恰当的执行过程是实现目标的关键。管理者和员工必须理解所选的计划，并且有足够的资源来保证该计划的顺利实施。在计划制订的前期步骤中，包括员工在内都已经为计划执行阶段铺平了道路，员工对于目标或计划的了解程度、认知程度越高，且目标或计划可能推动员工的发展的程度越大，该目标或计划对员工的激励性就越强。最后，计划还要与组织中的其他系统相联系，尤其是预算和奖励制度，这有助于确保其成功实现。如果管理者没有或无法找到充足的财务资源来执行这个计划，那么该计划就注定失败；同样，

✧ Implement goal and plan

Proper implementation is key to achieving goals.

将目标达成与组织的奖励系统相联系，如奖金、晋升等，则有助于激励员工正确地实现目标和实施计划。

（六）步骤六：监督与控制计划

⟡ Monitor and control plan

第六个步骤有时会被忽视，但对于计划制订全过程而言，监督与控制计划至关重要，没有它，人们无法判定计划是否取得了成功。如前所述，计划工作是一个循环工作，它不断地持续、重复。管理者必须持续监控各工作单位的目标和计划的实施过程，还要开发控制系统来衡量绩效以及采取相应的措施纠正计划实施过程中的不当行为，或者及时发现情境因素是否发生了变化。在足球杂志出版的例子中，报摊和线上订阅的销售报告是必要的，它可以让管理者知道新杂志推出后市场情况究竟如何，如果订阅销售没有预期的那样好，管理者就需要更改销售计划。关于控制的相关重要问题将在后续章节中进行详细讨论。

Although it is sometimes ignored, the sixth step in the formal planning process—monitoring and controlling—is essential. Without it, you will never know whether your plan is succeeding.

需要指出的是，在计划制订过程中，产生备选方案、评价备选方案以及选择备选方案这几个步骤，实际上也是决策的过程。由此可以看出，决策是计划活动的核心。只有经过决策，计划方案才能产生。计划就是不断决策的过程。所以从某种程度上来说，计划就是决策。

二、计划制定方法

✍ **Planning Methods**

计划工作的效率高低和质量好坏在很大程度上取决于所采用的计划方法。过去人们常常采用定额换算法、系数推导法以及经验平衡等方法制订计划。

● 定额换算法。这是根据有关的技术经济定额来计算确定计划指标的方法。例如，根据各人、各岗位的工作定额求出部门应完成的工作量，再加总各部门的工作量得到整个组织的计划工作量。

● 系数推导法。这是利用过去两个相关经济指标之间长期形成的稳定比率来推算确定计划期的有关指标的方法，也称比例法。例如，在一定的生产技术条件下，某些原材料的消耗量与企业产量之间有一个相对稳定的比率，根据这个比率和企业的计划产量，就可以推算出这些原材料的计划需用量；也可以根据上一年度完成计划情况，再乘以一个系数来确定计划年度的工作量，并以此确定该年度的计划指标。

● 经验平衡法。这是根据计划工作人员以往的经验，把组织的总目标和各项任务分解分配到各个部门，并经过与各部门的讨价还价最终确定各部门计划指标的方法。

这些方法已经不能满足现代计划工作的要求,因为现代组织面对更加复杂和动荡的外部环境,要保证组织能够稳定地、持续地、高速地发展,就要更加准确地预测环境的变化,制定出可靠的计划指标,同时要做好综合平衡。此外,还要考虑当前利益与长远利益的一致性,既能确保眼前的繁荣,又能顾及将来的发展。要做好这些工作,首要的一步就是要有切实可行的计划。现代计划方法可以帮助确定各种复杂的经济关系,提高综合平衡的准确性,并能采用计算机辅助工作,加快计划工作的速度,已被越来越多的计划工作者所采用。

下面简要介绍两种常用的现代计划方法。

（一）甘特图

甘特图（Gantt Chart）历史上是用于产品生产中进行计划与排序的一种常用工具,最早由美国工程师和社会学家亨利·甘特（Henry Gantt）于 1917 年提出。甘特图用横轴表示时间,纵轴表示要安排的活动,线条表示在整个期间上计划的指标和实际的活动完成情况。管理者可以通过甘特图来事先安排好项目各项活动的进度,然后再随着时间的推移,对比计划进度与实际进度,进行监控工作,调整注意力到最需要加快速度的地方,使整个项目按期完成。甘特图是基于作业排序的目的、将活动与时间联系起来的一种方法。图 5-5 是制造电动高尔夫车的甘特图。

甘特图的优点是直观地标明了各活动的计划进度和当前进度,能动态地反映项目进展情况,缺点是难以反映多项活动之间存在的复杂的逻辑关系。

✧ Gantt chart

A Gantt chart is a graphical scheduling technique historically used in production operations.

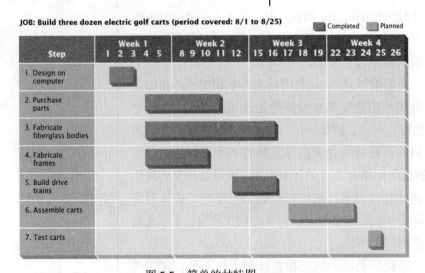

图 5-5　简单的甘特图

Figure 5-5　Sample Gantt Chart

（资料来源：Robert Kreitner. *Management* (11th edition). New York: Houghton Mifflin Harcourt Publishing Company, 2009, p. 165）

（二）网络计划技术

20 世纪 50 年代，为了适应科学研究和新的生产组织管理的需要，国外陆续出现了一些计划管理的新方法。1956 年，美国杜邦公司（DuPont）研究创立了网络计划技术的关键路径法（Critical Path Method，缩写为 CPM）。1958 年初，这一方法被用于一个价值 1000 万美元的新化工厂的建设，使整个工程的工期缩短了 4 个月。1958 年，美国海军特种计划局和洛克希德航空公司规划和研究在核潜艇上发射"北极星"导弹的计划时首次提出了计划评审方法（Program Evaluation and Review Technique，缩写为 PERT），这一方法的使用，使原定 6 年的研制任务提前两年完成。

如今，PERT 在国防和航天之外的领域也得到了广泛应用。PERT 是一个描述完成项目所需要的活动的顺序以及时间或成本的流程图。其核心技术为关键路径法。关键路径网络图是一种类似流程图的箭线图，它描绘出项目包含的各种活动（作业）的先后次序，标明每项活动的时间。其中，用圆圈表示作业的开始点和终结点；用黑色箭头表示作业，在其上面和下面分别标明各项作业的名称和时间，用红色向右面箭头表示关键作业，即关键路径（Critical Path），是 PERT 网络中的活动完成的最长路径，表示此路径上的作业必须按时开工和完成，否则会影响整个工期。

PERT 包括以下几个具体操作步骤。

第一步：对项目任务进行具体分析，确定完成任务所需要的各项作业，明确各项作业之间的相互关系，估计作业完成所需时间，画出作业分析表（表 5-3）。

◇ Network planning technique

One of the most widely recognized programming tools used by managers is a technique referred to simply as PERT.

An acronym for Program Evaluation and Review Technique (PERT) is a flowchart diagram showing the sequence of activities needed to complete a project and the time or cost associated with each.

Critical path is the longest sequence of activities in a PERT network.

Steps of PERT:

1. Determine the specific events and activities in the project, and clarify the relationships between each event and your estimate of the expected time to complete each by drawing a task analysis table.

表 5-3　任务分析表
Table 5-3　Task Analysis Table

Event	Preceding Event	Follow-on Event	Expected Time (Days)
a	—	b,c,d,e	60
b	a	j	45
c	a	f	10
d	a	g	20
e	a	g,h	40
f	c	j	18
g	d，e	i	30
h	d	j	15
i	g	j	25
j	b，f，h，i	—	35

第二步：根据作业分析表中各作业之间的前后关系绘制网络计划图，如图 5-6 所示。并计算各条路线的时间周期，如表 5-4 所示。

2. Draw a PERT network chart based on the data in the table. Calculate the length of time that each path of activities will take.

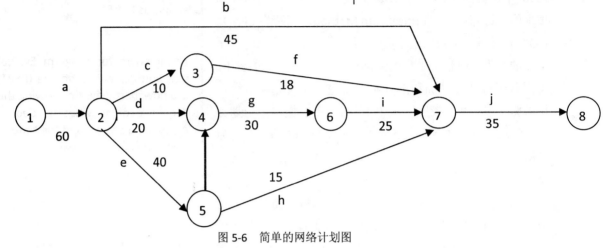

图 5-6　简单的网络计划图
Figure 5-6　A Simple PERT Chart

表 5-4　路线组成及工期
Table 5-4　Path and Time Limit for a Project

Path	Activities	Length of time (days)
1	①—②—⑦—⑧	60+45+35=140
2	①—②—③—⑦—⑧	60+10+18+35=123
3	①—②—④—⑥—⑦—⑧	60+20+30+25+35=170
4	①—②—⑤—④—⑥—⑦—⑧	60+40+30+25+35=190
5	①—②—⑤—⑦—⑧	60+40+15+35=150

第三步：根据图中确定的关键作业寻找关键路径。可以看出第 4 条路线是工期最长的，此即关键路径。关键路径上的作业我们称之为关键作业。关键作业是必须按时开工和完成的作业，否则将影响整个工期。

第四步：优化网络。即挖掘非关键路径上的潜力，重新平衡人力、物力，重新确定作业所需要的时间，以非关键作业的潜力支持关键作业，减少关键作业时间，从而缩短关键路径上的整个工期时间。

3. Decide the project's critical path (the longest sequence of activities).

4. Optimize the network to reduce the length of time in the project.

虽然通过网络图可以了解计划全貌，了解各项活动之间的依存制约关系，进而掌握关键路径，并对其进行有效控制，但是网络图也不是万能的。它推动了计划工作，但并不等于计划工作；它建立了一种正确理解和使用合理控制原则的工作环境，但不会使控制自动进行。如果计划本身模糊不清，并对时间进度做出不合情理的"瞎估计"，那么网络计划技术也许毫无用处。所以，网络计划技术的有效性取决于对该项技术的正确运用。

第三节　目标管理

An University's Standing Plan on Diversity

At the University of Western Australia, a process called the "Diversity Job Bank" (DJB) is aimed at implementing the university's Workforce Diversity Strategy. The DJB is specifically targeted at encouraging employment for three specific groups of people: indigenous Australians, people with disabilities, and people from culturally and linguistically diverse backgrounds. The job bank operates as a brokerage service to aid managers in the recruitment of general staff in all faculties, departments and administration units within the university. It endeavors to offer employment to the above groups as ongoing employment, fixed-term employment, casual employment, and traineeships and cadetships.

Traineeships are structured programs that are approved by the Department of Education and Training in fields of employment within business administration and information technology. They may involve all on-the-job training, or a mixture of on-the-job and off-the-job training, but trainees must work at least 20 hours per week. They must also undergo assessment of their progress related to defined training modules. Subsidies are available for people from the target employment groups.

The cadetship program within the priority employment group is the National Indigenous Cadetship Project (NICP), which is a Commonwealth government initiative designed to improve the professional employment prospects of indigenous Australians. Cadets receive a study allowance while undertaking full-time study and at least 12 weeks' paid work experience each year. There is a reimbursement of the study allowance available from the government to the employing organization, and the NICP provides help in finding suitable people to undertake the cadetships.

There is also a program called "Supported Teams", which is aimed at assisting the employment of people with disabilities. This program works on a "fair day's work for a fair day's pay" principle and usually involves employing people in this category in small teams of two to three people for periods of up to 20 hours per week. These employees are supervised at all times, and subsidies are available to employing units who offer work under this scheme. Managers and supervisors within the university can become involved in the university's Workforce Diversity Strategy by recruiting staff through the DJB utilizing one of the range of employment and training options outlined above. There are guidelines available for managers and supervisors, which are designed to explain the process involved in selecting staff through the DJB.

In terms of planning, the DJB at the University of Western Australia would be considered a standing plan for managers seeking to arrange the work and tasks required within his or her area of responsibility. The availability of a job bank of this nature also provides an incentive for a manager to develop plans that meet objectives of social responsibility, rather than just getting tasks achieved in the most efficient and economical way. As a result, the university won the Prime Minister's Award for the Employment of People with Disabilities in two successive years.

（案例来源：Stephen Robbins, Rolf Bergman, Ian Stagg and Mary Coulter. *Management* (6th edition). Melbourne: Pearson Australia Group Pty Ltd., 2012, pp. 303-304）

　　上一节中介绍了计划制订的过程，提出计划要明确目标，目标应该清晰且富有挑战性。但是，明确的目标并不意味着一个组织只可以设定或完成一个目标。事实上，一个组织可以同时设定多个目标。就像案例中所讲述的那样，一个组织可能存在着多样化的目标。那么，各个目标之间是什么样的关系？该如何管理这些目标？如何通过科学的管理，充分利用组织的资源来实现各种目标？本节将围绕目标管理相关理论来探讨解决上述问题的方法。

一、目标管理

目标管理（Management by Objectives）产生于 20 世纪 50 年代中期的美国，是以科学管理理论和行为科学理论为基础形成的一套管理制度。1954 年德鲁克(Peter Drucker）在其名著《管理实践》中提出了一个具有划时代意义的概念——目标管理。德鲁克认为，对每个企业员工分派目标并实行责任制度可以大大提高管理效率，企业的运作要求企业各项工作都必须以整个企业的目标为导向，尤其是每个管理人员的工作必须注重企业整体的成功。他提出，任何企业必须形成一个真正的整体。每个成员所做的贡献各不相同，但是，他们都必须为着一个共同的目标做贡献。他们的努力必须全都朝着同一方向，他们的贡献都必须融成一体，产生出一种整体的业绩，没有隔阂，没有冲突，没有不必要的重复劳动。德鲁克揭示了目标管理的内涵，至今在管理界仍有很大的影响，对深入研究目标管理具有指导意义。

美国行为科学家伦西斯·利克特（Rensis Likert）侧重于行为科学的理论研究，他认为要提高组织管理效率，必须为组织设立高标准的目标。一个组织的领导和每一个成员都要有高标准的志向，树立高标准的目标。通过这些目标的实现，既达到组织目标，又满足组织成员的个人需要。他对目标管理的贡献在于把个人目标与组织目标联系在一起，充分考虑了人在组织发展中的作用。同时，他还指出目标管理的实现与领导方式有关，组织在实施目标管理中必须考虑不同的领导方式与管理目标的融合，不能盲目照搬别人的做法。

加拿大的行为管理学家罗伯特·豪斯（Robert J. House）认为领导者的工作是帮助下属达到他们的目标，并提供必要的指导和支持以确保他们各自的目标与组织的总体目标一致。他从领导方式的角度说明了目标管理的应用不是孤立的，应贯彻从上到下、再从下到上的几个过程，这就要求组织领导者必须具有良好的民主作风，用好的领导方式去推动目标管理的开展。

简言之，目标管理就是一个全面的管理系统，将许多关键的活动连接在一起，使组织和个人目标得以高效率地完成。其实质是让组织的主管人员和员工亲自参加目标的制定，在工作中实行自我管理和自我控制，努力完成工作目标。其主要目的是以目标来激励员工的自我管理意识，激发员工行动的自觉性，充分发挥其智慧和创造力，以期最终形成员工与组织同呼吸、共命运的共同体。

☞ **Management by Objectives (MBO)**

Management by Objectives (MBO) is a comprehensive managerial system that integrates many key managerial activities in a systematic manner and is consciously directed toward the effective and efficient achievement of organizational and individual objectives.

The philosophy of MBO is self-direction and self-control.

The purpose of MBO is to motivate rather than to control subordinates.

二、目标管理的优缺点

目前很多企业都在应用目标管理法,因为多数管理者都认同它是一种有效的管理工具,但也有管理者指出,目标管理同样存在着许多弱点（见表 5-5）。当管理者及员工的工作重点聚焦在目标上时企业目标更容易实现,使用目标管理的绩效考核系统有助于员工了解自己的工作绩效对企业的贡献,从而给员工归属感。当员工承诺要达到某种目标时,将有助于改善其工作表现,而且一旦他们决定要实现期望目标时就更容易被激励。但当目标管理法使用不当时将会导致一系列问题,例如过分强调"完成目标"可能忽视了员工为达到目标而采取的方式,人们可能会偷工减料,忽略潜在问题,甚至做出不道德行为以实现目标。

✍ **Advantages and Disadvantages of MBO**

Any widely used management technique is bound to generate debate about its relative strengths and weaknesses, and MBO also has some shortcomings.

表 5-5　目标管理的优缺点
Table 5-5　MBO's Strengths and Limitations

Strengths	1.	MBO blends planning and control into a rational system of management.
	2.	MBO forces an organization to develop a top-to-bottom hierarchy of objectives.
	3.	MBO emphasizes end results rather than good intentions or personalities.
	4.	MBO encourages self-management and personal commitment through employee participation in setting objectives.
Limitations	1.	MBO is too often sold as a cure-all.
	2.	MBO is easily stalled by authoritarian (Theory X) managers and inflexible bureaucratic policies and rules.
	3.	MBO takes too much time and effort and generates too much paperwork.
	4.	MBO's emphasis on measurable objectives can be used as a threat by overzealous managers.

三、目标管理步骤

作为一种方法,目标管理的基本步骤如图 5-7 所示。要进行成功的目标管理,就必须完成以下 4 个主要步骤。

✍ **The Process of MBO**

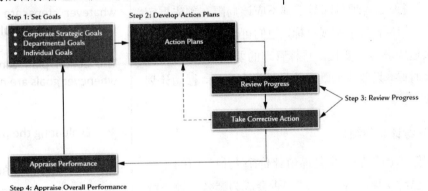

图 5-7　目标管理过程模型
Figure 5-7　Model of the MBO Process
（资料来源：Richard L. Daft. *Management* (12th edition). Boston: Cengage Learning, 2014, p. 230）

（一）确定目标

这是目标管理最困难的一步。确定目标涉及各个层面的员工，还要通过日常工作，回到"我们努力实现什么目标？"这个问题。一个优秀的目标应该是具体而现实的，有明确的对象和时限，责任落到实处。目标可以是定量的，也可以是定性的，这取决于结果是否可以测量。定量目标可用数值来表示，例如"推销员王勇12月份需要发展16位新顾客"。定性目标则用这样的陈述来表示："明年营销部将通过改善顾客服务来减少顾客的抱怨。"目标应该由组织和员工一起制定。员工与管理者之间的相互协调是实现目标最强有力的保证。如果任务由团队来完成，那么所有的团队成员都应该参与制定目标。

（二）制订行动计划

行动计划详细说明了实现一定的目标所需要的行动过程，个人和部门都要制订行动计划。虽然目标管理法强调员工的自我控制和自我管理，但是并不等于管理者可以完全放手不管。管理者应该根据组织或部门的整体目标，制订全面的行动计划，并以此为依据来判断和评价员工的个人行动计划是否准确。当发现员工个人的行动计划不够准确或与组织的整体目标相矛盾时，应及时采取措施，提出问题，协助和指导员工对其行动计划进行修订，以保证组织整体目标的实现。

（三）评估进程

要保证行动计划起作用，定期的进程评估是很重要的。进程评估可以在管理者和下属之间非正式地进行。组织可能希望，在年度的第3个月、第6个月或者第9个月时进行评估。这种定期检查可以使管理者和员工们了解工作状况，确定当前工作与目标的一致性，或者是否有必要采取纠偏行动。管理者和员工都不应该局限在预先框定的模式中；相反，为了实现目标，他们可以采取一切必要的措施来适应环境的变化。目标管理的要点是实现目标，不论什么时候，只要我们既定的目标没有实现，行动计划就可以改变。

（四）考评总体绩效

目标管理的最后一步是谨慎评价个人和部门的年度目标是否已经实现。目标的实现与否会成为绩效考评系统的一部分，也会成为加薪或其他奖励的依据。对部门和整

◇ Setting goals

Setting goals involves employees at all levels and looks beyond day-to-day activities to answer the question, "What are we trying to accomplish?"

However, goals should be derived jointly. Mutual agreement between employee and supervisor creates the strongest commitment to achieving goals. In the case of teams, all team members may participate in setting goals.

◇ Developing action plans

An action plan defines the course of action needed to achieve the stated goals. Action plans are made for both individuals and departments.

◇ Reviewing the process

A periodic progress review is important to ensure that action plans are working.
Managers and employees should not be locked into predefined behavior and must be willing to take whatever steps are necessary to produce meaningful results. The point of MBO is to achieve goals. The action plan can be changed whenever goals are not being met.

◇ Evaluating the performance

The final step in MBO is to evaluate whether annual goals have been achieved for both individuals

个组织绩效的考评结果，决定了明年的目标是否需要调整。一般来说，目标管理以年度为单位循环进行。如果目标顺利完成，上下级应在一起总结经验，讨论下一阶段的目标；如果目标没有完成，应分析原因，总结教训，并以此为基础，结合组织实际状况，明确下一阶段的目标。

and departments. Success or failure to achieve goals can become a part of the performance appraisal system and the designation of salary increases and other rewards. The appraisal of departmental and overall organization performance shapes goals for the next year. The MBO cycle repeats itself annually.

Global Perspective

From the Past to the Present：1954–1960s and 1970s–Present

All you need to know about MBO!

Management by objectives (MBO) isn't new—it was a popular management approach in the 1960s and 1970s. The concept can be traced back to Peter Drucker, who first popularized the term in his 1954 book *The Practice of Management*. Its appeal lies in its emphasis on converting overall objectives into specific objectives for organizational units and individual members.

How Is MBO Used?

- MBO makes goals practical and operational as they "cascade" down through the organization.

- Overall broad objectives are translated into specific objectives for each succeeding organizational level—division, departmental, individual.

- Result: a hierarchy that links objectives at one level to those at the next level.

- For each individual employee, MBO provides specific personal performance objectives.

- If all individuals achieve their goals, then the unit's goals will be attained. If all units attain their goals, then the divisional goals will be met until the organization's overall goals are achieved!

Does MBO Work?

- Assessing MBO effectiveness is not easy!

- Research on goal-setting research gives us some answers:
    ◇ Specific, difficult-to-achieve goals—an important part of MBO—produce a higher level of output than do no goals or generalized goals such as "do your best."
    ◇ Feedback—also an important part of MBO—favorably affects performance because it lets a person know whether his or her level of effort is sufficient or needs to be increased.
    ◇ Participation—also strongly advocated by MBO—has not shown any consistent relationship to performance.

Absolutely Critical to Success of MBO Program:

Top management commitment to the process. When top managers have a high commitment to MBO and are personally involved in its implementation, productivity gains are higher than without that commitment.

（案例来源：Stephen P. Robbins, David A. DeCenzo and Mary Coulter. *Fundamentals of Management: Essential Concepts and Applications* (9th edition). New York: Pearson, 2013, p. 135）

Planning

Unity

Continuity

Accuracy

Flexible

Corporate-level plan

Business-level plan

Functional-level plan

Mission

Strategic plan

Tactical plan

Operational plan

Situational analysis

SWOT analysis

Goals

Gantt chart

PERT

Management by objectives (MBO)

讨论问题 DISCUSSION QUESTIONS

1. Please explain why planning is beneficial. Will planning become more or less important to managers in the future? Why?

2. If planning is so crucial, why do some managers choose not to do it? What would you tell these managers?

3. "Organizations that fail to plan are planning to fail." Agree or disagree? Please give your reasons.

4. How do strategic, operational, and tactical plans differ?

5. What is a SWOT analysis, and why is it important to managers? Do a personal SWOT analysis. Assess your personal strengths and weaknesses (skills, talents, abilities). What are you good at? What are you not so good at? What do you enjoy doing? Not enjoy doing? Then, identify career opportunities and threats by researching job prospects in the industry you're interested in.

6. List the six steps in the planning process. Suppose you are a top executive of a bookstore and you want to launch a new company website. Provide examples of activities you would carry out during each step to create the site.

7. Many companies have a goal of becoming more environmentally sustainable. One of the most important steps they can take is controlling paper waste. Choose a company—any type, any size. You've been put in charge of creating a program to do this for your company. Set goals and develop plans. Prepare a report for your boss (that is, your professor) outlining these goals and plans.

8. What is network planning technique? Briefly explain the steps of PERT.

9. Define the Management by Objectives (MBO) and explain the philosophy and purpose of MBO. Is there any advantage or disadvantage of MBO?

10. Please describe the process of MBO. Could you give an example of MBO based on your experiences?

Icelandic Volcano, 1; Global Commerce, 0

Global businesses, including airlines, have had to develop plans, policies and procedures to handle a wide range of potential threats, such as the increased risk of terrorism, a worldwide influenza pandemic and global warming, just to mention a few. However, few global businesses or airlines thought to factor into their planning scenarios a volcanic eruption in Iceland. This volcano has a funny name—Eyjafjallajökull—but its impact on global businesses was no laughing matter. The eruption imposed the biggest airspace closure since the terrorist attacks in the US on 11 September 2001.

When the volcano erupted on 14 April 2010, the plume of volcanic ash that spread across thousands of kilometers disrupted air travel and global commerce for more than a week. The giant ash cloud affected most of northern and western European airspace, closing terminals from Dublin to Moscow. Because of the risk of possible engine shutdowns due to the ash cloud, airlines cancelled nearly 80 percent of their flights across Europe. At the event's peak, only about 5,000 out of a normal 22,000 flights went ahead. According to estimates by the International Air Transport Association (IATA), airlines were losing 200 million ($290 million) a day.

Qantas had to cancel numerous flights into and out of Europe, and more than 15,000 of its passengers were affected, costing Qantas about $1.5 million a day. An estimated 60,000 Australians were stranded either in or on their way to Europe, and became increasingly frustrated by the uncertain duration of the delay. Other airlines operating out of Australian airports also affected by the event in Europe were British Airways, Virgin Atlantic, Singapore Airlines, Thai Airways, Malaysia Airlines, Etihad Airways and Finnair.

As thousands of flights were cancelled across Europe, hundreds of thousands of air travelers could not reach their destination. Melbourne-based cosmetics entrepreneur Gillian Franklin was trapped in Geneva, Switzerland, for nearly a week. While she acknowledged that Geneva was a beautiful place to be stranded in, she also said it was costing her "a fortune." Although she could keep in contact with her office in Melbourne via email, she missed important meetings in Italy and in Melbourne. Also affected by the cancelled flights was Marthin De Beer, vice president of emerging technologies at Cisco Systems, who was due to fly to Oslo to discuss the final aspects of Cisco's acquisition of Tandberg, a Norwegian teleconferencing company. However, when his flight was cancelled, he and Tandberg's CEO, Fredrik Halvorsen, used their merged companies' equipment to hold a virtual press conference.

Other businesses, though, were not as lucky, especially those with high-value, highly perishable products such as berries, fresh fish and flowers, and medicines and pharmaceuticals. African farmers, European fresh-produce importers, and flower traders from Kenya to the Netherlands found their businesses threatened by the air traffic shutdown. Even garment manufacturers in Bangladesh and electronic component manufacturers in Europe and Southeast Asia were affected. For instance, BMW had to scale back its work hours, and had even prepared for possibly shutting down production, at its US assembly plant in Georgia because it depended on trans-Atlantic flights to bring transmissions and other components from German factories.

It could be argued that some of the havoc that was created during the period was caused by poor planning and little attention to risk management. For example, the International Organization for Standardization (ISO), which advocates the use of ISO 31,000 risk management standards, suggested that organizations with a strong culture of risk management seemed to have been better prepared. For example, United Parcel Service (UPS) quickly redirected air freight bound from Asia to Europe to Istanbul and then loaded it on to trucks for delivery to its final destination. According to ISO, UPS was one of the exceptions, as most other organizations that were affected just sat and wondered when the ash would blow away and aircraft would resume flying.

A volcanic event like the one that took place in Iceland does not appear to have been a risk that the airlines and many other companies and governments around the world had planned for. The eruption of Eyjafjallajökull and the blanketing of much of Europe in an ash cloud is a great example of how an event with a low probability of occurrence, but severe consequences if it does occur, tends to be overlooked by management when examining potential risk to corporate objectives. Considering the known impact on aviation of past volcanic eruptions in Asia (for example, in Indonesia and the Philippines), it is surprising that airlines, global companies and governments had made no plans to manage such a disruption-related risk. In an increasingly global economy with a high reliance on global business travel and "just-in-time" delivery of fresh goods and components in many industries, the need to plan for such events now seems quite obvious.

（案例来源：Stephen Robbins, Rolf Bergman, Ian Stagg and Mary Coulter. *Management* (6th edition). Melbourne: Pearson Australia Group Pty Ltd., 2012, p. 316）

Discussion Questions

1. Is it true that a company could do nothing in the face of the natural disaster? How could the company make such plans?

2. What could BMW, airline, a small flower grower do in this type of situation?

3. What types of plans do you see described in this case? Please explain it briefly. And what lessons can managers learn from this case?

第六章 组织

学习目标

1. 理解组织的类型和分类
2. 理解组织结构的内涵和影响因素
3. 掌握组织设计的原则、实施过程和基本步骤
4. 描述组织文化的作用以及组织文化建设的内容

Learning Outcomes

1. Understand the type of organization.
2. Understand the nature of organizational structure and its influential factors.
3. Master the principles and the steps for designing organizational structure.
4. Describe the functions and contents of organizational culture.

主要内容

第一节 组织的类型
第二节 组织结构
第三节 组织设计
第四节 组织文化

Contents

6.1 The Type of Organization
6.2 Organizational Structure
6.3 Organizational Design
6.4 Organizational Culture

第一节 组织的类型

Big Changes at Amoco

Amoco, like most other global oil companies, performs three major activities: (1) It explores for oil and pumps it out of the ground. (2) It refines the crude oil into gasoline and sells it through a nationwide system of gas stations. (3) It operates a chemicals company that uses the crude oil to manufacture plastics and other petroleum products that are sold to other companies. Throughout the 1970s, Amoco used a "three legged structure" to manage their three activities. Independent operating subsidiaries managed each activity.

Each of the three subsidiaries has its own hierarchy of top managers who are responsible for overseeing the many business divisions of the subsidiary. The top managers of each subsidiary reported to Amoco's corporate level managers, who oversaw their activities and made the final decision on what the subsidiaries should be doing. Under this setup, divisional managers within the subsidiaries are responsible for developing effective business-level strategies, but important decision making about whether to implement these strategies took place at the corporate level. As a result, strategy implementation often took a long time because of the many layers of managers separating Amoco's corporate managers from the managers of each division. The slow decision making hampered divisional managers' attempts to build a competitive advantage. The three-legged structure worked well enough in the good economic times of the early 1970s when oil prices steadily increased. Then, in the late 1970s, global oil companies experienced a shock. Oil prices tumbled and 20 years later were still flat. Amoco and other global oil companies—such as Exxon, British Petroleum, Mobil, and Elf Aquitane—experienced increased pressure to reduce costs and boost sales because of flat gasoline prices. In the attempt to boost profits, most large global oil companies—including Amoco—lay off thousands of employees; indeed, some analysts estimate that 500, 000 jobs were lost in the 1980s and early 1990s in the U.S. oil industry. Despite laying off over one-quarter of Amoco's workforce, managers were unable to boost profitability. As a result, in 1995, top management took a close look at Amoco's organizational structure to identify ways to increase both efficiency and effectiveness.

H. Laurance Fuller, Amoco's new chairman and CEO, decided that only a massive change in the way Amoco organized its activities would turn the company around and boost profits. Fuller decided that Amoco would completely eliminate the three-legged structure and remove the three top managers at the subsidiary level. The three subsidiaries would be divided into 17 independent business divisions, and decision-making authority would be decentralized to the managers of each division, who would be free to choose their own strategy for their division. Each division would be evaluated for its ability to reach certain growth targets set by corporate managers , but each division's managers would determine the approaches that the division took to reach those targets .

（案例来源：节选自王毅捷编著. *100 Cases for Management.* 上海：上海交通大学出版社，2003, pp. 254-255）

案例中阿莫科公司（Amoco）的组织结构是一种什么样的形式？不同组织结构可能会给企业带来哪些影响？这样的问题一直是众多管理者在企业实践中面临的"必答题"。组织理论已成为管理者们在管理过程方面的一门"必修课"。如何才能更好地通过改善和影响组织结构来提升组织绩效，如何充分发挥组织中非正式组织的力量，推动组织发展，是组织管理者们所必须认真思考的问题。本节将围绕组织的类型来进行讨论和学习。

一、按照组织目的分类：公共组织、非营利性组织和营利性组织

根据组织自身的目的可以把组织分为三大类：公共组织、非营利性组织和营利性组织。公共组织即负责处理国家公共事务的组织，包括政府部门、军队、司法机关等。非营利性组织是公共组织之外的一切不以营利为目标的组织。营利性组织当然是指以获利为主要目标的组织。

从实践发展来看，最初的管理实践多集中于公共组织的管理，例如国家管理、军队管理、宗教管理等。但是后来随着生产力的发展出现了手工作坊、家族式的商业企业和工业企业，再后来是大规模的公司，营利性组织就蓬勃发展起来了。于是管理领域开始细化，这种细化本身也是学科不断成熟的一个标志。它细化为两大类：一类是企业管理学，今天我们讨论的管理学更多意义上是企业管理；另一类是关于政府以及一些公共社会团体的管理，包括政治学、行政学等的传统研究范围以及现在正蓬勃发展的非营利性组织管理领域等内容。

二、按照组织内在结构分类：正式组织和非正式组织

按照组织内在结构可以将组织的类型分为正式组织和非正式组织两大类别。

（一）正式组织

正式组织一般就是在一个具有正式结构的组织中有目的地形成的职务结构。

尽管我们称某一组织为正式的组织，但并不意味着正式组织就一定是一成不变的，或者是存在着一些固定的限制不允许其改变现状。如果管理人员想要做好组织工作，组织的结构一定要提供这样一个环境，使个人不论是在现在或将来的工作中都能十分有效地为集体目标做出贡献。正式的组织必须具有灵活性，优秀的正式组织应留有酌情处置权，以充分发挥有创造力的人才的能力，尊重个人的喜好，挖掘员工的潜力。但必须把集体情境下的个人努力引向集体和组织的目标，组织中任何合作性的活动，都必须以实现组织目标为出发点。组织建构的目标性是我们建立有效正式组织必须遵循的指导原则。

优秀的正式组织一般具有如下特征。

第一，保持相对稳定性：存在稳定的秩序，人员流动性小，权责结构清晰。

✍ **Classification based on Organization Purposes: Public Organization, Non-profit Organization and Profit Organization**

Public organization is responsible for public affairs, including government, military, judiciary, etc.

Non-profit organization is non-profit oriented except for the public organization.

Profit organization is the organization which primary goal is making money (profit).

✍ **Classification based on Inner Structure of Organizations: Formal Organization and Informal Organization**

✧ Formal organization

Formal organization pertains to the intentional structure of roles in a formally-organized enterprise.

An excellent formal organization has following characteristics:
(1) Keep relatively stability of members and clear authority-responsibility structure.

第二，专业化分工：分成若干岗位及与之相应的职责。

第三，对不同管理层观念的协调：由于进行了专业化分工，并且分成一定结构和层次，所以在同级上要协调相互关系、在上下级工作链上也要协调关系，从而形成立体的协调层次。

第四，拥有法定的领导权威：其最高领导人的领导权是由法定规章制度确定的，并强制要求所有成员服从。

第五，建立起相对稳定的规章制度体系：优秀的正式组织将岗位分工、行为规范、奖惩措施、运营机制、产品范围、行动范围，都以明确的条文确定下来并公布给每个成员，要求他们去遵守。

第六，职位的可取代性：优秀正式组织的职位和职责要求不是针对某个具体的个人，某个人离开，其他人可以接替岗位继续工作。

（二）非正式组织

非正式组织是人们彼此联络而形成的一种人际关系网络。与正式组织相比较，非正式组织主要有以下几个特征。

第一，没有共同的组织目标：非正式组织并非是在完成一定任务的过程中形成的，而是在自然状态下形成的，所以这个群体并没有一个共识性的任务前提。

第二，没有明确的组织制度和规定：非正式组织的公共准则是通过一些约定俗成的、靠默契和非正式的契约来实现的。

第三，成员和形式不稳定，经常发生变动：非正式组织的边界是不清晰的，人员的进出是随意的，而且交互和影响过程也并不固定，有时表现为缺乏秩序。

非正式组织的研究可以追溯到哈佛大学梅奥教授（George Elton Mayo）所领导的"霍桑实验"。此后人们对组织内的非正式组织的特征及活动的正负面影响进行了充分研究，并取得了成果。起初大家都认为非正式组织是有负面影响的，例如拉帮结派、山头主义。后来行为学家通过研究发现，非正式组织其实也具有正面的推动作用，对非正式组织在管理中的作用要从正反两方面去认识。

切斯特·巴纳德（Chester Barnard）认为，任何没有自觉的共同目的的共同个人活动，都属于非正式组织，这些活动可能对于组织目标是有推动作用的。例如，午饭时棋友们所形成的非正式关系可能有助于实现组织的目标。当员工在工作中遇到问题时，与其去求助某个职位上并不认识的人，倒不如去求助认识的同事，哪怕他可能在另一个部门，这样沟通起来可能容易得多。

(2) Specialization by duties.

(3) Coordinate the concepts.

(4) Legal authority.

(5) The relative fixed rules.

(6) Professional job description.

✧ Informal organization

The informal organization is a network of interpersonal relationships that arise when people associate with each other.
The informal organization has following characteristics:
(1) Lack of common organization goals.
(2) Lack of clear organizational systems and rules.

(3) Instability of members and structures.

亚利桑那州立大学的基思·戴维斯（Keith Davis），把非正式组织描述为"并不是由正式组织建立或需要的，但由于人们互相联系而自发形成的个人和社会关系的网络"。因而，非正式组织并不存在于正式的组织图上，可能包括机械车间的班组，同在六层楼的邻居，星期五晚上玩保龄球的伙伴以及上午喝咖啡的常客。对非正式组织存在的原因、方式的探寻是社会心理学领域的一项特殊研究，这些动态的个体之间的关系受到集体中的人数、所涉及实际人员、与该集体有关的事物、该集体领导的变化以及人员不断变化过程的影响。管理人员必须要意识到非正式组织的存在，避免与之对立，并尽可能地利用非正式组织，发挥其作用。

非正式组织的正面影响见表 6-1 上栏。

第一，通过非正式组织活动，满足员工对正式组织的需求，消除员工对工作的抵触情绪，从而有利于正式组织的正常运作。

第二，通过非正式组织成员之间的感情交流，相互理解、相互信任，有利于组织成员间的协调与合作，加强集体凝聚力。

第三，促进信息沟通，避免正式组织僵化所导致的信息沟通不畅等情况，同时也有助于消除上下级之间的等级鸿沟。

第四，组织魅力，有利于利用本身的吸引力来提高员工的稳定度，保持组织的稳定和发展。

非正式组织的负面影响见表 6-1 下栏。

第一，观念差异。非正式组织成员形成的习俗、信仰，与正式组织的目标、行为规范有差异甚至背道而驰时，将影响组织运转。

第二，内部冲突。各层管理人员没能处理好正式组织与非正式组织的关系，会导致非正式组织成员不愿意听从指挥，甚至故意破坏既定的组织制度。

表 6-1　非正式组织的影响

Table 6-1　Impacts of Informal Organization

The impacts of informal organization	
Positive impact	1. Meet employees' needs and eliminate the dissatisfaction
	2. Enhance the unity of the organization and believe each other
	3. Eliminate the level gap between superior and subordinate
	4. Decrease staff turnover rate and keep the stability of the organization
Negative impact	1. Maybe against with the employees' beliefs
	2. Exist the conflict between formal organization and informal organization

Whom Do You Trust?

David Leers thought he knew his employees well. In 15 years, the company had trained a cadre of loyal professionals who had built a strong regional reputation for delivering customized office information systems. The field design group, responsible for designing and installing the systems, generated the largest block of revenues. For years it had been the linchpin of the operation, led by the company's technical superstars, with whom Leers kept in close contact. But Leers feared that the company was losing its competitive edge by shortchanging its other divisions, such as software applications and integrated communications technologies. When members of field design saw Leers start pumping more money into these divisions, they worried about losing their privileged position. Key employees started voicing dissatisfaction about their compensation, and Leers knew he had the makings of a morale problem that could result in defections.

To persuade employees to support a new direction for the company, Leers decided to involve them in the planning process. He formed a strategic task force composed of members of all divisions and led by a member of field design to signal his continuing commitment to the group. He wanted a leader who had credibility with his peers and was a proven performer. Eight-year company veteran Tom Harris seemed obvious for the job. Leers was optimistic after the first meeting. Members generated good discussion about key competitive dilemmas. A month later, however, he found that the group had made little progress. Within two months, the group was completely deadlocked by members championing their own agendas. Although a highly effective manager, Leers lacked the necessary distance to identify the source of his problem.

An analysis of the company's trust and advice networks helped him get a clearer picture of the dynamics at work in the task force. The trust map turned out to be most revealing. Task force leader Tom Harris held a central position in the advice network—meaning that many employees relied on him for technical advice. But he had only *one* trust link with a colleague. Leers concluded that Harris's weak position in the trust network was a main reason for the task force's inability to produce results.

In his job, Harris was able to leverage his position in the advice network to get work done quickly. As a task force leader, however, his technical expertise was less important than his ability to moderate conflicting views, focus the group's thinking, and win the commitment of task force members to mutually agreed-upon strategies. Because he was a loner who took more interest in computer games than in colleagues' opinions, task force members didn't trust him to take their ideas seriously or look out for their interests. So they focused instead on defending their turf.

With this critical piece of information, the CEO crafted a solution. He did not want to undermine the original rationale of the task force by declaring it a failure. Nor did he want to embarrass a valued employee by summarily removing him as task force head. Any response, he concluded, had to run with the natural grain of the informal organization. He decided to redesign the team to reflect the inherent strengths of the trust network. Leers looked for someone in the trust network who could share responsibilities with Harris. He chose Bill Benson, a warm, amiable person who occupied a central position in the network and with whom Harris had already established a solid working relationship. He publicly justified his decision to name two task force heads as necessary, given the time pressures and scope of the problem. Within three weeks, Leers could see changes in the group's dynamics. Because task force members trusted Benson to act in the best interest of the entire group, people talked more openly and let go of their fixed positions. During the next two months, the task force made significant progress in proposing a strategic direction for the company. And in the process of working together, the task force helped integrate the company's divisions.

（案例来源：David Krackhardt and Jeffrey R. Hanson. Informal Networks: The Company Behind the Chart, https://hbr.org/1993/07/informal-networks-the-company-behind-the-chart, 1993-7-8）

第二节　组织结构

Rules , Regulations, and You Say What ?

Rules and regulations often help to keep order in an organization by establishing the parameters in which organizational members operate. In most organizations, rules and regulations help members to plan, organize, control, and make decisions. And, depending on the size of the organization, these same rules and regulations can help to coordinate activities by keeping employees' work focused on goal attainment. But sometimes, rules become unwieldy and end up creating an amazing and inefficient runaround. Let's look at two such situations involving the Environmental Protection Agency (EPA) and the Department of Transportation (DOT).

The concern in the EPA situation revolved around testing for clean water at a site in Phoenix, Arizona. To do this testing, the EPA places flathead minnows and water fleas into storm water drains. These small creatures are then tracked as they float in the storm water making its way into streams and rivers. When the storm water reaches its destination, if the minnows and water fleas are alive, the water is considered to be not contaminated. If, however, the animals die en route, the water is considered to be polluted. Simple enough, right? Well, maybe not?

The problem in Phoenix is that the riverbed being tested is dry; there's absolutely no water in it, and there hasn't been any for years. The EPA spends about $500,000 annually on this aquatic life test—in a riverbed where no aquatic life exists. The EPA defends its actions on the grounds that they' are charged with protecting the groundwater, which will ultimately become drinking water for citizens in the general vicinity. Although no one says that this goal isn't important, the EPA regulations, ironically, don't focus on drinking water. Just on protecting aquatic life, so the test they're performing in Phoenix is worthless.

If you think testing a dry riverbed for aquatic life is counterproductive, just look at the rule imposed by the Department of Transportation and the Occupational Safety and Health Administration. These two government agencies require lumber companies to have specially designed gas cans to hold the fuel used in chainsaws. Each gas container (they usually hold five gallons of gas online) is required to have "a double roll bar on top, double-walled steel sides, and a screw filter on top, and it must be vented." A gas can that meets these regulations costs about $230. And, if the extra costs aren't enough, there are also the maddening results. The filler neck on the government approved gas can won't fit into the chainsaw, so about half of the gas poured spills out on the ground. But then, when it contaminates the ground it's not really the DOT' S responsibility. That would fall under the jurisdiction of the EPA.

（案例来源：节选自王毅捷编著. *100 Cases for Management*. 上海：上海交通大学出版社，2003，pp. 257-258）

根据案例描述，规则是组织有效运行的基础，有效的规则有助于组织整体发展。但与此同时，如果组织中制定了一些不合理或者与环境不相适应的规则，则可能阻碍组织的正常发展。作为一个优秀的组织，该如何设计自己的组织结构、制定合理的组织规则，才能不断提升企业效益？本节将围绕组织结构的相关内容进行讨论和学习。

一、组织结构的含义

组织结构（Organizational Structure）是指对于组织内的工作任务如何进行分工、分组和协调合作。组织结构是表明组织各部分排列顺序、空间位置、聚散状态、联系方式以及各要素之间相互关系的一种模式，是整个管理系统的"框架"。组织结构是组织的全体成员为实现组织目标，在管理工作中进行分工协作，在职务范围、责任、权利方面所形成的结构体系。组织结构是组织在职、责、权方面的动态结构体系，其本质是为实现组织战略目标而采取的一种分工协作体系，组织结构必须随着组织的重大战略调整而调整。就像人类由骨骼确定体型一样，组织也是由结构来决定其形态。在设计组织结构时，需要重点考虑三个要素：复杂性、正规化和集权化。

复杂性（Complexity）是指组织差异化的程度。一个组织愈是进行细致的劳动分工，就具有愈多的纵向等级层次。组织单位的地理分布愈是广泛，则协调人员及其活动就愈是困难。这种情况下我们认为组织的复杂性较高。

正规化（Formalization）是指组织依靠规则和程序引导员工行为的程度。有些组织只有很少的规范准则，而另一些组织却具有各种规定，指示员工可以做什么和不可以做什么。一个组织使用的规章条例越多，其组织结构就越正规化。

集权化（Centralization）指的是权力不被下放的程度，它考虑决策制定权的分布。在一些组织中，决策是高度集中的，问题自下而上传递给高级经理人员，由他们选择合适的行动方案。而另外一些组织，其决策制定权则授予下层人员，这被称作分权化（Decentralization）。

管理人员在设立或变革一个组织的结构时，他们所进行的就是组织设计（Organizational Design）工作，管理者做出的结构决策，如决定决策应该在哪一层次做出，或者需要有哪些标准规则让员工去遵循，就是组织设计结果的一个具体体现。

二、组织结构的影响因素

管理者在进行组织结构设计时，必须正确考虑 6 个关键因素：工作专门化、部门化、命令链、管理幅度、集权与分权、正规化。

✍ **The Nature of Organizational Structure**

Organizational structure is the formal arrangement of jobs within an organization.

Complexity refers to the degree of organizational differentiation.

Formalization refers to the degree of organization relying on rules and procedures to guide employees' behaviors.

Centralization refers to the degree to which authority is not delegated.

✍ **The Influential Factors of Organizational Structure**

（一）工作专门化

20世纪初，亨利·福特（Henry Ford）通过建立汽车生产线而富甲天下，享誉全球。他的做法是，给公司每一位员工分配特定的、重复性的工作，例如，有的员工只负责装配汽车的右前轮，有的则只负责安装右前门。通过把工作分化成较小的、标准化的任务，使工人能够反复进行同一种操作，福特利用技能相对有限的员工，平均每10秒钟就能生产出一辆汽车。福特的经验表明，让员工从事专门化的工作，其生产效率会提高。今天，我们用工作专门化（Work Specialization）这个术语或劳动分工这类词汇来描述组织中把工作任务划分成若干步骤来完成的细化程度。

工作专门化的实质是：一个人不是完成一项工作的全部，而是将全部工作分解成若干步骤，每一步骤由一个人独立去做。工人们完成的只是工作活动的一部分，而不是全部活动。20世纪40年代后期，工业化国家大多数生产领域的工作都是通过工作专门化来完成的。管理人员认为，这是一种最有效地利用员工技能的方式。在大多数组织中，有些工作需要技能很高的员工来完成，有些则经过简单的训练就可以做好。如果所有的员工都参与组织制造过程的每一个步骤，那么，就要求所有的人不仅具备完成最复杂的任务所需要的技能，而且还要具备完成最简单任务所需要的技能。结果，除了从事需要较高技能或较复杂任务以外，员工还需要在完成低技能工作上花费部分时间。由于高技能员工的报酬比低技能员工高，而工资一般是反映一个人最高技能水平的，因此，付给高技能员工高薪，却让他们做简单的工作，这无疑是对组织资源的浪费。通过实行工作专门化，管理层可以提高组织在其他方面的运行效率。通过重复性的工作，员工的技能会有所提高，在改变工作任务时或在工作过程中安装、拆卸工具及设备时所用的时间会减少。同样重要的是，从组织角度来看，实行工作专门化，有利于提高组织的培训效率，挑选并训练从事具体的、重复性工作的员工比较容易，成本也较低。

（二）部门化

一旦通过工作专门化完成任务细分之后，就需要按照类别对它们进行分组，以便各个任务之间的协调。工作分类的基础是部门化（Departmentalization）。

⬥ Work specialization

Work specialization is a process of dividing work activities into separate job tasks. Individual employees "specialize" in doing part of an activity rather than the entire activity in order to increase work outputs. It's also known as division of labor.

⬥ Departmentalization

How jobs are grouped together is called departmentalization.

Departmentalization patterns include: departmentalization by enterprise function, departmentalization by territory, departmentalization by process, and departmentalization by customers.

一般来说,组织会根据工作职能来对工作活动进行分类。例如,制造业的经理会将组织分为工程、会计、制造、人事、采购等部门;医院的主要职能部门可能包括诊疗部、护理部、财会部等;职业足球队则可能包括人事、票务部、运营部等。

还有一种部门化方法,即根据地域来进行部门划分。例如,就营销工作来说,根据地域,可分为东、西、南、北4个区域,分片负责。实际上,每个地域是围绕这个地区而形成的一个部门。如果一个公司的顾客分布地域较宽,这种部门化方法就有其独特的价值。

第三种部门化的方法是根据活动的过程划分,我们称之为过程部门化。该方法适用于产品的生产,也适用于顾客的服务。例如,人们去医院检查身体,往往需要跑好几个部门,因为医院的挂号、拍片、化验、检查、取药分别由不同的部门负责。

最后一种部门化方法是根据顾客的类型来进行部门化。例如,一家销售办公设备的公司可下设三个部门:零售服务部、批发服务部、政府部门服务部;比较大的法律事务所可根据其服务对象是公司还是个人来分设部门。根据顾客类型来划分部门的理论假设是,每个部门的顾客存在共同的问题和要求,因此通过为顾客分别配置有关专家,能够满足他们的需要。

One popular departmentalization trend is the increasing use of departmentalization by customers.

大型组织进行部门化时,可能综合利用上述各种方法,以取得较好的效果。例如,一家大型的日本电子公司在进行部门化时,根据职能类型来组织其各分部;根据生产过程来组织其制造部门;把销售部门分为七个地区的工作单位;又在每个地区根据其顾客类型分为四个顾客小组。但是,20世纪90年代以来,以顾客为基础进行部门化越来越受到青睐。为了更好地掌握顾客的需要,并对顾客需要的变化及时做出反应,越来越多的组织开始强调按照顾客类型来划分部门。

（三）命令链

命令链的概念是早期组织设计的基石。虽然今天它的重要性大大降低,不过在决定如何更好地设计组织结构时,管理者仍需考虑命令链的意义。命令链(Chain of Command)是一种不间断的权力路线,从组织最高层扩展到最基层,澄清谁向谁报告工作。它能够回答员工提出的这种问题:"有问题时,去找谁?""我对谁负责?"在讨论命令链时,必须讨论两个重要概念:职权和命令统一性。

✧ The chain of command

The chain of command is the line of authority extending from upper organizational levels to lower levels, which clarifies who reports to whom.
To understand the chain of command, you have to understand two important concepts: authority and unity of command.

职权（Authority）是指管理职位所固有的影响他人的决策权。为了促进协作，每个管理职位在命令链中都有自己的位置，每位管理者为完成自己的职责任务，都要被授予一定的职权。

命令统一性（Unity of Command）原则有助于保持职权链条的连续性。它意味着，一个人应该对一个主管，且只对一个主管直接负责。如果命令链的统一性遭到破坏，一个下属可能就不得不疲于应付多个主管不同命令之间的冲突或优先次序的选择。时代在变化，组织设计的基本原则也在变化。随着计算机的发展和给下属充分授权的潮流的冲击，命令链、职权、命令统一性等概念的重要性大大降低了，但是，仍然有一些学者认为，通过强化命令链可以使组织的生产率得到提高。

（四）管理幅度

一个主管可以有效地指导多少个下属？这种有关管理幅度（Span of Management）的问题非常重要，因为在很大程度上，它决定着组织要设置多少个层次、配备多少个管理人员。在其他条件相同时，管理幅度越宽，组织效率越高。

假设有两个组织，总员工数都是 30 人，如果所有管理者的管理幅度都是 4，那么这个公司至少需要 4 个组织层次；如果所有管理者的管理幅度都是 6，那么只要 3 个组织层次就够了。很显然，管理幅度越宽，组织层次越少，所需要的管理人员也越少。管理幅度宽的组织仅在管理人员薪水方面就可以节省一笔不小的开支。所以说，从成本方面考虑，管理幅度宽的组织效率更高。但是，从某些方面来说，宽的管理幅度也可能会降低组织的有效性。例如，如果管理幅度过宽，主管人员可能没有足够的时间为下属提供必要的领导和支持，如果下属员工的成熟度不高，其工作效率就会受到影响（参见图 6.1）。

Authority is the right in a position to exercise discretion in making decisions affecting others.

✧ The span of management

The span of management determines the number of levels and managers in an organization. If all other things being equal, the wider or larger the span, the more efficient an organization is.

194

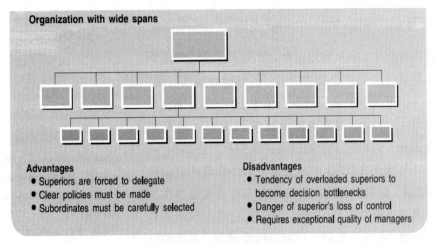

图 6-1　宽管理幅度组织的优缺点

Figure 6-1　Advantages and Disadvantages of Organization with Wide Spans

（资料来源：Heinz Weihrich, Mark V. Cannice and Harold Koontz. *Management: A global and Entrepreneurial Perspective* (12th edition). 北京：经济科学出版社，2008, p. 171）

　　窄的管理幅度同样具有一些优点，如管理者可以经常与下属沟通，可以为下属提供更多面对面的指导。但管理幅度过窄也存在着一些问题（参见图 6-2）。

　　第一，控制跨度过窄易造成对下属监督过严，妨碍下属的自主性。

　　第二，管理幅度过窄，管理层次会因此而增多，管理成本会大大增加。

　　第三，使组织的垂直沟通更加复杂。管理层次增多也会减慢决策速度，并使高层管理人员趋于孤立。

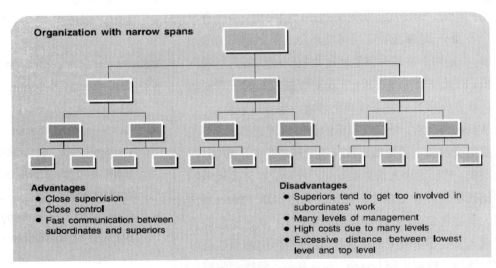

图 6-2　窄管理幅度组织的优缺点

Figure 6-2　Advantages and Disadvantages of Organization with Narrow Spans

（资料来源：Heinz Weihrich, Mark V. Cannice and Harold Koontz. *Management: A global and Entrepreneurial Perspective* (12th edition). 北京：经济科学出版社，2008, p. 171）

（五）集权与分权

在有些组织中，高层管理者制定所有的决策，低层管理人员只是执行高层管理者的指示。另一种极端情况是，组织把决策权下放到最基层管理人员手中。前者是高度集权式的组织，而后者则是高度分权式的组织。集权化（Centralization）是指组织中的决策权集中于一点的程度。这个概念只包括正式职权，也就是说，某个职位固有的权力。一般来讲，如果组织的高层管理者不考虑或很少考虑基层人员的意见就决定组织的主要事宜，则这个组织的集权化程度较高。相反，基层人员参与程度越高，或他们能够自主地做出决策，组织的分权化（Decentralization）程度就越高。集权式与分权式组织在本质上是不同的。在分权式组织中，采取行动、解决问题的速度较快，更多的人为决策提供建议，所以，员工与那些能够影响他们的工作生活的决策者隔膜较少，或几乎没有。企业所必须制定的主要战略决策与其结构的集权或分权程度有关。这通常取决于企业所处的特殊行业、环境和采用的技术。

集权式组织的优点主要有以下几个方面：一是易于协调各职能间的决策；二是对报告的方式进行了规范，例如可以使用公司内部的管理系统进行报告；三是能与企业的目标达成一致；四是危急情况下能进行快速决策；五是有助于实现规模经济，降低成本；六是这种结构比较适用于由外部机构（例如专业的非营利性组织）实施密切监控的企业，因为所有决策都能得以协调。

与此同时，集权式组织的缺点亦比较突出，主要有以下几个方面：一是高级管理层可能不会重视个别部门的不同要求；二是由于决策时需要通过集权职能的所有层级向上汇报，因此决策时间过长；三是对级别较低的管理者而言，其职业发展有限，工作缺乏热情，忠诚度较低。

从目前情况看，分权式决策的趋势比较突出，这与使组织更加灵活和主动地做出反应的管理思想是一致的。在大公司中，基层管理人员更贴近生产实际，对有关问题的了解比高层管理者更翔实。因此，像西尔斯（Sears）这样的大型零售公司，在库存货物的选择上，就对他们的商店管理人员授予了较大的决策权。这使得他们的商店可以更有效地与当地商店展开竞争。与之相似，蒙特利尔银行（Bank of Montreal）把它在加拿大的 1164 家分行组合成236 个社区，即在一个有限地域内的一组分行，每个社区设一名经理，他在自己所辖各行之间可以自由巡视，各个分行之间最长距离不过 20 分钟的路程。他对自己辖区内

✧ Centralization and decentralization

Centralization is the degree to which decision-making takes place at upper levels of the organization. If top managers make key decisions with little input from below, then the organization is more centralized.

Decentralization is the tendency to disperse decision-making authority in an organized structure.

Advantage of centralization:

- Better coordination among various operations.
- Standardization of work.
- Uniformity in action.
- Quick decision-making in a dangerous situation.
- Reduced cost.
- Easier control.

Disadvantages of centralization:

- No special attention is given to special work.
- Delay in work because of transmission of records from and to the central control office.
- Low loyalty of employees because of no involvement in decisions and absence of zeal.

的问题反应远远快于公司总部的高级主管，处理方式也会更得当。IBM 采取类似的办法把欧洲大陆的公司分成 200 个独立自主的商业单位，每个单位有自己的利润目标、员工激励方式、重点顾客，公司尽力使员工学会自我管理。

Global Perspective

Empowerment in Asia

The concept of empowerment is starting to spread into Asia, with a few younger Asian business leaders now espousing this style of management, too. An example is Ho Kwong Ping, the executive chairman and CEO of the Banyan Tree Hotels and Resorts Group, who wants to engage his staff and cultivate in them a set of core values that he hopes over time will take root and mature into an instantly recognizable Banyan Tree culture. Ho Kwong Ping was named "CEO of the Year" at the Singapore Corporate Awards 2008. The former chairman of India's Infosys, N.R. Narayana Murthy, and its present chief executive and managing director, Nandan Nilekani, are also two widely admired top managers who espouse empowerment of staff—a business practice not widely seen in India. However, as Asian companies start to rely more on professional employees of all sorts, and as professional services become more important in Asian economies, the less autocratic and more participative and even empowered style of leadership will emerge.

How can managers empower employees? They can begin by using participative decision making, in which employees provide input into decisions. Although getting employees to participate in making decisions is not quite taking the full plunge into employee empowerment, it is at least a way to begin tapping into the collective array of employees' talents, skills, knowledge and abilities.

Another way to empower employees is through delegation—the process of assigning certain decisions or specific job duties to employees. By delegating decisions and duties, the manager is turning over the responsibility for carrying them out. When a manager is finally comfortable with the idea of employee empowerment, fully empowering employees means redesigning their jobs so they have discretion over the way they do their work. It is allowing employees to do their work effectively and efficiently by using their creativity, imagination, knowledge and skills.

If a manager implements employee empowerment properly—that is, with complete and total commitment to the program and with appropriate employee training—results can be impressive for the organization and the empowered employees. The business can enjoy significant productivity gains, quality improvements, more satisfied customers, increased employee motivation and improved morale.

Employees can enjoy the opportunities to do a great variety of work that is more interesting and challenging. In addition, they are encouraged to take the initiative in identifying and solving problems and doing their work.

（案例来源：Stephen Robbins, Rolf Bergman, Ian Stagg and Mary Coulter. *Management* (6th edition). Melbourne: Pearson Australia Group Pty Ltd., 2012, p. 365）

（六）正规化

正规化（Formalization）是指组织中的工作如何进行标准化以及员工的行为受规章制度引导的程度。如果一种工作的正规化程度较高，就意味着做这项工作的人对工作内容、工作时间、工作手段没有多大自主权。管理者总是期望员工以同样的方式投入工作，能够保证稳定一致的产出结果。在高度正规化的组织中，有明确的工作说明书，有繁杂的组织规章制度，对于工作过程有详尽的规定。而正规化程度较低的工作，相对来说，工作执行者和日程安排就不是那么僵硬，员工对自己工作的处理许可权就比较宽。由于个人许可权与组织对员工行为的规定成反比，因此工作标准化程度越高，员工决定自己工作方式的权力就越小。

组织之间或组织内部不同工作之间正规化程度差别很大。某些工作正规化程度很低，如大学书商（向大学教授推销公司新书的出版商代理人）工作自由许可权就比较大，他们的推销用语不要求标准划一。在行为约束上，可能不过就是每周交一次推销报告，并对新书出版提出建议。而相反，那些处于同一出版公司的职员与编辑位置的人。他们上午 8 点要准时上班，而且他们必须遵守管理人员制定的一系列详尽的规章制度。

三、组织结构的制度形式

（一）直线制

大多数组织建立之初都是使用直线制结构。直线制是最早也是最简单的组织形式。它的特点是各级行政单位从上到下实行垂直领导，下属部门只接受一个上级的指令，各级主管负责人对所属单位的一切问题负责（参见图6-3）。

直线制组织结构的优点是：快速、灵活、维持低成本、责任明确。缺点是：对成长后的组织不适用，且过于依赖个人是有风险的。因此，直线制只适用于规模较小、生产技术比较简单的企业，对生产技术和经营管理比较复杂的企业并不适用。

✧ Formalization

Formalization refers to how standardized an organization's jobs are and the extent to which employee behaviors are guided by rules and procedures. In highly formalized organizations there are explicit job descriptions, numerous organizational rules, and clearly defined procedures covering work processes. Employees have little discretion over what's done, when it's done, and how it's done. However, where formalization is low, employees have more discretion in how they do their work.

✍ **Organizational Structure System**

✧ Simple structure

Most companies start as entrepreneurial ventures using a simple structure, which is an organizational design with low departmentalization, wide spans of control, authority centralized in a single person, and little formalization.

Simple structure is often used by small-scale and simple organizations.

事业部制是分级管理、分级核算、自负盈亏的一种形式，即一个公司按地区或按产品类别分成若干个事业部，从产品的设计、原料采购、成本核算、产品制造，一直到产品销售，均由事业部及所属工厂负责，实行单独核算，独立经营，公司总部只保留人事决策、预算控制和监督大权，并通过利润等指标对事业部进行控制。也有的事业部只负责指挥和组织生产，不负责采购和销售，实行生产和供销分立，但这种事业部正在被产品事业部所取代。

事业部制的优点是，它强调结果——事业部经理对特定产品或服务的经营负责；事业部制的缺点是，活动和资源重复配置导致成本上升、效率降低。

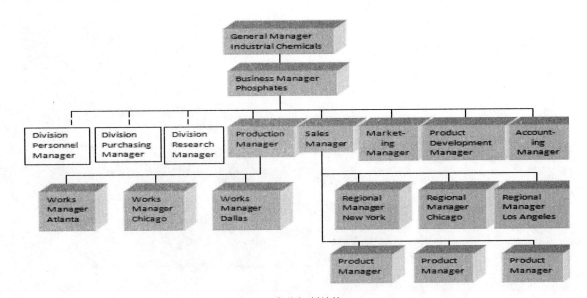

图 6-5　事业部制结构

Figure 6-5　Strategic Business Unit (SBU) Structure

（四）矩阵制

矩阵组织结构主要是指从不同职能部门抽调相关专家，分派他们在一个或多个由项目经理领导的项目小组中的组织结构形式。在组织结构上，把既有按职能划分的垂直领导系统又有按产品（项目）划分的横向领导关系的结构，称为矩阵组织结构（参见图 6-6）。矩阵制组织是为了改进直线职能制横向联系差、缺乏弹性的缺点而形成的一种组织形式。它的特点表现在围绕某项专门任务成立跨职能部门的专门机构上，例如组成一个专门的产品小组去从事新产品开发工作，在研究、设计、试验、制造各个不同阶段，由有关部门派人参加，以协调有关部门的活动，保证任务的完成。

✧　Matrix structure

Matrix structure assigns specialists from different functional departments to work on projects being led by a project manager.

矩阵制的优点是：由于这种结构是根据项目组织的，任务清楚，目的明确，因此，各方面有专长的人才在新的工作小组里，能沟通、融合，能把自己的工作同整体工作联系在一起，为攻克难关，解决问题而献计献策。由于从各方面抽调来的人员有被信任感、荣誉感，这使他们增加了责任感，激发了工作热情，促进了项目的实现。它还加强了不同部门之间的配合和信息交流，克服了直线职能结构中各部门互相脱节的现象。

矩阵制的缺点是：项目负责人的责任大于权力，因为参加项目的人员隶属关系仍在原单位，只是为"会战"而来，所以项目负责人对他们管理起来比较困难，没有足够的奖惩手段，这种人员上的双重管理是矩阵结构的先天缺陷；由于项目组成人员来自各个职能部门，当任务完成以后，仍要回原单位，因而容易产生临时观念，对工作有一定影响。

矩阵结构适用于一些重大攻关项目。企业可用来完成涉及面广的、临时性的、复杂的重大工程项目或管理改革任务，特别适用于以开发与实验为主的单位，例如科学研究，尤其是应用性研究单位等。

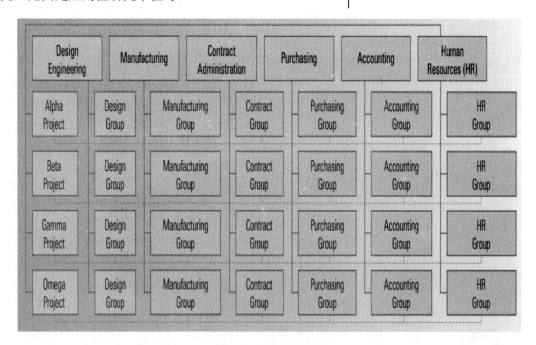

图 6-6　矩阵组织结构

Figure 6-6　Matrix Structure

一、组织设计

（一）组织设计的定义、要求及关键点

1. 组织设计的定义

所谓组织设计，是指建立或改造一个组织的过程，即对组织活动和组织结构的设计和再设计，是把任务、流程、权力和责任进行有效的组合和协调的活动。

2. 组织设计的一般要求

（1）精简：注意避免机构重叠，头重脚轻，人浮于事。

（2）统一：组织内权利应相对集中，实施"一元化管理"。

（3）高效：应使各部门、各环节、组织成员组合成高效的结构形式。

3. 组织设计的关键点

（1）组织的目标性：组织内各部门应在组织整体经营目标下充分发挥能力而达成各自目标。

（2）组织的成长性：考虑组织的业绩经营与持续成长。

（3）组织的稳定性：随着组织成长而逐步调整组织设计是必要的，但经常的组织变更将使员工信心动摇。

（4）组织的简单性：组织的简单将有助于内部协调与人力分配。

（5）组织的弹性：保持基本形态，又能配合各种环境条件的变化。

（6）组织的均衡性：各部门业务量的均衡，将有助于内部的平衡与分工。

（7）指挥的统一性：一个员工同时接受二位以上主管管理，将使其产生无所适从的感觉，组织设计应充分考虑统一指挥的问题。

（8）权责明确化：权责或职责不清将使工作发生重复或遗漏、推诿现象，易使员工产生挫折感。

（9）作业制度化：明确的制度与标准作业可减少冗余时间。

（二）组织设计的原则

1. 任务与目标原则

组织设计的根本目的,是为实现组织的战略任务和经营目标服务的,这是一条最基本的原则。组织结构的全部设计工作必须以此作为出发点和归宿点,即任务、目标同组织结构之间是目的同手段的关系;衡量组织结构设计的优劣,要以是否有利于实现任务和目标作为最终的标准。

✍ **Organizational Design**

✧ The definition, requirements and key points of organizational design

The organizational design is a process which establishes or renovates an organization, namely the combination and coordination of activities of designing or redesigning organizational task, process, authority and responsibility.

The basic requirements of organizational design:
(1) Simplification.
(2) Unity.
(3) Efficiency.

The key points of organizational design:
(1) The goal of the organization.
(2) The growth of the organization.
(3) The stability of the organization.
(4) The simplification of the organization.
(5) The flexibility of the organization.
(6) The balance of the organization.
(7) The unity of the organization.
(8) The correspondence of power and responsibility.
(9) Activity institutionalization.

✧ The principles of organizational design

1. The principle of goal orientation

从这一原则出发，当组织的任务、目标发生重大变化时，例如，从单纯生产型向生产经营型、从内向型向外向型转变时，组织结构必须作相应的调整和变革，以适应任务和目标变化的需要。又如，进行企业机构改革，必须从任务和目标的要求出发，该增则增，该减则减，避免单纯地把精简机构作为改革目的。

2. 专业分工和协作的原则

2. The principle of specialization and division cooperation

现代组织的管理，工作量大，专业性强，分别设置不同的专业部门，有利于提高管理工作的质量与效率。在合理分工的基础上，各专业部门只有加强协作与配合，才能保证各项专业管理的顺利开展，达到组织的整体目标。贯彻这一原则，在组织设计中要十分重视横向协调问题。可以实行系统管理，把职能性质相近或工作关系密切的部门归类，成立各个管理子系统，分别由各位副总经理负责管辖，也可以设立一些必要的委员会来实现协调，还考虑创造协调的环境，提高管理人员的全局观念，增进相互间的共同语言。

3. 有效管理幅度原则

3. The principle of effective management span

由于受个人精力、知识、经验条件的限制，一名领导者能够有效领导的直属下级人数是有一定限度的。有效管理幅度不是一个固定值，它受职务的性质、人员的素质、职能机构健全与否等条件的影响。这一原则要求在进行组织设计时，领导者的管理幅度应控制在一定水平，以保证管理工作的有效性。由于管理幅度的大小同管理层次的多少呈反比例关系，这一原则要求在确定组织的管理层次时，必须考虑到有效管理幅度的制约。

4. 集权与分权相结合的原则

4. The principle of combining centralization and decentralization of authority

在组织设计时，既要有必要的权力集中，又要有必要的权力分散，两者不可偏废。

集权是大生产的客观要求，它有利于保证组织的统一领导和指挥，有利于人力、物力、财力的合理分配和使用。而分权是调动下级积极性、主动性的必要组织条件。合理分权有利于基层根据实际情况迅速而正确地做出决策，也有利于上层领导摆脱日常事务，集中精力抓重大问题。因此，集权与分权是相辅相成的，是矛盾的统一。没有绝对的集权，也没有绝对的分权。组织在确定内部上下级管理权力分工时，主要应考虑的因素有：组织规模的大小，组织生产技术特点，各项专业工作的性质，各单位的管理水平和人员素质的要求等。

常用的影响利益相关者的策略有：第一，确定特定利益相关者的需要，并提供新方案给他们带来的好处的信息；第二，与别的有势力的个体和集团形成联盟或联合，直接与关键利益相关者交往，以及通过各种渠道来影响关键利益相关者，使其支持实施活动。

2. 制定行动计划

推行组织设计的实施，组织要制定一个行动计划，这个计划应当包括如何帮助组织每个人从自己目前的位置走向目标点的机制，应当涵盖情感、认知及行为等多个维度。行动计划应清晰、具体、有效，紧紧围绕组织设计的目标展开。

3. 建立协调机制

实施过程中，除了保证组织运营的各种组织和机制之外，还需要建立协调机制以协调组织各部分同时发生的转变。协调机制的另一个作用是使组织结构方面的调整尽量不要影响正在向客户提供的产品和服务，否则，组织设计的实施也就失去了其本意。

（三）评价阶段

一旦组织设计方案开始实施，就应着手对其进行评价，评价不但包括实施完成后对实施效果的评价，还包括实施过程中的评价。

1. 对组织设计实现的结果评价

组织设计新方案的总体效果是很难全面衡量的，常用的两类评价方法包括权变评价法和平衡评价法。

（1）权变评价法

权变评价法包括目标评价法、资源评价法和内部过程评价法。

①目标评价法。此方法包括识别组织的产出目标以及测评组织在何种程度上实现了这些目标。这种方法的优点是产出目标易于衡量。缺点是组织的目标是多重的，而且有些是难以定量的主观指标，因此，衡量这些目标完成程度的客观性问题是这一评价方法需要注意的。

②资源评价法。通过考察组织获取组织设计过程所需资源并成功加以整合和管理的能力来衡量组织的效能。这种评价方法的优点是简单易行，因为资源消耗和利用情况比较容易获得。缺点是这种方法对组织与外部环境中顾客需要的联系考虑不清。资源评价法最适合在目标达成情况从其他方面难以衡量时使用。

2. Design action plan.

3. Establish a coordination mechanism.

✧ The phase of evaluation

1. Evaluate outcomes of organizational design.

(1) Contingency evaluation approach.

The goal-based evaluation identifies the degree and nature of goal attainment.

The resource-based evaluation evaluates the efficiency by focusing on the resources needed for designing organization and the extent of utilization.

208

内部过程评价法。这种方法通过对组织内部的健康状况和效率来衡量组织效果。这种评价方法的优点是同时考虑资源利用率与内部功能的协调性,不足之处是它没有评价总产出和组织与外部环境的关系,另外对内部健康和运行状态的评价往往带有主观性。

（2）平衡评价法

平衡评价法包括利益相关者评价法和冲突价值评价法。

利益相关者评价法。它综合考虑组织的各种不同活动,把利益相关者的满意程度作为评价组织绩效的尺度。这种评价方法的优点是它能够全面地反映组织设计的效果。既考虑了组织内部因素也考虑到了环境因素,并且把对社会的责任也考虑了进去;不足之处是,有些指标难以衡量,如员工的满足、社区服务,只能采取主观方法进行评价,这影响了评价结果的准确性。

冲突价值评价法。它综合考虑了管理人员和研究人员所采用的各种不同的绩效标准,总结出能反映组织中不同人员的价值冲突。这种评价方法的主要贡献是:第一,它将效果的几个方面的不同认识有机地结合到一个模式中,它综合了产出目标、资源获取、人力资源开发等思想,把这些作为组织将要力图实现的目标;第二,这种方法将效果标准提高到了价值观的高度来认识,并说明了各种看似对立的价值观是如何可能并存的。其不足之处是组织中成员的类型很多,很难对所有类型人员的绩效标准进行考评。

2. 组织设计实现的过程评价

仅仅对组织设计实现的结果进行评价是不够的,还需要对改革过程本身进行评价。组织设计实现过程的评价包括两个方面的内容:一是组织设计实现过程是否按照原定规划进行;二是组织设计实现过程的效率和效果。组织设计实现过程中可能出现两类问题:一类是执行偏离原方案,一类是方案与实际脱节。组织设计的实施执行机构应该区分不同的问题,采取不同的办法解决这类问题。组织设计的实现过程的效率和效果可以通过对组织设计的实现成本、组织设计的实现速度、未预料到的行动和事件三个方面进行评价。

3. 建立有效的反馈机制

事实上,反馈机制并不仅仅是评价阶段的重要工作。在整个组织设计实现的三个阶段当中,为了获得有关实现进程的信息,组织需要建立超越日常经营所需的多种反馈机制。

The internal process-based evaluation keeps an eye on internal health and efficiency in an organization.

(2) Balance evaluation approach.

The stakeholder-based evaluation considers the satisfaction of stakeholders to evaluate the organization's performance.

The conflicted value-based evaluation considers the different performance criteria of managers and researchers to evaluate the conflicting values in the organization.

2. Evaluate the process of organizational design.

* The extent to follow plans.
* Efficiency and effectiveness during the process.

3. Establish an effective feedback mechanism.

第四节　组织文化

The Bean Queen

There's the Bean Queen. There are Bean Counters. And there are Human Beans. All can be found at Buckeye Beans and Herbs in Spokane, Washington. Jill Smith is the Bean Queen. She's a self-proclaimed hippie artist turned entrepreneur who started her company in 1983 with an investment of $1,000. From that small, inauspicious beginning, Buckeye Beans now has sales revenues approaching 8 million and employs 50 people (human beans). Buckeye Beans has been innovative in expanding its product line, which started out with one product, Buckeye Bean Soup, and now includes a line of all-natural soups, chili, bread mixes, and pasta. Buckeye Beans also pioneered special-occasion-shaped pasta: that is, pasta shaped like Christmas trees, hearts, bunnies, dolphins, leaves, grapes, baseballs, and even golf balls. But what strikes you most about Buckeye Beans isn't its unique products, it's the unusual organizational culture that melds this company together.

That unusual organizational culture is reflected in the company's simple mission statement: Make people smile. Smith's belief is that cooking should be fun and the experience of cooking can be a fun escape, not a drudgery. That's why the first ingredient listed on all Buckeye's product packages is a cup of good wine for the cook. Buckeye's strategy—that its products go beyond just a simple bag of beans and instead serve as entertainment—is also seen in the company's HEHE principle: Humor, Education, Health , and Environment. That's what Jill Smith, husband Doug, and other Buckeye employees believe in and value.

Shared values are very important to Smith and her employees. Not only are many of Buckeye's employees family and long-time friends, but they all share similar values. As Smith built Buckeye Beans, she felt it was important that her employees should have the same value systems. And although she admits that her approach wouldn't work for each organization, she does think it's important for managers to identify their basic values and what they're trying to accomplish. Smith suggests asking what kinds of values are important and what kind of organization is desired. For Buck-eye Beans, the approach has been to create a "different" type of company with a new model on which the business is run and the relationships between employee and customer operate on the basis of trust, confidence, loyalty, and working hard together to get something done. As Smith so earnestly stresses, it's easier to work hard when you have a philosophy like that.

（案例来源：节选自王毅捷编著. *100 Cases for Management*. 上海：上海交通大学出版社，2003, pp. 250-251）

案例中吉尔·史密斯（Jill Smith）为她的公司创建了一种独特的组织文化。这种文化不仅体现了创始人的思想和经营理念，更被多数员工接受和理解，形成了组织凝聚力，推动了企业的发展。组织文化能够给组织带来哪些意想不到的效果？这种效果是长期性的还是短期性的？该如何设计独特的组织文化？组织文化应该包括哪些内容？本节将围绕组织文化的相关知识进行讨论和学习。

一、组织文化的内涵

（一）组织文化的含义

组织文化（Organizational Culture）是一个组织由其价值观、信念、仪式、符号、处事方式等所组成的其特有的文化形象。从广义上讲，组织文化是指企业在建设和发展中形成的物质文明和精神文明的总和，包括组织管理中硬件和软件，即外显文化和内隐文化两部分。从狭义上讲，组织文化是组织在长期的生存和发展中所形成的为组织所特有的且为组织多数成员共同遵循的最高目标、价值标准、基本信念和行为规范等的总和及其在组织中的反映。具体来说，组织文化是指组织全体成员共同接受的价值观念、行为准则、团队意识、思维方式、工作作风、心理预期和团体归属感等群体意识的总称。

（二）组织文化的内容

组织文化的内容可以分为显性的和隐性的两大部分。

1．显性组织文化

所谓显性组织文化是指那些以精神的物化产品和精神行为为表现形式的，人通过直观视听器官能感受到、又符合组织文化实质的内容。它包括组织的标志、工作环境、规章制度和经营管理行为四个部分。

（1）组织标志。组织标志是指以标志性的外化形态，来表示本组织的文化特色，并且和其他组织明显区别开来的内容，包括厂牌、厂服、厂徽、厂旗、厂歌、商标、组织的标志性建筑等。

（2）工作环境。工作环境是指员工在组织中办公、生产、休息的场所，包括办公楼、厂房、俱乐部、图书馆等。

（3）规章制度。并非所有的规章制度都是组织文化的内容，只有那些以激发员工积极性和自觉性为目标的规章制度，才是组织文化的内容，其中最主要的就是民主管理制度。

（4）经营管理行为。再好的组织哲学或价值观念，如果不能有效付诸实施，就无法被员工所接受，也就无法成为组织文化。组织在生产中以"质量第一"为核心的生产活动、在销售中以"顾客至上"为宗旨的推销活动、组织内部以"建立良好的人际关系"为目标的公共关系活动等，这些行为都是组织哲学、价值观念、道德规范的具体实施，是组织文化的直接体现，也是这些精神活动取得成果的桥梁。

✍ **The Nature of Organizational Culture**

✧ The definition of organizational culture

Organizational culture is a cultural image consisted of value, faith, ritual, symbol, manner of an organization.

Specifically, organizational culture is commonly accepted group consciousness which includes value, code of behave, team work, way of thinking, style of work, expectation and sense of belonging.

✧ The contents of organizational culture

Organizational culture is consisted of explicit organizational culture and implicit organizational culture.

Explicit organizational culture is something accorded with the essence of organizational culture which is shown as the product and behavior connected with spirit, usually perceived by sight and hearing.

Explicit organizational culture includes four parts:

(1) Organizational symbol

(2) Working environment

(3) Regulations

(4) Management style

二、组织文化的类型分类

根据标准和用途的不同,理论界目前对组织文化有着不同的划分方法,其中,最常见的划分方法有以下几种。

(一) 按照组织文化的内在特征分类

艾莫瑞大学(Emory University)的杰弗里·桑南菲尔德(Jeffrey Sonnenfield)提出一套标签理论,这一理论有助于我们认识组织文化之间的差异,认识到个体与文化合理匹配的重要性。通过对组织文化的研究,他提出了 4 种文化类型(参见表 6-3)。

1. 学院型组织文化

学院型组织是为那些想全面掌握每一种新工作的人而准备的地方。在这里他们能不断成长、进步。这种组织喜欢雇用年轻的大学毕业生,并为他们提供大量的专门培训,然后指导他们在特定的职能领域内从事各种专业化工作。IBM 公司、可口可乐公司(Coca-Cola)、宝洁公司(P&G)等都是典型的学院型组织文化代表。

2. 俱乐部型组织文化

俱乐部型公司非常重视适应、忠诚感和承诺。在俱乐部型组织中,资历是关键因素,年龄和经验都至关重要。这类组织喜欢从内部提升员工。俱乐部型组织文化的例子有:联合包裹服务公司(UPS)、德尔塔航空公司(Delta)、政府机构和军队等。

3. 棒球队型组织文化

棒球队型这种组织鼓励冒险和革新。招聘时,从各种年龄和经验层次的人中寻求有才能的人。薪酬制度以员工绩效水平为标准。由于这种组织对工作出色的员工给予巨额奖励和较大的自由度,员工一般都拼命工作。在会计、法律、投资银行、咨询公司、广告机构、软件开发、生物研究等领域,这种组织文化比较普遍。

4. 堡垒型组织文化

棒球队型公司重视创造发明,而堡垒型公司则着眼于公司的生存。这类公司以前多数是学院型、俱乐部型或棒球队型,但在困难时期衰落了,现在尽力来保证生存。这类公司工作安全保障不足,但对于喜欢流动性、挑战的人来说,具有一定的吸引力。许多传统制造行业的组织文化都属于堡垒型。

✍ **Types of Organizational Culture**

✧ Classification based on internal features of organizational culture

Organizational culture can be divided into four types: academy culture, club culture, baseball team culture and fortress culture.

表 6-3　四种组织文化的特征

Table 6-3　Characteristics of Four Organizational Cultures

Academy Culture	Employees are highly skilled and tend to stay in the organization and work their way up the ranks. Stress Long-term career development and provide a stable environment in which employees can develop and exercise their skills.
Club Culture	To fit into the group is the most important requirement for employees. Emphasize commitment to the company and do things for the good of the group. Promote from within and highly valued seniority.
Baseball Team Culture	Seek out talents of all ages and experiences. Employees have highly prized skills and are rewarded on the basis of what they produce. Encourage innovation.
Fortress Culture	Companies are struggling to keep afloat. Many are academies, clubs, or baseball teams that have failed and trying to come back. Cannot promise job security or reward employees on the basis of how well they perform. Often undergo massive reorganization.

（二）按照组织文化对其成员影响力的大小分类

哈佛商学院的两位著名教授约翰·科特（John P. Kotter）和詹姆斯·赫斯科特（James L. Heskett）于 1987 年 8 月至 1991 年 1 月，先后进行了四个项目的研究，依据组织文化与组织长期经营之间的关系，将组织文化分为如下三类。

1. 强力型组织文化

在具有强力型组织文化的公司中，员工们方向明确，步调一致，组织成员有共同的价值观念和行为方式，所以他们愿意为组织自愿工作或献身，而这种心态又使得员工们更加努力。强力型组织文化提供必要的组织机构和严格的管理机制，从而避免组织对那些影响组织活力和改革思想的官僚们的依赖，促进了组织业绩的提升。

2. 策略合理型组织文化

具有这种文化的组织，不存在抽象的、绝对好的组织文化内涵，也不存在任何放之四海而皆准、适合所有企业"克敌制胜"的组织文化。只有当组织文化与组织环境相"适应"时，这种文化才是好的、有效的文化。不同的组织需要不同的组织文化，只有文化适应于组织，才能发挥其最大功能，改善组织经营状况。

3. 灵活适应型组织文化

市场适应度高的组织文化必须具有同时在组织员工个人生活中和组织生活中都提倡信心和信赖感、不畏风险、注重行为方式等特点，员工之间相互支持，勇于发现问题、解决问题。员工有高度的工作热情，愿意为组织牺牲一切。

◇　Classification based on the influence of organizational culture to members

Organizational culture can be divided into three types: strong culture, strategically appropriate culture and adaptive culture.
In order to create a strong culture, it is very important to align values of employees with the values of an organization.

Strong culture provides clear organizational structures and strict management systems.

Strategically appropriate culture is the corporate culture must be with the business environment, business strategy to adapt to and associated business performance, suitable for business growth culture.

Adaptive culture is characterized by managers paying close attention to all of their constituencies, especially customers, initiating change when needed, and taking risks.

（三）按照组织文化所涵盖的范围分类

组织作为一个系统，是由各种子系统构成的，各个子系统又是由单个的具有文化创造力的个体组成。

在一个组织中，除了整个组织作为一个整体外，各种正式的、有严格划分的子系统，或非正式群体，相对于组织来说也都能够作为一个小整体。从这个角度来说，组织文化又可以分为主文化和亚文化两类。

1．主文化

主文化体现的是一种核心价值观，它为组织大多数成员所认可。当我们说组织文化时，一般就是指组织的主文化。

2．亚文化

亚文化是主流文化中一个较小的组成部分。在组织中，主文化虽然为大多数成员所接受，但是，它不能包含组织中所有的文化。青年文化、老年文化、城市文化、乡村文化等都是组织中常见的亚文化。

组织中有各种小团体，它们有自己独特的亚文化。亚文化或者是对组织主文化更好的补充，或者是与主文化相悖的，或者虽然与主文化有区别，但对组织来说是无害的，在一定条件下又有可能替代组织的主文化。

（四）按照权力的集中或分散分类

卡特赖特（Cartwright）和科伯（Cooper）于 1992 年提出四种文化类型。这四种组织文化的区别在于权力是集中的还是分散的，以及政治过程是以关键人物还是以要完成的职能或人物为中心的。

1．权力型组织文化

权力型组织文化也叫独裁文化，由一个人或一个很小的群体领导这个组织。组织往往以企业家为中心，不太看重组织中的正式结构和工作程序。随着组织规模的逐渐扩大，权力型文化会很难适应转型，不得不开始改变。

2．作用型组织文化

作用型组织文化也叫角色型组织文化。在这样的组织里，你是谁并不重要，你有多大能力也不重要，重要的是你在什么位置，你和什么人的位置比较近，做每件事情都有固定的程序和规矩，人们喜欢的是稳重、长期和忠诚。这种文化看起来安全和稳定，但是当组织需要变革的时候，这种文化则会受到较大的冲击。

◇ Classification based on coverage of organizational culture

Organizational culture can be divided into two types: dominant culture and sub-culture.

An organization is a system which contains several sub-systems that is made up of cultural individual with creativity.

Dominant culture is the core value which is accepted by the majority of organization. Usually, it refers to dominant culture when mentioning the organizational culture.

Sub-culture is a component of dominant culture. The dominant culture is not the whole culture though is accepted by the majority.

◇ Classification based on the centralization and decentralization of authority

Organizational culture can be divided into four types: power culture, role culture, task culture and person culture.

A power culture concentrates power among a few. Control radiates from the center like a web. Power and influence spread out from a central figure or group.

In a role culture, people have clearly delegated authorities within a highly defined structure. It is controlled by procedures, roles descriptions and authority definition.

3．使命型组织文化

使命型组织文化也叫任务文化。在这种文化中，团队的目标就是要完成设定的任务。成员之间的地位平等，这里没有领导者，唯一的老板就是任务或者使命本身。有人认为这是最理想的组织模型之一，但这种文化要求公平竞争，而且当不同群体争夺重要的资源或特别有利的项目时，很容易产生恶性的组织内冲突。

4．个性型组织文化

个性型组织文化是一种既以人为导向，又强调平等的文化。这种文化富于创造性，孕育着新的观点，允许每个人按照自己的兴趣工作，同时保持相互有利的关系。在这样的组织里，组织实际上服从个人意愿，但是很容易被个人左右。

三、组织文化的作用

由于组织文化涉及分享期望、价值观念和态度，它对个体、群体及组织都有影响。组织文化除了提供组织的身份感之外，还有稳定感。具体来说组织文化有以下几个方面的作用。

（一）整合作用

强有力的组织文化能成为激发员工积极性、使员工全心全意工作的动力。在一个富有凝聚力的组织文化中，组织价值观念深入人心，员工把组织当成自己的家，愿意为了组织目标共同努力，贡献自己的力量，使得员工和组织融为一体。

组织文化能从根本上改变员工的旧有价值观念，建立起新的价值观念，使之适应组织正常实践活动的需要。一旦组织文化所提倡的价值观念和行为规范被接受和认同，成员就会做出符合组织要求的行为选择，倘若违反了组织规范，就会感到内疚、不安或者自责，会自动修正自己的行为。从这个意义上说，组织文化具有很强的整合作用。

（二）提升绩效作用

管理学大师彼得·德鲁克（Peter Drucker）说过："企业的本质，即决定企业性质的最重要的原则，是经济绩效。"如果组织文化不能对企业绩效产生影响，那么也就凸显不出它的重要性了。瑞士洛桑国际管理学院（IMD）对企业国际竞争力的研究显示，组织文化与企业管理竞争力的相关系数最高，为 0.946。组织文化在组织绩效的提升方面确实发挥着积极作用。

A task culture emphasizes the task. Teams are formed to solve particular problems.

A person culture exists where all individuals believe themselves superior to the organization. It allows employees to do what they like.

✍ **The Functions of Organizational Culture**

✧ Integrate different cultures

If the organizational culture is accepted by the group members, they will behave as what organization requires and feel guilty or shameful when their behaviors are against the organization requirements.

✧ Improve organization's performances

Organizational culture is an incredibly powerful factor in a company's long-term success.

约翰·科特（John P. Kotter）和詹姆斯·赫斯科特（James L. Heskett）在对企业的大量实地调研的基础之上，提出组织文化对企业长期经营业绩有着重要的作用。组织文化可以将组织目标细化，以便于员工进行日常决策；可以减少组织中的沟通成本，更利于员工合作；可以更有效地激励员工努力的工作。优秀的组织文化可以提升组织的效率，进而实现组织绩效的提高。

（三）完善组织作用

组织在不断的发展过程中所形成的文化积淀，通过无数次辐射、反馈和强化，会不断随着实践发展而更新和优化，推动组织文化从一个高度向另一个高度迈进。

也就是说，组织文化不断深化和完善，一旦形成良性循环，就会持续地推动组织本身上升和发展；反过来，组织的进步和提高又会促进组织文化的丰富、完善和升华。国内外多个成功的案例表明，组织的兴旺发达总是与组织文化的自我完善分不开。

（四）塑造产品作用

组织文化虽然是无形的，但可以通过有形的产品来体现。当组织的产品浸润了组织文化时，其产品的生命力是非常强大的，具有鲜明的个性特征。组织文化对于塑造组织产品有极为重要的作用，组织依据组织文化进行产品设计、生产和销售，只有符合组织文化的产品才能在市场上立足、立稳。反过来，组织产品的畅销则会使消费者进一步了解企业的组织文化，这是一种相互促进和发展的关系。

四、全球化背景下的组织文化

随着市场和生产的全球化进程不断加快，一个更加整体化而又相互依赖的世界经济趋势逐渐形成，市场已经不再是某一个国家内部的市场，组织所面对的外部经营环境愈加复杂。组织文化是内聚人心、外树形象和指导组织经营的灵魂，是组织在全球化背景下实现资源整合和文化融合的基础和动力。如何在全球化背景下，建立与宏观环境相适应的组织文化，是所有企业，尤其是跨国公司，必须认真考虑的问题。

（一）全球化环境下组织文化的复杂性

开展全球化经营的企业必须承认且准确理解各国之间的文化差异，要重视对他国语言、文化等的学习和了解，这是建设全球化背景下组织文化的必要条件。这种文化差

The culture specifies the goals of the firm and helps the employees make daily decisions easily; reduces the communication costs and facilitates coordination among employees; raises the employees' motivation.

Organizational culture can be a major source of efficiency in organizations and improve corporate performance.

✧ Improve organization development

The culture that generates with the development of organization updates and optimizes by radiation, feedback and reinforcement. It then pushes the organizational culture to a higher level.

✧ Shape product image

The organizational culture plays a significant role in shaping product image. The design, production and marketing of products are based on the spirit of organizational culture. Also, the consumers will understand the organizational culture by buying products.

✍ **The Organizational Culture in the Global Perspective**

✧ The complexity of organizational culture in the global perspective

异，不仅体现在不同群体具体的信仰、价值观等方面，而且还体现在各国人民对于组织文化内涵的理解上。人们普遍认为，组织文化会缓和甚至消除民族文化的影响，比如一家美国的跨国公司在中国开展业务，那么不久中国的雇员就会像美国人一样思考。但是，越来越多的证据表明，员工的民族文化价值观对组织绩效有着重要的影响，员工带到工作场所的文化价值观不易被组织所改变。南希·阿德勒（Nancy Adler）对此做了相关调研，发现当员工为同一家跨国公司工作时，似乎是德国人更加德国化，美国人更加美国化，瑞典人更加瑞典化，这说明组织文化并没有减少或消除民族文化差异。

例如，如图 6-8 和图 6-9 所示，一家美国跨国公司在美国和欧洲经营，但是当欧洲人对于美国分公司和欧洲分公司的文化维度进行评价时，他们的认知却存在着较大的差异。复杂的国际化环境增加了文化的多样性，在同一个组织中工作的人群如果来自不同国家，文化冲突可能会时常发生，进而形成一种缺乏信任、低生产率、不和谐的工作环境。当文化上有差异的团队成员一起工作时，常常会有先入为主的固定思维模式，进而造成偏见和沟通障碍。因此，在开展全球化经营的组织中，组织文化的作用尤为重要，组织文化不仅受到领导者的影响，还受到员工的文化偏好等众多因素的制约。管理者需要充分了解和剖析各个文化群体的特征，深入讨论员工之间的文化差异，并谨慎协调他们的行为，不断完善组织文化内容，提高团队凝聚力。如果组织的全球化是通过合并或收购来实现的，那么组织文化的整合就应该成为国际企业管理中的关键问题。

National cultural values of employees may significantly impact their organizational performance.

Cultural values employees bring to workplace are not easily changed by organization.

Organizational culture is shaped by numerous factors including cultural preferences of leaders and employees.

If the international expansion is via mergers or acquisitions, the integration of organizational culture is a key problem to solve.

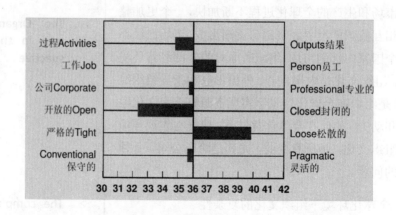

图 6-8 欧洲人对同一家跨国公司的美国分公司的文化维度的感知

Figure 6-8　Europeans' Perception of the Cultural Dimensions of U.S. Operations of the Same Multinational Corporation

（资料来源：Lisa Hoecklin. *Managing Cultural Differences: Strategies for Competitive Advantage*. England: Addision-Wesley, 1995, p. 147）

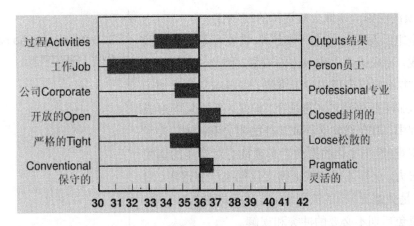

图 6-9　欧洲人对同一家跨国公司的欧洲分公司的文化维度的感知

Figure 6-9　Europeans' Perception of the Cultural Dimensions of European Operations of the Same Multinational Corporation

（资料来源：Lisa Hoecklin. *Managing Cultural Differences: Strategies for Competitive Advantage*. England: Addision-Wesley, 1995, p. 148)

（二）组织文化整合的步骤

⟡ Steps in the integration of organizational culture

在全球化背景下,组织文化整合是管理者必须考虑和解决的一个重要问题。但是由于组织和环境的复杂性,很难找到统一的适用于所有全球化组织的组织文化整合步骤。由于并购是许多组织实现全球化战略的重要途径,这里仅对进行了国际合并或收购的组织重点讨论。在实施并购时,管理者可以参考如下步骤进行组织文化整合。

1. 必须明确并购的目的、目标及重点

1. Establish purpose, goals, and focus of merger.

组织的并购带来的是思维模式的强烈变革和不同组织文化的巨大冲击,如果在文化整合中处理问题过于草率,缺乏有效的沟通和准确的判断,其结果是必然造成并购后组织内部更大的摩擦与消耗。因此,在酝酿并购的过程中,必须全面地考察双方原有文化状况,充分了解可能出现的文化差异及冲突,明确并购的目的和目标,对并购双方进行详细的评估和调研,划定工作重点,确定文化整合模式的选择及文化整合的总体思路。

2. 必须制定确定最重要的组织结构及管理者角色的机制

2. Develop mechanisms to identify most important structures and manager roles.

在现有文化基础上,整合或创造一种新的文化形态并不是一件容易的事情,在这个过程中,经常伴随着一些较大的改革举措,如新的组织结构的建立、管理层的调整、人员的精简等。这些改革都是非常敏感的问题,一定会影响某些人的利益,带来一定的阻力。管理者必须有一个完整的计划,制定明确的规则,健全与预期组织文化相吻合的内部管理制度和行为规范,让组织员工有明确的行为导向。这些制度规范应该是组织文化的具体贯彻和准确体现,应该能够被并购双方理解和接受。

3. 必须决定哪一方拥有对资源的控制权

并购是组织发展壮大的一种方式,它并不是一个谁输谁赢的游戏,而应该是并购双方的双赢。因此,在收购过程中,收购方不应该表现得过于强势,将组织文化强加于被收购方,那样不利于文化的融合。但是,新文化的形成和推广过程中,总会遇到这样或那样的阻力和困难,为了解决这些困难,组织文化的推动者必须拥有对资源的调配和使用的权力,这样才能够保证新文化的推广和落实。对资源(尤其是关键资源)的控制权,最好在并购之初明确,这样可以避免后期不必要的冲突和误解。

4. 必须了解所有利益相关者的期望,并使部门和人员之间易于沟通

并购不仅会影响并购双方的直接利益,还会为双方的客户、供应商等其他相关群体的工作和利益带来影响。在进行组织文化整合的过程中,决策者应该充分的考虑所有利益相关者的期望,综合各方面因素,尽量减少并购可能带来的文化冲突。同时,应建立一种便于理解、易被接纳的组织文化,通过理性化的行为和系统的传播方式,对新的组织文化不断进行推广,获得员工和公众的认可和支持。还可以辅以组织文化培训,增强员工对不同文化传统的了解和适应能力,促进不同文化背景的人之间沟通与理解,加强员工对新组织文化的认同。

3. Determine who has authority over resources.

4. Identify expectations of all involved participate and facilitate communication between departments and individuals.

Features of Apple's Organizational Culture

Apple's organizational culture is a key factor in the company's success. A company's organizational culture determines capabilities in supporting changes, new policies and new strategies. In Apple's case, employees are effectively developed and integrated into an organizational culture that facilitates rapid innovation.

Apple's organizational culture is effective in supporting the firm's leadership because of key features that fit the business. Different businesses have different requirements for their culture. In Apple's case, the following characteristics are the most significant in its organizational culture:

Top-notch excellence: Apple's organizational culture involves a policy of selecting only the best of the best workers. Steve Jobs was known to readily fire employees who did not meet his expectations.

Creativity: Apple employees are selected for their knowledge, skills, and creative abilities. The firm's organizational culture highlights the importance of creativity. Employees involved in product design and development processes are especially creative.

Innovation: Apple's organizational culture is also highly innovative. In fact, Apple is frequently appraised as one of the most innovative companies in the world. All employees are trained and encouraged to innovate in terms of individual work performance and by contributing ideas to the firm's product development processes.

Secrecy: Steve Jobs developed Apple to have an organizational culture of secrecy. This secrecy is part of the company's strategy to minimize theft of proprietary information or intellectual property. Upon hiring, Apple employees agree to this organizational culture of secrecy, which is reflected in the firm's policies, rules and employment contracts.

Moderate Combativeness: Apple's organizational culture has moderate combativeness. This feature is linked to Steve Jobs and his combative approach to leadership. He was known to randomly challenge employees to ensure that they have what it takes to work at Apple.

（案例来源：节选自 Pauline Meyer. Apple Inc. Organizational Culture: Features & Implications. http://panmore.com/apple-inc-organizational-culture-features-implications, 2015-9-8）

Public organization

Non-profit organization

Profit organization

Formal organization

Informal organization

Organizational structure

Centralization

Decentralization

Work specialization

Departmentalization

Chain of command

Authority

Unity of command

Span of management

Strategic business unit

Organizational design

Contingency evaluation approach

Resource-based evaluation approach

Internal process-based evaluation approach

Explicit organizational culture

Implicit organizational culture

Dominant culture

Sub-culture

Power culture

Task culture

讨论问题 DISCUSSION QUESTIONS

1. According to the inner structure, the organizations can be classified into 2 types: formal organizations and informal organizations. What characteristics do the above-mentioned organizations have respectively?

2. Describe a typical informal organization as you know. Please briefly explain the impacts of informal organization.

3. Explain the concept of the organizational structure. What factors should we consider when we design the organizational structure?

4. Please design the organizational structure for any student associations in your colleges. Explain

the reason why choose this kind of organizational structure.

5. Please describe the merits and demerits of the functional structure.

6. Briefly describe the influential factors of organizational structure.

7. Please explain the strengths and weaknesses of matrix structure.

8. Please explain the process of organizational design.

9. Describe the important role of organizational culture. Could you analyze the culture of your class?

10. Briefly describe the step of constructing organizational culture.

11. Please describe the key points of organizational design.

12. Explain the relationship between the cross-cultural management and corporation's competitive advantages in the global perspective.

Huawei's Culture Is the Key to Its Success

Today, Huawei is the only Chinese company—out of the 91 mainland Chinese companies listed on the Fortune Global 500 list—earning more revenue abroad than in China. Huawei's revenue from overseas markets exceeded that from the Chinese market for the first time in 2005. In 2012, Huawei surpassed Ericsson—at that time the world leader in telecommunications and networks—in terms of sales revenue and net profit, and this trend continued in the fiscal year of 2014 when Huawei reached an all-time high sales revenue of $46.5 billion and net profits of $4.49 billion (both in U.S. dollars). What makes it so successful? The foundation of Huawei's value-driven culture is the key to its success.

Customer-First Attitude

Strong leaders provide a sense of purpose to their people, and Ren Zhengfei is no exception. His first and foremost concern is the customer. An example of this customer-first attitude comes from an early episode in their history that's since become something of a company legend. In desert and rural areas in China, rats often gnawed the telecom wires, severing customers' connections. The multinational telecom companies providing service at that time did not consider this to be *their* problem, but rather that of the customer. Huawei, in contrast, viewed the rat problem as one the company had the responsibility to solve. In doing so, they acquired extensive experience in developing sturdier equipment and materials—such as chew-proof wires—which helped them later on to gain several big business accounts in the Middle East, where similar problems stymied the multinational firms. Since then, there have been other projects where Huawei experienced severe climate challenges, such as building the highest wireless communication base station in the world and building the first GSM network within the Arctic circle. These have helped acquire useful knowledge.

Employee Dedication

Huawei emphasizes that the only way to obtain opportunities is through hard work. For example, in the early years of the company, every new employee was given a blanket and a mattress. Many of them would work late into the night, then sleep in their offices, perhaps taking a catnap during lunch again the next day. Knowing that a dedicated and committed work force makes companies more competitive is not a too difficult concept to understand. The way to promote dedication and make it accepted by its employees—as it is the case in Huawei—is, however, a more difficult nut to crack. Huawei does it in part with the type of incentive performance system the company employs. Huawei is not a public company, and is in fact owned by the employees. Ren Zhengfei's shares account for nearly 1.4% of the company's total, and 82,471 employees hold the rest. This employee shareholding system is referred to within Huawei as the "silver handcuff." It is a system that is different from the more common stock option arrangement, which is often termed the "golden handcuff". The idea underlying this scheme is that Ren Zhengfei wants to share both responsibilities and benefits with his colleagues. As he puts it, he wants everyone to act like the boss. Important to note, however, is that that only those who perform well enough qualify to participate. The current employee-ownership structure is what helps the company maintain a strong collective fighting spirit.

Long-Term Thinking

The employee-ownership arrangement not only helps Huawei attract and retain dedicated employees, but also allows the company to plan for the long term. Ren Zhengfei has also credited it with allowing them to stay close to their goals and long-term vision. For example, Huawei plans the development of the company by decade, whereas most of their competitors such as Ericsson and Motorola plan it by financial quarter or year. Being privately held has allowed Huawei to work on its 10-year plans, while its competitors struggle to follow near-term fluctuations of the capital market.

For example, Huawei has introduced the use of a rotating CEO system in which three deputy chairmen take turns acting as CEO for six months each. At the same time Ren Zhengfei maintains his oversight role, acting as a mentor and coach for the acting CEO. This innovative management structure is inspired by a book on new leadership called *Flight of the Buffalo* (authors James Belasco and Ralph Stayer). While it will make the company less vulnerable if one chief fails or derails, it's hard to imagine a publicly held company getting away with such an unusual plan.

Gradual Decision-Making

Ren Zhengfei is known for avoiding quick decisions and forcing himself to take time to reflect. His company reflects these traits. Again, he ties this in part back to their ownership structure: it keeps the decision-making power under company control-no outside investor will gain relative control over Huawei. As we've seen, they have much more freedom and less pressure from the market to consider their next steps to take. Their system of rotating CEOs helps support a gradual, more democratic decision-making process. It also helps Ren Zhengfei make a gradual decision about his ultimate successor. Huawei also emphasizes what they call "the power of thinking." The company philosophy is that the most valuable thing is the power to think. For example, efforts are made to ensure that intellectual exchange happens as a matter of routine. Executives are urged to read books outside their area of expertise and books have to be present in each office. Furthermore, ideas are communicated frequently to every employee by both senior executives and Ren Zhengfei.

（案例来源:节选自 David De Cremer and Tian Tao. Huawei's Culture Is the Key to Its Success. *Harvard Business Review*. https://hbr.org/2015/06/huaweis-culture-is-the-key-to-its-success, 2015-6-11）

Discussion Questions

1. Are there any special characteristics of Huawei's organizational culture? Are they helpful to improve the development of Huawei? Please share your ideas with your classmates.

2. What's meaning of Customer-First Attitude in Huawei? Could you give some examples?

3. Is Huawei's culture strong culture or weak culture? How to maintain the culture in the development of organization? Is there any factor to influence the establishing of organizational culture?

4. What could other organizations learn from Huawei's experiences about the importance of organizational culture?

第七章 人员配备

学习目标

1. 理解人员配备的含义、原则、任务及程序
2. 解释人员选拔和人员培训的内涵
3. 描述人员绩效评估的基本内容

Learning Outcomes

1. Understand the definition, principle, task and process of staffing.
2. Explain the meaning of selection and training.
3. Describe the contents of performance appraisal.

主要内容

第一节 人员配备概述
第二节 人员选拔与培训
第三节 人员绩效评估

Contents

7.1 Introduction to Staffing
7.2 The Selection and Training
7.3 Performance Appraisal

第一节 人员配备概述

Global and Cultural Effectiveness: Recruiting Is Social and Talent Is Local

For years, we've been hearing about the importance of building recruiting tools that have full mobile capability, but this has not yet become main stream. According to data from Jobsite, Beyond.com and others, roughly three-quarters of job seekers are now using smartphones and other devices to research companies, review career resources and apply to jobs. The rise of social and mobile recruiting worldwide and the clarion call to build global talent pools for highly skilled labor have become an inevitable tendency. Understanding these developments is critical to cultivating one's competency in global and cultural effectiveness. The use of mobile recruiting tools to research and apply for jobs is becoming popular among midcareer professionals in such emerging markets as India, China and Vietnam. Thus, 2016 may be the year when mobile job-apply capability evolves from nice-to-have to must-have around the world.

Continued globalization and a widening skills gap will require global talent acquisition strategies. To compete, more companies are hiring skilled workers wherever the talent resides, even if it means dealing with complex immigration and taxation laws. This proactive might become even more critical in 2016, as tech innovations lead to more new job types and roles and as expertise may not be readily available in the country where a company is headquartered.

As candidates around the world become immensely more findable and more comfortable being found, recruiters will begin deploying social-centric search strategies. Meanwhile, job seekers are quickly learning that social monitoring can go two ways. Many are using social tools to learn more about the reputation of a company—or even a manager—by reaching out to their networks or perusing rating sites such as Glassdoor. The days when people blindly applied to open positions (the so-called spray and pray method) may be coming to an end.

（案例来源：改编自 Danielle Monaghan. Global and Cultural Effectiveness: Recruiting Is Social and Talent Is Local. http://www.shrm.org/publications/hrmagazine/editorialcontent/2016/0116/pages/0116-competencies-global-cultural-effectiveness-monaghan.aspx, 2015-12-16）

随着国际化水平的不断提高，企业对于国际化人才的争夺已近白热化。如何招聘、选拔优秀的员工，并为其提供必要的相关培训，提高员工素质，是确保员工队伍拥有良好素质的基础，也是管理理论中人员配备职能的核心内容。正如案例中所讲述的那样，网络与智能手机的出现和流行，催生了一些新型的招聘方式，也使得人才招聘和选拔的过程越来越透明。环境的变化为组织人员配备提出了新的要求和挑战。人员配备包括哪些内容？应遵循哪些基本的原则？会受到哪些因素的影响？本节将从人员配备的定义入手，围绕人员配备的原则和影响要素展开讨论。

一、人员配备的含义

管理学中的人员配备，是指对组织结构中的职位进行填补和不断充实的过程,其目的是为了选择合适的人员充实组织结构中所规定的各项职务,以保证组织活动的正常进行，进而实现组织的既定目标。很显然，人员配备必须与组织管理紧密相连，即有目的地确立角色和职位结构。传统的观点一般将人员配备狭义地理解为选人和用人,并将其作为人事部门的主要工作,而现代的观点则认为,人员配备不仅要包括选人和用人,还应该包括如何通过增强组织凝聚力来留住优秀员工,以及如何帮助员工制订职业生涯规划,培养员工。人才的选、用、留、育构成了广义的人员配备基本框架（参见图 7-1）。

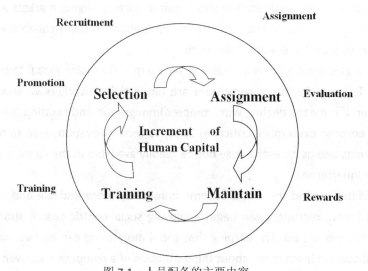

图 7-1　人员配备的主要内容
Figure 7-1　Main Contents of Staffing

二、人员配备的系统方法

许多学者将人员配备作为组织职能的一部分进行论述,但本教材认同孔茨（Harold Kootz）的观点,即人员配备应该作为一个独立的管理职能存在。组织职能更多地强调如何设立角色结构,对如何充实这些职位研究的较少。组织中的人作为一个重要资产,招聘、选拔和培训都花费巨大,管理实践要求组织在管理中要更关注人的因素。人员配备不应该仅是人事部门的职责,而应与整个组织运营战略联系起来,是整个管理系统的一部分。

✍　**The Definition of Staffing**

In management, staffing is defined as a process of filling, and keeping filled, positions in the organization structure.

Staffing must be closely linked to organizing, that is, the setting up of intentional structures of roles and positions.

✍　**Systems Approach to Staffing**

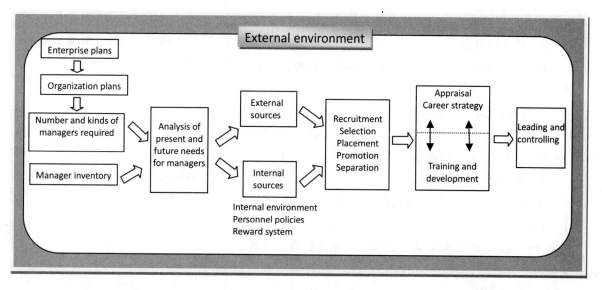

图 7-2 　人员配备的系统方法

Figure 7-2　Systems Approach to Staffing

（资料来源：改编自 Heinz Weihrich, Mark V. Cannice and Harold Koontz. *Management: A global and Entrepreneurial Perspective* (13th edition). 北京：经济科学出版社，2011, p. 245）

图 7.2 描述了人员配备的系统方法，解释了人员配备与整个管理系统的关系。首先，公司计划是组织计划的基础，公司根据整体的战略计划设计公司的组织架构，进而决定了所需要的管理人员的人数和类型；其次，管理者可以根据目前的管理人才储备情况，结合职位需求，对管理人员进行需求分析比较；最后，在分析比较的基础上，通过组织外部来源和内部来源两个渠道，来对人才进行招聘、选拔、替换、晋升和调离，并对新的员工或者将到新岗位上工作的员工进行培养和训练，帮助其制定职业生涯规划。

正如图 7-2 所示，计划是组织设计的基础，组织设计决定了人员配备的需求，而人员配备的结果又会直接影响管理者后续的领导工作和控制工作环节。合适的人员安排更有利于管理者进行领导和控制。因此，人员配备是整个管理系统中的必要一环，应该用一种开放的系统方法去进行人员配备管理，不仅要考虑组织内部需求，更要考虑外部环境的变化。

Planning is the basis for organizational design, and organizational design determines the number and kinds of managers required. Staffing affects leading and controlling. Therefore, staffing requires an open-system approach.

三、人员配备的原则

✍ **Principles of Staffing**

人员配备需要按照一定原则来实施有效管理，一般而言，人员配备的原则主要有如下几个方面。

1. 经济效益原则

1. Principle of economic benefit

组织中人员配备计划的拟定既不是为了盲目地扩大员工队伍，也不是单纯为了解决员工就业问题，而应该以组织需要为依据，以保证经济效益的提高为前提。应保证人员配备的经济性，保证组织效益的提高。

2．任人唯贤原则

在人员配备中，招聘和选拔是重要的核心内容。在人才选聘时，应该大公无私，实事求是地发现人才、爱护人才，本着求贤若渴的精神，重视和使用有真才实学的人。"举贤避亲"和"举贤不避亲"在特殊的情境下都可能是正确的选择，最终的目的是选用适合组织职位的人。

3．因事择人原则

正如前文所述，人员配备与组织职能是紧密相连的两个职能。因此，人员配备应该以职位的空缺和实际工作的需要为出发点，以职位对人员的实际要求为标准，选拔、录用各类人员。

4．量才使用原则

量才使用就是根据每个人的能力大小而安排合适的岗位。人与人之间的差异是客观存在的，只有将人放在最能发挥其才能的岗位上，才能干得最好。同时，对缺乏某个具体岗位的工作经验的人员，管理者应该能够挖掘和发现其潜能，有针对性地对其培训，以实现人才价值最大化。

5.程序化原则

人员配备必须遵循一定的标准和程序。制定科学合理的选聘程序、培训规范和绩效评价标准，通过员工培训、职业生涯规划与开发等手段，促进员工素质的提高，是人员配备顺利实施的重要保证。

6．动态平衡原则

处在动态环境中的组织，是不断变革和发展的。组织对其成员的要求也是在不断变动的，当然，工作中人的能力和知识也是在不断提高和丰富的。因此，人与事的配合需要进行不断的协调平衡。管理者应该充分了解内外部环境的变化，对不符合职位需要的人及时调整，最终实现人与职位、工作的动态平衡。

四、国际环境中影响人员配备的外部环境因素

随着国际化的进程不断加快，先进技术的不断涌现和跨国公司的不断崛起，为人员配备带来了新的挑战。大型跨国公司中的员工多来自不同国家，也可能会被派到其他国家去工作。全球化的核心思想就是将整个世界视为一个整体，从全球范围内去选择资源，并将其合理地分配到全球各个地方。在这样背景下，人员配备需要在全球化的背景下进行全球性人员决策，除了会受到公司规模、公司文化、公司组织架构等内部要素的影响之外，还必然会受到一些组织之外的环境因素直接或间接的制约。

---

2. Principle of appointing people by merits

3. Principle of following job requirements

4. Principle of person-position

5. Principle of following policies and procedures

6. Principle of dynamic balance

✍ **External Factors Influencing Staffing in the International Environment**

External factors are things from outside an organization that directly or indirectly influences it.

（一）政治法律环境

全球化背景下，跨国公司需要在多个国家运营，其东道国的管理人员可能由母公司所在国外派，也可能来自东道国本土选拔，还有可能是来自第三国的管理人员。不同国家的政治法律环境差异很大，这就要求跨国公司在进行人员配备时，应充分了解各国的政治法律制度，按照各国政府的政治和法律限制来制定公司的人员管理制度。例如，美国的法律禁止由于种族、肤色、宗教信仰、国籍、性别或年龄而在就业方面予以歧视，那么在美国进行招聘和挑选晋升人员时，就必须严格遵守这些法律规定。再如中国 2008 年颁布新的劳动法，对试用期、临时用工、违约金、裁员、劳动合同等人员管理都有了新的要求和标准，对员工的合法权益保护更加全面，组织在制定人员管理政策时，必须遵照新劳动法进行管理，充分考虑员工合法利益的保护，建立完善的用工制度和绩效管理体系。

工会的力量是国际化经营中企业必须关注的一项重要内容。工会是代表工人利益并通过集体谈判寻求保护工人利益的组织。在跨国并购过程中，对并购之后员工的管理和安置，必须考虑当地工会的影响，以免并购之后在员工的劳动关系、薪酬待遇、工作时间等方面引起员工和工会的不满，导致公司新政策无法顺利实施。例如，在德国，工会对经济的发展起着巨大的积极推动作用，集体谈判是德国工会的一项重要工作，是工会代表和维护职工权益的有效手段，德国法律规定，企业必须建立监事会、董事会、工人委员会，三者相互制约和监督，这就要求跨国企业在人员管理过程中，必须充分考虑工会的地位和作用。2006年明基并购西门子手机失败，提出破产保护并撤出欧洲手机市场，此举引起当地工会不满，组织工人们上街游行抗议，惊动德国政府，最终西门子推迟管理层加薪 30%的计划，以节省资金为 3000 名手机部门的前员工进行培训，以帮助他们找到新工作。

（二）社会文化环境

在国际化环境背景下，员工队伍的差异化特点越来越明显，民族、性别、年龄、教育背景上的差异不断加大。员工队伍的差异化会影响到人员配备的各个方面，不同的社会背景带来了较大的文化差异，如何调整不同的文化之间的冲突和矛盾、如何培育适当的组织文化、如何让管理者适应与不同文化背景员工相处的工作状态，是人员配备职能所必须考虑的问题。

❖ Political and legal environment

It is not unusual for large international firms to have top management teams composed of managers of many different nationalities.
Companies have three sources for staffing the positions in international operations: from the home country of the firm, from the host country, and from third countries.
Managers will have to be more oriented toward the public responding to the public's legitimate needs.
Legal and political constraints require that organizations follow laws and guidelines issued by various levels of government.

Labor union is an organization that represents workers and seeks to protect their interests through collective bargaining.
Labor unions have the goals of obtaining pay and working conditions that satisfy members and of giving members a voice in decisions that affect them. They influence the way which pay and promotions are determined.

❖ Sociocultural environment

In the international environment, organizations today have a very diverse workforce. The diversity in the workplace has implications for staffing.

Global Perspective

Amazon in Germany

Germany is one of Amazon's largest markets outside the United States, and the company has a big human resource (HR) responsibility there, with 8,000 permanent workers at eight distribution centers, along with more than 10,000 temporary workers for seasonal jobs. But the giant online retailer has become the latest symbol of everything that many Germans resent about American-style human resource management (HRM). A series of protests by ver.di, one of the largest labor unions in Germany, has raised the question of whether Amazon will become the latest company to run afoul of German labor laws, which are much tougher than those in the United States. Walmart abandoned Germany in 2006 after a number of setbacks, including a struggle with ver.di. The triggering event for Amazon was a documentary about third-party contractors hired to manage thousands of temporary immigrant workers. The documentary interviewed workers who said that security guards intimidate them, and even went so far as to imply that Amazon uses neo-Nazi thugs to keep workers in line. Amazon immediately stopped doing business with that security company. Amazon already pays above union wages, but ver.di has other complaints. Union officials say that a "Big Brother" atmosphere prevails at the company. "Everything is measured, everything is calculated, everything is geared toward efficiency," said Heiner Reimann, a spokesman for ver.di. "People want to be treated with respect."

（案例来源：改编自 Amazon Workers Strike in Germany Over Pay. http://www.bbc.com/news/business-25397316, Amazon Staff in Germany to Prolong strike. http://news.xinhuanet.com/english/europe/2014-12/18/c_133862362.htm; Amazon Germany http://Employees: Go on Strike,. http://timesofindia.india-times.com/tech-news/labour-union-to-Amazon-Germany-eemployee-Go-on-strike/articleshow/44946844.cms?）

社会文化环境的差异主要源于国家或地区文化差异。国家或地区文化对于人员配备的影响是非常巨大的，包括人员管理、绩效评价、战略决策、职业发展规划等多个方面。这种文化差异在跨国公司运营中表现得尤为明显。在制定人员配备战略时，保持与外部环境的一致是非常重要的。组织必须能够识别社会文化差异，并相应地调整薪酬等人事政策，以适应不同国家和地区的文化环境。

社会文化环境包括工作伦理、员工对工作的态度、员工的工作动机等内容。例如，在一些文化环境中，货币激励政策可能是很有效的政策，而在其他一些文化环境中，员工可能更关注较好的工作与生活的平衡关系。人员配备在制定相关政策时必须充分考虑不同的文化差异，以满足不同的工作动机。在更关注经济效益的文化环境中，高工资、直接的经济奖励等条件可能会吸引更多的优秀人才，而在更关注生活质量的文化环境中，带薪休假也许更具吸引力。

National culture influences numerous facets of a corporation's staffing policies, including human resource administration, performance appraisal, strategic decision-making, and provision of developmental opportunities.

It is crucial that the companies, especially multinational companies, recognize the cultural differences and adjust their compensation practices to the cultural specifics of a particular host country.

The cultural and social environment includes such things as work ethic, attitude towards work and employee motivations.

Staffing must assess cultural factors, find differences, and match motivators accordingly.

Global Perspective

Do Blondes Have More Fun in Japan

An American executive told the following story: "My first trip to Japan was pretty much a disaster for several reasons. The meetings didn't run smoothly because every day at least 20, if not more, people came walking in and out of the room just to look at me. It is not one thing to see a woman at the negotiation table, but to see a woman who is blonde, young, and very tall by Japanese standards (5'8" with no shoes) leading the discussions was more than most of the Japanese men could handle."

"Even though I was the lead negotiator for the Ford team, the Japanese would go out of their way to avoid speaking directly to me. At the negotiation table I purposely sat in the center of my team, in the spokesperson's strategic position. Their key person would not sit across from me, but rather two places down. Also, no one would address questions and/or remarks to me—to everyone (all male) on our team—but none to me. They would never say my name or acknowledge my presence. And most disconcerting of all, they appeared to be laughing at me. We would be talking about a serious topic such as product liability, I would make a point or ask a question, and after a barrage of Japanese they would all start laughing."

（案例来源：节选自 Philip R. Cateors and John L. Graham. *International Marketing* (12th edition). 北京：中国人民大学出版社，2005, p. 98）

伦理环境也是社会文化环境中一个重要的内容，社会伦理认知同样会影响人员配备决策选择。例如，在一些国家男女公平就业的呼声越来越高，社会改变了对工作女性的态度，那么公司就应该将有能力的女性安排在管理职位上，从而为自己树立一个较好的形象；再如，同性恋结婚已被十多个国家认定为合法，但是在一些国家和地区被认定是犯罪行为，那么跨国公司为了实现自己对所有员工一视同仁的承诺，在进行人员配备的时候，就应该有选择地将其派往适合他们工作和生活的地区。

Social and ethical attitudes in society will also influence how staffing operates.

For example, changing societal attitudes toward women in the workplace and same-sex marriage issue are new challenging ethical environments companies have to face.

（三）技术环境

21 世纪以来，技术的变化日新月异，尤其在计算机和通信领域，发生了翻天覆地的变化。互联网和智能手机的出现为企业管理的所有领域都带来了机遇和挑战，当然也包括人员配备这一职能。新的技术要求从事人力资源管理的专业人士必须了解、熟悉和掌握新的信息技术和方法，以新的方式雇用、管理、评价员工；同时也为人力资源管理提供了更便捷有效的方式，可以大大降低人力资源管理成本。

✧ Technological environment

Technology, especially Internet and smartphone, can present opportunities and challenges for staffing. New technologies may require HRM professionals to hire, manage or evaluate employees in the new technologies.

互联网的广泛使用改变了人们的工作方式。越来越多的公司开始雇用不同的工作形式的员工，包括全职员工和兼职员工，包括虚拟员工、现场员工、分布在全球的员工，这完全符合全球化的工作要求，人们不必在传统的办公室里或者同一个工作地点工作，他们可以通过互联网了解彼此的工作状态，很好地完成工作。这为人员配备提出了新的要求，人事管理者需要突破传统的用人思维，接受多种工作方式，并提出相应的绩效考评和培训办法。

同时，视频软件和社交网站的出现为人员配备提供了更多的选聘办法。越来越多的公司开始使用互联网作为招聘工具，因为互联网招聘可以节约成本，并且高效。人事管理者可以通过互联网发布简历、收集简历，将电话面试、视频面试和面对面面试整合起来，更好地选聘员工。

例如，耐克公司（Nike）在人员招聘时，在专业招聘网站上发布招聘信息，之后对应聘人员进行筛选，通过初选后的应聘者，首先要通过电话面试，回答 8 个问题；在一部分应聘人员通过了电话面试之后，他们将会接受计算机视频面试，一般会回答 3 个左右的问题；只有通过了计算机视频面试的人，才会获得最后的面对面面试机会。耐克公司通过这种方式，减少了人事管理人员的工作量，也节约了人事管理成本。

大数据技术作为社会科技发展的新方向，为人类生活带来了巨大的便利，为科技发展带来了深远的影响，对人力资源管理的影响也日益显著。将大数据技术应用到企业的人事管理当中，可以加强人事管理的效率。通过建立大数据技术应用平台，可以实现人才招聘、员工培养、员工关系、绩效管理等方面的信息化，为人力资源管理工作模式的创新提供可能。

Keeping up with new technological development is key to employee engagement and productivity.

Many global companies have full time and part time employees, virtual employees, field employees, and globally deployed employees.

It is not necessarily to work in the traditional office or the single location based staff.

Many companies are turning to the Internet as recruiting tool because it is cost effective and timely.

Staffing managers can combine interactive voice recognition technique and computerized interview with human interview to reduce recruiting costs.

Internet recruiting can conduct searches for specific areas and talents. Using some softwares to manage staffing process can reduce recruiting costs.

Big Data technique is indisputable valuable to staffing and organization decision-making.

Global Perspective

Big Data in Staffing

The talk about Big Data is getting louder by the minute. As companies shift their core systems to the cloud, more and more people-related data becomes available. Given the global recession and talent imbalances in the world, companies are focusing on replacing their legacy HR systems to help apply analytics reasoning to HR and talent. However, most HR teams today are not ready for this evolution. One research shows that only 6% of HR departments believe they are "excellent" in analytics and more than 60% feel they are poor or behind. Over the next few years we are going to see major investments in BigData analytics in all large companies, with huge returns on investment from the effort.

We are all flooded with data: employee data, location data, social data, compensation data, and much more. If you start an analytics project by collecting all the data you can find, you may never come to an end. One common talent problem, for example, may be sales productivity. What factors contribute to a predictable high-performing sales person? Every company would like to understand this better. And once you understand these characteristics, how can you better source, attract, and hire such people? These questions are worth millions of dollars to answer. If you have very smart statisticians working with a very senior manager to come up with the hypothesis, and they can explore all the possible data elements that might contribute to the answer, you can know how to do next.

Most HR data is quite dirty. Fields are filled with incorrect, duplicate, out of date, and inconsistent information. And you'll find one of your biggest challenges is clearly defining what various data elements mean (building the data dictionary). These problems can be solved by analysis. A major part of a talent analytics program is defining the data itself, and bringing together definitions from across your different HR functions.

So, do you apply big data to your human capital investment?

（案例来源：改编自 Josh Bensin. Big Data in HR: Why it's Here and What it Means. http://www.bersin.com/blog/post/BigData-in-HR--Why-its-here-and-what-it-means.asp 2012-11-17）

（四）经济环境

经济环境变化对人员配备的影响是显而易见的。许多专家提出，全球经济下滑的趋势对全球的人力资源管理实践活动产生了持续而显著的影响。例如，终身雇佣制曾经是日本的一种主流雇佣制度，日本的员工们曾经一直习惯于两件事情：终身雇佣和体面的退休金。但是，随着经济的整体下滑，终身雇佣已经不复存在，而公司退休金计划也开始表现不佳。再如，2014 年欧洲遭遇希腊债务危机，经济复苏步伐缓慢，欧洲经济遭到重创，与此相对应的是，2014 年欧洲失业率达到了 11.9%，而希腊更是达到了 27.5%。企业的发展前景与整个经济发展状况紧密相连，企业在制定人员配备战略时，必须依据企业发展前景对人力资源的需求做出合理的规划。

✧ Economic environment

The global economic downturn has left what many experts believe to be an enduring mark on HRM practices worldwide.

In Japan, workers used to count on two things: a job for life and a decent pension. Now, lifetime employment is long gone and corporate pension plans are crumbling.

互联网经济的迅速发展为人们提供了新型的工作方式，自主创业和网络兼职已成为中国两种新型的、发展迅速的就业途径。一些传统的行业逐渐衰败，造成员工失业，但是与此同时，一些新型行业的兴起又为员工就业提供了机遇。这些变化为组织的人员配备提出了新的要求。组织的人事管理人员需要根据行业的发展现状及未来走向，描画出组织所需的新型人才的特点，并积极做好人才储备，以适应组织未来的发展。

Many jobs lost during the recession and might not come back at all, but they may be replaced by other types of work in growing industries. All of these changes have affected staffing strategies.

Global Perspective

Bias against the Unemployed

As the economy has continued to perform poorly since the start of the Great Recession, a large number of individuals have joined the ranks of the long-term unemployed. The difficulties of unemployment are compounded because many employers either overtly or covertly prefer candidates who do not have gaps in their work history. For example, New York Times reporter Catherine Rampell found in hundreds of job postings on Monster.com, CareerBuilder, and Craigslist that employers prefer people who are either currently employed or only recently laid off. This makes it extremely difficult for qualified individuals to find work because it constitutes a bias against the unemployed.

Although federal regulators in the Equal Employment Opportunity Commission have voiced concerns about the practice, unemployment is not a protected status like age, race, or gender. Due to gaps in the law, some states like New Jersey, New York, and Michigan have considered or implemented laws prohibiting advertisements that discourage unemployed workers from applying. What can employers do to ensure they are giving qualified individuals who have been unemployed a fair shot at open positions? A few principles can help ensure they are recruiting ethically:

1. Always try to evaluate the whole candidate, including prior experience, ability, and personality. Don't get overly focused on a single detail of their employment history.

2. If you are concerned about an employment gap in the resume, ask about it directly. Don't assume it reflects a lack of initiative or interest in work.

3. Consider offering additional training to those who may have missed out on certain developments in the field during their spell of unemployment. Although it can add expense, your organization might benefit from securing someone other employers would overlook.

（案例来源：改编自 C. Rampell. The Help Wanted Sign Comes with a Frustrating Asterisk. *The New York Times*, www.nytimes.com, 2011-7-25; S. Kelly. Unemployed Not Wanted? The EEOC Scrutinizes Whether Companies' Recruiting Only Already Employed Application Could Be Discrimination. *Treasury and Risk*, www.treasurandrisk.com, 2011-4-1）

第二节 人员选拔与培训

Why Are Fewer and Fewer U.S. Employees Satisfied with Their Jobs?

Research by the Conference Board suggests that job satisfaction for U.S. employees is at a 23-year low. This appears to be occurring in the midst of a dramatic growth in information technology that was supposed to make work easier for employees. What is going on here? Are employers failing to consider an ethical responsibility to employees by providing a satisfying, fulfilling experience at work?

When Professor James Heskett of Harvard posted information about these low job satisfaction rates on his blog, respondents provided a variety of different explanations for why U.S. workers are less satisfied than they were in the past. They included economic pressures, instability in the business environment, and increased competition to get the best jobs. Others believe businesses have become so focused on stock prices and profitability that the personal relationship that used to exist between employers and employees has been lost. Still others proposed that in a poor economic environment, employees who wanted to switch to a new job aren't always able to find alternatives, leaving them "hostages" to a dissatisfying work situation. Whatever the explanation, there is cause for concern. Survey data from Towers Watson's global workforce study of 20,000 employees in 22 markets around the world found that employees are especially concerned about job security and feel they are entirely responsible for ensuring their long-term career prospects work out. In the current economic environment, it seems that in employers' minds, employee well-being and security have taken a back seat to coping with workplace realities.

What can managers do to ensure they are making ethical decisions about protecting the quality of the workplace in their organizations? As we have shown, managers can enact a variety of concrete steps—including improving working conditions and providing a positive social environment—that will make work more enjoyable for employees. Employers may also want to think about whether their efforts to achieve efficiency and productivity are creating a work environment that is not very satisfying for employees.

（案例来源：改编自 Jim Heskett. Why Are Fewer and Fewer U.S. Employees Satisfied with Their Jobs? Harvard Business School Working Knowledge. http://hbswk.hbs.edu/item/why-are-fewer-and-fewer-u-s-employees-satisfied-with-their-jobs, 2010-4-2）

多数企业的主要目标是追求企业绩效和企业价值的提升，企业员工是完成企业目标和提升企业绩效的最重要载体，员工的质量及员工满意度直接影响了企业的工作效果。但是正如案例中所描述的那样，如今越来越多的员工对工作现有状态表现出不满意。如何有效提高员工满意度、进而提升组织整体绩效已成为当今组织必须面对的重要问题。组织在进行人员配备的过程中，人员选拔和培训是两个重要的内容。一方面，组织可以通过不同的选拔方式，挑选出优秀的员工，委以重任；另一方面，也可以通过相关的培训来规划员工职业发展生涯，帮助员工增强自身竞争力，提升组织员工满意度。本节将主要围绕人员选拔和人员培训两个核心问题分别进行讨论。

一、人员选拔的定义及过程

（一）人员选拔的定义

人员选拔主要是指当组织出现人员短缺或是其他人员需求时，管理者采用一些方法对应聘者进行甄别和筛选的过程。

我们可以将人员选拔看作一种预测行为，在选拔过程中应该做出预测，聘用哪一位应聘者未来可能会取得成功，即哪一位应聘者在未来工作中可能完成组织所规定的绩效要求。例如，为某销售职位选拔人员，其甄选过程应当能够预测到哪位应聘者未来会给公司带来更大的销售额；为中学教师职位选拔人员，其甄选过程应该能够预测到未来哪位应聘者将会是优秀的教育者。

人员选拔过程将会产生四种可能的结果（如图 7-3 所示）。其中两种结果说明决策正确；另两种结果说明决策错误。如果选中的申请人在日后的工作中确实取得了成功，或者拒绝的申请人在日后的工作中表现的确实不尽如人意，就说明组织的人员选拔决策正确。在前一种情况下，组织成功地接受了合格的申请人；在后一种情况下，组织成功地拒绝了不符合资质的申请人。如果组织错误地拒绝了一位在后来的工作中可能有成功表现的申请人，或者错误地接受了在后来的工作中表现极差的申请人，那么人才选拔的过程就出现了问题。前者称为错误拒绝，后者称为错误接受。错误拒绝可能会因需要继续寻找其他合适的申请人而浪费人员选拔成本，错误接受可能会因不合资质的员工无法完成组织绩效要求而为组织带来损失，或者浪费培训成本。人员选拔应该尽量减少拒绝错误或接受错误的概率，增加做出正确选择的概率。

✍ **The Definition and Process of Selection**

◇ Definition of selection
The selection is the process of identifying and screening the applicants when an organization faces the personnel shortage or other talents demands. Selection involves predicting which applicants will be successful if hired.

A decision is correct when the applicant was predicted to be successful and proved to be successful on the job, or when the applicant was predicted to be unsuccessful and was not hired. In the first instance, we have successfully accepted; in the second, we have successfully rejected.

The major emphasis of any selection activity should be reducing the probability of reject errors or accept errors while increasing the probability of making correct decisions.

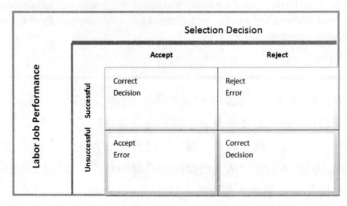

图 7-3　人员选拔结果

Figure 7-3　Selection Results

（资料来源：Stephen P. Robbins and Mary Coulter. *Management* (13th edition). New York: Pearson, 2016, p. 380）

（二）人员选拔的过程

人员选拔的具体步骤可能因职位和候选人自身情况而有所不同。例如，选择一个高级职业经理人和选择一个一线操作工人的过程可能会明显不同。但是总体上来说，典型的人员选拔过程可能包括如下步骤（如图 7-4 所示）。

1. 建立选拔标准

组织应根据当前职位的要求和未来可能的工作要求，提出该职位的选拔标准，包括教育背景、知识、技能、经验、个性特征等内容。选拔标准一般会在招聘启事上登出，以便应聘者查看。

2. 应聘者填写申请表格

在招聘或选拔标准公布之后，会有应聘者前来询问。这时候人事管理人员应该让应聘人员填写申请表格。当然，如果应聘人员来自本单位内部，可以省略掉该步骤，或者填写简略的申请表。

3. 进行筛选性面试

收到申请表之后，人事部门应该首先对申请人进行筛选性面试，对申请人的基本资质进行考核，筛选出符合本职位基本要求的候选者。

4. 组织正式面试

通过筛选性面试的候选者，应由管理人员、该职位的直接上级或者组织内的其他人员对其进行正式面试，对候选人所提供的材料进一步核对和核实，并对其能力做出评价，判断其是否符合该职位的要求。

5. 同意聘用或拒绝聘用

根据上述步骤所得到的结果，综合做出评价，是否同意聘用或拒绝聘用。有些单位对同意聘用的人还需要进行体检，体检合格后方可正式发出聘用通知。

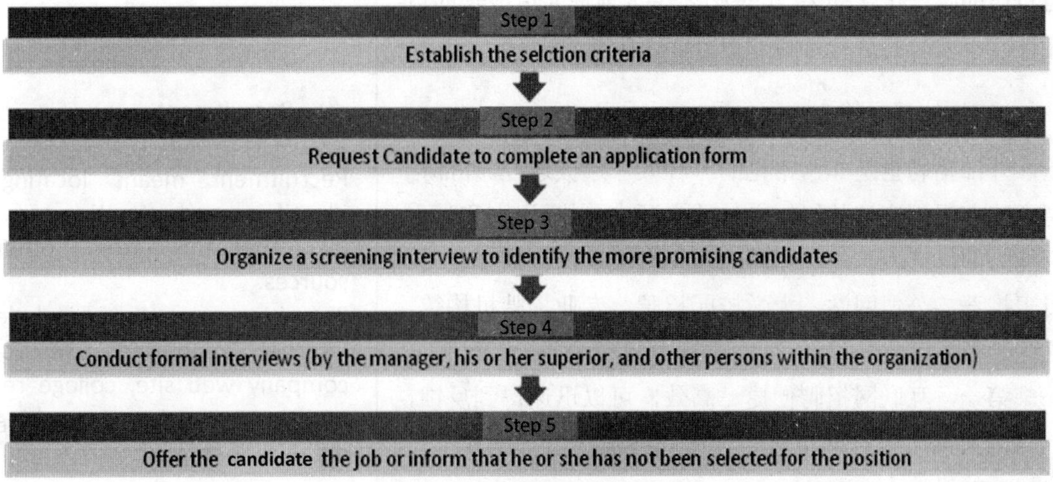

◇ Selection process

图 7-4　人员选拔过程

Figure 7-4　Selection Process

二、人员选拔的渠道

（一）内部提升

内部提升是许多组织（尤其是大型组织）常用的人员选拔途径。内部提升意味着员工进入基层一线主管的职位，然后按组织结构向上晋升。显然，组织内部的员工会非常赞成内部提升这种选拔政策，这样可以减少外部人员的竞争。内部提升也的确有很多的优点，它不仅在提高员工士气、增强员工对组织的忠诚度以及提高组织的声誉方面有积极的作用，而且还有助于组织挖掘内部员工中潜在的优秀管理人员。

但是，从内部提升也存在着一些局限性。当员工知道会从内部提升一个管理者时，可能会不惜一切争夺晋升机会，这种竞争有时可能不够理性，会影响组织的内部团结，不利于组织文化的建设。同时，内部提升还可能会导致领导者只挑选那些能够模仿他们的上司行事的人，因为从领导者的心理角度来讲，这样的人可能行为方式更像自己，因此更具有领导的才能。这样的结果就是会使组织缺少新的思想、新的做法，进而缺少创新能力。因此，组织不能单纯依靠内部提升这一种渠道来选拔人才。

在管理学中，有一个很著名的"彼得原理"，由管理学家劳伦斯·彼得（Laurence J. Peter）提出。他总结了诸多有关组织中不能胜任的失败实例之后，归纳说："在一个等级制度中，管理者可能被提升到他们并不胜任的岗位上。尤其当某个管理者在现有职位很成功的时候，常常会被提升到更高的职位上，但是他可能并不具有更高职位所需的技能。"对于人才选拔者来说，不应该将晋升作为对员工的主要奖励方式；对于员工来说，也不应该将晋升作为自己的唯一工作动力。组织必须注重管理人员成长的可能性，不要轻易进行选拔和提升。

（二）外部招聘

外部招聘也是非常常见的一种人才选拔途径。外部招聘意味着组织应该从组织之外的来源去寻找、识别和吸引有能力的候选人。外部招聘的途径有很多，包括互联网、员工推荐、公司网站、大学校园招聘、专业招聘机构等。这些途径各有优缺点。

第一，互联网招聘便捷、高效，可以迅速得到反馈，但是因为网络信息的不真实性可能会筛选出一些并不符合资质的候选人。

✍ **Selection Sources**

✧ Promotion from within

Promotion from within implies that workers proceeded into first-line supervisory positions and then flow upward through the organization structure.
Promoting from within the organization not only has positive values relating to morale, employees' long-run commitment to the organization, and the organizational reputation, but also allows the organization to take advantage of the presence of potentially fine managers among its employees.
A danger presented by a policy of exclusively promoting from within is that it may lead to the selection of persons who have, perhaps, only imitated their superiors.

Peter Principle implies that managers tend to be promoted to the level of their incompetence.
Specifically, if a manager succeeds in a position, this very success may lead to promotion to a higher position, often one requiring skills that the person does not possess.

✧ Recruitment

Recruitment means locating, identifying and attracting capable applicants from other sources.
Recruiting sources include Internet, employee referrals, company web site, college recruiting, professional recruiting organizations, etc.

第二，员工推荐有助于组织更好地了解候选人的资质，而且也可能因为了解而找到特别优秀的候选人。但是这种方法可能会造成同类人群太多，比如同学、同乡，影响了组织人员构成的多元化。

第三，公司网站的公开性很高，因此可以获得较多的候选人的关注，而且关注公司网站的人往往是某个领域的特定群体，因此使招聘更加有针对性。但是公司网站也属于一种互联网招聘，因此信息的真实性仍然会受到质疑。

第四，大学校园招聘可以获得很多的有潜质的候选人，但缺点就是大学生们多数没有行业经验，只能招聘到一些入门级的管理者。

第五，专业的招聘机构对于招聘有丰富的经验，了解行业和人才需求，可以更有效地完成招聘工作。但是因为是组织之外的机构代为招聘，可能对于组织的文化、组织的领导风格等无形的部分并不熟悉，影响了招聘效果。

随着互联网技术的不断发展，新型的招聘渠道越来越多，互联网招聘、智能手机招聘已成为被广为接受的招聘方式。另外，一些组织正在使用社交网站来招聘员工。组织可以结合多种招聘途径，取长补短，最终获得有潜质的候选人。

More and more organizations are using social networking sites to recruit new employees.

Global Perspective

Online Job Searching Has Doubled Since 2005

The survey on the job search methods of 2001 U.S adults by the Pew Research Center found that a majority of Americans (54%) have researched jobs on the Internet, and nearly as many (45%) have applied for a job online. That's more than double the number from 2005.

These days, many resources for job seekers are posted online and employers often expect applicants to find and apply for job using the Internet, e-mail or mobile applications. Creating a professional online profile is becoming more and more important. Job seekers should spend time finishing their resumes online.

The percentage of job seekers searching and applying for jobs using mobile devices and social media is also increasing. Some 28 percent of job seekers—including 53% of 18 to 29 years olds—have used a smartphone as part of a job search. Among these Americans who have looked for a new job in the last two years:

94 percent have used a smartphone to browse or research job listings.

74 percent have used a smartphone to e-mail about a job.

50 percent have used a smartphone to fill out an online job application.

23 percent have used a smartphone to create a resume or cover letter.

Mobile use will continue to change recruiting. Recruiters have to make it easier for job seekers to find, apply for and share the jobs they have available.

（案例来源：改编自 Roy Maurer, Online Job Searching Has Doubled Since 2005, http://www.shrm.org/hrdisciplines/staffingmanagement/articles/pages/online-job-searching-doubled.aspx, 2015-12-21）

（三）公开竞争

正如前文所述，内部提升和外部招聘各有优缺点，因此许多组织将二者结合，采用公开竞争的方式。公开竞争是指让最合适的人员公开竞争空缺职位，不论这些人员来自组织内部还是外部。

公开竞争最大的好处就是可以让组织有机会得到最好的候选人员。一方面，公开竞争可以避免内部提升的缺点，为内部人员引入外部人员的竞争，激励内部员工不断进取；另一方面，公开竞争仍然为内部员工保留了晋升的机会，并没有像外部招聘那样完全拒绝内部人员，在其他条件都一样的情况下，内部员工应该与外部人员展开竞争。这种方式总体上比较公平。但是，在实行公开竞争的招聘政策时，组织必须用公正和客观地评价和选拔办法，尽可能保持内外部平衡，科学的选拔优秀员工。

三、人员选拔方法

管理者可以使用各种选拔方法来减少接受错误和拒绝错误的发生。常用的方法包括：应聘者申请表分析、笔试、绩效模拟测试、面试、履历调查等。

（一）申请表分析

几乎所有的组织，在招聘时都会要求应聘者填写一份申请表。这可能只是一份让应聘者填上姓名、地址和电话号码的简表，也可能是一份综合性的个人简历表，要求仔细地填写个人的活动、技能和成就。

经历方面相关的、硬性的、可证实的资料（如在大学学习成绩的名次）可以作为某些工作绩效的衡量标尺。另外，组织可以依据与工作相关性的程度，对申请表的栏目进行加权评分，根据综合评分来初步判定该应聘者是否符合职位的基本资质。这种分析方法对于营业员、工程师、生产者、地区经理、办公室职员和技术员等技术性或操作性较强的工作尤为有效。

（二）笔试

笔试是一种与面试相对应的测试，包括对智商、悟性、能力、个性和兴趣等方面的内容的测试，测试内容应该与工作相关。笔试是考核应聘者学识水平的重要工具，可以较为客观地衡量应聘者在基本知识、专业知识、综合分析能力、文字表达能力等素质及能力方面的差异。

◇ Open competition

Principle of open competition means that vacant positions should be opened to the best-qualified persons available, whether inside or outside the organization.
Open competition gives the organization the opportunity to secure the services of the best-suited candidates.
When using open competition policy, the organization must have fair and objective methods of appraising and selecting its people.

✍ **Selection Tools**

◇ Application forms

Application forms are almost universally used and are most useful for gathering information.

◇ Written tests
Written tests must be job-related and include intelligence, aptitude, ability, personality, and interest tests.

此种方法曾经非常流行，但是因许多组织并不能验证所采用的笔试与工作效度之间的相关性。因此，笔试的有效性受到了一些管理者的质疑。不过，从 20 世纪 80 年代后期开始，笔试又重新得到了重视。管理者日益清醒地认识到，不良的选聘决策代价很大，希望经过科学设计的测试能减少决策错误发生的可能性。

典型的笔试测试类型包括：

智商——你有多聪明？

悟性——你能学会做事吗？

态度——你感觉怎么样？

能力——你能做吗？

兴趣——你想做吗？

笔试中，智商测试是争议较多的一项内容。有些学者认为，智商测试是评价候选人是否有发展潜力的一个重要指标，而有一些学者则认为，智商测试的高分并不能很好地预见应聘者会出色地完成某项工作。常见的智力测试维度如表 7-1 所示。

Types of Tests
Intelligence: how smart are you?
Aptitude: can you learn to do it?
Attitude: how do you feel about it?
Ability: can you do it?
Interest: do you want to do it?

表 7-1 智力测试维度
Table 7-1 Dimensions of Intellectual Ability

Dimension	Description	Job Example
Number aptitude	Ability to do speedy and accurate arithmetic	Accountant: Computing the sales tax on a set of items
Verbal comprehension	Ability to understand what is read or heard and the relationship of words to each other	Plant manager: Following corporate policies on hiring
Perceptual speed	Ability to identify visual similarities and differences quickly and accurately	Fire investigator: Identifying clues to support a charge of arson
Inductive reasoning	Ability to identify a logical sequence in a problem and then solve the problem	Market researcher: Forecasting demand for a product in the next time period
Deductive reasoning	Ability to use logic and assess the implications of an argument	Supervisor: Choosing between two different suggestions offered by employees
Spatial visualization	Ability to imagine how an object would look if its position in space were changed	Interior decorator: Redecorating an office
Memory	Ability to retain and recall past experiences	Salesperson: Remembering the names of customers

（资料来源：Stephen P. Robbins and Timothy A. Judge. *Organization Behavior* (15th edition). New York: Prentice Hall, 2013, p. 53）

（三）绩效模拟测试

绩效模拟测试主要测试应聘者的实际工作能力，即通过模拟实际工作中的表现证明其具备某项工作的知识和能力。有什么更好的办法能在应聘者实际做一项工作之前就可以发现他是否具备相应的能力？例如，某公司的市场推广职位的申请人能否进行新产品推广活动的设计？对这类问题的思考使得绩效模拟测试日益受到重视。绩效模拟测试是基于职务分析资料做出的，因此比笔试更能满足工作相关性的要求。绩效模拟测试考量的是候选者的实际工作行为，而不是其履历或表面看起来所具有的能力。

✧ Performance simulation tests

Performance simulation tests use actual job behaviors to test an applicant's ability.

Global Perspective

SAT and Recruitment

Many high school students probably believe that once they get into college, their SAT scores are a thing of the past. However, many job seekers are discovering their would-be employers are asking for their SAT scores as part of the selection process. Donna Chan, a 23-year-old graduate of New York's Wagner College, learned that one of the minimum requirements for many of the entry-level financial services jobs she was seeking was a combined SAT score of 1300. According to the College Board, the organization that administers the exam, the average combined math and verbal score of the freshman class of 2005 (the last class to take the old version of the SAT) was 1028. Donna Chan's score was "in the 1200s"—a good score to be sure, but not good enough to obtain any of the positions she was seeking, even though she earned a 3.9 GPA in college. "I think it's asking a bit much," says Chan. "That's something high school kids have to worry about. After four years of working hard, I think you've paid your dues, and unless you're applying to Princeton Review or some math-related, analytical job, I don't see the relevance."

Apparently, however, some recruiters do. Alan Sage, a vice president at systems management software company Configuresoft Inc., says SAT scores are a good predictor of success in his company, and he regularly has applicants submit their scores when applying for sales positions. He set the mark at a combined score of 1200—lower than Donna Chan faced but nonetheless well above average. Says Sage, "In my experience, people with high SAT scores tend to do better." He adds, however, that "we wouldn't exclude someone from an interview if he or she didn't score high." Similarly, Google has used SAT scores to identify individuals with higher levels of cognitive ability in the hiring process, but it also does not use an absolute cutoff. Some individuals, such as Kristin Carnahan, a spokesperson for the College Board, feel companies should use other measures of cognitive ability, such as college grades, which are also more recent indicators than SAT scores. Google uses grades in addition to SAT scores because it believes grades reflect motivation and discipline as well as intellectual ability. However, grades aren't standardized across institutions, so they can't be compared like SAT scores can. Grade inflation also may make it more difficult for recruiters to assess an applicant's GPA. Because OB research has shown cognitive ability is a strong predictor of job performance—and the SAT is supposedly a measure of cognitive ability—many companies may continue to use it as a benchmark for job applicants.

（案例来源：改编自 K.J. Dunham. Career Journal: More Employers Ask Job Seekers for SAT Scores. *The Wall Street Journal*. www.online.wsj.com, 2003-10-28; M. LaChapelle. Do You Hire People the Google Way? *Time Union*. www.timesunion.com, 2011-7-13）

最有代表性的绩效模拟测试方法有两种：工作抽样法和测评中心法。前一方法适用于常规的职务，后一种更适用于挑选从事管理工作的人员。

工作抽样法就是创造一个小型的工作环境，让应聘者完成某项职务的一个或多个核心任务。应聘者通过实际执行这些任务，来展示他们是否拥有职位所必需的才能。人事管理者借助于职务分析得来的资料对工作样本进行仔细设计后，可以确定该项职务需要哪些知识、技术和能力，并将这些工作样本因素与相应的职务绩效因素匹配起来。例如，一项要求使用电子表格（Excel）进行计算的职务，在设计工作样本时，就可以要求应聘者使用 Excel 来解决一个统计计算问题。工作抽样法的结果往往是令人满意的，其效度会高于申请表分析和笔试。

测评中心不是一个场所，而是一种选拔和晋升管理人员的方法。为了衡量一个潜在的管理人员在一个典型的管理环境中如何工作，测评中心往往会让应聘者参加一系列的模拟活动，在这段时间里，心理学家和富有经验的管理人员会对应聘者进行观察和评价。在测评中心测评期满时，评审人员要对每一应聘者的表现做出总评价，并与其他评审人员的评价进行比较，共同就应聘者的管理工作潜力给出结论，针对应聘者写出总结报告。尽管这一方法的使用成本并不低，但如果挑选了一位无效的管理者，其成本毫无疑问会更高。因此，测评中心法仍然被许多组织接受并使用。

（四）面试

面试是一种经过组织者精心设计，在特定场景下，以面对面的方式为主要手段，来评估应聘者在模拟情境中对角色的把控能力。面试与申请表分析一样，几乎是所有组织都要使用的一种人员甄选手段。但是，有趣的是，虽然面试被广为使用，但对其作为一种甄选手段的价值，却一直存在着争议。面试可以成为既有效度又有信度的甄选工具，如果面试设计安排得很好，面试者能够不断提问来获取信息，那么面试可以成为选择优秀人员的一个有效工具。但大多数面试的效果并不理想。一般的面试（在非正式的背景下对应聘者提出一些主题多变的、基本上随机的问题）通常不会提供多少有价值的信息。如果没有良好的组织并按标准化的方式进行，面试可能隐含着各种潜在的偏见和障碍。常见的偏见和障碍包括如下几个方面。

（1）先前对应聘者的认知可能影响面试者做出公正评价。

Performance simulation tests include work sampling and assessment center.

Work sampling requires applicants to actually perform a task or set of tasks that are central to successful job performance.

Work sampling is appropriate for routine or standardized work.

Assessment center is not a location, but a technique for selecting and promoting managers.

Intended to measure how a potential manager will act in typical managerial situations, the assessment center approach is to have candidates take part in a series of exercises.

During this period, they are observed and assessed by psychologists or experienced managers.

At the end of the assessment center period, the assessors summarize their own appraisal of each candidate's performance, then compare their evaluations, come to conclusions concerning each candidate's managerial potential, and write a summary report on each candidate.

✧ Interviews

Interviews are almost universally used by all kinds of organizations. It is to evaluate the candidates on how well they handle role play in mock scenarios.

（2）面试者通常对什么是"合格的"应聘者持有固定的框框。

（3）面试者倾向于支持与他持相同态度的应聘者。

（4）应聘者接受面试的顺序会影响到评价。

（5）面试中信息表达的顺序会影响到评价。

（6）面试者往往会更为重视听到的反面信息。

（7）面试者经常在面试的头四五分钟内对应聘者做出适合与否的判断。

（8）面试者经常在做出结论后的几分钟内忘记面试的多数内容。

为了尽量减少面试的偏见和障碍，在面试中应注意如下几个方面。

（1）对所有应聘者设计一些固定的问题。

（2）取得对应聘者面试的工作有关的更详细信息。

（3）尽量减少对应聘者履历、经验、兴趣、测试成绩或其他方面的先前认识。

（4）多提问那些要求应聘者对实际做法给予详尽描述的行为问题（例如，请举个惩戒员工的具体例子，描述一下你会采取什么行动，行动的结果会怎样）。

（5）采用标准的评价格式。

（6）面谈中要做笔记。

（7）避免面谈中造成过早形成决策。

面试过程中，还应该注意一些伦理问题，不要冒犯到应聘者的习俗或个人隐私。

表 7-2 列出了面试中一些恰当的和不恰当的表达方式。

表 7-2　申请和面试时：该怎样问？

Table 7-2　Employment Applications and Interviews: What Can You Ask?

Category	Okay to Ask	Inappropriate or Illegal to ask
National origin	The applicant's name If the applicant has ever worked under a different name	The origin of the applicant's name The applicant's ancestry/ethnicity
Race	Nothing	Race or color of skin
Disabilities	Whether the applicant has any disabilities that might inhibit performance on the job	If the applicant has any physical or mental defects If the applicant has ever filed a workers' compensation claim
Age	If the applicant is over 18	Applicant's specific age When the applicant graduated from high school
Religion	Nothing	The applicant's religious affiliation What religious holidays the applicant observes
Criminal record	If applicant has ever been convicted of a crime	If the applicant has ever been arrested
Marital/family status	Nothing	Marital status; number of children or planned children Childcare arrangements
Education and experience	Where the applicant went to school Prior work experience	When the applicant graduated Hobbies
Citizenship	If the applicant has a legal right to work in the United States	If the applicant is a citizen of another country

（资料来源：Richard L. Daft. *Management* (12th edition). Boston: Cengage Learning, 2014, p. 415）

Acting Your Interviews

An interview allows potential employers to solicit information about you and to see you "in action". You want to put your best foot forward and show that you're a good catch! Here are some suggestions for helping you "ace" that interview:

1. Research the company ahead of time.

Know the company's competitive advantages—what makes this company unique. Look closely at its financial health. Know the company's strategic initiatives. Find out what you can about the company's culture. Where do you find this information? Internet!

2. Research the industry and competitors.

Familiarize yourself with this industry and the main competitors, but only the big-picture stuff, not minute details.

3. Decide ahead of time how you will answer certain "standard" interview questions.

(1) "Tell me about yourself" question. One expert suggests a "present-past-future" approach. Describe where you are right now, describe a little about your past experiences and the skills you've gained, finish with describing the future and why you're excited about this particular job opportunity.

(2) "What's your greatest weakness" question. One expert suggests talking about weaknesses that don't relate to the job (e.g. if you know the job doesn't require public speaking and public speaking is one of your weaknesses, talk about that). This shows you're self-aware and realize you have weaknesses. Another approach is to talk about past weaknesses and how you dealt with them by getting advice or additional training.

4. Watch your body language.

You want to present a polished, poised, and professional demeanor. So, No: bad posture, too weak/too forceful handshake, lack of eye contact, fidgeting, appearing distracted or uninterested, not smiling. And definitely no cell phone going off in the middle of your interview!

5. Review the job description carefully.

Pay particular attention to stated requirements outside the standard "various duties as assigned." Come up with possible questions an interviewer might ask about those requirements and think about how you would answer those questions.

6. Review your resume with the critical eye of an interviewer.

What stands out? What would you ask a person who had those statements/descriptions on their resume?

（案例来源：节选自 Stephen P. Robbins and Mary Coulter. *Management* (13th edition). New York: Pearson, 2016, pp. 368-369）

（五）履历调查

履历调查是指对应聘者的资历、工作经历的信息的查询验证。雇主们出于安全的考虑，一般会通过履历调查来评价候选人过去的错误、个性特征、健康情况等方面，以确定潜在的雇佣风险。

✧ Background investigations

Background investigation is an investigation comprised of confirmation of credentials and confirmation of employment history.

履历调查有两种形式：申请资料核实和参考查询。

申请资料核实是指对已提交的各项申请材料进行一一核对。该方法已被证实是获取选拔人员相关信息的一个有价值的渠道。有研究证明，对申请表中填写的各项内容进行核实是非常有益的。有资料显示，超过 15%的应聘者对他们的就业日期、职务头衔、过去薪金或离开原工作岗位的原因描述不够准确。因此将这些申请表上的资料与其原来的雇主进行核对，是一种有意义的行为。

参考查询也为许多组织所采用，主要是指通过前雇主的推荐或评价，来更多的了解候选人的情况。但其效果很难得到验证。前雇主可能会因为担心给自己带来法律上的麻烦，而不愿意对其先前雇员的工作表现提供评价。另外，个人的喜恶也会对前雇主们所做出的推荐意见产生强烈的影响，因此个人的评价很可能提供了带有偏见的信息。

不同选拔方法可能带来不同的结果，因此选拔人员要结合不同方法对应聘者进行科学筛选。就上述几种方法而言，申请表能提供有限的信息；传统的笔试对技术类职务的选拔效度较高；工作抽样与笔试相比，准确度明显要高一些；从管理人员甄别角度来看，测评中心法是比较受广大人力资源经理推崇的一种方法；面谈则比较适用于管理类的职务，尤其是中高层的管理职位，是分辨智力和人际关系技能的一种相当有效的手段；对申请资料的核实适合于所有职务的招聘，可提供准确而有价值的参考信息。

The background investigations are often used by employers as a means of judging a job candidate's past mistakes, character, and fitness, so as to identify potential hiring risks for safety and security reasons.

Background investigations include verification of application data and verification of reference checks.

Global Perspective

HRM in India and Other Countries

Outsourcing has become very popular with globalization. India is often the favorite place for outsourcing. The benefits for outsourcing are obtaining a lower cost service which may increase the competitive advantage of the firm doing the outsourcing. But, outsourcing is not without risk because cultural differences may result in some difficulty in communication although English is widely spoken. Other considerations are the differences in time zones that may hinder, for example, providing assistance to Dell customers in the United States. On the other hand, communication through the internet is rather inexpensive. But India has no monopoly on the information technology and outsourcing. In Asia the work force in the Philippines also offers IT services and China is in the process of going into the IT business.

These developments have important implications on staffing and leading. Human resource managers have now a greater and more diverse tool for selecting suitable persons for the tasks. Traditional tools for selecting the right candidate may not be appropriate for candidates in other countries. Moreover, training and performance evaluation may have to be adapted to the local environment. Compensation, motivation, local needs, and requirements, as well as expectations differ among countries. Companies need to adapt to the local situation. This is true for India as well as for other countries.

（案例来源: Heinz Weihrich, Mark V. Cannice and Harold Koontz. *Management: A global and Entrepreneurial Perspective* (13th edition). 北京：经济科学出版社，2011, p. 265）

四、人员培训

（一）人员培训的含义

需要指出的是,管理学界对人员培训的研究中通常认为简单意义上的人员培训就是组织中对员工的"培养、训练",并不包括广义培训理论中的学校教育和工作中接受的再教育。人员培训注重增强组织员工完成某项任务的技能,它侧重于完成组织活动的经验而不是抽象出能够反映客观物体的概念化的过程。所以,管理学视角下的人员培训理论一般并不包含教育培训的范畴。所谓人员培训,是指长期性的、面向未来的、旨在改进人们管理能力的计划。

人员培训主要强调以下四个方面的特征:其一,重在培养员工的工作技能;其二,强调知识转化技能的学习过程;其三,强调对组织和员工个人的投资过程;其四,强调实现组织目标。

（二）人员培训效果的制约因素分析

1. 培训设计

不同形式的培训设计是影响受训员工学习效率的关键因素之一。传统的单一培训方式很难满足员工的多样化培训需求,无法提高员工的学习兴趣。丰富多彩的"因需而制"的培训设计形式不仅可以扩宽培训范围,丰富培训内容,而且还可以增强受训员工对所学知识的吸收和转化能力,同时也能够提高他们在同样的时间约束下有效利用更多学习资源的效率。人员培训设计应该基于工作情境的改变而做出相应的改变。培训设计创新不足、培训设计目标不明必然会在一定程度上制约组织最终的培训效果。

2. 培训制度

高效培训效果的产生不仅需要科学的培训设计,还需要依靠完善的人员培训制度。人员培训制度是培训得以顺利实施的重要支撑,同时也是凝聚受训员工士气、增加受训员工工作积极性的制度保障。如果人员培训制度不完善,必然影响组织文化的凝聚力,那么就可能会对组织文化的形成带来负向的影响,人员培训成果在组织中的转化也会受阻,进而降低人员培训的效果。

3. 高管对培训的支持

高层管理者的支持对人员培训顺利开展有重要的推动作用。在培训得到高管重视的组织中,受训员工在工作中使用培训所学知识的积极性更高,尤其是当受训员工在工作中因使用所学知识而受到高管领导奖励时,员工会表现出更好的培训迁移行为（Training Transfer）。

✍ **Employee Training**

✧ The definition of employee training

Employee training is the use of long-term, future-oriented programs to develop a person's ability in managing.

Employee training emphasizes 4 parts:
1. Training working skills.
2. Learning to transfer knowledge to skills.
3. Investment on organization and employees.
4. Achieving organization's goals.

✧ Factors affecting the training effectiveness

1. Training program design

2. Training system

3. Support from the top management

Training transfer enables employees to apply the skills learned in training on the job.

4．组织文化

不同的组织文化会对培训的实施产生不同的影响。例如，在强调高绩效的组织中，组织面临的风险任务、革新文化、质量文化会对培训的知识迁移起到明显的促进作用，反之则会降低培训对知识的迁移作用；在组织文化强调效率的组织中，高管对培训的关注更多地体现在培训实际效果方面，那么培训的整体规划就会与强调文化建设的组织有所不同。

5．培训评价机制

人员培训的最终目的是为了提高组织绩效，但是组织绩效的改善并不是判断人员培训效果成功与否的唯一条件。多数组织会通过一种或多种评估方式来考察培训效果，不同的评价机制会影响培训的方案设计和培训的效果。例如，采用员工满意度作为评价指标的组织中，人员培训计划会更多地关注员工的个人成长需求，而可能忽略对组织的长期发展的考虑；采用主管领导打分评价方式的组织中，人员培训可能过多地关注部门或组织的需求，而忽略对个人成长的需求。

6．受训员工的接受能力

人员培训主要是通过转化学习成果来增加学习的价值，进而改善受训员工的工作绩效，因此，受训员工自身的学习能力或是对所培训内容的接受能力对最终培训效果的发挥起到了重要作用。其实，组织对员工进行培训暗含的一个假设就是：培训所带来的利益（如改善工作绩效，提高员工工作效率等）会超过组织进行培训所投入的成本。如果受训员工由于自身原因（个体差异）或是其他原因（抱怨、负面情绪）导致其不愿或是不能很好地接受所培训的主要内容，那么对培训效果就会产生不良影响。

7．受训员工的积极性

受训员工积极的学习态度和工作热情被认为是保持组织竞争力的重要因素。个体积极性以及自我效能的变化能够显著地影响人员培训中员工的培训迁移动机及行为。当员工个体认识到培训能带来更多的工作和职业上的效用（例如职位晋升、工资增加）时，他们的培训迁移动机就会增强，产生更高的工作积极性；相反，如果受训者对他们参与的培训活动不满意，那么他们也不会乐于应用其在培训中所学的知识，难以达到培训预期效果。

（三）培训方法

人员培训的方式主要包括两大类：在职培训和组织内外部培训。

4. Organizational culture

5. Training appraisal mechanism

6. Capacity of trainees

7. Trainees initiatives

◇　Training methods

Employee training includes on-the-job training and internal & external training.

1. 在职培训

大多数的人员培训是以在职方式进行的,这主要是因为在职培训简单易行且成本通常较低。常见的在职培训方法包括以下几种。

（1）职务轮换

职务轮换是通过横向的交换,让员工从事某一领域内的不同工作,积累工作经验。职务轮换使员工在逐步学会多种工作技能的同时,也增强其对工作间相互依赖关系的认识,并对组织活动有更广阔的视角。

（2）预备实习

对于新员工而言,组织通常采取预备实习的方式,跟随经验丰富的老师傅学会如何工作。在实际工作中我们常称之为师徒关系、教练或导师关系。不论何种情况,实习者都是在富有经验的人的指导下开展工作的,这些师傅或教练可以成为实习者认真学习的榜样。

（3）临时性晋升

临时性的晋升是指在正式经理生病或较长时间出差,出现职位暂时空缺时,指派代理经理来行使缺位管理人员的职责。临时性晋升既可以培养管理人员,同时也给组织工作开展带来了便利。当代理经理独自完成决策并承担责任时,他所取得的经验是很宝贵的财富,也是对代理经理的一种培养和锻炼。

2. 组织内外部培训

组织内外部培训实际上是一种脱产培训,当然,脱产的时间可以很长,如去参加外部培训班,也可以很短,如工作日中的短暂培训。管理者可以向员工提供多种脱产培训。最常见的包括课堂讲座、电视录像、模拟练习。课堂讲座特别适用于传递具体的信息,因此可以用来有效地培训员工的技术能力及解决问题的能力。电视录像可以用来清晰地展示技术方面的技能,尤其对于一些不容易采用面授的内容,可以通过电视录像的方法详细说明。人际关系和解决问题方面的技能可以通过模拟练习得到更好的学习,诸如案例分析、实验演习、角色扮演和小组互动会议等。复杂的计算机模型,如航空中用以培训飞行员的那套模型,也是模拟练习的一种,它可以用来讲授技术方面的知识。类似的还有仿真培训（Vestibule Training）,让工人们在他们未来将使用的同类设备上学习操作,培训是在模拟的工作环境中进行的,而不是实际的工作场地。这种方法不仅提供了严格的学习过程控制,使受训者学会如何处理各种可能出现的问题,同时也避免了对实际进行中的作业的干扰和妨碍。

1. On-the-job training

Job rotation means that employees work at different jobs in a particular area, getting exposure to a variety of tasks.

Mentoring and coaching means that employees work with an experienced worker who provides information, support, and encouragement.

Temporary appointment means that an acting manager is used to cover the responsibilities of the absent manager.

2. Internal & external training

Internal and external training includes classroom lectures, CD-ROM/ DVD / videotapes / audiotapes, and simulations, etc.

第三节　人员绩效评估

Appraising Performance

The process of appraising performance is complicated and requires both assessing what employees are doing and communicating this information back to the employees. These are two highly social, context-dependent processes, so we might expect performance appraisal to vary dramatically depending on the country. Preliminary research suggests that management practices related to performance appraisal do indeed vary across borders. A structured interview study examined Chinese managers' beliefs about performance appraisal. Most respondents found it is a good way to build communication and believed performance levels are a function of each person's individual attributes. These attitudes were fairly similar to those of managers in the United States, where most research on performance appraisal has been performed. However, the Chinese managers believed a person in a position of power and control should run the appraisal meeting, unlike the more informal preferences of U.S. managers. One larger-scale study compared appraisal practices in the United States, Canada, the United Kingdom, Finland, Sweden, Hong Kong, and Singapore using the dimensions of culture identified in the global survey. Appraisals were more frequently used for communication and development in countries like Sweden and Finland that were low in assertiveness and power distance. Formal feedback was more frequent in highly assertive, low collectivist, and uncertainty avoidant cultures like the United States, the United Kingdom, and Canada. Finally, appraisals were more collaborative in nature in the United States and Canada, and more formal and top-down in Hong Kong and Singapore.

（案例来源：改编自 K. H. C. Cheng and W. Cascio. Performance-Appraisal Beliefs of Chinese Employees in Hong Kong and the Pearl River Delta. *International Journal of Selection and Assessment*, 2009, 17 (3): 329-333）

组织进行人员绩效评估是对现有人力资源状况进行科学评价的一个关键过程。如何建构一种良好的绩效评价体系以及采用何种科学的评估方法来反映组织的人力资源绩效，是所有组织必须深入思考的一个问题。正如上述案例所述，绩效评估的方法有很多，影响绩效评估方法选择和评估效果的因素也有很多。如何在各种方法中进行选择和平衡，在绩效评估中坚持公平和客观地反映组织人员的实际业务水平，是组织面临的一项重要挑战。本节将主要围绕人员绩效评估的含义和评估方法进行分析和讨论。

一、人员绩效评估的含义

绩效评估（Performance Appraisal）是对员工的工作绩效进行评价，以便形成客观公正的人事决策的过程。组织可以根据绩效评估结果做出许多有关人员配备的决策。例如，绩效评估可以用来决定谁将得到涨工资的机会，谁将得到职位的晋升。绩效评估的结果也为员工的工作提供了反馈，使员工了解组织如何看待他们的工作绩效表现。绩效评估还确定了下一步培训和发展的需要，根据绩效评估发现的不足，制定适合员工发展和组织发展的培训计划。绩效评估可为人力资源规划提供依据，并辅助做出晋升、岗位轮换及解聘的决策。绩效评估有时还被用来作为验证人员选拔手段和培训发展方案效度的一个标准，来验证人员选拔方法是否合适，培训发展方案是否恰当。

二、人员绩效评估的标准

绩效评估需要有所依据，即确定标准之后，根据实际工作的结果来判定是否与目标存在差距，因此标准的选择在进行人员绩效评估过程中至关重要。总体来说，人员绩效评估的标准包括两类：按照可考核的目标进行评估和按照管理人员的标准进行评估。

（一）按照可考核的目标进行评估

这是最常用的一种绩效评估方式，即通过检验是否完成了最初制定的可考核的目标，来评估人员绩效。这种方法简便、易行、相对客观。只要确定了具体的目标，那么管理者就可以将评估标准确定为目标的完成程度。前面章节中所讲述的目标管理，就是一个非常典型的按照可考核的目标进行评估的方法。

但是，这种方法也存在弊端。首先，目标必须是可考核的，而且评估人要首先确定这些目标是科学合理、切实可行的。如果环境改变了，目标却没有及时调整，那么就可能出现不合理的目标，而依据不合理的目标进行的评估当然也就不够准确。其次，有时候目标没有完成，并不能归因于被考评人的个人能力问题，遇到自然灾害或突发事件，也可能导致目标无法达成，这个时候仍然用目标是否达成来评估管理者的绩效，就不够合理和准确。另外，有些管理者可能只关注目标的完成，尤其是可量化的结果，但是对于管理者应承担的其他职能，如计划、组织、领导、控制，却并不关注，这样的管理者不能算作合格的管理者。考评应该针对结果，但是必须要避免"数字游戏"。

✍ **The Definition of Performance Appraisal**

Performance appraisal is the process of evaluating the employee performance to help managers to make fair staffing decisions.

☞ **Appraisal Criteria**

Appraisal criteria include appraising managers against verifiable objectives and appraising managers as managers.

✧ Appraising managers against verifiable objectives

Appraising managers against verifiable objectives is a widely used approach to managerial appraisal. It is the system of evaluating managerial performance against the setting and accomplishing of verifiable objectives.

Appraisal should focus on results, but one must be careful to avoid the "number game."

（二）按照管理人员的标准进行评估

按照管理人员的标准来进行评估实际上是按照可考核的目标进行评估的一种补充。按照可考核的目标去考核可能忽略了管理中的一些隐性要素，这方面可以通过按照管理人员的标准进行考核来弥补。按照管理人员的标准进行评估，最合适的依据就是管理的基本原则，即查看管理者在工作中是否尽到了计划、组织、人员配备、领导、控制的责任。为了让管理的基本原则变得易于评价和相对客观，许多学者给出了具体的评价标准，如表7-3所示。

✧ Appraising managers as managers

The system of measuring performance against preestablished objectives should be supplemented by an appraisal of a manager as a manager.

表 7-3　按照管理人员标准考评管理人员的要点问题示例

Table 7-3　Sample Questions for Appraising Managers as Managers

Planning
● Does the manager set for the department both short-term and long-term goals in verifiable terms that are related in a positive way to those of the superiors and of the company?
● In choosing from among alternatives, does the manager recognize and give primary attention to those factors that are limiting or critical to the solution of a problem?
● Does the manager check plans periodically to see if they are still consistent with current expectations?
Organizing
● Does the manager delegate authority to subordinates on the basis of results expected of them?
● Does the manager refrain from making decisions in that area once authority has been delegated to subordinates?
● Does the manager regularly teach subordinates, or otherwise make sure that they understand the nature of line and staff relationships?

（资料来源：Heinz Weihrich, Mark V. Cannice and Harold Koontz. *Management: A global and Entrepreneurial Perspective* (13th edition). 北京：经济科学出版社，2011, p. 280）

这些评价标准将基本原则具体化，更便于管理者进行绩效评估。这种方法可以将评估重点放到管理的核心问题上，让人们了解真正的管理工作是应该怎样进行的。但是，这种方法的适用范围有限，它只适用于对一定职位的管理工作方面进行评估，而不能适用于技术素质的评估（如营销、研发能力）。而且，这种方法主观性较强，可能会影响评估的准确性。

The most appropriate standards to use for appraising managers as managers are the fundamentals of management.

三、绩效评估方法

绩效评估是非常重要的。那么，如何对一个员工的工作绩效进行评估呢？下面将介绍几种主要的绩效评估方法。

✍ **Performance Appraisal Methods**

（一）书面描述法

书面描述法是最简单的绩效评估方法，是指评估人员写一份材料，描述一个员工的优点和缺点、过去的绩效和潜能，并提出改进和提高的建议。书面描述不需要采取复杂的格式，完成书面描述不需要经过特殊的培训。但是，一种"好"或"差"的评价结果，可能不仅取决于员工的实际绩效水平，也与评估者的写作技能有很大的关系。

✧ Written essays

Evaluator writes a description of employee's strengths and weaknesses, past performance, and potential, then provides some suggestions for improvement.

（二）关键事件法

使用关键事件法，评估者是将注意力集中在那些特别有效的和非常无效的工作绩效的关键行为方面。评估人员记录下一些能说明员工所做的特别有效果的或无效果的事件，然后据此评估绩效。这种方法要注意的是，记录时只描述具体的行为，并不对员工的个性特质进行评价。通过一系列的关键事件作为具体评估示例，为员工指出哪些行为合适，哪些行为不合适。

❖ Critical incidents
Evaluator focuses on critical behaviors that separate effective and ineffective performance.

（三）评分表法

评分表法是一种最古老也最常用的绩效评估方法。它列出一系列绩效因素，如工作的数量与质量、职务了解程度、合作、出勤、忠诚、诚实和首创精神等，然后，评估者逐一对表中的每一项给出评分。评分尺度通常采用 5 分制，如对职务了解程度这一因素的评分可以是 1 分（"对职务职责的了解很差"）至 5 分（"对职务的各方面有充分的了解"）。评分表法虽然不像前两种方法那样可以提供详细的信息，但其设计和执行的总时间耗费较少，而且便于做定量分析和比较。

❖ Graphic rating scales
A popular method that lists a set of performance factors and an incremental scale; evaluator goes down the list and rates employee on each factor.

（四）行为定位评分法

行为定位评分法是近年来日益得到重视的一种绩效评估方法。这种方法综合了关键事件法和评分表法的主要要素，考评者按某一评分量表进行打分，但是不是针对个人特质，而是某人从事某项职务的具体行为事例。行为定位评分法侧重于具体且可衡量的工作行为。它将职务的关键要素分解为若干绩效因素，然后为每一绩效因素确定有效或无效果行为的一些具体示例。其结果可以形成诸如"预测""计划""实施""解决眼前问题""贯彻执行命令"以及"处理紧急情况"等的行为描述。此种方法关注具体的可测量的工作行为，因此测量相对量化，但是操作起来比较耗时。

❖ Behaviorally anchored rating scales (BARS)
A popular approach that combines elements from critical incident and graphic rating scale; evaluator uses a rating scale, but items are examples of actual job behaviors.

（五）多人比较法

多人比较法是将一个员工的工作绩效与一个或多个其他人做比较。这是一种相对的而非绝对的衡量方法。该类方法最常用的三种形式是：分组排序法、个体排序法和配对比较法。分组排序法要求评价者按照某个要素（如表现、业绩等）进行分组，然后对小组进行排序；个体排序法要求评价者将员工根据业绩按照从高到低的顺序排列；配对比较法是将每个员工都一一与比较组的其他每一位员工结对进行比较，评出其中的优者和劣者。

❖ Multiperson comparisons
Employees are rated in comparison to others in work group. Multiperson comparisons include group order ranking, individual ranking and paired comparison.

（六）目标管理法

此方法已在第五章有详细介绍，此处不赘述。

❖ Management by objectives （MBO）

（七）360 度评分法

360 度评分法是多角度进行的比较全面的绩效考核方法，也称为全方位考核法或全面评价法。它的基本原理是：员工的工作是多方面的，业绩体现也是多维度的，不同的个体对同一工作得出的结论和评价也不相同。因此，通过上级、下属、同事、顾客、供应商及其他部门的员工对其进行综合评价，更能全方位的准确的考核员工的工作业绩（参看图 7-5）。但是由于此种方法操作起来比较复杂，且定性考核比重较大，因此收集和评价信息的成本较高。

◇ 360-Degree evaluations
360-Degree evaluations utilize feedback from supervisors (top management and manager), subordinates, co-workers, clients, suppliers and other department representatives.

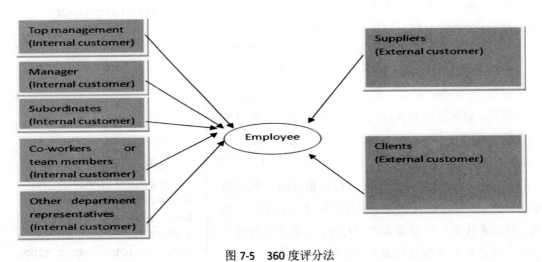

图 7-5　360 度评分法

Figure 7-5　360-Degree Evaluations

（资料来源：作者根据相关资料整理）

Staffing

Principles of staffing

External factors

Big Data technique

Selection

Selection results

Selection process

Promotion from within

Peter principle

Recruitment

Open competition

Application forms

Written tests

Performance simulation tests

Interviews

Background investigations

Employee training

Job rotation

Mentoring and coaching

Temporary appointment

Performance appraisal

Appraising managers against verifiable objectives

Appraising managers as managers

Written essays

Critical incidents

Graphic rating scales

Behaviorally anchored rating scales

Multiperson comparisons

360-degree evaluations

讨论问题 **DISCUSSION QUESTIONS**

1. In management, staffing is defined as a process of filling, and keeping filled, positions in the organization structure. Briefly describe the main contents of staffing.

2. Explain the principles of staffing with specific examples.

3. As we all know, it's important for multinational firms to train international professionals and

strengthen their international competitiveness. Describe the external factors influencing staffing in the international environment.

4. Big Data technique is indisputable valuable to staffing and organization decision-making. Talk about your idea.

5. The selection is the process of identifying and screening the applicants when an organization faces the personnel shortage or other talents demands. Briefly describe the main process of selection.

6. Human resources are important factors in the modern society. Setting position by employee or setting employee by position is one of the main concerns for HRM personnel. What's your opinion?

7. What are the dangers and difficulties in applying a policy of promotion from within? What is meant by a policy of open competition? Do you favor such a policy? Why or why not?

8. What is assessment center? How does it work?

9. What are the sources to recruit? Explain the strengths and weaknesses of these recruiting sources.

10. Divide the class into several groups to discuss, and act interview after discussion.

11. Employee training is the use of long-term, future-oriented programs to develop a person's ability in managing. Briefly describe the significance of employee training.

12. Describe the two main types of training. How do you think these tend to be delivered?

13. How do you feel about an appraisal system based on results expected and realized? Would you prefer to be appraised on this basis? If not, why?

14. Explain the different performance appraisal methods.

Haidilao Hotpot: You Can Never Learn His Way!

China is in any sense a big cake for almost every industry. Adding the fact that most Chinese have constant interest in finding new delicious food, the restaurant industry can never relax for a moment or they will lose their customers. While most competitors struggle to win the favor of the clients in such a stringent environment, a hotpot chain brand named Haidilao seems light and easy in gaining the popularity among the critical customers. It has opened more than fifty chain restaurants spread in more than 10 biggest cities in China and its revenue in fiscal 2010 has reached 238 million dollars. Even a book was published to discuss the success of its managing and marketing strategy, "Haidilao, you can never learn his way," not to mention the numerous topics and reports it has created in both mass media and social websites.

The most legendary success can always been destructed into several pieces of normal marketing concepts, just with extraordinary usage. In this case, the vital factor that leads the brand is its positioning. When Haidilao asked itself what kind of restaurant it wanted to make, the answer was a great hotpot cooker with unique experience. Great hotpot cookers can be found all over the country but they share most similarities like any crowded place, full of noise and sweaty customers. In contrast, Haidilao hotpot extremely exploits the word "service" and by that way they create one great consuming experience that strongly impresses every new customer. This kind of difference exactly accounts for the big applause for this new brand.

The emphasis on service is an old word but only when someone really believes in that way can the tradition concept refresh the marketing history. In Haidilao, even waiting for seats can be enjoyable. There are different drinks and kinds of chess on the desk, newest play cards aside and services like nail care for women and shoe care for men available all the time. During dining, you are provided frequently with warm hand towels, a pinafore with ethnic feature, hair string for girls, glass cloth in case that the drop splits to your glasses and a small plastic bag to put your big screen cell phone in. Every waiter and waitress has the right to give you a free meal in particular situation. These uncommon attributes attract more and more interest.

The execution of the brand positioning is valid through every single effort done by the employees and consequently conformed by the public. That is the interesting part of this case. Haidilao promotes itself by only two ways: indoor experience and online discussion. It is unlike KFC or McDonald. Normally the restaurant chain will not put advertisements on TV. Giving out coupons is the most used way for this industry. However, the reputation of Haidilao relies on the personal recommendation within its clients. Meanwhile, clients will talk about the exciting experience in Haidilao like what kind of service they have enjoyed. For example, one day a tweet in Weibo (the Chinese version of Twitter) was forwarded for thousands of time. It said that "Today when I had dinner in Haidilao, I found the pieces of watermelon taste good so I asked the waiter if I can bring the rest home. The waiter said no. But after a while the waiter brought a whole watermelon and gave it to me. Human Cannot Stop Haidilao!" This kind of little story was a free promotion automatically done by the customers themselves. And this kind of recommendation enjoys high credit than TV commercials because it comes from people who you are familiar with.

Choosing a restaurant is not a low-involvement consumer behavior especially when you are finding an eating place on purpose rather than grabbing some stuff to fulfill your stomach. People who are in favor of the hotpot and the spicy flavor are a whole segment for the hotpot industry. Haidilao has its own comparable advantage of its unique formula of the bottom soup. What's more important, it has an excellent managing group including thousands of passionate waiters and waitresses. Every worker there sincerely loves their work because the company treats them like family and offers great career skill training and health insurance to everyone, including their children's entrance to kindergarten. The loyalty of their group is the most crucial advantage of Haidilao. Marketing is everyone's responsibility in this company instead of limited within the marketing department. Concerning the external environment the spicy hotpot is becoming more and more popular in China but old chain brand is stuck by their unchanged product and service. The opportunity is that customers are looking for hotpot with higher and decent service. That is a combination of advantage and the opportunity and where exactly Haidilao puts itself in.

However, opportunity always goes with a threat. The threat for Haidilao is that it is difficult to maintain the perfect quality of service when the scale is expanding. More and more new workers are recruited but before they get understood in the company's culture they start in their position. One normal mistake can easily take down the legend because of the focus from the media. The word of mouth is an economical way of marketing but they are not passively under control. It is a sword of double edges. Additionally, the food safety issue is an old problem in China. Many restaurants use chemical additives and forbidden stuff in making the food. Famous food brands are always in monitoring. In hotpot area, the quality of the bottom soup is always questioned. Haidilao is no exception. In August 2011, a news report pointed that the bottom soup of Haidilao, which is declared to be boiled with pure pig bone, is actually blended with other artificial additives. A brand with good reputation will suffer more in this kind of situation if they cannot deal with this credit crisis on time. And this report just reflects the problems brought with expansion.

This kind of brand always presents us with a good case to learn. Haidilao found out and grabbed the changing need of the hotpot fans and positioned itself in a potential market area. The communication channel is creative because every employee and every client with satisfaction becomes the advertiser automatically. The social media offers a great platform for the quick spread of word of mouth. Meanwhile, Haidilao needs to care for its reputation by guarantee its high quality in products and service because it still faces the threat of food safety issue and the problems brought by the expansion.

What should Haidilao do next? Within the current popularity, it would like to make full use to promote its brand for sure. But as to expansion, the managing group needs to slow down its pace to validate every chain restaurant opened. Meanwhile the training process for every new member is as equal importance with hiring a new marketing agency. A better capability in controlling the media agenda is also required because when the brand is always in the center of discussion every little change will be magnified especially the bad news. Given that, keeping low profile for a period of time would not be a bad choice. Back to the root service is part of the brand product and that is the secret for restaurant industry that is firstly figured out by Haidilao and it should insist on. It is not the truth that anybody can copy the way Haidilao operates but the developer always has an advantage over the follower.

（案例来源：Shan Lu. A New Fairy Tale of Chain Restaurant: Haidilao Hotpot, "You Can Never Learn His Way!" http://press.emerson.edu/imc/2011/12/19/a-new-fairy-tale-of-chain-restaurant-haidilao-hotpot-you-can-never-learn-his-way/ 2011-12-19）

Discussion Questions:

1. According to the case, talents are very important factors in the development of Haidilao. Is there any special method for Haidilao to attract excellent employees? How to keep the good employees?

2. Why did Zhangyong, the founder of Haidilao, give his employees more rights of making decisions than other bosses in the hotpot industry? How to evaluate employees' performances?

3. Does Haidilao have any special way to train its employees? Is there any plan for its employees' long-term development? If yes, please explain the detailed plans.

4. Haidilao's food wins high marks and its good services are very famous. What are Haidilao's core competitive competences? Discuss with your classmates.

第八章　领导

学习目标

1. 解释激励的含义，描述各种激励理论及其优缺点
2. 描述领导力及其构成要素
3. 描述各种领导力方法理论
4. 解释组织中沟通的作用

Learning Outcomes

1. Explain the meaning of motivation, and describe the various theories of motivation and their strengths and weaknesses.
2. Describe leadership and its ingredients.
3. Describe various leadership approaches.
4. Explain the flow of communication in an organization.

主要内容

第一节　领导与权力
第二节　激励理论
第三节　沟通

Contents

8.1 Leading and Power
8.2 Motivation Theories
8.3 Communication

第一节　领导与权力

Jack Ma and His Alibaba

Jack Ma—whose net worth is $21.9 billion according to the Bloomberg Billionaires Index—now stars in the coming-out party for China's private sector onto the world stage. He praises and uses Western management techniques but also quotes regularly from Chairman Mao Zedong. He is a fan of China's kung fu novels and made those legends part of his company's culture. He travels the world with a tai chi trainer. With the help of more than a dozen friends who pooled their resources—just $60,000—he founded Alibaba, a business-to-business online platform. The company now makes more profit than rivals Amazon.com and e-Bay combined, as China's burgeoning middle class are big spenders online, and small companies rely on Alibaba and its online payment system.

Jack is responsible for the overall strategy and focus of Alibaba Group. He has been described as feisty, with keen entrepreneurial instincts. In China, Jack has been called the entrepreneur's entrepreneur. In 2000, he became the first mainland China entrepreneur to appear on the cover of Forbes. Barron's named him one of the World's Top 30 CEOs in 2008. Jack believes that, if a company wants to succeed, it has to confront social needs and solve social problems instead of just catching one or two opportunities. And his role as a business leader is to decide on which opportunities to focus. As a leader, Jack is not afraid of making mistakes. He has said: "If you want to learn how other people succeed, it's very difficult because there are so many things they do that are the result of luck. If you learn how people fail, you'll benefit a lot." Jack has admitted that "I have made many mistakes. The book I really want to write about is Alibaba's 1001 mistakes."

（案例来源：根据 Calum Macleod. Alibaba's Jack Ma: From Crazy to Chin's Richest Man, www.usatoday.com, 2014-9-19 和 Jack Ma, www.worldofceos.com 相关内容改编）

对于组织的成功来说，领导是一项非常重要的内容。从一定程度上说，领导者及其领导方式决定了组织的发展战略及成败。马云在中国是家喻户晓的成功企业家，他的阿里巴巴（Alibaba）支持了无数微小企业的运营。2014 年，马云凭借 200 多亿美元的净资产问鼎中国首富。阿里巴巴的成功与马云的领导战略及领导风格有密切关联。关于马云的传记有很多，许多人，尤其是许多年轻的创业者，期望能够效仿马云，成为一名优秀的企业家。但是，马云的领导魅力是与生俱来的还是后天形成的？马云对公司员工的影响力是来源于他作为董事长的权力，还是个人的独特魅力？他的成功是否能够总结成为可以借鉴的管理模式？这些都是管理学中领导职能所要研究的问题。本节将围绕领导与权力相关理论，深入剖析领导职能的内涵。

一、领导的本质

（一）什么是领导？

领导的概念有很多种定义。从字面上看，领导包括两种词性含义：一是名词（Leader），指领导人、领导者，即一个组织中确定和实现组织目标的首领；二是动词，意为领导职能（Leading），是一项管理工作、管理职能，通过该项职能的行使，领导者能促成被领导者努力地实现既定的组织目标。在所有关于领导的思想和著作中，有三个方面的研究是非常突出的，即：人、影响力和目标。领导出现于人群之中，涉及影响力的应用，领导职能就是通过影响力来达到组织的目的或目标。而领导者所具有的领导力（Leadership）就是为了实现组织目标而对他人施加影响力的能力。

领导活动对组织绩效具有重要的影响，这种作用具体体现在三个方面：指挥作用、协调作用和激励作用。

1. 指挥作用

指挥作用是领导最突出的作用，是指在组织活动中，需要领导综观全局、高瞻远瞩、运筹帷幄地帮助组织成员认知环境和形势，指明活动的目标和达到目标的路径。领导者发挥指挥作用一般有两条途径：一是运用领导权力强制引导下属人员的行为；二是通过个人效力来影响下属的行为，使下属自觉服从领导者的指挥。

2. 协调作用

协调就是使企业的一切工作都互相配合，以便组织运转能够顺利进行。在领导中，协调作用是指领导者需要在各种因素的干扰下，来协调部下之间的关系和活动，朝着共同的目标前进。有效的协调是提高组织效率的路径。

3. 激励作用

激励作用是指领导者通过为部下主动创造能力发展空间和职业发展生涯等行为，来影响部下的内在需求和动机，引导和强化部下为组织目标而努力的行为活动。物质激励、精神激励或惩罚都可以作为领导激励员工的手段。

（二）领导职能所包括的内容

领导作为一种人际间相互交往和作用的过程，它由以下三个方面的工作构成。

1. 权力或影响力

这是有关领导工作最狭义的理解。在一个组织内部，一个人可能会利用职权的合法性而采用强制手段来发布指挥和命令，这里他所依仗的只是自己所处的职位和职权

✍ **The Nature of Leading**

✧ What is leading?

Leader is someone who can influence others and who has managerial authority.

Leading is the process of influencing people so that they will contribute to organizational and group goals.

Leadership is the ability to influence people toward the attainment of organizational goals.

The Influence of leading activities includes command, coordination and motivation.

✧ Ingredients of leading

1. Power or influence

266

的权威性，这样的人称不上是一个优秀的领导者。在某些情况下，某个人可能根本就没有合法的地位所赋予的职权，但是他却能形成和发挥影响力，能以个人的才能、魄力、威望来影响和促进他人努力工作。可见，领导者借以影响他人的权力有多方面的来源。有效的领导者应该设法扩宽自己的权力或影响力的来源。

2. 激励

激励与领导密切相关。领导者要取得被领导者的追随与服从，首先必须能够了解被领导者的愿望并帮助人们实现各自的愿望，即了解能够对追随者起到激励作用的要素。管理者如果能够很好地了解激励要素，并懂得如何让这些激励要素发挥作用，则他们就更有可能成为有效的领导者。

3. 沟通

沟通是领导者和被领导者进行交往的不可或缺的活动。通过沟通，领导者不仅可以使所发布的命令、指示得到下属准确的理解和贯彻执行，而且还能更好地察觉下属需要什么以及他们为什么会如此行事。虽然管理工作的各个方面都离不开信息沟通，但在领导职能中，沟通的作用尤其重要。

综上所述，权力、激励、沟通是领导职能的三个重要内容，本章的后面部分将围绕这三个重要内容展开讨论。

二、领导的权力基础

从前面的内容中我们已经知道，狭义的领导工作，就是领导者运用其拥有的权力，以一定的方式来对他人施加影响的过程。因此，权力是领导者影响力的来源，是领导者对他人施加影响的基础。

（一）权力与职权

在日常工作中，提起权力，经常容易混淆的是职权。事实上二者是有区别的。

所谓权力，是个人或群体影响其他人或群体的能力。这种能力可能来源于职位，也可能与职位无关，而是来源于领导者的个人魅力、经验等其他影响力。所谓职权是赋予某个正式职位影响他人的合法权力。它与组织结构和组织管理联系在一起，范围要小于权力。职权存在于上下级之间，而权力可以存在两个人或更多人之间，可以在纵向和横向上使用，并不仅仅局限于组织的所有者或管理者。管理者如何能够有效地运用他的职权，取决于他对职位的理解力，而权力的实质内容就是向他人施加影响的能力。

2. Motivation

3. Communication

✍ **The Foundation of Power**

✧ Power and authority

Power is the ability of individuals or groups to induce or influence the beliefs or actions of other persons or groups.

Authority is the right in a position to exercise discretion in making decisions affecting others.

现代组织中,有的人可能能够影响他人,即具有权力,但是不一定具有法定职权。

（二）权力的类型

在一个组织内部,权力可以按其来源分为以下五种类型。

1. 法定权力

所谓法定权力,是指组织内各领导职位所固有的合法的、正式的权力。这种权力可以通过领导者利用职权向直属人员发布命令、下达指示来直接体现,有时也可以借助于组织内的政策、程序和规则等得到间接体现。例如,作为公司的财务主管,他有管理和监督各项资金流动的权力,可以要求相关人员严格按照财务管理制度开展业务活动;作为人事部经理,有招聘员工和选拔员工的权力。下属必须服从上司的指挥,这种权力是法定的,是组织的等级指挥链所固有的。

2. 奖赏权力

所谓奖赏权力,是来自职位的、对他人实施奖励的权力。包括提供奖金、加薪、升职、赞扬、理想的工作安排和其他任何令人愉悦的东西的权力。当被领导者感觉到领导者有能力给予他们奖赏,可以满足他们的需求时,就会更愿意追随和服从领导者。领导者所控制的奖赏手段越多,而且这些奖赏对下属越发重要,那么他拥有的影响力就越大。

3. 强制权力

强制权力是与奖赏权力对应的,同样来源于职位,是一种实施处罚或建议进行处罚的权力,包括扣发工资奖金、降职、批评、开除等惩罚性措施。例如,当员工业绩很差或违反公司规定时,总经理拥有辞退该员工的权力,即为强制权力;交通警察有权对违反交通规则的驾驶员发出违章罚款单或扣留驾驶执照,这也属于强制权力。

4. 专家权力

所谓专家权力是来自领导者在下属从事的任务领域所具有的专业知识或者专门技能的权力。如律师、大学教授、企业中的工程师在其组织中都可能拥有很大的影响力,他们的这种影响力即为专家权力。如果领导者的确是专家,那么下属就会从心底佩服该领导的能力,进而遵从他的指示。专家权力与职位没有必然关联。

5. 参考和感召权力

所谓参考和感召权力是指与个人的品质、魅力、经历、背景等紧密相关的权力。

◇ The type of power

Legitimate power is the power that stems from a formal management position in an organization and the authority granted to it.

Reward power is the power that results from the authority to bestow rewards on other people.

Coercive power is closely related to reward power and normally arises from legitimate power; it is the power to punish.

Expert power is the power that stems from special knowledge or skill in the tasks performed by subordinates.

268

领导者的某些个性特征、特殊经历可能会受到下属的爱戴和拥护，甚至可以让下属去效仿领导者，这样当领导者发出指令时，下属也会遵从他的指示。感召权力不依赖于正式的头衔或职位，它多见于魅力型领导者身上。参考权力则多出现在某些有特殊社会关系的人身上。例如，董事长夫人，虽然不在公司担任职务，但也可能对该企业的员工产生影响。

由上述内容可以看出，权力的构成是多种多样的。由于法定权力、奖赏权力和强制权力都与职位有关，我们将其统称为职位权力。职位权力来源于组织。专家权力与参考和感召权力与职位没有必然关联，与个人因素紧密相关，我们将其统称为个人权力。个人权力多来自内部因素。正式组织中的有效领导者应该是兼具职位权力和个人权力的领导。仅有职位权力的领导者只会是指挥官，而不能成为令人信赖和敬佩的领袖。个人权力是领导者不可或缺的主要工具，正式组织的领导者应该加强个人素质的修炼，在拥有职位权力的同时，也拥有更大的个人权力。

三、领导特质理论

领导理论是管理者理论研究的热点之一，中外许多管理学家们围绕着领导问题展开了大量的研究，其研究的核心在于领导的有效性。在管理理论的发展过程中，主要的领导理论有领导特质理论、领导行为理论和领导权变理论。下面将围绕领导特质理论展开讨论。

正如本节的开篇案例所讨论的那样，马云的成功是否可以复制？到底什么样的领导者才是成功的领导者？比尔·盖茨（Bill Gates）、史蒂夫·乔布斯（Steve Jobs）、杰克·韦尔奇（Jack Welch）、李彦宏、马云等成功的领导者身上是否存在共性？他们的领导战略是否适用于其他人或组织？这些问题正是促使领导特质论形成的动因。

领导特质理论首先是由心理学家开始研究的。一些心理学家最早对领导活动及行为进行系统的研究，希望从这些优秀的伟大人物身上寻找共同的东西。所谓特质，即领导者身上与众不同的个性特征，如智慧、价值观、自信等。领导特质论尝试说明，领导者的个人特质是决定领导效能的关键因素。

特质论的研究主要集中在领导者与被领导者以及有效的领导者与无效的领导者之间的素质差别上。研究表明，伟大的人物和普通的人有很大的差异。

Reference power is the power that people or groups may exercise because other people believe in them and their ideas.

Position power includes legitimate power, reward power and coercive power.

Personal power includes expert power and reference power.

Personal power is the primary tool of the leader.

✍ **Great Man Approach**

The early research focused on leaders who had achieved a level of greatness, and hence was referred to as the Great Man approach.

有的研究将有效领导者的特质归纳为身体特质、智力特质、性格特质、工作相关特质、背景特质以及社交特质（参见表 8-1）。对有效领导者的特质研究，不同国家、不同学者结论并不完全相同，但是却都有这样一个共识，即领导者是先天赋予的，而不是后天培养的，即便某些特质可以通过学习来获得，但人们学习能力的差异也是与生俱来的。

领导特质理论系统地分析了领导者所具备的条件，对于选拔、培养、考核领导者具有积极的意义。但是，领导特质理论也存在着一些显而易见的缺陷。

首先，到目前为止，研究者对有效领导者具备的特质，以及各种特质相对重要性的认识，并不一致，甚至存在着相互冲突；其次，领导特质理论忽视了被领导者对领导有效性的影响；最后，领导特质理论忽视了情境因素对领导有效性的影响。

Traits are the distinguishing personal characteristics, such as intelligence, values, and appearance.

Leadership trait theories have attempted to identify certain traits that all leaders have.

Find out what made these people great, and select future leaders who already exhibited the same traits or could be trained to develop them.

The appropriateness of a trait or set of traits depends on the leadership situation.

The same traits do not apply to every organization or situation.

表 8-1 有效领导者的特质
Table 8-1 Personal Characteristics of Effective Leaders

Physical Characteristics	Personality	Work-Related Characteristics
Energy	Self-confidence	Achievement drive, desire to excel
Physical stamina	Honesty and integrity	Conscientiousness in pursuit of goals
	Enthusiasm	Persistence against obstacles, tenacity
	Desire to lead	
	Independence	
Intelligence and Ability	**Social Characteristics**	**Social Background**
Intelligence, cognitive ability	Sociability, interpersonal skills	Education
Knowledge	Cooperativeness	Mobility
Judgment, decisiveness	Ability to enlist cooperation	
	Tact, diplomacy	

（资料来源：Richard L. Daft and Dorothy Marcic 著．高增安，马永红改编．*Management* (6th edition). 北京：机械工业出版社，2010，p. 400）

四、领导行为理论

20 世纪四五十年代对领导效能的研究主要侧重在领导者特质方面。但是慢慢的，研究者们发现了领导特质理论的局限性。从 20 世纪 60 年代开始，对领导研究的重点开始从领导者可能具有哪些特质转向领导者应当如何行为，并将各类领导行为和领导方式进行比较，产生了领导行为理论。领导行为理论的研究目的是寻求最有效的领导行为模式。

✍ **Leadership Behavior Theories**

Leadership behavior theories are theories that identify behaviors that differentiate effective leaders from ineffective leaders.

（一）勒温的领导风格分类

美国心理学家勒温（Kurt Lewin）是最早研究领导作风问题的心理学家，他以权力定位为基本变量，通过各种试验，从领导者如何运用其职权的角度来划分领导风格，将领导风格分为专制式、民主式和放任式三种。

1. 专制式

专制式亦称为专权式或者独裁式。这种领导者喜欢命令，并期望下属服从，属于比较教条的领导者。他们的权力定位于领导者个人，靠权力和强制命令让人服从。这种领导风格主要表现为：

（1）独断专行，很少考虑别人意见，领导者独自做出决策；

（2）领导者亲自设计工作计划，制定工作内容，很少与下属沟通，下属几乎没有参与决策的机会；

（3）领导者主要依靠行政命令、纪律约束、训斥和惩罚来进行管理，只有偶尔的奖励；

（4）领导者与下属保持一定的心理距离，很少参加群体活动。

专制式领导风格的优点体现在决策制定和执行速度快，可以使问题在短时间内得到解决。但是在专制型领导的团体中，下属的依赖性大，领导者负担较重，容易抑制下属的创造性和工作积极性。此类领导风格较适用于简单且重复性较高的任务，以及突发性紧急任务。

2. 民主式

民主式亦称为群体参与式。这种领导者喜欢鼓励下属参与决策的制定。他们在采取行动方案或做出决策之前常常听取下属意见。他们不会靠职位权力和命令来使人服从，主要以非正式的权力和职权来管理下属。这种领导风格主要表现为：

（1）大多数决策都是在领导者的鼓励和协助下，由群体讨论决定的，领导者不会个人决定；

（2）领导者在分配工作的时候，会尽量照顾到下属个人的能力和兴趣；

（3）领导者给下属较大的工作自由，下属工作有较强的灵活性，领导者对下属的工作并不做特别具体的安排；

（4）领导者会与下属打成一片，积极参加团体活动，与下属无距离感，谈话时多使用商量和建议的口气。

◇　Average leadership style (ALS)

Average Leadership Style (ALS) classifies the leadership styles on the basis of how leaders use their authority. The basic styles include autocratic leader, democratic leader and free-rein leader.

Autocratic leader commands and expects compliance, and he or she is dogmatic and positive, and leads by the ability to withhold or give rewards and punishments.

Democratic, or participative leader consults with subordinates and encourages their participation.

民主式领导风格可以使成员对团体活动有较高的满足感，有利于完成工作目标，并且可以使群体成员不仅彼此间关系融洽，而且工作积极主动，富有创造性。但是在民主式领导的团体中，决策制定的过程过长，耗费时间较多，领导者周旋于各派意见之间，容易优柔寡断。虽然民主式领导风格备受人们推崇，但是它不是无条件适用的，需要考虑领导工作所处的具体环境，以便扬长避短。

3. 放任式

放任式亦称为放任自流式。这种领导喜欢将权力分散给组织中的每个成员，工作事先无布置，事后无检查，毫无规章制度而言。放任式领导者很少使用职权，他们会留给下属很大的自由度，他们认为领导者的职责仅仅是为下属提供信息并与组织外部进行联系，以此有利于下属的工作。这种领导风格主要表现为：

（1）领导者在工作中缺乏积极性和主动性，极少运用其权力；

（2）在决策过程中，领导者不插手、不干扰，一切决策由团队成员自我摸索，自我决定；

（3）领导者在工作中对下属放任自流，既不布置任务，也不监督执行，更不检查任务完成情况。

放任式领导者风格虽然能够培养下属的独立性，但是在执行过程中，往往要求下属有极高的个人素质和成熟度。这种领导风格常常会因为领导无为、下属各自为政，最后难以做出统一决策。因此，放任式领导很难得到提倡，除非被领导者是专家人物且有高度的工作热情，才可在少数情况下采取这种"无为而治"的领导方式。

以上三种领导风格中领导与成员的关系见表8-2。

上述三种领导风格哪种方式最好？美国有学者做了一项实验，将一群儿童分成三组来进行堆雪人活动，各组的组长被事先分别训练成专制式、民主式和放任式领导者。实验结果表明，放任式领导的第一小组工作效果最差，雪人的数量和质量都排在最后一名。采取专制式领导方式的第二小组，堆的雪人数量最多，说明工作效率最高，但质量不如民主式领导下的小组。最后一个小组采用民主式领导，参与的儿童们积极主动发言，显示出很高的工作热情和创造性思维，小组长又在旁边引导和鼓励，结果堆出的雪人质量最高，但是由于讨论的时间过长，效率不及第二组。这次实验表明，专制式和民主式领导是利弊并存的，而放任式领导风格对下属要求较高，轻易不要采用。具体哪一种领导风格更好，应取决于所处的环境。

Free-rein leader uses power very little, if at all, giving subordinates a high degree of independence.

The use of any style will depend on the situation.

272

表 8-2　不同领导风格下领导与成员的关系

Table 8-2　Relationship between Styles of Leadership and Group Members

Autocratic Style

Leader
1.　The individual is very conscious of his or her position.
2.　He or she has little trust and faith in members of the group.
3.　This leader believes pay is a just reward for working and the only reward that will motivate employees.
4.　Orders are issued to be carried out, with no questions allowed and no explanations given.

Group members
1.　No responsibility is assumed for performance, with people merely doing what they are told.
2.　Production is good when the leader is present, but poor in the leader's absence.

Free-rein Style

Leader
1.　He or she has no confidence in his or her leadership ability.
2.　This leader does not set goals for the group.

Group members
1.　Decisions are made by whoever in the group is willing to do it.
2.　Productivity generally is low, and work is sloppy.
3.　Individuals have little interest in their work.
4.　Morale and teamwork generally are low.

Democratic Style

Leader
1.　Decision making is shared between the leader and the group.
2.　When the leader is required or forced to make a decision, his or her reasoning is explained to the group.
3.　Criticism and praise are given objectively.

Group members
1.　New ideas and change are welcomed.
2.　A feeling of responsibility is developed within the group.
3.　Quality of work and productivity generally are high.
4.　The group generally feels successful.

（资料来源：L. B. Bradford and R. Lippitt. Building a Democratic Work Group. *Personnel*, 1945, 11(2): 2）

（二）基于态度和行为倾向的领导风格分类：管理方格理论

管理方格理论（Managerial Grid Theory）是研究领导方式及其有效性的理论，由美国行为科学家布莱克（Robert R. Blake）和莫顿（Jane S. Mouton）在著作《管理方格》一书中提出。他们认为以生产为中心的管理风格和以人为中心的管理风格都是极端情形，在此基础上，他们发展了领导风格的二维观点，提出了管理方格理论。

管理方格理论有两个维度：纵坐标表示对人的关心程度，横坐标表示对生产的关心程度。两者按程度大小各分为九等份，每个方格就表示"关心人"和"关心生产"以不同程度相结合的一种领导风格，共有 81 种不同领导方式的管理方格。在这 81 种领导风格中，最具代表性的有贫乏型、任务型、乡村俱乐部型、中庸型和团队型五种领导方式（见图 8-1）。

◇　Managerial grid theory

Managerial grid is a two-dimensional framework rating a leader on the basis of concern for people and concern for production.

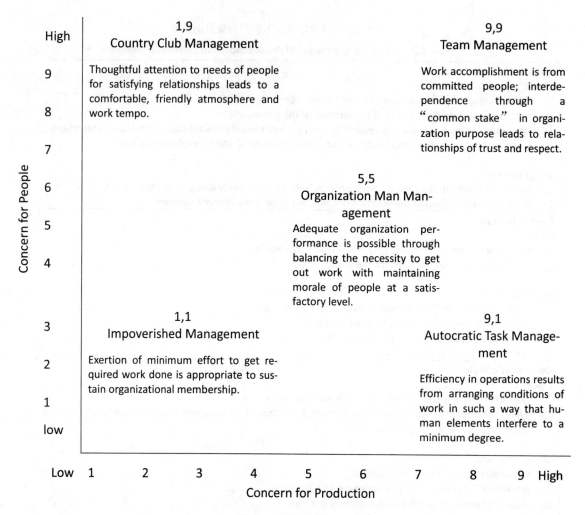

图 8-1 管理方格图

Figure 8-1 The Managerial Grid

（资料来源：改编自 Leslie W. Rue and Lloyd L. Byars. *Management: Skills and Application* (13th edition).
北京：北京大学出版社，2013，p. 290）

1. （1,1）型领导风格

（1,1）型也被称为"贫乏型的管理者"。这种领导者对于工作和人都极不关心，管理工作几乎处于放任状态，领导者希望以最低限度的努力来实现组织目标和维持人际关系，只要工作不出差错就会满足。这种管理者事实上根本没有发挥领导的作用，实际工作中这样的领导者很少见。

2. （1,9）型领导风格

（1,9）型也被称为"乡村俱乐部型的管理者"。这种领导者对于人高度关心，但是对生产却很少关心。他们不关心工作效率，也不注重工作结果，只是注意搞好人际关系，关心下属的需求是否获得满足，组织内员工们能够轻松、友好、愉快地相处，工作中强调自己与周围同事的关系一定要和谐，属于一种轻松的领导风格。

(1,1): Impoverished Management

Exertion of minimum effort to get required work done is appropriate to sustain organizational membership.

(1,9): Country Club Management

Thoughtful attention to needs of people for satisfying relationships leads to a comfortable, friendly atmosphere and work tempo.

3. （9,1）型领导风格

（9,1）型也被称为"任务型的管理者"。这种领导者对工作极为关心，强调有效地控制下属完成各项工作；但是对人却很不重视，不关心工作人员的需求及其满足，不关注下属的成长及团队的士气。在工作中，下属只能奉命行事，员工容易失去进取精神，不愿创造性地工作，不能施展所有的才能，属于独裁的重任务型的领导风格。

4. （5,5）型领导风格

（5,5）型也被称为"中庸型的管理者"。这种领导者既对工作关心，也对人关心，二者兼顾，程度适中。在工作中追求正常的效率和令人满意的士气，既对工作质量和数量有一定的要求，同时又通过引导和激励使下属完成工作。但是这样的领导往往缺乏进取心，没有远大的追求目标安于现状是他们多数的心态，工作缺少创新，是一种中间型的领导风格。

5. （9,9）型领导风格

（9,9）型也被称为"团队型的管理者"。这种领导者对人和生产都极其关心，在工作中既关心工作的效率及结果，又关心员工的士气和满意度，通过管理促进组织目标与个人目标的有效结合，高度重视组织的各项工作，同时又通过沟通和激励使群体合作，下属人员共同参与管理，使工作成为组织成员自觉自愿的行动，提高士气促进生产。这是一种最理想的管理方式。

布莱克（Robert R. Blake）和莫顿（Jane S. Mouton）对于各种领导风格进行了多次研讨，认为（9,9）型是一种最佳的领导风格。但是事实上，现实工作中能够实现（9,9）型管理风格的领导者凤毛麟角，人们都会或多或少受到管理环境的限制。

管理方格论提供了一种衡量领导者所处领导形态的模式，可以作为培养有效领导者的工具，使领导者较清楚地认识到自己的领导行为，向（9,9）型管理风格努力转变，以获得最好的效果。

管理方格理论说明了领导行为类型与群体工作绩效之间的关系，但是没有重视影响领导成功或失败的情境因素。领导权变理论有效地弥补了行为理论的不足。

（三）领导权变理论

领导特质理论着重研究领导的品牌、素质和修养，领导行为理论着重分析领导者的领导行为和领导风格。在运用特质论和行为论的过程中，人们发现，实际工作中何种领导方式最为有效，要视具体的工作环境而定。

(9,1): Autocratic Task Management

Efficiency in operations results from arranging conditions of work in such a way that human elements interfere to a minimum degree.

(5,5): Organization Man Management

Adequate organization performance is possible through balancing the necessity to get out work with maintaining morale of people at a satisfactory level.

(9,9)：Team Management

Work accomplishment is from committed people; interdependence through a "common stake" in organization purpose leads to relationships of trust and respect.

The grid provides a framework for conceptualizing leadership style.

In fact, little substantive evidence supports the conclusion that a 9,9 style is most effective in all situations.

✧ Contingency theory

没有唯一的领导特质为所有有效的领导者所共有，也没有哪一种领导风格适用于所有的工作情境。于是很多学者开始将研究目光投向情境因素的影响方面，产生了领导权变理论（Contingency Theory）。领导权变理论认为，领导是一种动态的过程，领导在实际工作中是否有效，不仅取决于领导者本身的领导行为方式，还取决于具体的情境和场合，其领导有效性会随着领导者的特点和所处情境的变化而变化。

1. 菲德勒权变模型

菲德勒权变模型是第一个综合的领导权变模型，由美国著名心理学家弗雷德·菲德勒（Fred E. Fiedler）于1962年提出。他的模型当中，把领导者的特质研究与领导行为研究有机地结合起来，并将其与情境分类联系起来，综合研究领导效果。其研究结论受到许多人的肯定和认同。他认为，任何领导形态均可能有效，其有效性完全取决于是否与所处的环境相适应。

（1）菲德勒模型第一步：确定领导方式

菲德勒认为，领导者个体的基础领导方式是影响领导成功的关键因素之一。因此，他设计了一种称为"最难共事者问卷"（Least Preferred Coworker Questionnaire, LPC）的工具，通过问卷来确定领导者的基础领导方式。

LPC问卷包括18组对应的形容词，让被测者先回忆一个自己曾遇到的最难相处的同事，然后根据18组形容词对该同事进行评价。通过分析被测试者的答案，可以看出被测试者所属的领导风格。如果一个领导者用较为积极的词语描述最难共事的同事，即LPC分高，那么就认为该领导者对人宽容、体谅、注重人际关系，其领导方式是关系导向型领导方式；反之，如果一个领导者用相对不积极的词语描述最难共事的同事，即LPC分低，那么就可以认为该领导习惯于命令和控制，注重工作，其领导方式是任务导向型的领导方式。

（2）菲德勒模型第二步：确定情境

在评估过个体的基础领导风格之后，就需要确定情境。菲德勒将影响领导风格的情境因素分为三个方面：职位权力、任务结构和上下级关系。

①职位权力

职位权力是指与领导者职位相关的正式职权，及其从上级和整个组织各个方面所得到的支持程度，包括领导者的地位、权威与责罚、升职加薪、任免、指派等能力。职位权力越充分，在上级和整个组织中所得到的支持越有力，对领导的有效性影响越大。一般来说，领导

Contingency theories of leadership: People become leaders not only because of their personality attributes but also because of various situational factors and the interactions between leaders and group members.

Fiedler Contingency Model is a leadership theory proposing that effective group performance depended upon properly matching the leader's style and the amount of control and influence in the situation.

Step 1: Define the basic leadership style

Fielder proposed that a key factor in leadership success was an individual's basic leadership style.

Least Preferred Coworker Questionnaire (LPC) is a questionnaire that measures whether a leader is task or relationship oriented.

Step 2: Define the different types of situations

Three critical dimensions of the leadership situation: position power, task structure and leader-member relations.

Position power arises from organizational authority. It describes the degree of influence a leader has over activities such as hiring, firing, discipline, promotions, and salary increases.

者拥有明确的职位权力时，组织成员会更顺从其领导，有利于提高工作效率。

②任务结构

任务结构是指下属所从事的工作或任务的明确程度，以及有关人员对工作任务的职责明确程度，包括目标对成员来说是否清晰、成果是否可测量、解决问题的方法是否具有正确性、完成任务的途径或手段多少等方面。当工作任务本身十分明确，且组织成员对工作任务的职责也十分明确时，领导者对工作过程易于控制；相反，如果任务复杂而又没有先例，工作规定不清楚，没有标准和程序，那么领导就处于被动地位，任务结构不明确。

③上下级关系

上下级关系是指领导者得到被领导者拥护和支持的程度，即下属对领导者的情感，包括尊重、友谊、信任、合作、支持、拥护、忠诚等方面；以及领导者对下属的关心和爱护程度。领导者越受下属的喜爱、尊敬和信任，领导者的权力和影响力就越大；反之，其影响力就越小。

这三种情境因素的不同组合导致领导方式发生权变，会形成 8 种不同类型的情境。其中，若三个情境因素的组合是职位权力强、任务结构高、上下级关系好，即为领导最有利的情境；若三个情境因素的组合是职位权力弱、任务结构低、上下级关系差，即为领导最不利的情境。按照这个三维结构模式，可以将 8 种不同类型的情境分为 3 类：有利的、中间状态的、不利的。

（3）菲德勒模型第三步：领导方式与情境的匹配

当领导方式与情境相匹配时，领导的有效性会达到最高。因此，菲德勒根据领导情境的 8 种分类，对 1200 个团队进行了抽样调查，得出结论：在环境较好的 1、2、3 和环境较差的 7、8 情境下，采用低 LPC 领导方式，即工作任务型的领导方式比较有效；在环境中等的 4、5、6 情境下，采用高 LPC 领导方式，即人际关系型的领导方式比较有效（见图 8-2）。

2. 情境领导理论

情境领导理论（Situational Leadership Theory, SLT）亦称为领导生命周期理论，是由科曼（A. K. Korman）首先提出的，后由保罗·赫塞（Paul Hersey）和肯尼斯·布兰查德（Kenneth Blanchard）予以发展。情境领导理论是一种重视下属成熟度的权变理论，认为随着下属的成熟度不断提高，结构行为应该减少；而社会情感支持行为应该先增加，然后逐渐减少。

Task structure describes the degree to which tasks can be clearly spelled out and people held responsible for them.

Leader-member relations describe the degree of confidence, trust, and respect employees had for their leader.

Step 3: Identify the appropriate combinations of style and situation

Situational Leadership Theory (SLT) is a leadership contingency theory that focuses on followers' readiness.

As the maturity of followers increases, structure should be reduced while socio-emotional support should first be increased and then gradually decreased.

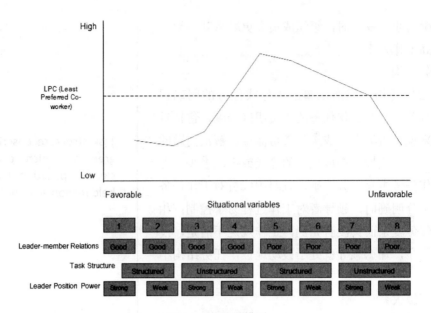

图 8-2　菲德勒模型

Figure 8-2　Fiedler Model

（资料来源：改编自 Heinz Weihrich, Mark V. Cannice and Harold Koontz. *Management: A global and Entrepreneurial Perspective* (13th edition). 北京：经济科学出版社, 2011, p. 364）

情境领导理论中，依旧使用菲德勒模型中的两个维度，即任务和关系，但是加入了对下属成熟度的考虑。下属成熟度（Readiness）是指人们对自己的行为承担责任的能力和愿望的大小。它取决于任务成熟度和心理成熟度。任务成熟度即胜任度，包括一个人的知识和技能，工作成熟度高的人拥有足够的知识、能力和经验完成他们的工作任务，而不需要他人的指导。心理成熟度即认同度，指的是一个人做某事的意愿和动机。如果下属无须领导者的直接控制和监管，具有自我激励和完成高质量工作的渴望，能自觉地去做，则认为他具有较高的心理成熟度。心理成熟度高的个体不需要太多的外部激励，主要靠内部动机激励。该理论将下属的成熟度分为以下四种程度。

Readiness is the extent to which people have the ability and willingness to accomplish a specific task.

R1（不成熟）：下属缺乏接受和承担任务的能力和愿望。

R2（初步成熟）：下属愿意承担任务，但缺乏足够的能力。

R3（比较成熟）：下属具有完成领导者所交给任务的能力，但没有足够的积极性。

R4（成熟）：下属愿意并且有能力去做领导者要求他们完成的任务。

R1: People are both unable and unwilling to take responsibility for doing something.
R2: People are unable but willing to do the necessary job tasks.
R3: People are able but unwilling to do what the leader wants.

R4: People are both able and willing to do what is asked of them.

根据情境领导理论，随着员工的成长，成熟度会发生变化，领导者与员工之间的关系也会相应地发生变化。因此，该理论提出了四种领导方式：命令式、说服式、参与式和授权式（见图 8-3）。

（1）命令式（Telling）

命令式的领导风格具体表现为高任务、低关系。领导者来定义下属角色，并具体告知下属应当做什么、如何做、何时以及何地去完成不同的任务。在员工进入组织的最初阶段，管理者采用任务导向的领导风格最为合适。

（2）说服式（Selling）

说服式的领导风格具体表现为高任务、高关系。领导者既给予下属一定的指导，又为下属提供一定的支持，注意保护和鼓励下属的积极性。在此种领导方式下，领导会与下属共同商讨工作的进行，比较重视领导与下属的双向沟通。

（3）参与式（Participating）

参与式的领导风格具体表现在低任务、高关系。在此种领导风格下，领导者很少发号指令，直接指挥员工工作，而是与下属共同参与决策。领导者的主要角色是为下属提供便利条件与协调沟通。

（4）授权式（Delegating）

授权式的领导风格具体表现为低任务、低关系。领导者在实际工作中几乎不提供指导或支持，管理者的主要工作就是授权，不需要做太多的事情，鼓励下属自主做好工作，由下属独立地开展工作，完成任务。

(1) Telling (high task and low relationship)
The leader defines roles and tells people what, how, when, and where to do various tasks.

(2) Selling (high task and high relationship)
The leader provides both directive and supportive behavior.

(3) Participating (low task and high relationship)
The leader and followers share in decision making; the main role of the leader is facilitating and communicating.

(4) Delegating (low task and low relationship)
The leader provides little direction or support.

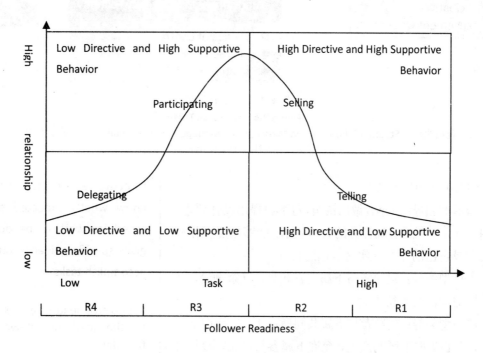

图 8-3　情境领导理论

Figure 8-3　Situational Leadership Theory

（资料来源：改编自 Kathryn M. Bartol and David C. Martin. *Management* (3rd edition).
北京：机械工业出版社，1998，p. 430）

3. 路径–目标理论

路径–目标理论由加拿大多伦多大学教授罗伯特·豪斯（Robert House）提出，其研究基础是领导期望理论。该理论的基本观点是，领导者的工作实质就是帮助下属达到他们的目标，并提供必要的指导和支持，以确保他们各自的目标与组织总目标一致。

该理论的核心是要求领导者用抓组织、关心生产的办法帮助员工理清达到目标的道路，用体贴精神关心人，满足人的需要，帮助员工通向自己预定的目标。该理论提出了指示型、支持型、参与型、成就导向型四种领导方式，并提出，这四种领导方式必须根据下属的不同情况分别选择，选择时主要考虑两个方面的因素：下属的人格特征和环境因素（见图 8-4）。

Path-goal theory is a leadership theory that says the leader's job is to assist followers in attaining their goals and to provide direction or support needed to ensure that their goals are compatible with the goals of the group or organization.

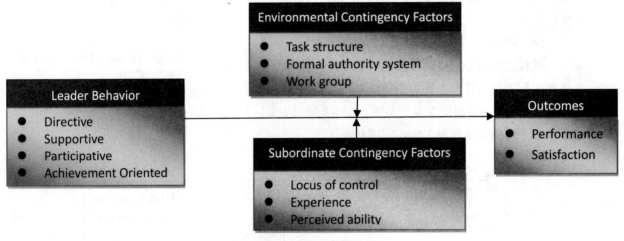

图 8-4　路径–目标理论

Figure 8-4　Path-goal Theory

（资料来源：Stephen P. Robbins and Mary Coulter. *Management* (11th edition). 北京：清华大学出版社, 2013, p. 468）

（1）4 种领导方式

指示型领导：领导者做出决策，对下属提出具体要求，指明方向，让下属明确任务的具体要求，能够按照工作程序去完成自己的任务，实现自己的目标。

支持型领导：领导者与下属友善相处，气氛融洽，关注下属需求，公平待人。

参与型领导：领导者与下属共同商量工作，征询下属建议，虚心听取下属的意见，允许下属参与决策，参与管理。

成就导向型领导：领导者提出有挑战的目标，要求下属有高水平的表现，鼓励下属并对下属的能力表现出充分的信心，激励下属想方设法去实现目标，迎接挑战。

Directive leader lets subordinates know what's expected of them, schedules work to be done, and gives specific guidance on how to accomplish tasks.

Supportive leader shows concern for the needs of followers and is friendly.

Participative leader consults with group members and uses their suggestions before making a decision.

（2）两个权变因素

下属的权变因素：包括下属的控制点、经验、感知能力。控制点分为内在控制点和外在控制点，内在控制点类型的人相信他们所遇到的一切是他们自己造成的；外在控制点类型的人相信他们所遇到的一切都是运气或命运。经验和感知的能力是指人们对自己从事工作的能力的信心。

环境的权变因素：包括人物结构、正式权力系统、工作群体。

下属的权变因素和环境的权变因素共同决定了适当的领导方式产生的有效业绩。

Achievement oriented leader sets challenging goals and expects followers to perform at their highest level.

Subordinate contingency factors include locus of control, experience and perceived ability.

Environmental contingency factors include task structure, formal authority system and work group.

Global Perspective

Leadership at the Chinese Haier Group and Volkswagen

Mr. Zhang Ruimin is the founder and CEO of the Haier Group, the most widely recognized home appliances manufacturer in China. Its many products include refrigerators, air conditioners, freezers, and microwave ovens. During China's Cultural Revolution, Mr. Zhang was sent to work in a metal processing plant, which may have helped him later in leading the appliance firm.

With the opening of China, Zhang became familiar with Harvard professor Michael Porter's book on competitive strategy, which emphasizes the importance of recognizing customer needs. Moreover, General Electric's approach to quality management and the emphasis on corporate culture illustrated by its CEO, Jack Welch, also influenced Zhang's view of managing.

Quality was Mr. Zhang's major concern. When visiting his refrigerator company, he noted that many of the products were defective. To demonstrate his passion for quality, he had the brand new refrigerators destroyed in a dramatic fashion. Needless to say, the workers were impressed, not only by Zhang's commitment to quality but also by his 14-hour daily work schedule. Uncommon in China at that time, he tied good performance of employees to monetary rewards and promotions. He also adopted other managerial practices learned from his German partner company, Liebherr.

His leadership by example transformed the bureaucratic enterprise into the Haier Group, which is now the best-known Chinese refrigerator company and operates in many countries, including the United States. But a leader cannot rest on accomplishments; a leader must articulate a vision for the future. Guided by Mr. Zhang's foresight, Haier ventured into computers and pharmaceuticals. The entrance of China into the World Trade Organization in 2001 not only has opened opportunities but also presents new challenges for the Haier Group. Mr. Zhang's leadership illustrates that Western management practices can be transferred to countries such as China.

While Mr. Zhang Ruimin may have benefited from German managerial practices, Volkswagen's Top manager Wolfgang Bernhard adopted some managerial approaches from the Americans.

Bernhard received his MBA from the Columbia Business School. He worked for the McKinsey consulting firm and later DaimlerChrysler. He then was hired by Mercedes being put on the fast-track promotion path. When this path was cut short, he got a top management position at Volkswagen being responsible for the VW brand. His task was to reduce the cost and develop new models, a task he did previously at Chrysler. Using his Chrysler experience, he ordered a study that found that VW needed twice the time to assemble a car when compared with its most efficient competitor.

Rather than following the traditional German way of delegating tasks to the appropriate departments, Bernhard assembled 200 VW people in an auditorium with the objective to reduce the costs of the newly planned Sport Utility Vehicle by $2500. They were not to go back to their workplace until the objective was reached. Each evening, Bernard watched the progress of the teams who worked until late at night to complete their task. After four weeks of hard work the goal was achieved through team effort. This illustrates that German managers as they gain international experience, can transfer their skills and approaches to their home country.

（案例来源：Heinz Weihrich, Mark V. Cannice and Harold Koontz. *Management: A global and Entrepreneurial Perspective* (12th edition). 北京：经济科学出版社，2008, p. 362）

第二节 激励理论

Youku: The Tao of Fun

Victor Koo is the founder and CEO of Youku. His resume includes stints at Bain & Co., P&G, the VC firm Richina, and Internet portal Sohu.com, where he rose to president. He said, "while we can learn from U.S. models, we certainly can't practice them in China." They must be modified because the culture is just different.

Hip Hop Office Quartet, which is produced by Youku, draws 4 million viewers per episode with its satire of the prevailing Chinese corporate culture, its hierarchy, discipline and paranoia. And it spotlights everything that Youku CEO Victor Koo does not want his office to be.

Koo has a less hierarchical view of his workers than exists at a typical Chinese company. He has dispensed with the titles and the offices that remind people of the traditional hierarchy. Youku employees work on teams, not in departments, and they refer to one another as classmates and to supervisors as teachers. And unlike the stereotypical Chinese CEO, who sequesters himself away from his underlings in a C-suite, Koo sits in a spartan cubicle.

Koo emphasizes the idea that work should feel as much as possible like play. While Youku's corporate culture is among the most casual, open , and egalitarian in the Chinese corporate world, the emphasis on fun is probably its most American aspect—though it's manifested in utterly Asian ways. Take the Youku offices, which employees have turned into a toy zoo gone wild: giraffes arching over cubicle dividers, computer screens vying for space with larger-than-life stuffed chickens, bobbleheads (mostly human) lined up in tidy rows. Plant sprout everywhere and motivational slogans shout from the walls.

According to Koo, the idea at Youku has always been "to get people I like to work on something I like to do. If you don't like what you do, you're probably dragging your feet. If you do like what you do, you're cooperating and sharing." "There's not the strong hierarchy that normally appears in a Chinese company," says Zhou Sheng, who worked at Microsoft for more than a decade before joining Youku as a senior product director. "At Youku the work is driven by the people here, not by the boss."

（案例来源：改编自 April Rabkin. Leaders at Alibaba, Youku and Baidu are Slowly Shaking up China's Corporate Culture. *Fast Company*, 2012, (2): 1-4）

　　激励下属对于管理者来说是一项挑战，因为激励需要找寻下属的工作动机，激励源于员工内心深处，而且不同的员工激励效果也会有所不同。优酷作为中国知名的视频分享网站，它注重用户体验，强调快者为王的产品理念，为传统媒体的发行和推广提供新的平台。创始人古永锵信奉平等简单的领导理念，作为圈内有名的好脾气老板，他放手让员工大胆工作，给予下属极大信任，激发其工作热情。古永锵对下属的激励方式与传统的物质激励方式不同，但是也都取得了卓越的成效。人是组织中非常重要的要素，如何实现员工激励，鼓励员工高质量的工作？每个人的动机是不一样的，管理者应该如何洞察员工激励动机并采取切实有效的激励方式？本节将介绍一些经典的领导激励理论，探讨如何提高员工满意度和生产效率。

一、管理中人的因素

（一）角色的多样性

领导的本质是影响他人，激发人们为组织提供有益贡献的工作热情，去实现管理者为组织制定的目标。因此，人是组织中非常重要的一个构成要素。因其社会属性的存在，对人管理的复杂程度远高于其他生产要素。人在一个组织中，可能是经理或员工；同时，也会购买其他产品，是其他组织的顾客，其购买行为会影响行业需求；他们也是家庭的一分子，如父母；也会是社会组织的一分子，如协会、政治团队的成员。管理者及其下属作为广义的社会系统中的一分子，其角色是多样的。而且，不同组织有不同的目标，与之相伴的，是员工的需要和目标的多样化和差异化。管理者必须意识到人的角色多样性这个特点，才能够更好地制定激励政策。

（二）个人尊严的重要性

人在社会组织中扮演着不同的角色，他们的喜好、个性、追求等各不相同，体现在工作中的目标也不尽相同。对管理者来说，实现组织目标是非常重要的，但是，这并不意味着要以牺牲员工个人尊严为代价。所谓个人尊严，是指人们必须被尊重，无论在组织中的职位高低。总经理、部门经理、一线员工，对组织的发展和目标的实现都功不可没，他们都有独特的贡献。在制定激励方案时，必须考虑员工个人尊严的保障。而且，我们无法通过单独的讨论或评价人的某一个方面，来实现对人的整体评价。在激励方案的制定过程中，我们必须将人视为一个整体来考虑，对其知识、态度、技能、个性等要素进行综合评价。

二、激励的内涵与过程

（一）激励的内涵

"激励"一词最早来源于古代拉丁语 movere，意为"移动"。后来在管理过程中被广泛应用，许多学者都给出了自己对"激励"一词的理解。学者们对激励内涵的理解，可以概括为以下三个方面。

首先，激励是一个过程。激励的主要作用是为了实现对人行为的激励。

其次，激励的目的性。激励是为了引起某种行为，进而实现特定的目标。

最后，激励的持续性。激励是一种持续的手段，需要保证行为持续发生。

✍ **People in Management**

✧ **Multiplicity of roles**

Managers and the people they lead are interacting members of a broad social system.

✧ **The importance of personal dignity**

Individual dignity: people must be treated with respect, no matter what their position in the organization is.

Managers must consider the whole person, not just separate and distinct characteristics such as knowledge, attitude, skills, or personality traits.

✍ **The Nature and Process of Motivation**

✧ **The nature of motivation**

The definition of motivation normally includes three common characteristics:

1. Motivation is concerned with what activates human behavior.

2. Motivation is concerned with what directs this behavior toward a particular goal.

3. Motivation is concerned with how this behavior is sustained.

所以，综上所述，激励是鼓舞、指引和维持个人努力行为以实现组织目标的过程。

（二）激励的过程

心理学家发现，人之所以会产生某种特定的行为，是由其动机决定的，而动机是由需求引起的，人之所以愿意做某事，是因为做这件事本身能满足其个人的某种需求。激励就是要激发人的需要，在满足个体需要的过程中同时实现组织目标，进而激发人的行为。简单地说，激励就是刺激需要、引发行为、满足需要、实现目标的一个动力过程，其核心目标是使组织中的成员充分发挥出其潜在的能力（如图 8-5 所示）。

Motivation is the process by which a person's efforts are energized, directed, and sustained toward attaining a goal.

✧　The process of motivation

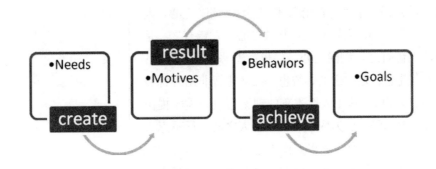

图 8-5　激励的过程
Figure 8-5　Simple Model of Motivation

在激励过程中，需要、动机和行为是三个重要构成要素。

需要是人们对某种目标物的欲望，如冷了需要衣服保暖，饿了需要食物果腹。需要是产生这种行为动机和行为的原动力，是激励的基础。因此在激励过程中，应该首先研究和了解人们具有哪些需要，这些需要在什么情况下能够成为推动人的行为的动力，再依此设计激励方案，才能发挥激励的作用。

动机是建立在需要基础之上的，其形成有两个基本条件：一是人的内在需求和愿望；二是外部提供的诱导和刺激，因此，并不是任何情况下需要都会引发行为的动机。当人们需要某种东西而没有得到，身体或心理会产生某种紧张和不安，这些不安会促使人们去寻找他们所需要的东西。管理者需要了解动机的形成、动机的强弱，以及动机与行为的关系，可以通过激励措施来引发动机，进而控制人的行为，实现管理目的。

Needs, motives and behaviors are three key factors in the process of motivation.

行为是指人类所特有的、由一定原因引起的、为了实现一定目的所进行的活动。行为是由某种需要的动机引起的，又是达到一定目标使需要得到满足的手段和过程。行为既是某种需要和动机的结果，又是这种需要和动机的反映。管理者要想方设法的做好需要引导和目标引导，强化员工动机，刺激员工的行为，进而实现组织的目标。

三、早期激励理论：人性假设理论

（一）中国古代的人性假设

中国古代的人性假设是从伦理学、社会学的角度来探讨人的本性问题，比较有代表性的观点是性善论、性恶论和人性可塑论。

1. 性善论

孟子最先提出了"性善论"。他认为："恻隐之心，人皆有之；羞恶之心，人皆有之；恭敬之心，人皆有之；是非之心，人皆有之。恻隐之心，仁也；羞恶之心，义也；恭敬之心，礼也；是非之心，智也。仁义礼智非由外铄我也，我固有之也。"基于人性本善的理论假设，孟子提出了"仁政"的主张，认为应该"以不忍人之心，行不忍人之政"，强调在管理中应该将人作为管理核心，运用道德的教化，恢复人的善良本性，依靠人内在因素去提高人们自律性，使各方面和谐统一，达到管理目的。

2. 性恶论

"性恶论"的代表人物是荀子，是中国古代人性假设理论的重要学说之一。荀子认为人性本来就是恶的："性之好恶、喜怒、哀乐，谓之情。"人都有"饥而欲食，寒而欲暖，劳而欲息，好利而恶善"的本性。因此，需要管理者加强对人的管理，防止社会混乱。基于人性本恶的理论假设，荀子提出了"礼义之治"的管理模式，提出管理者应该制定必要的规章制度，调节人们的欲望，以礼义来教育人民，建立法制以治理国家，推行刑罚以限制百姓，使社会变得安定而有秩序。

3. 人性可塑论

"人性可塑论"的首倡者应该属孔子。孔子提出"性相近也，习相远也"，认为管理不仅是对于人性的适应过程，而且是对于人性的塑造过程。他并没有提及人性的善或者恶，只是肯定的主张，人性是可以改变的，环境不同，行为的善恶也会不同。因此孔子提出了"仁学"，认为做出某种人性的判断虽然必要，但是更重要的在于如何改造这种人性，即去恶扬善。

✍ **Early Motivation Theories: Assumptions about Human Nature**

✧ Assumptions about the nature of people in ancient China

（二）道格拉斯·麦克雷戈的 X 理论和 Y 理论

美国社会心理学家道格拉斯.麦克雷戈（Douglas McGregor）1957 年在其发表的《企业的人性面》中，首次提出了著名的 X 理论和 Y 理论。麦克雷戈认为，管理者在管理中首先必须清楚地认识到身边人的本质,他们对员工的不同看法，决定了他们采取哪种管理方式。因此,他提出了两个人性假设,即 X 型人假设和 Y 型人假设,并将这两种人性假设概括为"X 理论"和"Y 理论"。

1. X 理论

麦克雷戈认为，持 X 理论观点的管理者对人的基本判断有以下几个观点（参见表 8-3）:

- 一般人都是好逸恶劳的，尽可能地逃避工作；
- 人生来就是以自我为中心的，对组织漠不关心；一般人缺乏进取心，不愿承担责任，宁愿被人领导；
- 一般人天生就反对变革，把安全看得高于一切；一般人易轻信，不机灵，容易受欺骗和煽动。

基于 X 理论对人的认识，管理者对下属的管理必须采用强制、惩罚、解雇等手段来迫使他们工作，对员工应当严格监督和控制,在领导行为上应当实行高度控制和集中管理，在领导模式上应采取集权的领导方式。这种对员工严加监督和控制的方式,实际体现在泰勒科学管理思想的奉行者及其之前的传统的管理方式上。

2. Y 理论

麦克雷戈认为,持 Y 理论观点的管理者对人的基本判断有以下观点（参见表 8-3）:

- 人们并不都是天生就厌恶工作的，他们热爱工作，从工作中获得满足感和成就感；人们能够对所参与的目标实行自我指挥和自我控制；
- 对目标的参与是同获得成就的报酬直接相关的，其中最重要的是自我实现需要的满足；
- 在适当条件下，人们不但能接受，而且能主动承担责任；
- 大多数人都具有相当高度的解决企业问题的想象力和独创性；
- 但在现代社会条件下，一般人的智慧潜能只是部分地得到了发挥。

◇ McGregor's Theory X and Theory Y

McGregor's Theory X and Theory Y: two sets of assumptions about the nature of people.

Theory X: the assumptions that employees dislike work, are lazy, avoid responsibility, and must be coerced to perform.

Theory Y: the assumptions that employees are creative, enjoy work, seek responsibility, and can exercise self-direction.

基于 Y 理论对人的认识,管理者应该对下属采取民主型和放任自由型的领导方式,在领导行为上必须遵循以人为中心的、宽容的和放权的领导原则,使下属目标和组织目标很好地结合起来,为人的智慧和能力的发挥创造有利条件。

表 8-3　麦克雷戈的 X-Y 假设

Table 8-3　McGregor's Theory X and Theory Y

Theory X Assumptions	Theory Y Assumptions
• Average human beings have an inherent dislike of work and will avoid it if they can. • Because of this human characteristic of disliking work, most people must be coerced, controlled, directed, and threatened with punishment to get them to put forth adequate effort toward the achievement of organizational objectives. • Average human beings prefer to be directed, wish to avoid responsibility, have relatively little ambition, and want security above all.	• The expenditure of physical and mental effort in work is as natural as play or rest; • External control and the threat of punishment are not the only means for producing effort toward organizational objectives. People will exercise self-direction and self-control in the service of objectives to which they are committed; • The degree of commitment to objectives is in proportion to the size of the rewards associated with their achievement. • Average human beings learn, under proper conditions, not only to accept responsibility but also to seek it. • The capacity to exercise a relatively high degree of imagination, ingenuity, and creativity in the solution of organizational problems is widely, not narrowly, distributed in the population. • Under the conditions of modern industrial life, the intellectual potentialities of the average human being are only partially utilized.

（资料来源：改编自 Heinz Weihrich, Mark V. Cannice and Harold Koontz. *Management: A global and Entrepreneurial Perspective* (13th edition). 北京：经济科学出版社，2011, p. 329）

显然,不同的人性假设有着根本的区别。实际工作中,管理者会受到自身价值观判断的影响,必然会在人性假设的认识上相对偏向于其中某一种。而管理者的人性假设的信奉,将会直接影响管理者的管理和领导方式。所以了解人性假设理论有现实的意义。麦克雷戈本人更推崇 Y 理论,但是事实上,这两种人性假设究竟谁对谁错,很难简单地得出结论。

Assumptions are not prescriptions or suggestions for managerial strategies; they do not imply hard or soft management. They are completely different views of people, not extremes on a continuous scale.

四、内容激励理论

人的未满足的需要是动机产生的根源,内容激励理论重点研究激发动机的诱因,由于其理论的内容基本都是围绕着如何满足需要进行研究的,故又被称为需要理论。主要包括：马斯洛需要层次理论,赫茨伯格双因素理论,奥尔德弗 ERG 理论和麦克莱兰成就需要理论。

✍ Content Theories

Content theories focus on people's underlying needs and label those particular needs that motivate behavior.

（一）马斯洛需要层次理论

亚伯拉罕·马斯洛（Abraham Maslow）是美国著名的社会心理学家，出生于美国纽约市布鲁克林区，1926年考入康奈尔大学，3 年后转至威斯康星大学攻读心理学，并获得博士学位。他于 1935 年在哥伦比亚大学任心理研究工作助理，1937 年任布鲁克林学院副教授，第二次世界大战后转到布兰戴斯大学任心理学教授，开始对健康人格或自我实现者的心理特征进行研究。在《人的动机理论》一书中，马斯洛提出了需要层次理论。该理论将人类纷繁复杂的需要从低到高分为五个层次：生理需要、安全需要、社交需要、尊重需要和自我实现的需要（图 8-6）。

✧　Hierarchy of needs theory

Hierarchy of needs theory is the Maslow's theory that human needs—physiological, safety, social, esteem, and self-actualization—form a sort of hierarchy.

图 8-6　马斯洛需要层次理论
Figure 8-6　Maslow's Hierarchy of Needs

1.　生理需要

生理需要是维持人类生存所必需的身体需要，包括对食物、空气和水的需要，这是最低的需要层次，人们在转向较高层次需要之前，总是尽力满足这一需要。在组织中，生理需要表现在对基本工资、基本工作条件的保障上的需要上。

Physiological needs: a person's needs for food, drink, shelter, sex, and other physical requirements.

2.　安全需要

安全需要是对人身安全、生活稳定以及免遭痛苦、威胁或疾病等保证身心免受伤害的需要。在组织环境中，安全需要体现为人们对工作的安全性、额外福利和工作保障的需要。

Safety needs: a person's needs for security and protection from physical and emotional harm as well as assurance that physical needs will continue to be met.

3.　社交需要

社交需要是对感情、友谊、爱情以及隶属关系等归属和爱的需要。在组织中，社交需要表现为人们希望与同事建立良好的人际关系、参与团队工作的需要。

Social needs: a person's needs for affection, belongingness, acceptance, and friendship.

4.　尊重需要

尊重需要是人们需要树立良好的自我形象，得到他人认可、受人尊敬等需要。在组织中，尊重需要主要体现为期望得到认同，职责的扩大以及地位的提高都可以实现尊重需要。

Esteem needs: a person's needs for internal esteem factors such as self-respect, autonomy, and achievement and external esteem factors such as status, recognition, and attention.

5. 自我实现需要

自我实现需要是人类最高级别的需要，包括个人成长、发挥个人潜能、实现个人理想等需要，一般体现为成就感和胜任感。在组织中，可以通过为员工提供成长机会、给予员工发挥创造力的机会、给员工培训以使他们能够承担有挑战性的工作任务等方式，来获得自我实现需要的满足。

根据马斯洛需要层次理论，低层次的需要应该首先得到满足。一旦某种需要得到了满足，这种需要的重要性就下降了，不再具有激励作用。

（二）赫茨伯格双因素理论

美国行为科学家弗雷德里克·赫茨伯格（Fredrick Herzberg）在马斯洛需要层次理论的基础上，提出了另一个广受欢迎的理论：双因素理论。他对匹兹堡地区多家工商企业机构的工作人员进行了大样本调查，主要围绕两个问题进行访谈：在工作中，哪些事项是让他们感到满意的，并估计这种积极情绪可以持续多长时间；有哪些事项是让他们感到不满意的，并估计这种消极情绪持续多长时间。访谈结果发现，与工作不满意有关的工作特性，截然不同于与工作满意相关的工作特性。在此基础上，赫茨伯格提出了"双因素理论"（也叫作"激励-保健理论"）如图 8-7 所示。

Self-actualization needs: a person's needs for growth, achieving one's potential, and self-fulfillment; the drive to become what one is capable of becoming.

When one set of needs is satisfied, this kind of need ceases to be a motivator.

✧ Two-factor theory

Two-factor theory (motivation-hygiene theory) is the motivation theory that intrinsic factors are related to job satisfaction and motivation, whereas extrinsic factors are associated with job dissatisfaction.

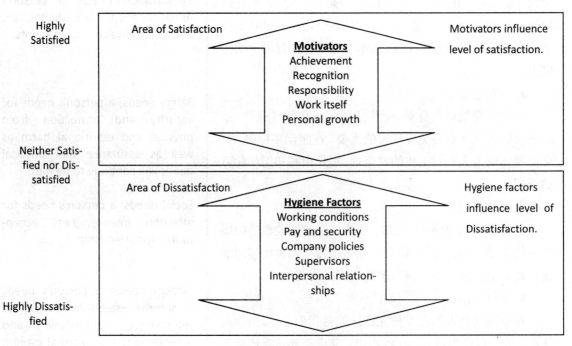

图 8-7　赫茨伯格双因素理论
Figure 8-7　Herzberg's Two-Factor Theory
（资料来源：Richard L. Daft. *Management* (7th edition). 北京：清华大学出版社，2006, p. 702）

290

赫茨伯格认为,有两种完全不同的因素在影响着员工的工作行为：一个是保健因素,一个是激励因素。

保健因素是指那些可能导致员工对工作不满意的因素,包括工作环境、工作薪水、工资政策、人际关系等。赫茨伯格认为,当保健因素得到满足后,员工对工作就没有不满的感觉,但是也不会导致其积极的态度,并不能对员工起到激励作用。但是如果这些因素得不到满足,就会引发员工的不满情绪。

Hygiene factors are factors that involve the presence or absence of job dissatisfiers, including working conditions, pay, company policies, and interpersonal relationships.

激励因素是高层次的需要,属于工作内容和工作本身的,包括成就、赏识、责任和发展机会等。赫茨伯格认为,当激励因素被满足了之后,员工就会感到满意,就能够激发员工的热情和积极性。但是如果这些因素得不到满足,员工只是没有满意感,但也不会产生不满。

Motivators are factors that influence job satisfaction based on fulfillment of high-level needs such as achievement, recognition, responsibility, and opportunity for growth.

赫茨伯格的双因素理论和马斯洛的需要层次理论有相似之处。双因素中的保健因素相当于马斯洛需要层次理论的生理需要、安全需要和社交需要这些较低层次的需要,这些因素的主要作用在于提供人们生活的基本保障,没有这些因素会引起人们的不满,但是并不能激励人们内在潜力、激励人们更好的工作；双因素中的激励因素相当于马斯洛需要层次理论的尊重需要、自我实现的需要等较高级的需要,可以激励人们去更好的完成任务。但是,双因素理论更强调保健因素与激励因素的本质作用,该理论认为,保健因素的需要得到满足,对人的激励作用是非常有限的,只有那些激励因素得到满足,才会最大限度的激发员工工作积极性。

20 世纪 60 年代以来,双因素理论的研究越来越受到人们的重视。管理者们逐渐意识到,管理的主要任务是消除员工的不满意因素,即为员工提供基本的保健因素,然后再运用激励因素来满足员工较高层次的需要,进而推动员工工作热情,获得更大程度的满意感。

（三）奥尔德弗 ERG 理论

✧ ERG theory

耶鲁大学的克莱顿·奥尔德弗（Clayton Alderfer）继续发展了马斯洛的需要层次理论,他对五个需要层次进行了修改和简化,提出了需要的"生存、关系、成长"理论（ERG 理论）,并通过实证研究验证了 ERG 理论的实用价值。该理论提出,员工有三类核心的需要：生存（Existence）、关系（Relatedness）、成长（Growth）。

ERG theory is an alternative to Maslow's hierarchy of needs theory which argues that there are three levels of individual needs.

生存的需要是与人们的基本物质生存相关的需要,包括食物、水、基本工资、工作条件等,类似于马斯洛需要层次理论中的生理需要与安全需要。

Existence needs include the various forms of material and physiological desires, such as food and water, as well as work-related forms such as pay, fringe benefits, and physical working conditions.

关系的需要是指人们对保持重要的人际关系的需要，包括人们同家庭、朋友、同事、同行的关系，类似于马斯洛需要层次理论中的社交需要。

成长的需要是指个人谋求发展的内在愿望，激励员工创造性地、有效地改变自身和环境，类似于马斯洛需要层次理论中尊重需要和自我实现需要。

ERG 理论并不是马斯洛需要层次理论的简单修改，它证实了不同类型的需要可以同时起作用。ERG 理论认为，人在同一时间可能有不止一种需要起作用，满足程度越低的需要，对人的行为影响越强烈。较低需要的满足越充分，对较高层次需要的渴望、追求越强烈。如果高一层次的需要满足程度很低或受到挫折，就会退化为对较低层次需要的更强烈追求，即使这一层次的需要已经得到了基本满足。人的需要的升级也不一定严格由低到高的顺序逐级递进，可以越级。

ERG 理论比马斯洛需要层次理论有更多的科学支持，而且与人们关于个体差异的常识认知更加一致，因此，ERG 理论在理论界和实践界更为流行。

（四）麦克莱兰成就需要理论

美国心理学家戴维·麦克莱兰（David C. McClelland）提出了成就需要理论，也称为三种需要理论或后天需要理论。该理论认为在人类基本生理需要得到满足的基础上，人的需要主要有三种：成就需要、归属需要和权力需要。这些需要是后天获得的，在个体中如何达到平衡也因人而异。

成就需要是对挑战性工作及事业成功的追求，是对成就的强烈愿望和对成功及目标实现的执着。有些人追求的成就，并不是事情做好之后的报酬，而是有一种欲望比以前做得更好、更有效率，这种内驱力就是成就需要。有成就需要的人有以下主要特征：有个人承担责任、解决问题、寻求答案的需要；寻求挑战，并为自己设立既有一定难度又不是高不可攀的目标；希望自己所做的事情能得到快速且明确的反馈；对工作热诚，执着于所从事的工作。

归属需要是对与他人建立和睦友好关系的愿望。有高归属需要的人可能是成功的整合者，能够协调各部门的工作，建立积极的工作关系。有归属需要的人有以下主要特征：寻求建立并保持和他人的友谊和亲密的感情关系；希望自己获得他人的好感；喜欢参加各种社交活动，结交知心朋友；乐于帮助和安慰危难中的伙伴。

Relatedness needs address our relationships with significant others, such as families, friendship groups, work groups, and professional groups.

Growth needs impel creativity and innovation, along with the desire to have a productive impact on our surroundings.

ERG theory argues that we can be concerned with more than one need category at the same time. And it acknowledges that some individuals' needs may occur in a different order than that posited by the ERG framework.

✧ Acquired-needs theory

Acquired-needs theory is a theory (developed by McClelland) stating that our needs are acquired or learned on the basis of our life experiences.

Need for achievement is the desire to accomplish challenging tasks and achieve a standard of excellence in one's work.

Need for affiliation is the desire to maintain warm, friendly relationships with others.

权力需要是指影响和控制别人的一种愿望或驱动力。有权力欲望的人往往对能否施加影响和控制他人表现出极大的关切，而且往往更容易获得机会晋升到组织的高级管理层。有权力需要的人有以下主要特征：对领导地位有强烈的渴求，要求取得并行使权力；喜欢争辩，很健谈，直率，头脑冷静并善于提出要求；竞争意识很强，喜欢支配、教训人。

麦克莱兰成就需要理论的重要性在于它揭示了员工与工作相匹配的重要性。对归属需要较高的员工更喜欢安定、保险系数高和可预见的工作场所，对成就需要较高的员工更喜欢有挑战性的、富于变幻的工作内容。对权力需要较高的员工更喜欢充满竞争、具有晋升机会的工作岗位。而且，员工的三种激励需要是可以通过培训来培育和激发的，因此，管理者可以通过识别出那些对人的行为有激励作用的特定需要，来围绕着满足人的需要进行工作设计，进而提高员工工作的效率和效果。

五、过程激励理论

过程激励理论主要研究管理者所提供的激励因素是否能够发挥作用，以及如何发挥激励作用。重点研究激励实现的过程和机制，使管理者了解人们在实际工作中是如何选择其所要进行的行为过程，以及行为过程是怎样产生的，是朝着哪个方向发展，以及如何将这个行为保持下去的发展过程。其代表理论包括期望理论、公平理论和强化理论。

（一）期望理论

美国心理学家维克多·弗鲁姆（Victor Vroom）在《工作与激励》一书中提出了期望理论。该理论认为，人们是否受到激励，取决于他们对努力后所取得的成果的价值以及实现目标的可能性的估计。用公式可以表示为：

激励力＝效价×期望值

其中，激励力是指激发出人的内在潜力的程度，即激励强度；效价是个人对结果的偏好程度；期望值是主观估计实现既定目标的可能性。

根据期望理论，目标对于人们的激励程度受到目标效价和期望值两个因素的影响。目标效价更多的来自人们的主观判断，如果他们认为实现这个目标的意义很大，对他们来说很有价值，那么效价就高，反之，效价就低；期望值来源于人们对实现该目标可能性大小的主观估计，如果估计实现的可能性很大，那么就会很努力地完成，激励效用增加，反之，激励效用下降。

Need for power is the desire to influence others and control one's environment.

✍ **Process Theory**

Process theories explain how employees select behaviors with which to meet their needs and determine whether their choices were successful.

✧ Expectancy theory

Expectancy theory proposes that motivation depends on individuals' expectations about their ability to perform tasks and receive desired rewards.

Force=Valence × Expectancy
Force: the strength of a person's motivation.
Valence: the strength of an individual's preference for an outcome.
Expectancy: the probability that a particular action will lead to a desired outcome.

在运用期望理论进行激励时，应重点处理好以下三个方面的关系。

1. 努力和绩效的关系

许多管理者认为，只要鼓励员工努力工作，就一定会提高工作绩效。其实不然。绩效和员工个人努力之间并不是一一对应的关系，而是随机的。人们总是希望通过一定的努力能够达到预期的目标，当员工认为，通过自己的努力实现预期目标的概率较大时，就会有强大的内部激励，努力工作；反之，当他主观判断即使自己努力工作也很难实现预期目标的时候，就会失去内在的动力，工作消极。因此，管理者不仅要提供必要的工作条件和工作指导，提高员工完成工作的信心，还必须调整评价标准，让员工经过一段努力之后可以取得一定的绩效，才会真正起到激励作用。

2. 绩效与奖励之间的关系

奖励包括物质奖励和精神奖励，是组织设定的行为强化物。员工努力的取得绩效，会理所当然地认为应该获得相应的奖励；如果奖励是合理的，就有可能产生工作热情。否则，就可能没有工作积极性。所以，管理者在日常工作中，必须要为绩效设置奖励，而且奖励必须公平合理，对奖励的承诺必须可信，才会提高员工的工作热情。

3. 奖励与满足个人需要的关系

同一种奖励对不同的人所起到的激励作用是不同的，人们总是希望自己所获得的奖励能够满足自己某方面的需要，但由于年龄、性别、资历、社会地位和经济条件等方面的差异，对于不同的员工，同一种奖励的效用会不同。而且，即使是对同一员工，不同的奖励对其吸引力也是不同的。因此，管理者应当寻求和采用多数员工认为的效应最大的奖励形式。

弗鲁姆期望理论识别了个人需求和激励的关系，有助于管理者们理解和分析员工们的激励状况，并识别有关的变量因素。管理者不应泛泛地抓各种激励措施，而应当抓多数员工认为效价最大的激励措施，需要综合分析和考虑员工们的具体需求和动机，了解动机之后再因人而异地选择和设置激励机制。同时，在设置激励目标时，应尽可能加大效价的综合值，既要考虑目标实现的实际概率，又要考虑员工目标实现的期望概率。期望概率虽然是员工的主观估计，但是会受到实际概率的影响。实际概率应该能够使大多数人受益，最好大于平均的个人期望概率。

Vroom's expectancy theory recognizes the importance of individual needs and motivations.

（二）公平理论

美国心理学家斯泰西·亚当斯（J. Stacy Adams）在《社会交换中的不公平》一书中，提出公平理论，又称为社会比较理论。公平理论是基于人们希望自己与别人相比能得到公平对待的激励理论，侧重研究工资报酬分配的合理性、公平性及其对员工产生积极性的影响。

根据公平理论，如果人们感觉自己获得报酬与他人的类似业绩所获取的报酬是相等的时候，那么他们就会认为自己受到了公正和公平的待遇。人们用投入产出比来衡量是否公平。工作投入是员工所理解的他对组织的贡献，包括受教育程度、智力水平、经验、所受培训、技能以及所付出的努力；工作产出是员工得到的报酬，包括薪水、晋升机会、上级赏识、地位等。当一个人感觉自己的投入报酬比比其他人的投入报酬比低时，就会产生不公平的感觉。明显的不公平感会使员工个体内心出现紧张情绪，进而激发他们重新回到公平状态（参见图 8-8）。

✧ Equity theory

Equity theory is a process theory based on the idea that people want to be treated fairly in relationship to others.

Inputs are what an employee perceives are his or her contributions to the organization, including education, intelligence, experience, training, skills, and the effort exerted on the job, etc.

Outputs are the rewards received by the employee, including pay, promotion, seniority benefits, and status, etc.

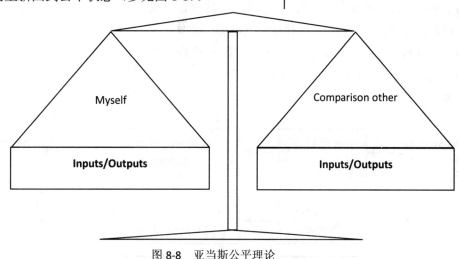

图 8-8　亚当斯公平理论

Figure 8-8　Adams's Equity Theory

不公平情绪的产生有两种情况。一种是奖励不足，即员工们认为他们的投入产出比比其他人的投入产出比要低，因而会产生不公平的感觉。这种情况下，员工们会重新评估形势并考虑通过实际做一些事情来改变投入产出比，他们往往会通过减小努力程度、降低工作水平或者停止工作来减少他们的投入，或者试图通过增加自己的产出来恢复公平。另一种是奖励过度，即员工们认为他们的投入产出比要比其他人的投入产出比高，也会产生不公平的感觉。这种情况下的员工往往会继续更加努力，增加自己的投入来恢复公平。

公平理论的研究结论表明，工作任务、公司的管理制度都有可能产生某种关于公平性的影响作用，而这种作用

Inequity exists when a person perceives his or her job inputs and rewards to be less than the job inputs and outcomes of another person.

Underreward: employees perceive their inputs-outcomes relation to be less than the inputs-outcomes ratio of a comparison other.

Overreward: employees perceive their inputs-outcomes relation to be greater than the inputs-outcomes ratio of a comparison other.

对于仅仅起维持组织稳定性的管理人员来说，是不容易察觉到的。影响激励效果的不仅是报酬的绝对值，还有报酬的相对值，管理者在设置激励措施的过程中，应该力求公平，使投入产出比相差不要过高。同时，投入和产出的评价是员工的一种主观判断，而人们总是倾向于过高估计自我的付出，过低估计自己所得到的报酬，但是对他人的估计恰恰相反。这种主观性对管理者的压力是比较大的，管理者应该注意实际工作绩效与报酬间的合理性，并留意重要员工的心理平衡。

（三）强化理论

强化理论由美国心理学家和行为学家博尔赫斯·斯金纳（Burrhus Fredric Skinner）于 20 世纪 50 年代首先提出，也叫作操作条件反射理论、行为修正理论。该理论认为，在既定行为和结果之间存在着一定的关系。斯金纳提出，人或者动物为了达到一定的目的，会采取一定的行为作用于环境，当这种行为的后果对其有利时，这种行为就会在以后重复出现，不利时，这种行为就减弱或消失。人们可以用这种强化的办法来影响行为的后果，从而修正其行为。根据强化的性质和目的，斯金纳将其分为四种类型，如图 8-9 所示。

◇ Reinforcement theory

Reinforcement theory is a motivation theory based on the relationship between a given behavior and its consequences.

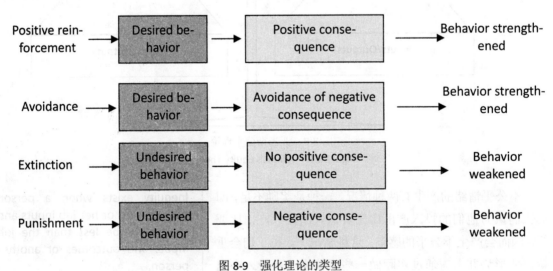

图 8-9 强化理论的类型
Figure 8-9 Types of Reinforcement
（资料来源：Leslie W. Rue and Lloyd L. Byars. *Management: Skills and Application* (13th edition).
北京：北京大学出版社，2013, p.273）

1. 正强化

正强化也称作鼓励，是给所希望发生的行为提供一个积极的结果，通过对某种行为的肯定和奖励，来鼓励这种行为重复发生，包括发放奖金、及时的表扬、改善工作环境和人际关系、晋升、给予学习和成长的机会等方式。在

Positive reinforcement involves providing a positive consequence as a result of desired behavior.

正强化的激励下员工会因为原有的行为受到鼓励和肯定而自觉加强该行为。

2. 负强化

负强化也称为趋避,是通过展示所希望发生的行为给人机会,避免消极结果的发生。负强化强调的是事前规避,通过展示某种不符合要求的行为所引起的不愉快的后果,来对该行为予以否定。俗语"杀一儆百"就是典型的负强化。如果员工能够按照要求的方式行动,就可以减少或消除令人不愉快的处境。因此,员工会因为取消或避免不希望的结果发生,就会对自己的行为进行约束。

Negative reinforcement, also called avoidance, involves giving a person the opportunity to avoid a negative consequence by exhibiting a desired behavior.

3. 自然消退

自然消退也称为冷处理,是指给不希望发生的行为提供非积极的结果或取消先前提供的积极结果。换句话说,就是当不希望出现的行为出现时,采用冷处理的方式,在一定时间内不予强化,达到无为而治的效果。例如,开会时会有一些员工可能提出无关的问题或干扰性的问题,如果管理者不打算处理这些问题,就可以采用自然消退的方式,当员工举手发言时,无视他们的表现,这样举手行为就会因为得不到强化而自行消失。

Extinction involves providing no positive consequences or removing previously provided positive consequences as a result of undesired behavior.

4. 惩罚

惩罚是指为不希望发生的行为提供一个消极的结果,如扣薪资和奖金、批评处分、降职甚至开除。通过惩罚,可以削弱不希望发生的行为。当员工出现一些不符合组织目标的行为时,采取惩罚的方法,可以约束这些行为不再发生或者减少发生频次。

Punishment involves providing a negative consequence as a result of undesired behavior.

强化理论对实践有较强的指导意义。在实际工作中,正强化虽然是一种较为有效的行为激励方式,但是应该注意与其他方式配合使用。如果频繁使用正强化,可能会导致人们对它形成越来越高的期望,同时,也可能会使人们产生"正强化是理所当然"的感觉。因此,在实际工作中,应该明确强化的目的和目标,及时奖励,正强化与负强化并举,同时还要因人而异,根据员工的实际情况和需求,来采取合理的强化措施。

第三节 沟通

How WeChat Changed the Way We Communicate?

WeChat is a multi-purpose messaging App made by Chinese Internet portal company Tencent. More and more people begin to use WeChat as an instant messaging tool. There are several features that attract users to WeChat. First, it can help send voice messages. Second, you can also publish microblogs on it or share your pictures and life events with your WeChat friends. Third, if you want to make friends with someone new, you can use one of these features: shake, scan QR code, nearby user awareness or WeChat ID. Fourth, you can also attach cards and bank accounts to the WeChat account, and with its GPS location awareness, you can call a nearby taxi when everyone around you is struggling to find one. Besides, WeChat payment, games and other neoteric plug-ins have made WeChat the most used microblogging application in the world. All of the elements of WeChat are free. WeChat launched in October 2010 and had about 5 million users by May 2011. By January 2013, it had exploded to 300 million users.

WeChat has a major impact on our social life, and also on organization's management. The employees can communicate by sending messages on WeChat instead of talking face to face. It allows employees to be connected in real time, all the time, even when not at the same location. But it is also a challenge for organizations. How to control the information flow?

（案例来源：根据 www.asmarterplanet.com 和 www.businessinsider.com 相关内容改编）

沟通在社会生活中无处不在。在管理实践中，沟通是领导职能的一个非常重要的环节，是信息传递与理解的过程，是两人或多人之间思想、意见和情感的交流。任何组织的有效运行都是建立在良好的沟通基础上的，没有沟通，就无法实现高效的合作，信息传递就会失效，组织会陷入混乱之中。但是，组织在沟通过程中会遇到许多的沟通障碍，如案例中提到的微信，对传统媒体而言，"微世界"里发生的一切都是颠覆性的，它不仅改变了媒介形态，也改变了传播方式乃至生活方式。越来越多的人开始习惯使用微信。面对这样一种新型的沟通工具，在组织管理过程中，是该利用其传递信息，更好地提高沟通效率，还是该控制该种即时信息在工作中的使用，避免负面信息的传递？这是管理者们需要面对的新的挑战。本节将围绕着沟通的概念、分类、过程以及如何克服沟通中的障碍，来对沟通相关理论进行详细阐述。

一、沟通的概念和作用

　　沟通在管理过程中有多重要？管理者每个工作日要花费 80%以上的时间去与其他人进行直接沟通，包括会议、电话、在线、面对面等多种方式。剩下的 20%左右的时间，管理者在处理文件，但是大多数也是通过读或者写的方式与其他人进行沟通。所以可以说，沟通无处不在，管理工作的方方面面都离不开沟通。沟通是信息传递和理解的过程，是在两个或更多人之间进行的事实、思想、意见和情感等方面的交流。有效的沟通管理不仅要了解复杂的沟通过程，还要制定合理的沟通策略，对沟通网络与沟通方式进行选择。

　　沟通在管理工作中的重要性可以体现在以下几个方面。

　　首先，沟通是组织的润滑剂，可以改善组织的员工关系。组织是由若干个个性不同的差异化个体所组成的，不同的员工对问题的理解、对生活的需求、对事物的态度差异很大。通过良好和有效的沟通，可以澄清事实，倾诉情感，了解员工的需求和愿望，改善组织内的工作关系；也可以让员工了解组织，参与管理，增进员工对组织目标的认同，建立相互信任的融洽的工作关系。

　　其次，沟通是激励下属的基本途径，有利于提高管理效能。一个管理者不管其技术水平多么高超，或者眼光多么远大和独到，如果不把自己的意图和想法准确地告诉下属，那么目标是很难实现的。同时，为了更好地实现目标，管理者也必须认识和了解员工对于公司目标的想法和态度，才能更好地激励下属。通过良好和有效的沟通，可以让领导者了解下属的愿望并为此采取合适的激励措施，同时，也可以让下属更好地领会领导的意图，降低信息的模糊性，提高管理效率。

　　最后，沟通是组织与外部环境建立联系的桥梁。组织是在一个动态的多元的环境中生存的，在经营过程中必然要与顾客、政府、公众、供应商、竞争者等利益相关者发生各种各样的关系。而且，它必须遵守政府的法令，遵循顾客的需求，综合考虑各方面的要素，来制定战略。通过良好和有效的沟通，组织可以更好地了解外部环境的变化，可以降低交易成本，实现资源的有效再配置；而且，良好和有效的沟通，对于顾客忠诚度、产品知名度的提升也至关重要。

✍ **The Concept and Functions of Communication**

Communication is the process of transferring information, meaning, and understanding from sender to receiver.

Effective communication can improve the relationships among employees.

Effective communication can motive employees and increase efficiency.

Effective communications can strength the relationship with external environment.

Communication Helps Southwest Airlines Excel

The CEO of Southwest Airlines, Herb Kelleher, is known for his unorthodox management approach that has helped set the standard for productivity in the airline industry. He frequently impersonates Elvis at employee gatherings, has dressed up as a leprechaun to entertain customers on St. Patrick's Day, and sometimes makes appearances as the Easter Bunny. Such antics help set the culture of humor and camaraderie that underlies Southwest Airlines' success.

Southwest attempts to hire people with a good sense of humor and a bent toward teamwork. Such individuals fit well with the culture that Kelleher works hard to create. According to Kelleher, communication with employees should be a top priority. He remembers being invited to a company to talk about what could be learned from Southwest Airlines' success. While riding in an elevator with the CEO, two employees got on and the CEO did not say a word to them. When Kelleher and the CEO got off the elevator, Kelleher suggested, "You might start by saying hello to your people."

Kelleher notes that a great deal is said about communication, but he believes it must come from the heart and be spontaneous. Kelleher likes to spend a great deal of time with Southwest employees. Each year, he helps load baggage on the Wednesday before Thanksgiving, typically the airline's busiest day of the year. He is the type of manager who will stay up talking with mechanics until 4 a.m. to find out their problems and will follow up to make sure the problems are solved. Kelleher's father was general manager of Campbell Soup Co., and he learned great respect for workers during his six summers working on the factory floor.

Kelleher says the people in headquarters are the supply corps, not the heroes. "We supply the heroes, period. The heroes are out there." He argues that before you implement an idea generated at headquarters, you should take it to the field and ask for input. "Pretty soon," he says, "the idea will look like Swiss cheese— full of holes. They know what they're doing and we don't. We may supply the idea, but they know how to implement and execute it." Southwest doesn't use surveys to check how managers are doing. "We are individually connected enough to each other so we can call and say, 'You've got a problem in your area.'" Southwest faces growing competition as other airlines attempt to emulate its innovative approach.

（案例来源：改编自 Kathryn M. Bartol and David C. Martin. *Management* (3rd edition). 北京：机械工业出版社, 1998, pp. 444-445）

二、沟通的过程

任何沟通都要有四个基本的构成要素：信息的发送者、信息的接收者、所沟通信息的内容、信息沟通的渠道。所谓有效沟通，就是指发出的信息与对方收到的信息在内容上能够达成一致，或者基本上相近。如果沟通中双方不能达成正确的理解，就说明信息沟通过程中发生了障碍。

沟通是个复杂的过程，图 8-10 描绘了基本的沟通过程。具体地说包括以下七个组成部分。

第一，信息发送者发出信息。信息发送者也称为信息源，是沟通中的主动者，是发出信息的一方。

第二，编码。编码是将要传递的信息转换为沟通双方都能理解的信息的过程。发送者具有某种意思或想法，但需要以一种对方可以理解的方式去传达，即编码。编码最常用的是口头语言和书面语言，有的时候也会借助于非言语语言。

第三，信息通过传递渠道进行传递。渠道是信息的载体，在编码之后仍然需要一定的传递渠道，才能将其传递给接收者。渠道可以是单一的，也可以是多样化的，发送者应该根据沟通双方的现有条件、沟通内容的本身属性等方面，来考虑渠道的选择。

第四，信息到达信息接收者。信息接收者即信息发送者传递信息的对象。从沟通渠道和路径传来的信息，需要经过接收者接收，并接受之后，才能达成共同的理解。

第五，解码。接收者收到了信息，但并不一定能够真正接受，而需要将收到的信息进行理解、翻译，转换成自己能够理解的信息，即解码。必须注意的是，在信息接收和解码的过程中，可能出现偏差。信息接收者的个体特质以及沟通时所处的环境等因素均会导致解码的过程出现差错，影响沟通的效果。

第六，反馈。为了核实、检查沟通过程中是否出现了偏差，信息沟通过程中需要有反馈环节。信息接收方将信息接收结果提交给信息发送者，从而便于发送者修正可能存在的误差，以达到最好的沟通效果。如在发出信息之后，询问"您听懂我的话了吗？"那么接收者的回复就是一种反馈。

第七，沟通中的噪声。在信息沟通的各个环节，都可能受到噪声的干扰。例如，双方价值观的差异、外界的噪声、语言的差异等。这些声音会妨碍信息沟通，导致信息传递错误。

✍ **The Process of Communication**

Four factors in the communication: receiver, sender, message, and channel.

Encode is to select symbols with which to compose a message.

Message is the tangible formulation of an idea to be sent to a receiver.

Channel is the carrier of a communication.

Decode is to translate the symbols used in a message for the purpose of interpreting its meaning.

Feedback is a response by the receiver to the sender's communication.

Noise is the interference with the transmission or decoding of a message.

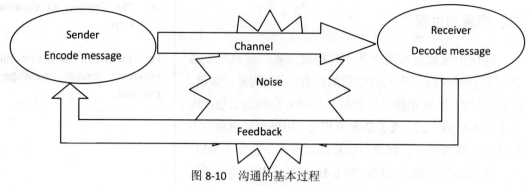

图 8-10　沟通的基本过程

Figure 8-10　Basic Communication Model

三、沟通的类型

（一）正式沟通和非正式沟通

按照沟通的组织系统分类，可以分为正式沟通和非正式沟通。

正式沟通是按照既定的组织工作程序和安排进行交流信息的过程，主要用于正式组织的各种沟通，如各部门之间的文件传递、会议召集、情报交换等。正式沟通传递的信息往往更为准确、可靠、重要，具有权威性和严肃性，但是正式沟通信息传递的形式比较刻板，传递速度较慢。

非正式沟通是不按照组织的结构层级进行交流，泛指正式沟通之外的所有沟通形式。例如，上下级之间的闲聊、朋友之间的交流、公司中的小道消息（Grapevine），等等。非正式沟通的自由度更大，信息扩散速度更快，但信息可能准确度不够高，缺乏权威性。但是，对于组织来说，非正式沟通所提供的信息是非常重要的，必须引起管理者的重视，在领导活动中，应该将非正式沟通作为正式沟通的一个必要补充。

（二）语言沟通和非语言沟通

按照沟通的中介或渠道的不同，可以分为语言沟通和非语言沟通。

语言沟通就是通过书面或口头表达的方式来进行的沟通，又分为口头沟通和书面沟通。口头沟通是以口语为媒体的信息传递，主要包括面对面的交谈、电话交谈、开会、讲座、讨论会等。口头沟通的优点是比较迅速、灵活并且反馈及时，但是信息越多、越复杂，经过的人越多，失真的概率也比较大。书面沟通是以文字为媒介的信息传递，主要包括文件、报告、信件、书面合同等。书面沟通的优点是规范、正式、准确度高、传递范围广，但是耗费时间较多，缺乏反馈。

♯　**The Types of Communications**

♢　Formal communication and informal communication

Formal communication takes place within prescribed organizational work arrangement.

Informal communication is not defined by the organization's structural hierarchy.

Grapevine is another term for informal communication.

♢　Verbal communication and nonverbal communication

Verbal communication is the written or oral use of words to communicate.

非语言沟通是指非口头和书面的沟通方式，主要通过动作和行为来传递信息，而非语言。例如，演讲时候的手势、说话的眼神、十字路口的红绿灯等都是非语言沟通。非语言沟通的优点是可以强化语言沟通内容，有的时候管理者的一些身体语言可以体现其高深的文化素养，增加管理者的个人魅力。但是，由于每个人的风格不同，非语言沟通有的时候容易引起误会和错觉，在传递信息时可能不够准确（参见表8-4）。

Nonverbal communication is a communication transmitted through actions and behaviors rather than through words.

表 8-4　语言沟通和非语言沟通

Table 8-4　Verbal Mode and Nonverbal Mode

	Verbal Mode		Nonverbal Mode
	Oral	Written	
Examples	<ul><li>Conversation</li><li>Speeches</li><li>Telephone calls</li><li>Videoconferences</li></ul>	<ul><li>Letters</li><li>Memos</li><li>Reports</li><li>Email</li><li>Fax</li></ul>	<ul><li>Dress</li><li>Speech intonation</li><li>Gestures</li><li>Facial expressions</li></ul>
Advantages	<ul><li>Vivid</li><li>Stimulating</li><li>Commands attention</li><li>Difficult to ignore</li><li>Flexible</li><li>Adaptive</li></ul>	<ul><li>Decreased misinterpretation</li><li>Precise</li></ul>	<ul><li>Effectiveness of communication increases with congruence to oral presentation</li><li>Can emphasize meaning</li></ul>
Disadvantages	<ul><li>Transitory</li><li>Subject to misinterpretation</li></ul>	<ul><li>Precision loss in translation</li><li>Inflexible</li><li>Easier to ignore</li></ul>	<ul><li>Meanings of nonverbal communication not universal</li></ul>

（资料来源：Michael A. Hitt，J. Stewart Black, and Lyman W. Porter. *Management* (3rd edition). 北京：中国人民大学出版社，2013，p.278）

（三）上行沟通、下行沟通、平行沟通和斜向沟通

按照沟通的流动方向，可以分为上行沟通、下行沟通、平行沟通和斜向沟通。

上行沟通是按照组织层级从下向上的一种沟通方式，是指下属部门或员工按照组织的层级关系与上级部门或领导者进行沟通。上行沟通是组织成员向上级部门提供信息的正常渠道，这在组织成员需要反映自己的合理要求以及对组织的批评建议时尤为重要。管理者可以通过上行沟通，来获取下属的真实想法，了解任务的实时进程。管理者应该力求在上行沟通中获得更多的真实信息。在一个提倡授权和开放的内部，员工之间比较公平，相互信任，上行沟通更容易获得成功。

❖ Upward, downward, horizontal and diagonal communication

Upward communication flows upward from subordinates to superiors and continues up the organizational hierarchy.

下行沟通是信息沿着组织的等级链自上而下进行传递的方式，是较高层级的领导者依照组织的层级关系与下级部门进行的沟通。命令的发送、计划的下达、程序规则的颁布等都属于下行沟通。下行沟通有利于上情下达，有助于下属了解和领会领导者的意图，也可以使员工对公司的发展计划和愿景有更好的理解，明确自己的工作任务。

Downward communication flows downward from people at higher levels to those at lower levels in the organizational hierarchy.

平行沟通也称为横向沟通，指信息在同级别或相似级别的部门或员工之间传递。在实际工作中，平行沟通的频率远远高于其他形式的沟通。它的主要优点是可以节省沟通成本，增进同级间的交流，有利于加强组织内部的联系，便于协调组织内部的各种横向关系。但同时，平行沟通如果过于频繁，也可能造成信息冗余，甚至引起不必要的组织冲突。

Horizontal communication takes place among any employees on the same or similar organizational levels.

斜向沟通是指不同层级不同工作部门的员工之间的沟通。这种沟通方式更为灵活，员工可以通过多样化的沟通渠道和组织内部的所有人员实现信息交换，是对其他渠道的一种补充。例如，公司的销售人员直接向财务总监汇报销售情况就属于斜向沟通。在一些情况下，斜向沟通可以提高沟通效率，但是同时，斜向沟通也容易造成部门之间尤其是直线职权与参谋职权之间的矛盾。

Diagonal communication takes place among persons at different levels who have no direct reporting relationships with one another.

（四）链式、Y 式、轮式、环式和网式

✧　Chain, Y, wheel, circle and all-channel

领导者除了要选择合适的沟通渠道之外，还要善于以沟通信息的渠道来有效组织周围相关人员，形成一个相互关联的网络，即沟通网络。沟通网络实际上是任务群体成员之间信息流向的组合模式。按照正式沟通渠道所形成的网络分类，可以将沟通分为链式、Y 式、轮式、环式和网式沟通（见图 8-11）。

Communication network is the pattern of information flow among task group members.

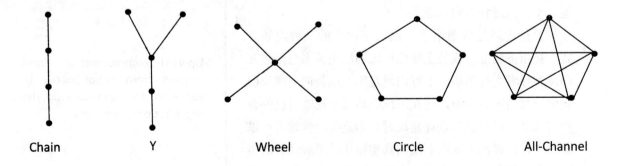

| Chain | Y | Wheel | Circle | All-Channel |

图 8-11　组织沟通网络

Figure 8-11　Group Communication Networks

在链式沟通中，信息的传递是自上而下或者自下而上的，这是一种最传统的纵向沟通网络。链式沟通的优点在于单向传递，因此易于掌控，比较直接。但是缺点在于，如果层级过多，仅依靠链式沟通，信息经过层层过滤后可能会失真。

Y 式沟通也属于一种纵向沟通，但是比链式沟通更为复杂一些。Y 式沟通中，有一个成员位于沟通网络的中心，处于上传下达的位置。如组织中的秘书，可能就处在沟通网络的中心位置上，一方面要对几个主管的意思理解透彻，另一方面又要对下面职能部门传递准确的信息。此种方式能够减轻组织中主要领导者的负担，但是由于中间有过滤和中转环节，容易导致信息失真。

在轮式沟通中，有一个信息中枢，它是组织内部各类信息和咨询的汇集中心，其他成员之间没有相互交流关系，所有信息都是通过他们共有的领导者进行交流的。这种沟通方式的准确率是很高的，几乎不存在失真现象，解决问题的速度也较快，主管人员对问题的控制能力较强。但是，由于主管人员需要应付和处理各种信息沟通，可能会造成信息超载的负担，其他成员的满意度也会降低。

在环式沟通中，没有中心人物，信息在成员之间依次以平等的地位相互联络，组织的集中化程度较低。这样的沟通方式会让员工感受到尊重，因此组织的满意度和员工士气比较高。但是同时，由于缺少中心人物，沟通渠道较少，信息传递的速度较慢，准确性也较低。

网式沟通是一个完全开放式的沟通网络，沟通渠道多，成员之间的地位也平等，合作气氛浓厚，组织中成员的满意度较高，士气也较高。而且由于渠道较多，信息的传递速度和准确程度也比较高。但是，此种网络的缺点是网络中主管人员不明确，集中化程度较低。

四、沟通的障碍

要提高组织沟通的效率和效果，就必须分析组织中可能存在的各种沟通障碍，并实施有效的沟通管理。

（一）组织中的沟通障碍

1. 个体层面的沟通障碍

个体层面的沟通主要体现在沟通双方。在沟通过程中，以下三个方面的问题可能会造成沟通障碍。

（1）选择性感知

信息接收者在接收信息过程中，可能会因选择性感

✍ **The Barriers of Communication**

✧ Communication barriers in organization

Individual barriers include selective perception, emotions, nonverbal signals, etc.

知而造成信息理解不准确。所谓选择性感知，是指接收者在处理信息时的一种选择性倾向，他们会根据自己的价值观或需求，过滤掉一些信息。

例如，某个员工在工作中特别关注劳动生产率的提高，而老板则关注项目的成本。那么在信息接收过程中，员工可能就特别关注老板关于生产率的命令和指示，而对成本的指示自动过滤掉，最终影响了沟通的效果。

还有另一种表达选择性感知带来的沟通障碍的方式，即参照标准。参照标准是指对于复杂信息给予一种快速的理解办法的现存的态度。人们在接收信息的时候，总是倾向于适应自己的参照标准，或者以一种简单的方式来理解复杂的信息，但是这种方式是基于自己的参照标准所选择的，这样也会影响沟通的效果。

（2）个人情绪

信息接收者在收到信息时的情绪和感受也会影响沟通的效果。例如，某个员工刚被领导批评过，情绪很低落，这个时候如果其他人与他开玩笑，他可能会表现出很反感的情绪。

（3）非语言暗示

在沟通过程中，许多人会使用一些非语言的表达方式，如手势、表情等，而且常常会有一些下意识的动作。这些非语言的表达可能会造成一些沟通上的误解。例如，有些人在与其他人沟通的时候，总是逃避直视对方的眼睛，这种非语言的行为会让信息接收者感到不信任或没有信心。另外，同一种手势在不同的人眼里可能会有不同的含义，也同样会影响沟通的准确性。

2. 组织层面的沟通障碍

组织层面的沟通障碍主要源于沟通渠道和沟通网络。在沟通过程中，以下三个方面的问题可能会造成沟通障碍。

（1）组织结构

组织结构指的是一个组织如何对于工作任务进行分工、分组和协调合作，它表明了组织各要素之间的相互关系，是整个管理系统的框架。组织结构限定了组织内部人员的部门归属，如果一个公司的组织结构过于繁杂，那么在沟通中可能流向较多，员工沟通起来比较困难，形成沟通障碍。

（2）组织层级

组织层级是公司从最高管理层到最低管理层之间的层次。组织规模越大，层级往往越多。随着层级的增加，人员之间的沟通传递干扰因素越来越多，就可能造成信息的失真，形成沟通障碍。

Selective perception is the process of screening out some parts of an intended message because they contradict our beliefs or desires.

Frame of reference is an existing set of attitudes that provides quick ways to interpret complex messages.

Emotions can be another barrier. How the receiver feels at the time can influence what gets heard or how it gets interpreted.

People can send nonverbal signals without being aware of them, and create unintentional consequences.

Organizational barriers include organizational structure, organizational hierarchy, communication channels, etc.

（3）沟通渠道

一个组织中可能同时存在多种沟通渠道，但是如果正式沟通渠道不畅通，就会激发人们打听小道消息的欲望，通过非正式渠道来获取信息，影响了信息的权威性和准确性。组织的规模越大，正式渠道越多，但是正式渠道沟通的效率却不高，妨碍了信息在组织的各个层次间的自由流动。

3. 文化层面的沟通障碍

文化与沟通是相辅相成、密不可分的。沟通一定是在一定的文化情境下进行的。相同或相似文化背景下，沟通起来更容易一些，信息接收方和发送方的理解一致性也会比较高。但是在文化差异很大的信息发送方和接收方之间，沟通起来难度会比较大。例如，一个美国的主管与一个加拿大的下属去沟通，就比与日本的下属去沟通要更容易一些。如果管理者没有很好地处理文化差异，那么可能就会因文化背景的不同而带来沟通障碍。

另外，组织文化本身也存在差异。不同的行业之间存在着文化差异，例如娱乐业和制造业，金融业和房地产业，文化差异都较大；同时，同一个行业内部，各个组织之间的文化也存在着差异，例如百度和谷歌，维珍航空和西南航空。这些文化差异也会形成沟通障碍。

（二）如何克服沟通障碍

有效沟通是组织中所有人的职责，无论是不是高层管理者，都应该为进行有效沟通而努力。评价沟通是否有效，要依据信息接收者与发送者对信息的理解的一致程度来判断。为提高沟通的效率和效果，组织管理者可以从以下几个方面着手。

1. 阐明信息传递的目的

信息的发送者对沟通的目的必须要清楚，而且对于信息的内容要理解准确。也就是说，在信息传递之前，就应该尽可能地消除掉那些可能造成信息不准确的因素，信息发送者保证对信息的理解准确，这样才能够保证后续的沟通顺畅。

2. 进行有效的编码

有效的沟通需要对沟通内容进行编码和解码，将信息内容转换成信息发送方和接收方都熟悉的语言。因此，管理者在沟通过程中，尤其是一些技术型的管理者，在面对非专业人士的时候，应尽量避免使用过于专业的行业术语。

Cultural barriers

Communication and culture are tightly intertwined. Similarity in culture between senders and receivers facilitates successful communication—the intended meaning of a message has a higher probability of getting transferred if the sender and receiver share the same culture.

Organizational cultures can also influence communication.

✧ How to overcome communication barriers

Guidelines for improving communication:

1. Clarify the purpose of the message

2. Use intelligible encoding

3. 参考其他人的意见

在组织沟通过程中，应该考虑多人的意见，鼓励其他人参与信息的沟通。例如，管理者在发布一个重要的信息之前，可以请其他相关同事或下属先阅读一遍信息，看看是否能够表达真实含义、没有歧义。信息的内容应该与信息接收者的知识水平和组织氛围相匹配。

4. 充分考虑接收者的需求

在信息传递过程中，充分考虑接收者的需求是非常重要的。接收者当时的情绪状态、在组织中的职位、价值观、文化教育背景等都可能影响沟通的有效性。而且，在信息的组织过程中，应站在接收者的角度去考虑，如何更好地让接收者理解信息。

5. 恰当使用非语言沟通

非语言沟通是一把双刃剑，有的时候会起到画龙点睛的作用，着重强调信息内容，有助于接收者理解；有的时候又会起到反作用，传递错误信息，影响信息的准确沟通。因此，在沟通过程中，信息发送者应该关注自己所使用的非语言方式，如手势、眼神、表情，尽量避免使接收者产生误解。

6. 及时获取反馈

在信息沟通中，只有接收者真正理解了信息的内容，沟通才算完成。而反馈正是沟通过程中的一个非常重要的环节，可以让信息发出者更加理解接收者对信息的接受程度。信息发送者可以通过询问"明白了吗？"或者再次简短重复概括信息内容，来获得对方的反馈。

7. 积极倾听

说与听在沟通中是一对无法分离的过程。有效的沟通不仅要靠信息发送者的努力，还要靠信息接收者的倾听。学会倾听的技巧，是理解信息内容的关键。在信息发送方发言时，要认真聆听对方所传递的信息，在发言结束时，要尽量给予对方积极的回应。同时，应当进一步寻找可能存在的共鸣点，针对这些共同点，双方可以分享各自的看法和体会。积极倾听还意味着在沟通中应当尽可能关注和把握细节，尽可能地抓住对方语言和肢体表达中的细微之处，挖掘更深层次的信息，以达成有效的沟通效果。

3. Consult others' views.

4. Consider receivers' needs.

5. Use appropriate nonverbal communication.

6. Get feedback.

7. Listening.

Leader

Leading

Leadership

Power

Authority

Leadership trait theories

Leadership behavior theories

Autocratic leader

Democratic or participative leader

Free-rein leader

Managerial grid

Contingency theories of leadership

Situational leadership theory

Path-goal theory

Individual dignity

McGregor's Theory X and Theory Y

Maslow's hierarchy of needs theory

Herzberg's two-factor theory

Alderfer's ERG theory

McClelland's acquired-needs theory

Vroom's expectancy theory

Equity theory

Reinforcement theory

Motivation

Communication

Formal communication

Informal communication

Grapevine

Verbal communication

Nonverbal communication

Upward communication

Downward communication

Horizontal communication

Diagonal communication

Communication network

Selective perception

Frame of reference

1. Please explain the ingredients of leadership.

2. Outline the major types of power available to managers, and differentiate between position power and personal power.

3. What is difference between trait theories and behavioral theories of leadership?

4. What is Managerial Grid? Explain the 5 extreme styles in the grid.

5. Please describe briefly the personal characteristics of effective leaders.

6. Outline the basic ideas in Fielder's contingency model of leadership.

7. What are the advantages and limitations of the path-goal approach to leadership?

8. What is motivation? Please explain the simple model of motivation.

9. What are Theory X and Theory Y assumptions? State your reasons for agreeing or disagreeing with these assumptions.

10. Please explain Maslow's Hierarchy of Needs Theory.

11. Compare and contrast the Maslow and Herzberg theories of motivation.

12. What is ERG theory? Please explain the basic ideas briefly.

13. Explain McClelland's theory of motivation.

14. Explain Vroom's expectancy theory of motivation.

15. Outline the equity theory. What potential difficulties does the perceptual aspect of equity judgments present for manager?

16. Explain the four main types of reinforcement.

17. Briefly describe the communication process model.

18. Is it necessary to use informal communication in an organization? Why or why not?

19. Discuss the advantages and disadvantages of verbal mode and nonverbal mode communication.

20. What are some problems in upward communication? What are some problems in downward communication? Please explain the importance and problems of horizontal communication and diagonal communication in an organization.

21. What kinds of barriers will be met in organization communication?

22. How to improve the organization communication?

Lei Jun, Founder of Xiaomi, Might Just Be "China's Steve Jobs"

China's Xiaomi Technology is a fairy tale for entrepreneurs. Less than three years after its founding, the smartphone maker is valued at $4 billion and evokes Apple-like adoration from its fans, some of whom are desperate enough to skip work for a shot at buying the latest product the day it goes on sale. Founder Lei Jun dresses like the late Steve Jobs, in jeans and a black top. He has created a fervent fan base for Xiaomi's moderately priced high-end smartphones by mimicking Apple Inc's marketing tactic of attaching an aura of exclusivity around its products.

Before Xiaomi, the 42-year-old Lei was a key investor in China's early Internet scene, co-founding startups including Joyo.cn, which was eventually sold to Amazon.com Inc, and the recently listed YY Inc. Born in Xiantao, a small city in China's central Hubei province better known for breeding Olympic gymnasts than billionaire technocrats, Lei brushes off comparisons to Jobs but concedes that the Apple visionary was an inspiration.

"China's media say I am China's Steve Jobs," Lei told Reuters in an interview. "I will take this as a compliment but such kind of comparison brings us huge pressure," said Lei, who grew up assembling radios as a hobby. "Xiaomi and Apple are two totally different companies. Xiaomi's based on the Internet. We are not doing the same thing as Apple."

Xiaomi has already sold 300,000 of its latest phone model, launched in October. The Xiaomi phone 2 has specifications similar to those of Samsung Electronics' Galaxy S3 and Apple's iPhone5 but a top-of-the-line model sells for about $370, half the price of an iPhone 5. Unlike the big domestic smartphone players which work with telecom carriers to sell a large volume of smartphones, Xiaomi sells most of its phones online and in small batches. This small volume strategy creates pent-up demand that gives Xiaomi free marketing buzz. The first batch of 50,000 phones released on October 30 sold out in less than two minutes. Subsequent larger batches have also sold out in minutes.

Lei, who has nearly 4 million followers on China's popular microblogging platform, Weibo, feeds the buzz by dangling teasers about new products and launch dates. "We're not a company that chases sales volume. We chase customer satisfaction. We look for ways to give the customer a great surprise," Lei said.

His vision for an exclusive mid-tier brand that builds up incrementally, rather than swamping the market, has found financial backers. In June, Xiaomi raised $216 million from Singapore's sovereign wealth fund, the Government of Singapore Investment Corp, and a few of Lei's friends, local media reported, giving it a valuation of $4 billion.

"China is ripe for its own Apple, HTC or Samsung," said Hans Tung, managing partner at Qiming

Venture Partners, a venture firm backing Xiaomi. "The country is big enough, there are enough mobile Internet users and mobile phone consumers. Therefore having its own mobile ecosystem built up by a domestic brand makes sense."

Xiaomi, which was founded in April 2010 and only started selling smartphones in October 2011, is on track to sell 7 million units this year, exceeding its target of 2 million. Xiaomi is already profitable and is expected to rake in sales of up to 13 billion Yuan ($2 billion) this year.

"Our product only sold for a year and hit sales of $2 billion. That is pretty impressive," Lei said, adding Xiaomi was not considering an initial public offering within the next five years.

Tung said Xiaomi's net margins were 10 percent. This suggests its net profit could hit $200 million this year.

Mo Xiaohua, a 24-year-old accountant, is a proud Xiaomi fan who only recently bought her first Xiaomi phone. For many who use Xiaomi phones, the customizable themes and the weekly updates are a big draw. "I like Xiaomi because among China's brand smartphones, its value is the best," Mo said. "Now that we have such a good China branded phone, we need to support it."

Xiaomi has its fair share of detractors who doubt it will have a happy ending. They say the smartphone game in China can only be won with wide distribution and high volume or a big brand with distinctive designs. Xiaomi, whose attraction is its price and high technical specifications, does not win points for cutting-edge design.

"This is a world where people are now cranking out 'black back flats', that's what all these phones are when you put 10 on the table ... Xiaomi is not going to stick out," said Michael Clendenin, managing director at RedTech Advisors. "In this world, the market is driven by two things: one is massive volume and two huge brands."

"Xiaomi had great headline appeal a year ago... but the problem is now you have got guys like ZTE and Huawei and Meizu with phones that are priced in a similar range," Clendenin said.

China is expected to surpass the United States as the world's largest smartphone market this year with 165-170 million unit sales, up from 78 million last year. Analysts said Xiaomi had to ramp up volume and address technical problems and a shortage of customer service centers if it wanted a shot at the big league. Lei is resolute that he will prove the naysayers wrong. "In this industry, I think the most important thing is to get love from your customers," he said. "If you are popular with your customers, you succeed."

（案例来源：节选自 Melanie Lee. Lei Jun. Founder of Xiaomi, Might Just Be "China's Steve Jobs". http://www.huffingtonpost.com/2012/12/07/lei-jun-xiaomi_n_2255953.html, 2012-12-7）

Discussion Questions

1. What leadership style do you see in this case? What aspects of personality do you see in this case about Lei Jun? List and describe.

2. Could you assess the Xiaomi's work environment? What might be the challenges for managers in motivating employees in Xiaomi?

3. How did Leijun influence members of the group to follow the organization's vision?

4. What do you think of Xiaomi's exclusive mid-tier brand strategy? What are the advantages and risks for the company?

第九章 控制

学习目标

1. 识别控制的基本概念及类型
2. 解释控制的作用及原则
3. 理解控制过程四个阶段的主要内容
4. 认识不同控制方法的应用范畴

Learning Outcomes

1. Identify the definition and various types of control.
2. Explain the functions and principles of control.
3. Understand the four stages of the control process.
4. Recognize the application of different control tools.

主要内容

第一节　控制概述
第二节　控制的过程
第三节　控制的方法

Contents

9.1　The Control System
9.2　The Control Process
9.3　The Control Tools

第一节 控制概述

The Zappos Holacracy

How can a company be controlled without becoming rigid? Zappos has always been a zany place to work. Before an employee even starts, the Las Vegas based company offers the employee $2,000 to leave. The company believes it saves money if an employee takes the offer because the company gets rid of someone who would be there only for the paycheck. The CEO wrote a book called *Delivering Happiness* about how concepts from happiness can be applied to business.

Then there's the call center. Rather than running a lean call center, Zappos encourages its employees to spend lots of time talking to customers and going the extra mile to resolve their issues. There are stories of the great lengths to which customer service representatives will go. For example, one employee went to a rival shoe store, bought a pair of shoes that Zappos did not have in stock, and delivered the shoes to the customer's Las Vegas hotel.

This different way of doing things is reflected in the Zappos core values, like "deliver WOW through service", "embrace and drive change", "create fun and a little weirdness", "pursue growth and learning", "be adventurous, creative, and open-minded", "build a positive team and family spirit", "build open and honest relationships with communication", "be passionate and determined", and "be humble".

And while the book and the active call center do not sound like trappings of a traditional lean company, another of the Zappos core values is "do more with less." The company claims that while it may have an informal culture, it is serious about operating efficiently. On its web page the company states, "We believe in operational excellence and realize that there is always room for improvement in everything we do. This means that our work is never done. In order to stay ahead of the competition (or would-be competition), we need to continuously innovate as well as make incremental improvements to our operations, always striving to make ourselves more efficient, always trying to figure out how to do something better. We use mistakes as learning opportunities." Now the company is getting even leaner by removing the traditional chain of command, job titles, and managers.

The change is designed to prevent the company from becoming too rigid as it grows. "Research shows that every time the size of a city doubles, innovation or productivity per resident increases by 15 percent. But when companies get bigger, innovation or productivity per employee generally goes down," said CEO Tony Hsieh. "So we're trying to figure out how to structure Zappos more like a city, and less like a bureaucratic corporation. In a city, people and businesses are self-organizing. We're trying to do the same thing by switching from a normal hierarchical structure to a system called holacracy, which enables employees to act more like entrepreneurs and self-direct their work instead of reporting to a manager who tells them what to do."

A holacracy is different from a traditional organization in three important ways. First, the former hierarchy is replaced with overlapping and self-governing circles of employees. Second, employees are assigned several roles in different circles where they perform different functions. There are no job titles because holacracy organizes around the work to be done instead of the workers who do it. Decisions about what each role involves are made within the circle. Third, managers are redefined as "lead links" who assign employees to roles but do not tell them what to do. Despite this lack of formal structure, Zappos says employees will still be appraised. The constitution of holacracy begins with roles, which it defines as "an organizational entity with a 'purpose' to express, 'domains' to control, and 'accountabilities' to perform." From this definition of roles, the constitution builds to include a circle structure that contains and integrates roles; a governance process that defines roles and policies, and an operational process in which members of the circles rely on one another to do operational work.

John Bunch, who is leading the change for Zappos, was quoted in The New York Times as saying that people see the holacracy as removing managers. However, Bunch explains that they are "decoupling the professional development side of the business from the technical getting-the-work-done side." Zappos was acquired by Amazon in 2009 but is run as a mostly independent unit. Zappos expects to transition to holacracy by the end of 2014.

（案例来源：Gareth R. Jones and Jennifer M. George. *Contemporary Management* (9th edition). New York: McGraw-Hill Education, 2014, pp. 313-314）

正如上述案例中所述，大量企业在管理实践过程中都必然会面临管理控制问题。如何将控制职能和管理有机结合起来？怎样实现人员管理控制与效率管理控制？这些问题的存在是制约组织长足发展的关键所在。本节将主要围绕控制的内涵、类型、原则、作用、目的等内容进行探讨和分析。

一、控制的内涵

（一）控制的含义

控制是对组织计划工作的一种后续推进。管理学中的控制主要是指能够保证组织活动按照预定计划顺利执行且能够在执行过程中及时得到纠偏的一项管理职能。

实践中，管理中的控制工作就是按设定的标准去衡量计划的执行情况，并通过对执行偏差的纠正来确保计划目标的正确实现。计划和控制是实现组织目标密不可分的一对辩证统一体。此外，控制还是指管理者影响组织中其他成员以实现组织战略的过程。在这个过程中，需要利用控制职能去影响计划组织的行动、协调组织中各部分的活动、交流信息、决定采取的行动以及促使成员去改变其行为。所以，管理控制的目的是使战略被执行，从而使组织的目标得以实现，强调的是战略执行。

（二）管理控制与一般控制

管理控制与一般控制的共同之处体现在以下四个方面。①同属于一个信息反馈过程：通过信息反馈，发现管理活动中存在的不足，促进系统进行不断的调整和改革，使其逐渐趋于稳定、完善，直至达到优化状态。②同有两个前提条件：计划指标在控制工作中转化为控制标准；有相应的监督机构和人员。③均包含三个基本步骤：拟订标准、衡量成效和纠正偏差。④都是一个有组织的系统。

管理控制与一般控制的不同之处在于：①一般控制所面对的往往是非社会系统，如机械系统，其衡量成效和纠正偏差过程往往可以按照给定程序而自动进行，其纠正措施往往是在接收到反馈信息后即刻就付诸实施，而在管理控制中，主管人员面临的是一个社会系统，其信息反馈、识别偏差原因、制定和纠正措施的过程比较复杂；②一般控制的目的在于使系统运行的偏差不超出允许范围，维持系统活动在某一平衡点上。管理控制活动不仅要维持系统活动的平衡，而且还力求使组织活动有所前进、有所创新，使组织活动达到新的高度和状态，或者实现更高的目标。

二、控制的类型

不同组织结构和组织活动会影响管理者采取不同的控制方式。按照对象不同、目标不同、范围和重点不同，管理实践中所运用的控制方式和类型也有所差异。总体而言，较为常用的控制类型主要有以下几个方面。

✍ **Control System**

✧ The definition of control

In management, control is a management function which ensures and rectifies the scheduled organization's activities.

✧ Management control and general control

General control and management control are similar in the following aspects:
(1) a process of information feedback;
(2) two premises;
(3) three steps;
(4) an organizational system.

General control and management control are different in the following aspects:
(1) General control belongs to non-social system; management control belongs to social system.
(2) General control is to keep the balance of all system activities; management control is to keep innovation of the organization besides the balance.

✍ **The Type of Control**

（一）按照系统思维划分

系统思维强调组织运行的"输入—转换—输出"过程。为了避免系统在运行过程中产生偏差，或在系统产生偏差时能及时地发出警告并进行修正，系统中一般设置有效的监控机制以保证该系统的正常运作。按照系统思维可以将控制分为事前控制、事中控制及事后控制。

1. 事前控制

事前控制是在问题发生前做出预测，防止问题在随后的转换中出现。事前控制重点关注组织的各种资源或工作的投入。它可以防止组织使用不合要求的资源，保证组织投入的资源在数量上和质量上达到预定的标准，在整个活动开始之前剔除那些在事物发展进程中难于挽回的先天缺陷。这个资源是广义的，包括人力、物力、财力、信息、时间、技术等所有与活动有关的因素。

采用事前控制的关键是要在实际问题发生之前就采取管理行动。事前控制是期望用来防止问题的发生而不是当出现问题时再补救。事前控制有许多优点。首先，事前控制是在工作开始之前进行的控制，因而可防患于未然，避免事后控制对于已铸成的差错无能为力的弊端。其次，事前控制是针对某项计划行动所依赖的条件进行的控制，不针对具体人员，不会造成心理冲突，易于被员工接受并付诸实施。但是，实施事前控制的前提条件也较多。它要求管理者拥有大量准确可靠的信息，对计划行动过程有清楚的了解，懂得计划行动本身的客观规律性，并要随着行动的进展及时了解新情况和新问题，否则就无法实施事前控制。由于事前控制所需要的信息常常难于获得，所以在实践中还必须依靠其他两类控制方式。

2. 事中控制

事中控制又称同期控制、现场控制或同步控制，是在系统进行到转换过程中，即组织生产或经营的过程中，对活动中的人和事进行指导和监督，以便管理者在问题出现时及时采取纠正措施。这类控制工作的纠正措施作用于正在进行的计划执行过程。事中控制的职能是对正在进行的活动给予指导与监督，以保证活动按规定的政策、程序和方法进行。监督是按照预定的标准检查正在进行的工作，以保证目标的实现；指导是管理者针对工作出现的问题，根据自己的经验指导下属改进工作，或与下属共同商讨纠正偏差的措施，以便使工作人员能正确地完成规定的任务。例如，制造活动的生产进度控制、学生的期中考试都属于此种控制。

✧ Classification based on systematic thinking: pre-control, spot control and afterwards control

Pre-control is to make prediction in order to prevent the transitional problems.

Control in process, also called real-time control, spot control or synchronous control. It focuses on the information about what is happening while it is happening.

事中控制一般都在现场进行，管理者亲临现场视察就是一种最常见的现场控制活动。它是一种基层主管人员经常采用的控制工作方法。主管人员通过深入现场亲自监督检查、指导和控制下属人员的活动。

事中控制包括的内容有：

①向下级指示恰当的工作方法和工作过程；

②监督下级的工作，以保证计划目标的实现；

③发现不合标准的偏差时，立即采取纠正措施。

事中控制具有指导职能，有助于提高工作人员的工作能力和自我控制能力。但是，事中控制也有很多弊端。

首先，运用这种控制方法容易受管理者的时间、精力、业务水平的制约。管理者不能时时对事事都进行事中控制，只能偶尔使用或在关键项目上使用。

其次，事中控制的应用范围较窄。对生产工作容易进行事中控制，而对那些问题难以辨别、成果难以衡量的工作，如科研、管理工作等，几乎无法进行事中控制。

最后，事中控制容易在控制者与被控制者之间形成心理上的对立，容易损害被控制者的工作积极性和主动性。

3．事后控制

事后控制是最常用的控制类型。按照系统思维理论，当系统最后阶段输出产品或服务时，来自系统内部对产生结果的总结和系统外部顾客与市场的反应，都是在计划完成后进行的总结和评定，具有滞后性的特点，但可为未来计划的制定和活动的安排，以及系统持续的运作提供借鉴。事后控制主要是把注意力集中于工作结果上，通过对工作结果进行测量、比较和分析，采取措施，进而矫正今后的行动，避免已发生的或即将出现的偏差今后再度发生或继续发展。

如企业对不合格产品进行修理，发现产品销路不畅而减产、转产或努力促销，学校对违纪学生进行处理等，都属事后控制。事后控制具有稳定系统、跟踪目标和抗干扰的特性。这些主要的性质可以用来改善管理控制工作。当系统不稳定时，就加强事后控制。例如，当员工对某些问题意见纷纷且情绪不稳定时，通过开辟对话渠道，加强领导与员工的对话，能够在一定程度上起到稳定员工情绪的作用；还可以利用事后控制的随机性质，当要控制某个变量时，就以这个变量作为反馈变量；此外，还可以利用事后控制抗干扰的性质，当某个环节受到多种不确定性干扰的影响时，不必逐一排除干扰，而要设法建立一个局部反馈回路，将此环节置于其中。

(1) instruct subordinates to work in a proper way;
(2) supervise the fulfillment of assigned tasks to ensure achieving goals;
(3) correct variations from standards and plans.

Afterwards control is very common in organizational operations.

Afterwards control focuses on outcomes to rectify the future actions by measurement, comparison, and analysis.

Afterwards control is to prevent the recurrence of deviation.

The characteristics of afterwards control include keeping the system stable, tracking goals, and anti-interference.

事后控制类似于"亡羊补牢"。它的最大弊端是在采取纠正措施之前，活动中出现的偏差已在系统内造成无法补偿的损失，例如已出的废品所费的原材料、工时等已无法补偿。

上述三种控制方式互为前提、互相补充。在实际工作中，不能只依靠某一种控制方式，必须根据实际情况综合使用这三种控制方式，对各种资源的输入、转换和输出进行全面的全过程控制，以提高控制效果。

（二）按控制源划分

按照控制源不同，可将控制工作分为正式组织控制、群体控制和自我控制三种类型。

1．正式组织控制

正式组织控制是指根据组织明文规定的政策、程序并通过正式的组织机构进行控制，如规划、预算和审计部门等是正式组织控制的例子。正式组织控制系统使得管理者能够利用正式组织的结构，使组织成员遵循和执行这些政策和程序。这些组织结构、政策和程序的正式文件帮助组织成员实施他们的职责。

2．群体控制

群体控制是指不通过正式控制过程进行的控制。它基于非正式组织的价值观念和行为准则，由员工组成参与并采取控制行动。

非正式组织的行为规范，虽然没有明文规定，但成员都十分清楚它的内容，都知道如果自己遵循这些规范就会得到奖励，获得其他成员的认可，可能会强化自己在非正式组织的地位。如果违反这些规范就可能遭到惩罚。这种惩罚可能是遭到排挤、讽刺，甚至是被驱逐出该组织。例如，一个新来的员工常常会主动将生产量控制在某个群体可接受的水平，就是遵守非正式组织行为规范的一个例子。

3．自我控制

自我控制是指个人有意识地去按某一行为规范进行活动。例如，一个人不把公家的东西据为己有，可能是由于他具有诚实、廉洁的品质，是有意识的自我控制，而不单单是怕被抓住受惩罚。自我控制的能力取决于个人的素质。具有良好修养的人一般自我控制力较强，顾全大局的人比仅看重自己局部利益的人有更强的自我控制能力，具有高层次需求的人比具有低层次需求的人有更强的控制能力。

◇ Classification based on sources of control: formal organization control, group control and self control

Formal organization control is controlled by the formal organization according to the written policies and procedures.

Group control is not controlled by formal control process. It is based on the values and codes of informal organizations. It's controlled by all members of the group.

Self control is restraint of one's emotion, desires, or actions by one's own will.

三、控制的原则

孔茨（Harold Koontz）曾说过："可以把计划工作和控制工作看成一把剪刀的两个刃。缺少任何一个刃，剪刀也就没有用了。没有了目标与计划，也就不可能实施控制，这是因为必须要把业绩同某些已规定的标准相比较。"控制的目的是为了实现计划，计划是控制所采用的绩效衡量标准的原始依据。因此，管理者在制订计划时要考虑到相关的控制因素。管理控制的主要原则有以下几个方面。

（一）关键点原则

✧ The principle of key point

所谓关键点原则是指控制工作要突出重点，不能只从局部利润出发，要针对重要的、关键的因素实施重点控制。

The principle of key point means that the control should highlight the key point and focus on the critical factors in the management.

事实上，组织中的活动往往错综复杂，管理者无法对所有方面实施完全的控制，他们应该且只能将注意力集中于计划执行中的一些关键影响因素上。因此，找出或确定这些关键因素，并建议重点控制，是一种有效的控制方法。控制住了关键点，也就控制住了全局。

选择关键控制点的能力是管理工作的一种艺术，有效控制在很大程度上取决于这种能力。目前，已经存在一些有效的方法，能帮助管理人员在某些控制工作中选择关键点。例如，计划评审技术就是一种在有多种平行作业的复杂管理活动网络中寻找关键活动和关键路径的方法。

（二）例外原则

✧ The principle of exception

所谓例外原则，是指控制工作应着重于计划实施中的例外偏差（超出一般情况的特别好或特别坏的情况）。这可使管理者把精力集中在他们应该注意的问题上。

The principle of exception means that the control should focus on the abnormal deviation (extremely good or extremely bad).

但是，只注意例外情况是不够的，对例外情况的重视程度不应仅仅依据偏差的大小而定，同时需要考虑客观实际情况。在偏离标准的各种情况中，有一些是无关紧要的，而另一些则不然，某些微小的偏差可能比某些较大的偏差影响更大。因为在一个特定的组织中，不同工作的重要程度各不相同。例如，某一企业中，对"合理化建议"的奖励超出 20%可能无关紧要，而产品的合格率下降 1%却可能使所有产品滞销。在实际工作中，控制的例外原则必须与控制关键点原则相结合，把注意力集中在对关键点的例外情况的控制上。关键点原则强调选择控制点，而例外原则强调观察在这些控制点上所发生的异常偏差。

（三）及时性原则

一个有效的控制系统必须能够提供及时的信息。信息是控制的基础。为提高控制的及时性，信息的收集和传递必须及时。如果信息的收集和传递不及时，信息处理的时间又过长，则偏差就不能及时纠正。当采取纠正措施时，如果实际情况已经发生了变化，这时采取的措施如果不变，不仅不能产生积极作用，反而会带来消极影响。

控制信息滞后往往会造成不可弥补的损失。时滞现象是反馈控制系统一个难以克服的困难。较好的解决办法是要用前馈控制，使管理者尽早发现甚至预测到偏差的产生，采取预防性措施，使工作的开展在最初阶段就能够沿着目标方向进行，即使有了偏差，也能及时纠正，把损失降到最低程度。控制要做到及时，必须依靠现代化的信息管理系统，随时传递信息，随时掌握工作进度，如此才能尽早发现偏差，进而及时采取措施进行控制。

（四）客观性原则

所谓客观性原则是指在控制工作中，管理者不能凭个人的主观经验或直觉判断，而应采用科学的方法，尊重客观事实。

控制工作的客观性要求控制系统应尽可能提供和使用无偏见的、详细的、可以被证实和理解的信息。同时，还要求必须具有客观的、准确的和适当的控制标准。管理难免有许多主观的因素在内，但是对于下属工作的评价，在整个控制过程中，不应仅凭主观判断来决定。那样不仅可能使绩效的衡量无法得到明确的结论，而且还会难于把握纠正偏差的力度，从而使现实工作更加混乱。为了保证控制的客观性，就要求尽可能将衡量标准加以量化。量化程度越高，控制越规范。但是，在诸多衡量标准中总有一些是定性的和难以量化的。客观标准可以是定量的，也可以是定性的，但要做到客观，关键问题是使标准在任何情况下都是可测量和可考核的。

（五）准确性原则

所谓准确性原则是指一个控制系统要想行之有效，必须具备准确性。一个提供不准确信息的控制系统将会导致管理者在应该行动的时候没有行动，没有出现问题时反而采取了行动。基于不准确信息的种种决策，往往是错误的决策，会使整个组织蒙受损失。

◇ The principle of timely feedback

The principle of timely feedback means that the deviation should be found and corrected in time.

◇ The principle of objectivity

The principle of objectivity means that the control should use scientific methods and not be driven by subjective experiences and intuitive judgments.

◇ The principle of precision

The principle of precision means that the control system should be precise.

在现实中，由于各种因素的影响，常常会将不准确性带入控制系统之中。有时可能是因为衡量绩效的工具精确度不够，使衡量结果的误差过大；有时则可能是工作人员出于个人利益，人为地虚报数据。因此，管理者需要选择适用的、精确的绩效衡量方法和工具来避免产生误差，同时还要采取预防措施，运用先进的管理技能避免出现弄虚作假行为。

（六）灵活性原则

所谓灵活性原则是指有效的控制系统应具有足够的灵活性，以适应各种不利的环境变化或利用各种新的机会。

如今技术进步日新月异，顾客需求也在不断变化，组织所处的内外部环境中的干扰性、复杂性越来越大。如果没有一个灵活的系统对这些变化做出准确的预测或反映，并据此调整组织活动，那么任何一个组织的生存都难以维系下去。一个灵活的控制系统能在计划变化以及发生未曾预见事项的情况下继续发挥作用。一项管理计划方案在某种情况下可能会出现问题，控制系统应能报告这种失常的情况，同时还应有足够的灵活性来保持对运行过程的管理控制。例如，假设预算是根据预测的销售量制定的，如果实际销售量远远高于或低于预测的销售量，原来的预算就变得毫无意义，这时就要求修改甚至重新制定预算，并根据新的预算制定合适的控制标准。通常，对各种可能出现的情况都应尽量准备好各种可选择的方案，以使控制更具有灵活性。

（七）经济性原则

所谓经济性原则是指控制活动需要节约经费。是否进行控制，控制到什么程度，都要考虑费用问题。将控制所需的费用同控制所产生的结果进行比较。当通过控制所获得的价值大于它所需费用时，才有必要实施控制。所以，从经济性的角度考虑，控制系统并不是越复杂越好，控制力度也不是越大越好。控制系统越复杂，控制工作力度越大，意味着控制的投入也越大。而且在许多情况下，这种投入的增加并不一定会推动计划更顺利地完成。管理者应尝试使用能产生期望结果的最少量的控制。如果控制能够以最小的费用或其他代价来实现预期的控制目的，那么这种控制系统就是最有成效的。

◆ The principle of flexibility

The principle of flexibility means that the control system should be flexible to adapt rapidly to a changing environment and take advantage of new opportunities.

◆ The principle of economy

The principle of economy means that the control should avoid wasting resources.

Global Perspective

Controlling Success at McDonald's

The original McDonald's drive-in restaurant in San Bernardino, California, was doing a brisk business in 1955 when Ray Kroc, a milk-shake-mixer salesperson, bought the franchising rights. At the time, Kroc did not know the restaurant business and was not wealthy. Nevertheless, he was going into competition against well-established fast-food chain, such as Kentucky Fried Chicken, Burger King, Dairy Queen, and Big Boy.

While selling milk-shake mixers, Kroc had witnessed many franchised outlets go out of business because of poor management, uneven quality, and financial draining by parent companies. On the basis of his observations, Kroc believed that an organization could run a successful franchising operation if it could control the quality of both the food and the service offered at the franchised outlets. Offering franchisees good financial incentives for adhering to a fair, but closely controlled, system would be another essential element for success.

To develop the kind of controls needed, Kroc designed training programs that were unusual at the time and remain the best in the fast-food industry. He also put together a training manual that has grown to about 600 pages. The manual detailed operating procedures for virtually every aspect of outlet management. Instructions ranged from the cooking time for french fries to expected standards of cleanliness for rest rooms. To help ensure that employees followed the provisions outlined in the manual, Kroc had field inspectors visit outlets and grade their operations against the standards set forth.

Kroc also demanded that suppliers conform to high standards. For example, potato distributors were shocked to learn that McDonald's technicians measured the moisture levels in potatoes by using devices called hydrometers and rejected batches in which the solids content did not meet requirements. Because cheating on hamburger quality was a common practice in the meat industry at that time, McDonald's inspectors would sometimes show up at a meat-packing plant at 3 a.m., ready to cancel contracts if they found anything amiss. McDonald's still keeps close tabs on suppliers, right down to conducting laboratory tests on the thickness of pickle slices.

Another unique aspect of the McDonald's operation was Kroc's approach to granting franchises. While other chains, such as Dairy Queen and Burger King, usually licensed whole territories in return for sizable front-end payments, Kroc sold franchises one outlet at a time. Only if an operator demonstrated a willingness and an ability to live up to McDonald's standards would that operator be considered for additional outlets. Kroc also made sure that the franchisees would be able to keep a good chunk of the fruits of their labors, giving them ample incentive to work hard.

Because he had the foresight to concentrate on the long run, Kroc began to achieve a vision that would ultimately prove difficult for the competition to duplicate: nationwide standardization. Gradually, customers started to notice that regardless of where they were, they could count on the local McDonald's restaurant to offer reliable food, quick service, and clean rest rooms.

Today, there are more than 20,000 McDonald's outlets located in the United States and in almost 100 other countries, including Japan, Canada, Germany, England, Australia, and France. On average, a new McDonald's outlet opens every 3 hours someplace in the world.

（案例来源：Kathryn M. Bartol and David C. Martin. *Management* (3rd edition). 北京：机械工业出版社，1998，p. 510）

四、控制的作用和目的

控制在管理中的作用有两方面：一方面起检验作用，它检验各项工作是否按预定计划进行，同时也检验计划的正确性和合理性；另一方面起调节作用，在计划的执行过程中，对原计划进行修改，并调整整个管理过程。

在现代的管理活动中，控制工作要达到两个方面的目的（参见图9-1）。

一是对于经常发生变化的而又直接影响组织活动的"急症问题"，控制应随时将计划的执行结果与标准进行比较，若发现有超过计划允许范围的偏差时，则及时采取必要的纠正措施，使组织内部系统活动趋于相对稳定，实现组织的既定目标。

二是对于长期存在着的影响组织素质的"慢性病症"，控制要根据内外环境变化对组织新的要求和组织不断发展的需求，打破执行现状，重新修订计划，确定新的现实和管理控制标准，使之更先进、更合理。

✍ **The Functions and Purposes of Control**

The functions of control include evaluating and adjusting.

The purposes of control:
1. To achieve the goals of organization by stabilizing the systematic activities of internal organization.

2. To create a better organization by adjusting plans that are for the past and existing conditions, and renew the criteria.

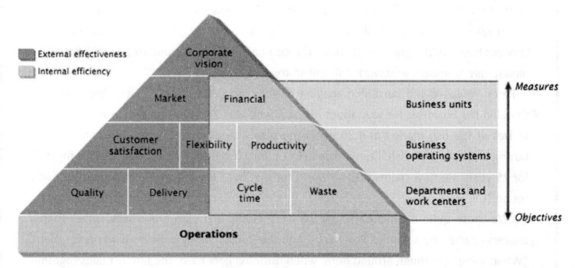

图 9-1　战略控制效果金字塔

Figure 9-1　Performance Pyramid for Strategic Control

（资料来源：Kit Fai Pun and Anthony Sydney White. A Performance Measurement Paradigm for Integrating Strategy Formulation: A Review of Systems and Frameworks. *International Journal of Management Reviews*, 2005, 7 (1): 54）

第二节　控制的过程

Peter Poulos, **Managing Director, Poulos Bros Seafood**

Poulos Bros Seafoods Pty Ltd. is part of the Poulos Bros Group, the largest seafood company on Australia's eastern seaboard. The company has successfully established itself as one of the most prominent wholesale seafood suppliers in Australia. It was founded in 1955 by two brothers, Con and Denis Poulos, who migrated from Greece, and is still a family-run business, which operates out of the Sydney suburb of Pyrmont. The Poulos Bros Group is a privately owned and operated business involved in all aspects of the seafood industry on the east coast of Australia. It is one of the country's largest distributors, processors, importers, exporters and retailers of fresh and frozen seafoods and related food products.

The group's competitive advantage is its ability to ensure continuity to be a reliable supplier of high quality seafood. One of its key strengths is its access to markets and relationships with customers. Much emphasis has been placed on acquisition and alliances which it believes will ensure reliable supply lines into the future.

Members of the family—for it is very much a family concern—call their business "The Fish Shop," but what a fish shop! The company turns over $100 million annually and has a factory and distribution business in Queensland. There are three wholesale outlets in New South Wales, and a retail outlet and wholesale and processing facility in Tasmania, which services basically the entire east coast. The company employs about 165 people, including nine family members who work full-time in the business.

Peter Poulos is the current managing director and son of one of the brothers who founded the business. He says about his dad, who was 74 at the time of writing, "He still arrives at the fish market at 4.30 every morning. He loves trading his fish and he loves buying and selling his fish. I've worked in the family business with my dad, not for my dad, for 25 years. He now claims that he works for me, but I think it's still kinda the other way round."

"We chose quite a while back that we were family first with a business, rather than a business owned by a family," Peter says. And the Poulos family believes it works for them. "When things get tough around here, when business gets hard, the family rallies together first," Peter explains proudly. "If there is a disaster, if there is a problem, I don't have to worry about who do I call? They are all there. We are all in front, and everybody is pulling in the same direction in that respect. Having lost my uncle [one of the original founding brothers] a few months ago has really put a different spin on things, because it has changed the dynamic within the business. It has also shown everybody that it is time to mature, to make that extra step."

Succession is as much a tool of control as it is a planning activity. After all, it establishes what is to happen in the event of certain conditions such as the death or retirement of key people within a business.

However, it is not only about what happens following the event; it is also about preparation for certain eventualities. It is also about preparing individual people, training and gaining experience, and this is very much a control activity. Referring to the death of his uncle Denis, one of the company's founders, Peter Poulos says: "That has been a challenge all on its own, coping with that and the succession plan that we had in place. It has been a very interesting few months 'surviving' in the family business in these times."

（案例来源：Stephen Robbins. Rolf Bergman. Ian Stagg and Mary Coulter. *Management* (6th edition). Melbourne: Pearson Australia Group Pty Ltd., 2012, pp. 657-658）

在组织运行过程中，管理者要时刻关注目标完成情况，将实际绩效与目标进行对比，并及时做出调整。这是控制职能在管理中的具体应用的过程。组织控制是一个系统工程，正如案例中所讲述的那样，不仅需要对结果进行控制，还需要未雨绸缪，考虑不同阶段可能出现的各种问题。那么，组织控制的过程是如何实现的呢？本节将围绕控制过程的不同阶段进行深入分析和探讨。

一般而言，控制过程的基本工作可分为四个阶段：建立控制标准；衡量实际业绩，根据预定的标准检查或衡量业绩，即监控阶段；鉴别并分析偏差，即检查阶段；采取纠正措施，即纠偏与执行阶段（参看图9-2）。

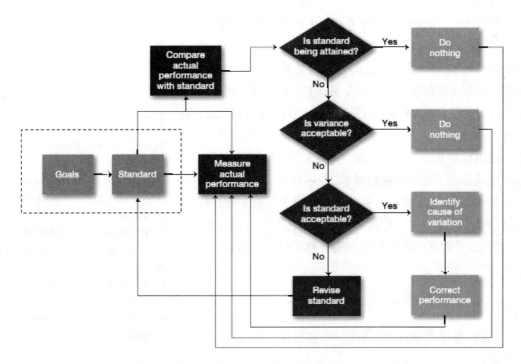

图 9-2　控制过程流程图

Figure 9-2　Control Process

一、建立控制标准

管理学中的标准是指所期望的业绩水准,它构成了控制过程的基础。建立控制标准是第一个阶段。控制标准的制定是控制能否有效实施的关键。对照标准,管理人员可以判断绩效和成果,标准是控制的基础,离开标准实施控制只能流于形式,对工作绩效和成果的评估会变得毫无意义。然而,当工作繁杂并包括许多难以琢磨的因素时,建立具体的标准来衡量业绩变得比较困难,例如在衡量一个高层管理者的业绩时就是这样。而对于生产或经营者来说,建立工作标准相对简单。如一些常见的标准包括数量、质量、时间和成本。标准的类型很多,它的建立取决于所需衡量的绩效和成果领域。一般而言,控制标准有定量和定性两大类之分。而控制标准主要是以效率、质量、对顾客响应和创新等具有竞争优势因素作为评估目标来制定的。

企业管理中较为常用的定量的控制标准主要有:①物理标准,如企业中的产品产量、工时定额等;②货币标准,如产品成本、销售收入、应交税金、利润等;③时间标准,如生产周期、交货期、维修间隔等;④综合标准,如劳动生产率、废品率、市场占有率、投资回收率等。比较典型的标准是衡量财务业绩的四种标准:利润率(投资收益率、销售毛利率);现金比率(流动比率、速动比率);杠杆比率(资产负债率、长期偿还比率);周转率(存货周转率、平均收账率)。

一般而言,在企业中,为了避免主观性和个人对控制过程的影响,对控制标准尽量采取数字化和定量化,但是对于某些不能用数量来衡量的方面只是采取定性的控制标准。如企业的信誉,人员的发展、工作能力等。较为常见的有目标管理(MBO)方法。控制工作的范围很广泛,因而为进行控制制定的标准也可以有多种。通常,比较理想的控制标准是可考核的标准。一般来说,所制定的控制标准应满足以下几个方面的要求:

第一,应使标准便于对各部门甚至每个人的工作进行衡量,当出现偏差时,能找到相应的责任单位或责任人;

第二,所建立的具体标准应该有利于组织整体目标的实现;

第三,标准应与未来发展相结合,应有利于组织的长期兴旺发达;

第四,标准要根据工作而定,不能根据完成工作的人来制定;

第五,标准应是经过努力可以达到的,标准过高,人们可能会放弃努力,标准太低,人们的潜力难以充分发挥;

✍ Establishing the Control Criterion

In management, the criterion is the expected performance which is the basis of control.

The criteria:
(1) physical criterion: output, time quota; (2) monetary criterion: cost, revenue, tax, profit; (3) time criterion: production cycle, delivery, maintenance interval; (4) comprehensive criterion: the labor productivity, rejection rate, market share and return on investment.

Usually, the control criterion should meet the following requirements:
1. It should easier to evaluate the performance of departments and individuals.
2. It should be helpful to the achievement of organizational goals.
3. It should focus on the future development.
4. It should be determined by task requirements.

5. It should be achievable.

第六，标准应具有一定的弹性，当环境发生变化时有一定的适应性，特殊情况能够做到例外处理。

二、衡量实际业绩

控制过程的第二阶段是将实际工作成绩与控制标准进行比较，并做出客观的评价，从中发现二者的偏差，为进一步采取有效的控制措施提供全面准确的信息。为了确定实际工作的绩效如何，管理者首先要收集必要的信息，然后开始比较衡量。这时应该考虑的是衡量什么与如何衡量这两个问题。

衡量什么，这是处理有效控制的关键。在计划实施过程中并不是所有的步骤都要进行控制，而是选择一些关键点作为控制点，以控制关键点来控制全局，一般来说，控制关键点是计划实施过程中起决定性作用的点，或是容易出现偏差的点、起转折作用的点、变化大而又不容易掌握的点、有示范作用的点。所以选择控制关键点的过程是快捷、准确实施控制的有效过程。那么关键的控制点如何选择，即衡量什么可与相应的控制标准进行比较，这是首先要解决的问题。

在管理者处理衡量什么的时候，很大程度上是依据人们的追求，这是一个导向。例如衡量管理者的领导能力，可以从员工的满意度、营业额、出勤率等定量与定性多方面进行衡量；衡量政府机关公务员的工作效能，可以从是否患有"机关病"入手，从机关的不良作风"懒"（懒于学习，维持现状）、"满"（自我满足）、"慢"（办事拖沓）、"难"（畏难无为）、"软"（对问题视而不见，官官相护）、"老"（因循守旧）、"空"（脱离实际，弄虚作假）设置控制关键点，整顿机关工作人员的工作作风，并实施控制监督。

如何衡量是指对实际情况实施的具体方法，即通过什么渠道收集必要的信息进行衡量。管理者在衡量实际工作绩效时，常采用四种收集信息的方式：个人观察、统计报告、口头汇报和书面报告。这四种方式各有千秋，但是，它们一旦综合起来使用就能大大扩宽信息来源，并提高信息的可靠性。

三、鉴别并分析偏差

在衡量实际绩效后，若没有偏差发生，或偏差在规定的"容限"之内，则该控制过程只需前两个阶段即可完成。但是如果有偏差，且超出范围，就要采取措施加以纠正。

✎ **Measuring Performances**

The second stage of control is to compare actual performance against the standard.

Ways of collecting information for measuring performance include observation, statistics, oral reports and written reports.

✎ **Identifying and Analyzing Deviation**

If there is not deviation or the deviation is within the "acceptable range", the control ends with the first two steps. But deviations outside an acceptable range of variation need attention.

在控制过程前两个步骤完成后，便可以将衡量结果与所建立的标准进行比较，鉴定出偏差的大小和方向。比较的结果可能是实际工作的绩效高于、低于或正好符合标准。如果实际工作与标准相符，便没有任何偏差产生。然而，在某些管理活动中，偏差是在所难免的，而且也不需要做到完全没有偏差。因此基于工作标准确定出一个可接受的偏差范围是非常重要的。以一家电话机生产厂为例。该厂设定每位工人每小时应该生产 50 部电话机的生产率标准，可接受的偏差是每人每小时正负 5 部。可接受的偏差为控制过程确定了界限。如果实际产量在 45 部至 55 部之间，那么就认为生产处于正常控制之下，超出这一范围则表示情况失控。

除了偏差的大小，管理者还应对偏差的方向给予重视和分析。还以电话机厂为例，如果实际产量是每人每小时 42 部，就意味着负向的偏差超出了可接受的范围，应该采取纠正措施。再假设现在的产量是每人每小时 58 部，偏差超出了可接受的范围，但偏差是正向的。有人可能会认为这种正向的偏差是求之不得的，不应该采取纠正措施。但是，如果该厂对超出的产量没有市场需求或没有库存空间，那么这一偏差就会带来问题；而且超出的产量可能占用了应用于其他方面的资源。因此，偏差的允许范围要视具体工作的实际情况确定。

此外，偏差鉴定频率也很重要。这主要取决于控制对象的重要性和复杂性。例如：对于那些较为长期、较高水平的标准，适合采用年度的偏差鉴定；而对产量、出勤率等短期、基础性的标准，则需要比较频繁的偏差鉴定。

四、采取纠正措施

在得出实际工作与标准进行比较的结果之后，管理者便可以对实际工作进行评价，并依据偏差的程度和性质分析产生的原因，采取相应的措施。或维持现状，或纠正偏差，或修改标准。当没有偏差或偏差在允许范围之内时，便不需要采取任何纠正性措施。对这样一个成功的控制循环也应分析其中的原因，以便积累经验，为今后的控制活动提供借鉴。同时，管理者还应向具体工作人员及时反馈信息，必要时可给予适当的奖励，激励他们继续努力工作。

如果发现存在超出允许范围的偏差，就应该认真分析偏差产生的原因。在实践中，管理者出于各方面的原因时常只采取一些临时性的纠正措施，而不去分析偏差产生的真正原因。这种治标不治本的做法也许会收效一时，但对以后的工作往往容易产生不良影响。

Taking Corrective Actions

After measuring the actual performance against control criteria, managers should evaluate the results, analyze the reasons and take corrective actions to solve the problems. They can choose among three possible courses of action: do nothing, correct the actual performance, or revise the standards.

出现超出允许范围的偏差表明工作未能按预期进展。为了能从根本上解决问题,管理者必须把精力集中于查清问题的原因上,既要查内部因素,又要查外部环境的影响,寻找问题的本质,以求治标治本之策。其实,问题之中孕育着机会,查明问题原因本身就代表着成就。

在分析偏差原因的基础上,针对那些可以控制的因素采取相应的纠正措施,把实际工作拉回到计划的轨道上来。导致偏差的原因往往是多种多样的,但一般认为,造成实际工作结果出现偏差的原因可以归纳为以下几类。

1. 计划操作原因

这是指计划执行者自身的原因造成偏差,如工作不认真,没有责任心,玩忽职守,或能力不够,不能胜任工作等。这时可采取一些措施加以纠正:重申规章制度,明确责任,明确激励措施,奖惩分明;或调整工作人员,加强员工培训,改组领导班子等。

2. 外部环境发生重大变化原因

如国家政策法规发生变化,国际政治风云突变,发生自然灾害,某个关键合作伙伴突然破产,遭遇某个突发事件（如 2003 年春 SARS 流行病在多个省市的蔓延）等,这些因素往往是不可控的,只能在仔细研究分析的基础上采取一些补救措施,以尽量减少不良影响,然后改变策略,避开锋芒,另辟蹊径。

3. 计划不合理原因

指计划制订时不切合实际,使得标准是基于错误的假设和预测制定的,难以达到。所以在设定目标时,管理者应注意既不能把目标定得太高,也不能将目标设置在很低的水平上,这样会导致不利的影响,更谈不上有效控制了。太高的目标,如过高的利润目标、过高的市场占有率,根据具体情况根本实现不了,这样轻则挫伤员工的积极性,重则面临整个计划失控,甚至葬送整个企业;太低的目标,低估自己的实力,无法对员工起到激励作用,这时就应根据企业或组织的具体情况进行调整,制订出切实可行的计划。

归纳起来,当出现如下三种情况时,就需要采取措施。

①控制标准不存在问题,环境也没有发生大的变化,偏差是由于组织和领导工作不力等原因造成的。对于这类偏差,所应采用的措施是纠正工作行为。在这种情况下,管理者有较大的能动性。例如,可以通过改进领导作风、调整人员、实施奖惩等方法来减小或消除偏差。

②控制标准本身没有问题,但由于环境发生了较大的变化,使原本适用的标准不合时宜。如银行大幅度提高贷

The reasons for deviation include:

1. Unsatisfactory work

2. Great changes in external environment

3. Improper plans

The actions to be taken when the following conditions occur:

(1) Deviation is caused by ineffective organizing and leading.

(2) Deviation is caused by external environment changement.

款利率，可能会使组织计划期内的资金筹措目标不能实现。这些由于组织外部环境因素造成的偏差，对于一个特定组织来说，是管理者所无法控制的。因此，管理者可以采取修改控制标准甚至调整组织的计划目标的措施，使之与组织的外部环境相适应。

③控制标准本身不合理，过高或者过低。这时必须对控制标准进行修改。如果是由于计划本身的不合理或不完善造成的，就有必要对计划本身甚至目标进行修改，然后根据修正了的计划制定出合理的控制标准。

(3) Deviation is caused by improper criterion (too high or too low).

Global Perspective

Steps in the Control Process

UPS, which employs 99,000 U.S. drivers, has established intergard, an 11,500-square-foot training center 10 miles outside Washington, D.C. There trainees practice UPS-prescribed "340 Methods" shown to save seconds and improve safety. Graduates of the training, who are generally former package sorters, are eligible to do a job that pays an average of $74,000 annually. (Because about 30% of driver candidates flunk training based on books and lectures, UPS now uses video games, a contraption that simulates walking on ice, and an obstacle course around an artificial village.)

Establishing Standards. UPS establishes certain standards for its drivers that set projections for the number of miles driven, deliveries, and pickups. For instance, drivers are taught to walk at a "brisk pace" of 2.5 paces per second, except under icy or other unsafe conditions. However, because conditions vary depending on whether routes are urban, suburban, or rural, standards vary for different routes.

Measuring Performance. Every day, UPS managers look at a computer printout showing the miles, deliveries, and pickups a driver attained during his or her shift the previous day. In general, drivers are expected to make five deliveries in 19 minutes.

Comparing Performance to Standards. UPS managers compare the printout of a driver's performance (miles driven and number of pickups and deliveries) with the standards that were set for his or her particular route. For instance, the printout will show whether drivers took longer than the 15.5 seconds allowed to park a truck and retrieve one package from the cargo. A range of variation may be allowed to take into account such matters as winter or summer driving or traffic conditions that slow productivity.

Taking Corrective Action. When a UPS driver fails to perform according to the standards set for him or her, a supervisor then rides along and gives suggestions for improvement. If drivers are unable to improve, they are warned, then suspended, and then dismissed.

（案例来源：Angelo Kinicki and Brian K. Williams. *Management: A Practical Introduction* (7th edition). New York: McGraw-Hill Education, 2015, p. 516）

第三节 控制的方法

Technology and the Manager's Job

Technological advances have made the process of managing an organization much easier. But technological advancements have also provided employers a means of sophisticated employee monitoring. Although most of this monitoring is designed to enhance worker productivity, it could, and has been, a source of concern over worker privacy. These advantages bring with them difficult questions regarding what managers have the right to know about employees and how far they can go in controlling employee behavior, both on and off the job. Consider the following:

• The mayor of Colorado Springs, Colorado, reads the e-mail messages that city council members send to each other from their homes. He defended his actions by saying he was making sure that e-mails to each other were not being used to circumvent the state's "open meeting" law that requires most council business to be conducted publicly.

• The U.S. Internal Revenue Service's internal audit group monitors a computer log that shows employee access to taxpayers' accounts. This monitoring activity allows management to check and see what employees are doing on their computers.

• American Express has an elaborate system for monitoring telephone calls. Daily reports provided to supervisors detail the frequency and length of calls made by employees, as well as how quickly incoming calls are answered.

• Employers in several organizations require employees to wear badges at all times while on company premises. These badges contain a variety of data that allow employees to enter certain locations in the organization. Smart badges, too, can transmit where the employee is at all times!

Just how much control a company should have over the private lives of its employees also becomes an issue. Where should an employer's rules and controls end? Does the boss have the right to dictate what you do on your free time and in your own home? Could your boss keep you from engaging in riding a motorcycle, skydiving, smoking, drinking alcohol, or eating junk food? Again, the answers may surprise you. Today many organizations, in their quest to control safety and health insurance costs, are delving into their employees' private lives. Although controlling employees' behaviors on and off the job may appear unjust or unfair, nothing in our legal system prevents employers from engaging in these practices. Rather, the law is based on the premise that if employees don't like the rules, they have the option of quitting. Managers, too, typically defend their actions in terms of ensuring quality, productivity, and proper employee behavior.

（案例来源：Stephen P. Robbins, David A. DeCenzo and Mary Coulter. *Fundamentals of Management: Essential Concepts and Applications* (9th edition). New York: Pearson, 2013, p. 404）

科学合理的控制方法对促进组织发展具有重要意义，但是，没有任何一种方法完全适用于所有类型的组织，在控制过程中，组织的管理者不得不考虑采用哪种恰当的控制方法，来满足环境的需求，适应环境的变化。随着科技的不断进步，新的控制工具不断涌现，但正如案例中所描述的那样，控制工具是否使用得当，会直接影响控制的效果。本节将针对管理实践中常用的控制方法进行系统分析和探讨，描述不同控制方法的适用条件和环境。

组织管理实践中运用着多种控制方法,管理人员常用的控制方法主要有以下几种。

一、预算控制方法

预算主要是一种计划方法,但是它也履行控制职能。预算是以数字来表示未来某个时期的计划。在实际工作中,预算是以财务术语(如收支预算和资本预算),或者以非财务术语(如直接工时、物资、实际销售量或生产量)来表述预期的结果。

通常,预算的各个子部分是由组织中各层成员参与共同制定的。合并这些子部分形成一个综合财务计划。这个计划可以成为衡量业绩的标准。在许多组织中,预算都包括资金总数额的分配和指定在某一期间专用于某些特定活动的资金数额。控制方面包括针对计划结果衡量和确定计划期间费用的支出情况。

但是,许多企业在预算控制方面还存在着不足。

(一)不恰当的预算

常见的预算不当有如下几种情况。

1. 过度预算

过度预算是指组织过于强调预算的作用,限制了管理者工作的自由。

例如,在一个预算规定过于严格的公司中,某个部门经理由于其办公费用支出超过了预算估计,而不得不放弃一项重要的促销活动。在一些部门中,详细的费用支出预算毫无实用价值,过于细致的成本控制要求使得许多项目在实际操作中很难维持在预算控制之内,影响了实际工作的灵活性。

2. 无视组织目标

存在的另一个误区是使预算目标变得比组织目标更为重要。只是热衷于保持不要超过预算限制,管理者却可能忘记了他们应该为组织目标的实现付出努力。例如,某企业拟开拓新的市场,必须不断推出新的产品,但是该企业的预算控制程序很严格,产品研发部门可能为了不超出预算控制,而减少新产品的开发。这样,虽然最后完成了预算目标,却没有达成企业目标。

由于计划应该组成一个相互支持和相互联结的网络系统,而且每一个计划都应该能以一种有助于实现组织目标的方式反映在预算中,因此部门和总体控制目标之间的冲突、部门之间的过分独立性以及缺乏协调都是管理不当的一种表现。

✍ **Budgeting**

Budgeting is the formulation of plans for a given future period in numerical terms.

Budgets are statements of anticipated results, either in financial terms—as in revenue and expense as well as capital budgets—or in nonfinancial terms—as in budgets of direct-labor-hours, materials, sales volume, or units of production.

✧ Improper budget

Overbudget means that organizations overemphasize budget so that the flexibilities of management are limited.

Ignore the organizational goals when conducting budgeting.

3．隐瞒无效率

预算中的另一个弊端在于它可以用于隐瞒无效率。预算有一种沿用前例的方法，即过去支付某项费用的事实在现在可能成为它合理性的证据。例如，某个部门曾经为供货花的一笔钱，可能会成为未来预算的最低限度。管理者有时认为，最终审批时已做的预算会被削减，因而故意将预算做高。除非预算的制定是通过经常对标准实行再检验和运用转换因子将计划活动转换成数字项目来完成的，否则预算可能成为隐藏拖沓和无效管理的保护伞。

Another disadvantage of improper budgeting is hiding inefficiency.

4．导致不灵活

非灵活性可能是预算中最大的弊端。即使预算并未用来代替管理，过多地根据预算数字来苛求项目计划无疑会产生一种误导。事实证明，资金的分配可能会随着市场状况的变化而变化，实际销售额可能超出或低于预测量。这样的差别可能使得预算在刚制定出来时就成为过时了的东西，要求管理者及时对预算做出调整；如果管理者面对这样的事件而又必须受预算的束缚，那么预算的作用将会被削弱或变得无效。尤其是事先制定长期预算时更是如此。

Excessive budget number will be the standard for a project which may mislead, even the budget is not in charge.

（二）提高预算有效性的方法

1．有效实施预算控制

要想使预算控制良好运行，管理者必须记住，预算仅仅是一种控制工具，不能用于替代管理，它有局限性，并且它必须是为每项工作所制定的。

进一步来说，预算是所有管理者的工具而不仅仅是预算管理人员或预算财务控制人员的工具。由于预算是计划的一种，那么唯一可以管理预算的人就是那些对预算负有职责的管理者，而不是预算程序。预算管理人员可以协助负有责任的管理者准备和使用预算，但是，除非整个组织的管理是由预算管理人员掌管，否则此人绝对无权做预算实施或费用支出决策工作。

◇ The method of improving budgeting

Budget is a useful tool, but it also has limitations. Budget cannot replace other management methods, and it should be formulated based on specific jobs.

2．高层管理支持

为了使预算控制效果达到最佳，预算的制定和管理必须得到高层管理全心全意的支持。命令成立预算管理部门却又不重视它，所制定的预算必然杂乱无章。相反，如果高层管理者积极支持预算的制定，使预算科学地以计划为基础，要求各部门制定并执行它们的预算，并参与预算的审核，那么预算将在整个组织中起到警示的积极作用。

The budget must be supported by the top management, such as the boards, CEO, CFO, etc.

3．参与

另一个使预算有效的方式就是确保所有与预算有关的管理者都能参与预算的准备和制定。实际参与预算制定过程对于确保成功是必要的。实际工作中，虽然大部分预算管理人员和财务控制人员都能认识到这一点，但许多情况下参与仅仅等同于被迫接受已定的预算。

一些高层管理者相信，给予管理者最好的预算就是把一段时期内所允许的费用支出都归在某一总额中，然后给予他们完全的自由，去考虑在追求组织目标的过程中如何使用这些资金。尽管这种方式不够科学，但是通过部门经理积极参与预算的制定，的确可以实现更好的计划和控制，因此这种授权方式仍很值得推荐。只要他们不超出预算总额，高层管理者完全可以多给予部门经理一些自由，来决定预算的用途。

4．标准

成功预算的一个关键点就是制定可利用的一些标准，通过这些标准程序，工作量可以转换成对劳动力、经营支出、资本支出、场地和其他资源的需求量。许多预算就是由于缺乏这样的标准而失败，一些高层管理者由于担心他们不具备审查预算要求的逻辑基础，在允许其下级提供预算计划时犹豫不决。

事实上，如果能够科学地制定标准程序，高层管理者就能够审查这样的预算要求，并合理地做出批准或否决预算的决定。进一步来说，通过关注那些为完成计划任务所需要的资源，管理者就可以把他们的要求建立在为了满足产出目标和提高业绩所必须具备的方面上。他们也不必再去应付预算委员会对预算所采取的削减计划。

5．信息

最后，要想使预算控制有效，管理者需要关注他所在的部门在预算内的实际业绩和预测业绩方面的信息。这些信息必须能向管理者显示出他们管理工作的效果如何。但是，这样的信息通常无法及时得到，即使得到了这些信息，对管理者来说，要想避免预算偏差可能已经为时太晚了。

因此，管理者必须实时关注预算实施过程中的各种信息，及时获得，有效处理，才能保证预算控制的准确。

（三）常用的预算方法：零基预算

常见的一种预算方法是零基预算法，它与运行良好的变动预算系统有许多共同点，该方法的思想是将组织规划分成由目标、活动和所需资源组成的一些"包"（Packages），然后以零为基础开始计算每一个包的成本。

In practical, participation is a good method to improve budgeting results.

Lack of standards may lead to failure of budgeting.

The managers should focus on the information about actual performance and expected performance to check the effectiveness of budgeting.

✧ Zero-base budget

The zero-base budget divides the programs into packages composed of goals, activities, and needed recourses, and calculates the costs for each package from base zero.

通过从零基础上开始对每一个包进行预算,成本在每一预算期重新计算,从而避免了预算仅仅是寻找前一时期变化的这种共同倾向。这种预算方法通常应用于支持领域的部门,而不是实际生产领域,它所基于的假设对大部分规划,诸如市场、研究与开发、人事、计划和财务及其费用支出等都具有自行处置的余地。预算中对各种被认为是需要的规划按其带给组织的效益进行成本核算和审查,然后将其效益进行排序,并根据这个包将产生所期望的效益来进行挑选。该方法的主要优点显然在于它迫使管理者重新规划每一个包。一旦管理者这样做了,他将对新规划及其成本与已确定的规划及成本一道进行全面审查。

二、生产控制方法

生产控制是生产系统的主要组成部分。生产控制的目标是以最低成本及时生产出质量和数量都符合要求的产品。

生产控制中一个最基本的活动就是在生产过程中监督和指导工人。生产控制包括根据订单计划生产批量、安排产品的生产顺序、进行生产监督直到产品生产完成以及协助管理控制的执行。

近年来,生产计划和控制集合成为一个系统。计划部分就是生产路径设计、作业计划和生产指令。在生产路径设计中,需要确定生产作业的具体顺序,即从接受原材料一直到产品生产的完成这一生产过程的路径。作业计划指的是在生产过程中作业的时间安排,即什么时候开始生产、完成日期,以及在开始和完成之间的各种作业的开始时间和完成时间。生产指令并不只是简单发布开始生产的命令,它还包括从销售部门得到顾客订单到对生产部门的要求之间的一系列转换过程。

控制包括按要求进行生产。这些生产活动包括生产订单的实际发放、跟踪生产进度和采取纠偏措施。这些活动又被称为调度、监控和纠偏措施。调度是将实际工作任务单派发给工人,准许他们开始工作。监控活动是与调度紧密相连的,包括跟踪观察生产作业的准备(如原材料和零件的供应,工具分派等)、生产过程(开始和完成时间、数量、工作流程等)、进度报告、向管理高层汇报任何相对于标准和计划的显著偏差,并在出现偏差时,遵照高层管理的建议,采取相应的纠偏措施。

✏ **Production Control**

Production control is the main part of production system, which aims at that the quantity and quality of production meet the requirements at the lowest cost.

一些生产控制工具、诸如甘特图、CPM、PERT 和其他方式都广泛应用于生产控制之中。通过这些工具，我们可以很容易地看出哪个部门或机器是按照作业计划工作的，哪些是落后于作业计划的。PERT（计划评审技术）是以箭头描绘的图形来表示各类活动及其之间的联系、这些活动所占用的时间及成本因素。该图有助于确定 CPM（关键路径法），从而更有效地完成目标。

下面我们着重讨论与投入活动相关的对供应商的控制和库存控制，以及与产出相关的质量控制。

1. 对供应商的控制

毫无疑问，供应商即为本企业提供了所需的原材料或零部件，根据波特的竞争模型，他们又是本企业的竞争力量之一。供应商供货及时与否、质量的好坏、价格的高低，都会对最终产品产生重大影响。

因此，对供应商的控制可以说是从企业运营的源头抓起，能够起到防微杜渐的作用。

目前比较流行的做法是在全球范围内选择供应商，其原因是为了能够有保障地获得高质量低价格的原材料，同时也可避免只选择少数几个供应商可能构成的威胁。大型公司多采用这种方法。许多企业正在改变与供应商之间的竞争关系，试图建立一种长期的、稳定的、合作的双赢局势。传统的做法是在十余家、甚至数十家供应商中进行选择，鼓励他们互相竞争，从中选取能够提供低价格高质量产品的供应商。现在，企业也在更广范围内挑选供应商，但是，一旦选了 2～3 家供应商，就和他们建立长远的、稳定的联系，并且帮助供应商提高原材料的质量，降低成本。这时企业和供应商就形成相互依赖、相互促进的新型关系，双方都降低了风险，提高了效益，真正做到双赢。还有一种控制供货商的方法是持有供货商一部分或全部股份，或由本企业系统内部的某个子企业供货。这常常是跨国公司为了保证货源而采用的做法。很多日本的大型企业采用这种方法控制供货商。

2. 库存控制

对库存的控制主要是为了减少库存，降低各种占用，提高经济效益。管理人员使用经济订购批量模型（Economic Order Quantity，简称 EOQ）计算最优订购批量，使所有费用达到最小。在全年需求可预测且相当稳定的情况下，这种方法在确定订购批量时尤为有效。

The timely delivery, the quality, and price of suppliers have impact on final productions.

The inventory control is to reduce the inventory, save the cost and increase profits.
The EOQ model to determining inventory levels has been used by firms for many years.
The EOQ model works reasonably well for finding order quantities when demand is predictable and fairly constant throughout the year.

这个模型考虑三种成本：一是订购成本，即每次订货所需的费用（包括通信、文件处理、差旅、行政管理费用等）；二是保管成本，即储存原材料或零部件所需的费用（包括库存、利润、保险、折旧等费用）；三是总成本，即订购成本和保管成本之和。

当企业在一定期间内总需求量或订购量为一定时，如果每次订购的量越大，则所需订购的次数越少；如果每次订购的量越小，则所需订购的次数越多。对第一种情况而言，订购成本较低，但保管成本较高；对第二种情况而言，订购成本较高，但保管成本较低。通过经济订购批量模型，可以计算出订购量多大时，总成本（订购成本和保管成本之和）为最小。图 9-3 为经济订购批量示意图。

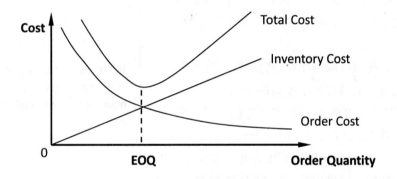

图 9-3　经济订购批量示意图

Figure 9-3　Economic Order Quantity Model

假定企业在一定期间内总需求量为 *D*，每次订购所需的费用为 *O*，库存物品单价为 *P*，保管成本与全部库存物品价值之比为 *C*，则最优订购批量为

$$EOQ = \sqrt{\frac{2 \times D \times O}{P \times C}}$$

下面举例具体解释最优订购批量模型。假设某企业一年对某种材料的总需求量为 5000 件，每件价格为 20 元，每次订购所需的费用为 250 元，保管成本与全部库存物品价值之比为 12.5%，则最优订购批量为

$$EOQ = \sqrt{\frac{2 \times D \times O}{P \times C}} = \sqrt{\frac{2 \times 5000 \times 250}{20 \times 0.125}} = 1000 \ （件）$$

因此，一年最优订购批量为 5 次，每次 1000 件，此时，订购成本为 1250 元，保管成本为 1250 元，总成本最低，为 2500 元。

一般说来，企业除了最优订购批量外，为了预防万一会保留一个额外的储存量，这个储存量被称为安全库存。

日本企业发明了一种准时制库存系统（Just-in-time Inventory Systems，简称 JIT-IS），其目标是实现零库存。它的基本思路是企业不储备原材料库存，一旦需要时，立即向供应商提出，供应商只是在需要和适时装配时才把零部件准时送到生产企业的生产线。JIT 的具体做法如下。

企业收到供应商送来的装有原材料的集装箱，卸下其中的原材料准备用于生产装配，同时把箱中的"看板"（Kanban，日语中指卡片或标牌）交回给供应商；供应商接到"看板"后立即进行生产，并将新生产出来的原材料再送来。如果双方衔接得好的话，这时，上次的原材料刚好用完。

准时制库存系统可以减少库存，降低成本，提高效益。但是，该种方法对供应商提出了很高的要求。

供应商必须在规定的时间，按照规定的质量和数量，将原材料或零部件生产出来，并且准确无误地运输到规定的地点。但是，许多研究指出准时制库存系统事实上将库存及带来的风险转嫁给了供应商，供应商所能做的是自己消化或再次转嫁给那些为自己供货的供应商。另外，准时制库存系统对企业选择和控制供应商提出了更高的要求。

3．质量控制

所谓的质量有广义和狭义之分。狭义的质量指产品的质量；而广义质量除了涵盖产品质量外，还包括工作质量。产品质量主要指产品的使用价值，即满足消费者需要的功能和性质。这些功能和性质可以具体化为下列五个方面：性能、寿命、安全性、可靠性和经济性。工作质量主要指在生产过程中，围绕保障产品质量而进行的质量管理工作的水平。

迄今为止，质量管理和控制已经经历了三个阶段，即质量检验阶段、统计质量管理阶段和全面质量管理（Total Quality Management，简称 TQM）阶段。

质量检验阶段大约发生在 20 世纪 20—40 年代，工作重点在产品生产出来之后的质量检查。

统计质量管理阶段发生在 20 世纪 40—50 年代，管理人员主要采用统计方法作为工具，对生产过程加强控制，提高产品的质量。

JIT inventory systems mean that the supplier delivers the components and parts to the production line only when needed and "just in time" to be assembled.

JIT is good for reducing inventory and cost. This method, however, is difficult for suppliers.

So far, quality management and control has experienced three stages: quality inspection, statistical quality management and total quality management.

从 20 世纪 50 年代开始的全面质量管理是以保证产品质量和工作质量为中心，企业全体员工参与的质量管理体系。全面质量管理涉及整个组织系统内长期对持续质量改善的承诺，各个层次所有员工的积极参与，以及满足并超出客户的期望值。它具有多指标、全过程、多环节和综合性的特征。如今，全面质量管理已经形成了一整套管理理念，风靡全球。常用的全面质量管理技术有 7 种，如图 9-4 所示。

Total quality management is the long-term commitment to continuous quality improvement, throughout the organization and with the active participation of all members at all levels, to meet and exceed customer expectations.

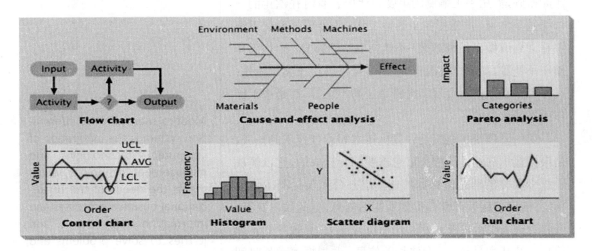

图 9-4　7 种常用的全面质量管理技术

Figure 9-4　Seven Basic TQM Tools

（资料来源：Robert Kreitner. *Management* (11th edition). New York: Houghton Mifflin Harcourt Publishing Company, 2009, p. 479）

质量控制方法用了一些技术，如统计质量控制。概率论也被用来检验产品质量。抽样方法是指对有限数量产品或原料的所有或部分规格指标进行检查。抽样方法所依据的假设是随机抽取的样本的质量将反映全部产品的质量。问题在于我们如何知道所选取的样本能真实地反映整体。为了解决这个问题，统计方法被用来确定样本和检查质量。通过这样的方法，可以在容许的风险程度下进行选择，也就是说，在某一比率下容忍不合乎质量标准的产品。统计质量控制使我们确定质量低劣产品掺入检查计划中的可能程度。质量统计员必须在为降低该风险所需增加的成本与承担该风险所带来的损失之间进行权衡。

三、管理信息控制系统

随着信息时代的来临，信息在管理控制中发挥的作用越来越大。能否建立有效的管理信息系统，及时有效地收集、处理、传递和使用信息，是衡量管理控制系统的标准之一。

✍ **Management Information Control**

With the coming of information age, information in the management control is increasingly important.

管理系统模型表明沟通对于执行管理职能和将组织与其外部环境联系起来是必不可少的。管理信息系统（MIS）提供了这种沟通和联系，使得管理职能的顺利执行成为可能。

管理信息系统存在于任何一个组织中，这是因为每个组织自身都有一套传输、处理信息的渠道，只不过传统的管理信息系统多是通过手工操作运行的，有一系列的弊端：处理速度缓慢，常常要等到结果出来后经过很长时间才能得到，如用手工编制的年度会计报表有时在次年的三月都做不出来，严重影响了其他工作；不能根据变化迅速调整计划或做出预测结果；不能得到实时信息；查询工作操作不便等，如库存情况查询，常常通过盘点才能查清楚；又如工作程序的不合理和出错率居高不下等，都是手工操作所不能避免的。

现代管理信息系统是计算机技术和管理技术的集成，是根据组织的业务流程和信息需要综合构成的，它以解决组织中面临的问题为目标，使基层办公人员提高工作效率，并能向各级管理部门提供所需的信息，据此做出决策，增强管理人员的决策水平和快速反应能力。高效率的管理信息系统能大量收集、存储相关信息，并根据要求长时间保存；能迅速对信息进行加工，使信息更加精练、准确、集中；能快速传递信息，同时由于计算机网络技术的发展，使得在线服务、远程控制成为可能。

现代管理信息系统不仅具有优势，也使管理者的工作发生了一些变化。首先是信息的获得渠道有了变化，它可以在信息系统上直接获得大量的、第一手信息。根据这些信息能够快速做出决策或改变计划，使应变能力增强，控制反馈速度提高；组织的结构可以向扁平化发展，使管理层减少，管理幅度加大，同时控制力度却不会削弱。另外，管理者和属下的信息交流也增加了通道，他们不必事事面对面地交流，汇报和指令都可以通过该系统双向传递，尤其在双方相距遥远时，可以节省大量的时间和金钱。当然，建立管理信息系统要有一笔不小的投资，对管理者及员工的计算机操作水平也有一定的要求，这些在初期应加以考虑。

Modern management information system is the integration of computer technology and management technology, which meets the needs of the organizational business processes and information requirements, and it tries to solve problems and improve the work efficiency.

Modern management information system can help managers get more primary information.

Modern management information system provides convenient communication tools between managers and subordinates.

Global Perspective

RFID: The Ultimate Tracker?

Technological devices over the years have always been of major assistance to the control systems of organizations of all types—business companies, government agencies, and health care institutions, to name a few. Recent years have seen the development of a technological method that holds great promise for reducing costs of control and, especially, for increasing accuracy. It is radio-frequency identification (RFID), and automatic identification method using tags or transponders to send data that can be remotely retrieved and stored. RFID tags with silicon chips containing antennas are small enough to be inserted into—or attached to—a person, animal, or product for identification purposes using the emitted radio waves. Larger transponders are used currently in everyday activities, such as the automatic identification of cars on toll roads.

Initially, there were no agreed-upon standards for "passive" RFID tags (that is, tags with no internal power source), and this fact was a major hurdle that had to be overcome before RFID could be more widely used, particularly by global companies. Until countries could agree on those standards, the technology would enjoy only minimal efficiencies and costs would be prohibitively high. However, this problem was mostly resolved when a number of countries—including China, a significant exporter—agreed to an RFID standard in 2006.

As with any technology, especially relatively new ones, there are always pluses and minuses. On the positive side: RFID opens up many new approaches for managers and organizations—in industries as diverse as cleaning, auto manufacturing, aircraft, coal mining, and retail stores—to enhance their control actions. For example, two major retail chains, Wal-Mart and Marks & Spencer, have been especially active in adopting this technology. Wal-Mart has applied it to the issue of how to avoid the perennial "out-of-stock" problem that plagues all stores of any size. Shortly after trying out RFID technology, the firm was able to reduce the incidences of the problem by 13 percent in its inventory of mid-price items. A few years later, that percentage reduction was 62 percent and is still improving. Wal-Mart has also used RFID tags to track high-cost items in its stores to prevent them from being shoplifted. Likewise, Marks & Spencer uses the technology to help manage inventory turnover by precisely tracking its merchandise. As a Marks & Spencer executive explained: "Most people think that the benefits of RFID are around cost reduction and speed, but the main benefit is control. Sending the right product in the right quantity to the right depot at the right time is far more important."

In the health care industry, RFID is being increasingly used. Specifically, the tagging procedure has been used to control the supply chain flow of pharmaceuticals from their point of origin through their dispensation to patients. As in retail stores, the technology has been used in hospitals to keep track of, and reduce the theft of, high-cost drugs and other items. Additionally, RFID has been used to keep track of patients and the location of personnel within the hospital.

On the downside, three major concerns have slowed down wide-scale adoption of RFID technology. The first of these, as we mentioned, was the lack of agreed-upon standards. To some extent, this problem has been solved. A second deterrent has been the high costs related to purchasing the tags and their sophisticated readers. Experience has shown, however, that if the initial investment can be made, the subsequent return-on-investment results of RFID have more than justified the costs. Finally, and perhaps the most difficult problem to solve, has been the public's concerns with privacy: It is one thing to track the movement of goods, and quite another thing to track the movement and activities of individual people. This "Big Brother is watching you" issue is likely to be a continuing topic of discussion in the coming years.

（案例来源：Michael A. Hitt, J. Stewart Black, and Lyman W. Porter. *Management* (3rd edition). 北京：中国人民大学出版社，2013，pp. 372-373）

关键概念 **KEY IDEAS AND CONCEPTS**

Control

Pre-control

Control in process

Afterwards control

Formal organization control

Group control

Self control

Control process

Budgeting

Budget

Overbudget

Zero-base budget

Production control

Economic order quantity model

Just-in-time inventory systems

Total quality management

Management information systems

讨论问题 **DISCUSSION QUESTIONS**

1. What's control in management?

2. What are the main differences and similarities between general control and management control?

3. By systematic thinking, control in management can be divided into 3 types: pre-control, control in process and afterwards control. Please explain the differences among them. Can you give some examples?

4. Control plays an important role in business administration. Explain the principles of control.

5. Why is control so important for managers and organizations, and how is it related to planning?

6. Briefly describe the four steps of the control process.

7. Budget should be formulated based on specific jobs. How to improve effectiveness of it?

8. What is zero-base budget? Are there any advantages or disadvantages? Please explain it briefly.

9. Briefly describe the three stages of quality management and control.

10. Which is more critical for success in organizations: continuous improvement or quality control? Support your position.

11. "Every individual employee in an organization plays a role in controlling work activities." Do you agree with this statement? Or do you think control is something that only managers are responsible for? Explain.

Continuous Improvement at Toyota

Deep inside Toyota's car factory in Georgetown, Kentucky, is the paint shop, where naked steel car bodies arrive to receive layers of coatings and colors before returning to the assembly line to have their interiors and engines installed. Every day, 2,000 Camrys, Avalons, and Solaras glide in to be painted one of a dozen colors by carefully programmed robots. Georgetown's paint shop is vast and crowded, but in two places there are wide areas of open concrete floor, each the size of a basketball court. The story of how that floor space came to be cleared—tons of equipment dismantled and removed—is really the story of how Toyota has reshaped the U.S. car market. It's the story of Toyota's genius: an insatiable competitiveness that would seem un-American were it not for all the Americans making it happen. Toyota's competitiveness is quiet, internal, self-critical. It is rooted in an institutional obsession with improvement that Toyota manages to instill in each one of its workers, a pervasive lack of complacency with whatever was accomplished yesterday.

The result is a startling contrast to the car business. At a time when the traditional Big Three are struggling, Toyota is thriving. Just in the year of 2006, Ford and GM have terminated 46,000 North American employees. Together, they have announced the closing of 26 North American factories over the next five years. Toyota has never closed a North American factory; it will open a new one in Texas this fall 2007 and another in Ontario, Canada in 2008. Detroit isn't being bested by imports: 60% of the cars Toyota sells in North America are made here.

Toyota doesn't have corporate convulsions, and it never has. It restructures a little bit every work shift. That's what the open space in the Georgetown paint shop is all about. Chad Buckner helped clear the space. Buckner, 35, has a soft Southern accent and an air of helpfulness. He is an engineering manager in the painting department, where he arrived straight out of the University of Kentucky 13 years ago. His whole career has been spent at Toyota. As recently as 2004, a car body spent 10 hours in painting. Robots did much of the work, then as now, but they were supplied with paint through long hoses from storage tanks. "If we were painting a car red, before we could paint the next car white, we had to stop, flush the red paint out of the lines and the applicator tip, and reload the next color," Buckner says. Georgetown literally threw away 30% of the pricey car paint it bought, cleaning it out of equipment and supply hoses when switching colors.

Now, each painting robot, eight per car, selects a paint cylinder the size of a large water bottle. A whirling disk at the end of the robot arm flings out a mist of top-coat paint. When a car is painted—it takes just seconds—the paint cartridge is set back down, and a freshly filled cartridge is selected by each robot. No hoses need to be flushed. There is no cleaning between cars. All the paint is in the cartridges, which are refilled automatically from reservoirs. Cars don't need to be matched by color—a system that saved paint but caused constant delays. Cars now spend 8 hours in paint, instead of 10. The paint shop at any moment holds 25% fewer cars than it used to. Wasted paint? Practically zero. What used to require 100 gallons now takes 70.

The benefits ripple out. Not only does Georgetown use less paint, it also buys less cleaning solvent and has dramatically reduced disposal costs for both. Together with new programming to make the robots paint more quickly, Buckner's group has increased the efficiency of its car-wash-sized paint booths from 33 cars an hour to 50. "We're getting the same volume with two booths that we used to get with three," Buckner says. "So we shut down one of the booths." If you want to trim your energy bill, try unplugging an oven big enough to bake 25 cars. Workers dismantled Top Coat Booth C, leaving the open floor space available for some future task.

So what do Buckner and his crew do with a triumphant operational improvement like that? By way of an answer, he walks to the second area of open space, where the sealer-application robots used to sit. They've been consolidated, too. Buckner points to another undercoating booth that the engineering staff is now working to eliminate. Indeed, shutting down Top Coat Booth C liberated a handful of maintenance engineers—who turned their attention to accelerating the next round of changes. Success, in that way, becomes the platform for further improvement. By the end of this year, Buckner and his team hope to have cut almost in half the amount of floor space the paint shop needs—all while continuing to paint 2,000 cars a day.

For Buckner, the paint-shop improvements aren't "projects" or "initiatives." They are the work, his work, every day, every week. That's one of the subtle but distinctive characteristics of a Toyota factory. The supervisors and managers aren't "bosses" in any traditional American sense. Their job is to find ways to do the work better: more efficiently, more effectively. "We're all incredibly proud of what we've accomplished," says Buckner, a little puzzled that his attitude might be considered unusual. "But you don't stop. You don't stop. There's no reason to be satisfied."

What is so striking about Toyota's Georgetown factory is, in fact, that it only looks like a car factory. It's really a big brain—a kind of laboratory focused on a single mission: not how to make cars, but how to make cars better. The cars it does make—one every 27 seconds—are in a sense just a by-product of the larger mission. Better cars, sure; but really, better ways to make cars. It's not just the product, it's the process. The process is, in fact, paramount—so important that "Toyota also has a process for teaching you how to improve the process," says Steven J. Spear, a senior lecturer at MIT who has studied Toyota for more than a decade. The work is really threefold: making cars, making cars better, and teaching everyone how to make cars better. At its Olympian best, Toyota adds one more level: It is always looking to improve the process by which it improves all the other processes.

There's a certain Zen sensibility to that—but also a relentlessly capitalistic, tenaciously competitive quality. If your factory is just making cars, once a day the whistle blows and it's quitting time, no more cars to make that day. If your factory is making a new way to make cars, the whistle never blows, you're never done. Without fanfare, in fact, Toyota is confounding conventional wisdom about U.S. manufacturing. Toyota isn't outsourcing; it's creating jobs in the United States. It isn't having trouble manufacturing complicated products here—it's opening factories as quickly as its systems and quality standards allow. It's offering union wages and good health insurance (to avoid being unionized) and selling the products its American workers make to Americans, profitably and more inexpensively than its U.S. competitors.

So put aside everything you think you know about the current state of the car business in the United States. Sure, Toyota enjoys some structural advantages in the form of lower health care and pension costs. But the real reason it is thriving is because of people like Chad Buckner saying, "There's no reason to be satisfied." It's not just the way Toyota makes cars—it's the way Toyota thinks about making cars. That thinking is hardly novel: Lean manufacturing and continuous improvement have been around for more than a quarter-century. But the incessant, almost mindless repetition of those phrases camouflages the real power behind the ideas. Continuous improvement is tectonic. By constantly questioning how you do things, by constantly tweaking, you don't outflank your competition next quarter. You outflank them next decade.

Toyota is far from infallible, of course. In the past two years, recalls for quality and safety problems have spiked dramatically—evidence of the strain that rapid growth puts on even the best systems. But those quality issues have seized the attention of Toyota's senior management. In the larger arena, when the strategy isn't to build cars but to build cars better, you create perpetual competitive advantage. By the time you best your competitors, they aren't just a bit behind you, in need of a reorganization and a sales surge to regain the lead. They are a decade behind. They just don't realize it.

What happens every day at Georgetown, and throughout Toyota, is teachable and learnable. But it's not a set of goals, because goals mean there's a finish line, and there is no finish line. It's not something you can implement, because it's not a checklist of improvements. It's a way of looking at the world. You simply can't lose interest in it, shrug, and give up—any more than you can lose interest in your own future. "People who join Toyota from other companies, it's a big shift for them," says John Shook, a faculty member at the University of Michigan, a former Toyota manufacturing employee, and a highly regarded consultant on how to use Toyota's ideas at other companies. "They kind of don't get it for a while." They do what all American managers do—they keep trying to make their management objectives. "They're moving forward, they're improving, and they're looking for a plateau. As long as you're looking for that plateau, it seems like a constant struggle. It's difficult. If you're looking for a plateau, you're going to be frustrated. There is no 'solution.'" Even working at Toyota, you need that moment of Zen.

"Once you realize that it's the process itself—that you're not seeking a plateau—you can relax. Doing the task and doing the task better become one and the same thing," Shook says." This is what it means to come to work."

（案例来源：节选自 N. Charles Fishman. No Satisfaction at Toyota. http://www.fastcompany.com/58345/no-satisfaction-toyota, 2006-12-1）

Discussion Question

1. What roles does control play in Toyota's manufacturing strategy?
2. Is production control an evident in this case? And why? Please explain.
3. Please explain the four steps of the control process in this case.

参考文献

1. 陈传明，周小虎．管理学原理（第二版）[M]．北京：机械工业出版社，2012

2. 托马斯·S. 贝特曼，斯科特·A. 斯奈尔著，于淼等评注．管理学：全球竞争中的领导与合作（英文注释版·第10版）[M]．北京：电子工业出版社，2014

3. 王毅捷编著．*100 Cases for Management* [M]．上海：上海交通大学出版社，2003

4. 赵丽芬．管理学——全球化视角[M]．北京：中国人民大学出版社，2013

5. 周三多．管理学——原理与方法（第六版）[M]．上海：复旦大学出版社，2014

6. Angelo Kinicki and Brian Williams. Management: A Practical Introduction (7th edition) [M]. New York: McGraw-Hill Education, 2015

7. Fred R. David. Strategic Management, Concepts and Applications (11th edition) [M]. New Jersey: Prentice Hall, 2006

8. Gareth R. Jones and Jennifer M. George. Contemporary Management (9th edition) [M]. New York: McGraw-Hill Education,2014

9. Heinz Weihrich, Mark V. Cannice and Harold Koontz, Management: A global and Entrepreneurial Perspective (12th edition) [M]．北京：经济科学出版社，2008

10. Heinz Weihrich, Mark V. Cannice and Harold Koontz, Management: A global and Entrepreneurial Perspective (13th edition) [M]．北京：经济科学出版社，2011

11. Kathryn M. Bartol and David C. Martin, Management (3rd edition) [M]．北京：机械工业出版社，1998

12. Leslie W. Rue and Lloyd L. Byars. Management: Skills and Application (13th edition) [M]．北京：北京大学出版社，2013

13. Lisa Hoecklin. Managing Cultural Differences: Strategies for Competitive Advantage [M]．England: Addision-Wesley, 1995

14. Michael A. Hittv, J. Stewart Blackv, and Lyman W. Porter. Management (3rd edition) [M]．北京：中国人民大学出版社，2013

15. Philip R. Cateors and John L. Graham, International Marketing (12th edition) [M]．北京：中国人民大学出版社，2005

16. Richard L. Daft. Management (5th edition) [M]．北京：机械工业出版社，2000

17. Richard L. Daft. Management (7th edition) [M]．北京：清华大学出版社，2006

18. Richard L. Daft. Management (12th edition) [M]. Boston: Cengage Learning, 2014

19. Richard L. Daft and Dorothy Marcic著．高增安，马永红改编．Management (6th edition) [M]．北京：机械工业出版社，2010

20. Ricky W. Griffin. Management (11th edition) [M]. Boston: Cengage Learning, 2012

21. Robert Kreitner. Management (11th edition) [M]. New York: Houghton Mifflin Harcourt Publishing Company, 2009

22. Stephen P. Robbins. Management (4th edition) [M]．北京：人民大学出版社，1996

23. Stephen P. Robbins, David A. DeCenzo and Mary Coulter. Fundamentals of Management: Essential Concepts and Applications (9th edition) [M]. New York: Pearson, 2013

24. Stephen P. Robbins and Mary Coulter. Management (11th edition) [M]. New Jersey: Prentice Hall, 2012

25. Stephen P. Robbins and Mary Coulter. Management (11th edition) [M]．北京：清华大学出版社，2013

26. Stephen P. Robbins and Mary Coulter. Management (13th edition) [M]. New York: Pearson, 2016

27. Stephen Robbins, Rolf Bergman, Ian Stagg and Mary Coulter. Management (6th edition) [M]. Melbourne: Pearson Australia Group Pty Ltd., 2012

28. Stephen P. Robbins and Timothy A. Judge. Organization Behavior (15th edition) [M]. New York: Prentice Hall, 2013

29. Thomas S. Bateman. Management: Leading & Collaborating in a Competitive World (8th edition) [M]. New York: McGraw-Hill Education, 2009

30. Thomas S. Bateman and Scott A. Snell. Management: Leading & Collaborating in a Competitive World (9th edition) [M]. New York: McGraw-Hill Irwin, 2014

31. Thomas S. Bateman and Scott A. Snell. Management: Leading & Collaborating in a Competitive World (11th edition) [M]. New York: McGraw-Hill Irwin, 2015

32. 何军. 大数据对企业管理决策影响分析[J]. 科技进步与对策, 2014（4）: 65—68

33. 林泉, 邓朝晖, 朱彩荣. 国有与民营企业使命陈述的对比研究[J]. 管理世界, 2010（9）: 116—122

34. 卢颖. 管理者的十个角色[J]. 经济与信息, 1998（7）: 48—51

35. 田硕, 李春好. 复杂管理决策分析的系统思维整合工具: Srop分析矩阵[J]. 经济管理, 2015（6）: 133—142

36. 汪国银, 刘芳, 陈传明. 中层管理者战略决策参与对战略绩效的影响路径研究[J]. 当代财经, 2013（2）: 67—73

37. 王军, 王菲. 管理决策中的归因偏差及其纠正[J]. 沈阳工业大学学报（社会科学版）, 2010（1）: 52—54

38. 张桂英. 管理者角色新探, 商业研究[J]. 2005（19）: 94—96

39. 张健东, 肖洪钧, 洪勇. 高层管理者前瞻性行为与组织绩效关系的案例研究[J]. 管理案例研究与评论, 2012（6）: 438—446

40. 中国企业家调查系统. 中国企业家成长 20 年: 能力、责任与精神——2013 中国企业家队伍成长 20 年调查综合报告[J]. 管理世界, 2014（6）: 19—38

41. 中国企业联合会课题组. 中国职业经理人年度报告（摘编）[J]. 企业管理, 2014（2）: 12—14

42. April Rabkin. Leaders at Ailibaba, Youku and Baidu are Slowly Shaking up China's Corporate Culture [J]. Fast Company, 2012 (2): 1-4

43. D. Argus. It's Human Nature [J]. AFR Boss, 2010 (3): 32–33

44. R. Turner. You'll Never Make it On Your Own [J]. The Australian Deal, 2009 (8): 38–39

45. Hambrick, Donald C. and Phyllis A. Mason, Upper Echelons: The Organization as a Reflection of its Top Managers [J]. Academy of Management Review, 1984, 9 (2): 193-206

46. Harold Koontz. The Management Theory Jungle [J]. The Journal of the Academy of Management, 1961, 4 (3): 174-188

47. Heinz Weihrich. Management Practices in the United States, Japan, and the People's Republic of China [J]. Industrial Management, 2012 (32): 3

48. K. H. C. Cheng and W. Cascio. Performance-Appraisal Beliefs of Chinese Employees in Hong Kong and the Pearl River Delta [J]. International Journal of Selection and Assessment, 2009, 17 (3): 329-333

49. L. B. Bradford and R. Lippitt. Building a Democratic Work Group [J]. Personnel, 1945, 11(2): 2

50. Li, P. L. and Lu, H. L. Research on Initiative Turnover Rate of the Post-90s Workforce—Taking

Labor-Intensive Enterprises as an Example [J]. Journal of Human Resource and Sustainability Studies, 2014 (2): 12-25

51. Marian C. Schultz and James J. Schultz. Corporate Strategy in Crisis Management: Johnson & Johnson and Tylenol [J]. Essays in Economic and Business History, 1990 (7): 164-172

52. Michel, John G. and Donald C. Hambrick. Diversification posture and Top Management Team Characteristics [J]. Academy of Management Journal, 1992, 35 (1): 9-37

53. Midred Golden Pryor and Sonia Taneja. Henri Fayol, Practitioner and Theoretician—Revered and Reviled [J]. Journal of Management History, 2010, 16 (4): 489-503

54. Mikhail Grachev and Boris Rakitsky. Historic Horizons of Frederick Taylor's Scientific Management [J]. Journal of Management History, 2013, 19 (4): 512-527

55. Philip D. Olson. Choices for Innovation-Minded Corporations [J]. The Journal of Business Strategy, 1990, 11 (1): 42-46

56. Thomas V. Bonoma and Joseph C. Lawler, Chutes and Ladders: Growing the General Manager [J]. Sloan Management Review, 1989, Spring: 27–37

57. 史玉柱：中国"最著名的失败者" [EB/OL]. 中国网，http://www.china.com.cn/economic/txt/2009-07/23/content_18190312.htm

58. Amazon Germany Employees: Go on Strike [EB/OL]. http://timesofindia.indiatimes.com/tech-news/labour-union-to-Amazon-Germany-eemployee-Go-on-strike/articleshow/44946844.cms?

59. Amazon Workers Strike in Germany Over Pay [EB/OL]. www.bbc.com/news/business-25397316.htm

60. Amazon Staff in Germany to Prolong strike [EB/OL]. http://news.xinhuanet.com/english/europe/2014-12/18/c_133862362.htm

61. Big Data in HR: Why it's Here and What it Means [EB/OL]. http://www.bersin.com/blog/post/BigData-in-HR--Why-its-here-and-what-it-means.asp, 2012-11-17,

62. Calum Macleod. Alibaba's Jack Ma: From Crazy to Chin's Richest Man [EB/OL]. www.usatoday.com, 2014-9-19

63. C. Rampell. The Help Wanted Sign Comes with a Frustrating Asterisk [J/OL]. The New York Times, www.nytimes.com, 2011-7-25

64. Cross-functional Innovation Teams at Harley-Davidon [EB/OL]. http://www.1000ventures.com/business_guide/cs_innovation_cft_harleydavidson.html

65. Danielle Monaghan. Global and Cultural Effectiveness: Recruiting Is Social and Talent Is Local [J/OL]. http: //www. shrm. org/publications/hrmagazine/editorialcontent/2016/0116/pages/0116-competencies-global-cultural-effectiveness-monaghan.aspx, 2015-12-16

66. David De Cremer and Tian Tao. Huawei's Culture Is the Key to Its Success, Harvard Business Review [EB/OL]. https://hbr.org/2015/06/huaweis-culture-is-the-key-to-its-success, 2015-6-11

67. David Krackhardt and Jeffrey R. Hanson. Informal Networks: The Company Behind the Chart [EB/OL]. https://hbr.org/1993/07/informal-networks-the-company-behind-the-chart, 1993-7-8

68. Li, D. Do in China as the Chinese Do: An Overview of KFC's Localization Strategies in China [EB/OL]. http://lidan.y3k.org/blog/en/2004/04/kfcs-localization-strategies-in-china/, 2004-4

69. Jack Ma [EB/OL]. www.worldofceos.com

70. Jim Heskett. Why Are Fewer and Fewer U.S. Employees Satisfied with Their Jobs? [J/OL]. Harvard Business School Working Knowledge, http://hbswk.hbs.edu/item/why-are-fewer-and-fewer-u-s-employees-satisfied-with-their-jobs, 2010-4-2

71. Johnson & Johnson and Tylenol [EB/OL]. http://www.mallenbaker.net/csr/crisis02.php

72. K. J. Dunham. Career Journal: More Employers Ask Job Seekers for SAT Scores [EB/OL]. The Wall Street Journal, www.online.wsj.com, 2003-10-28,

73. Lawrence Gregory, Starbucks Coffee's Operations Management: 10 Decisions, Productivity [EB/OL]. http://panmore.com/starbucks-coffee-operations-management-10-decisions-areas-productivity, 2015-9-15

74. M. LaChapelle. Do You Hire People the Google Way? [J/OL]. Time Union, www.timesunion.com, 2011-7-13

75. Melanie Lee. Lei Jun, Founder of Xiaomi, Might Just Be "China's Steve Jobs" [EB/OL]. http://www.huffingtonpost.com/2012/12/07/lei-jun-xiaomi_n_2255953.html, 2012-12-7

76. N. Charles Fishman. No Satisfaction at Toyota [EB/OL]. http://www.fastcompany.com/58345/no-satisfaction-toyota, 2006-12-1

77. Pauline Meyer. Apple Inc. Organizational Culture: Features & Implications [EB/OL]. http://panmore.com/apple-inc-organizational-culture-features-implications, 2015-9-8

78. Qu Yunxu and Wang Qionghui. E-commerce Giants, Gov't Create New Markets in China's Rural Areas [EB/OL]]. 财新网，http://english.caixin.com/2015-03-05/100788403.html，2015-3-5

79. Roy Maurer, Online Job Searching Has Doubled Since 2005[EB/OL]. http://www.shrm.org/hrdisciplines/staffingmanagement/articles/pages/online-job-searching-doubled.aspx, 2015-12-21

80. Shan Lu. A New Fairy Tale of Chain Restaurant: Haidilao Hotpot, "You Can Never Learn His Way!" [EB/OL]. http://press.emerson.edu/imc/2011/12/19/a-new-fairy-tale-of-chain-restaurant-haidilao-hotpot-you-can-never-learn-his-way/, 2011-12-19

81. S. Kelly. Unemployed Not Wanted? The EEOC Scrutinizes Whether Companies' Recruiting Only Already Employed Application Could Be Discrimination [J/OL]. Treasury and Risk, www.treasurandrisk.com, 2011-4

82. Starbucks Coffee Company's Organizational Structure [EB/OL]. http://panmore.com/starbucks-coffee-company-organizational-structure, 2015-9-13

83. The New Model of Open Innovation "Haier Star Box" to Create Intelligent Home First Entry [EB/OL]. http://www.fireinews.com/news-9523347.html, 2015-3-12

84. World of CEOs. Jack Ma: Executive Chairman, Alibaba Group [EB/OL]. http://www.worldofceos.com/dossiers/jack-ma, 2015-10-27.

85. http://sc.winshang.com/news-524737.html

86. http://en.wikipedia.org/wiki/catfish_effect

87. www.asmarterplanet.com

88. www.businessinsider.com

89. www.ecommercetimes.com/story/81788.html

90. www.enwyorker.com/business/currency/coca-colas-happiness-machines

91. www.foxconn.com.cn

92. www.hiltonworldwide.com

93. www.indigodev.com/Circular1.html

94. www.jnj.com

95. www.pandaexpress.com

96. www.patagonia.com

97. www.retailindustry.about.com